The Triumph of

ROMANTICISM

The Triumph of

ROMANTICISM

Collected Essays
by MORSE PECKHAM

UNIVERSITY OF SOUTH CAROLINA PRESS
Columbia, South Carolina

PN
603
.P43x

First Printing, August 1970
Second Printing, October 1971

International Standard Book Number: 0-87249-182-X
Library of Congress Catalog Card Number: 73-120574
Suggested Library of Congress classification furnished by
McKissick Memorial Library of the University of South Carolina:
PN603.P

Manufactured in the United States of America

Preface

This collection of papers, essays, and addresses, about two-thirds in bulk of what I have published, consists of those pieces I think worth republishing. Reappearance is at least in part justified by the fact that so many originally came forth in journals of small circulation, some of which have by now ceased to exist. I have made no attempt to revise these essays or to make them consistent one with another. The few changes are the result of house-styling and the sharp eye of a professional editor. With much of what is presented here I no longer agree. Though I think I was wrong then and right now, for all I know I may have been right then and wrong now. At any rate, a number of people have told me that they continue to find various essays valuable which I no longer care for. Since they still seem to be useful, I have included them. Usefulness is all I hope for. To hope to be right in such matters as are discussed here would be foolish. If any reader finds something useless, as practically every reader will, I hope he will either forget it or attack it, providing he thinks it worth the trouble. In the second essay presented here, I myself attack much that I said in the first.

I have included after each title the date the essay was written and in a footnote, when appropriate, the occasion for which it was prepared. Thus I express my gratitude for those colleagues in the profession who have trapped me into doing what otherwise I probably would not have done.

Columbia, S.C.
December 29, 1969

Contents

I THEORY

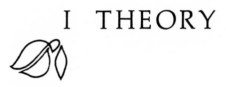

1

TOWARD

A THEORY OF ROMANTICISM

[1950*]

Can we hope for a theory of Romanticism? The answer, I believe, is, yes. But before proceeding further, I must make
quite clear what it is that I propose to discuss.

First, although the word "Romanticism" refers to any number
of things, it has two primary referents: (1) a general and permanent characteristic of mind, art, and personality, found in all
periods and in all cultures; (2) a specific historical movement in
art and ideas which occurred in Europe and America in the late
eighteenth and early nineteenth centuries. I am concerned only
with the second of these two meanings. There may be a connection between the two, but I doubt it, and at any rate whatever
I have to say refers only to historical Romanticism.

Second, in this historical sense "Romanticism" as a revolution
in art and ideas is often considered to be only an expression of a

* Delivered before the English Graduate Club, University of Pennsylvania,
January, 1950. Reprinted by permission from *PMLA*, LXVI (March, 1951),
pp. 5–23. Copyright 1951 by the Modern Language Association of America.

general redirection of European life which included also a political revolution, an industrial revolution, and perhaps several others. There may be a connection between the revolution in ideas and the arts and the more or less contemporary revolutions in other fields of human activities, but for the time being, at any rate, I think it is wise to dissociate the Romanticism of ideas and art from these other revolutions. Just as one of our greatest difficulties so far has arisen from assuming an identity between general and historical Romanticism, so much of our difficulty in considering the nature of historical Romanticism has come from assuming its identity with all of the other more or less contemporary revolutions. Let us first isolate the historical Romanticism of ideas and arts before we beg any questions about the nature of history. For example, I think it is at present wiser to consider Romanticism as one of the means then available for hindering or helping the early nineteenth-century movement for political reform than it is to assume that Romanticism and the desire for political reform and its partial achievement are the same thing.

With these two distinctions in mind, I repeat, Can we hope for a theory of the historical Romanticism of ideas and art? Such a theory must be able to submit successfully to two tests. First, it must show that Wordsworth and Byron, Goethe and Chateaubriand, were all part of a general European literary movement which had its correspondences in the music, the painting, the architecture, the philosophy, the theology, and the science of the eighteenth and early nineteenth centuries. Second, it must be able to get us inside individual works of literature, art, and thought: that is, to tell us not merely that the works are there, to enable us not merely to classify them, but to deliver up to us a key to individual works so that we can penetrate to the principles of their intellectual and aesthetic being. Can we hope for such a theory? *Dare* we hope for such a theory? To this question I answer, "Yes, we can." I feel that we have it almost within our grasp—that one or two steps more and we shall have mastered this highly perplexing literary problem.

Certainly there is no generally accepted theory of Romanticism at the present time. Twenty years ago, and for more than twenty years before that, the problem of Romanticism was debated passionately, not least because of the redoubtable but utterly mis-directed attacks of Babbitt and More. In his *Romanticism and the Modern Ego* (1943), Jacques Barzun has made a good collection of some of the definitions that have been more or less widely used in the past fifty years: a return to the Middle Ages, a love of the exotic, the revolt from reason, a vindication of the individual, a liberation of the unconscious, a reaction against scientific method, a revival of pantheism, a revival of idealism, a revival of Catholicism, a rejection of artistic conventions, a return to emotionalism, a return to nature—and so on. The utmost confusion reigns in the whole field. In the past fifteen or twenty years, most scholars have done one of two things. Either they have given up hope for any sense to come out of this tangle and have stoutly denied that there was such a movement, or, less pessimistically, they have continued to use one or more concepts or ideas—theories which they feel to be unsatisfactory yet which they continue to employ because there is nothing better. Most students are convinced that something happened to literature between the death of Pope and the death of Coleridge, but not very many are willing, when you question them sharply, to tell you exactly what happened. The situation is all the more discouraging in that it is generally conceded that Romanticism is a central problem in literary history, and that if we have failed to solve that problem, we can scarcely hope to solve any general problems in literary history.

Too many scholars, then, will try either to avoid the term entirely, or failing that strategy—and it always fails—will isolate some idea or literary effect and will say, "This is Romanticism." Or such a scholar will use the term with the full knowledge that the reader will recognize the difficulties involved and will charitably permit him to beg the question. He will very rarely begin with a theory of Romanticism and seek to place a particular poem or author in relation to that theory or seek to use the theory in unlocking a baffling and complex work, or even a simple one for that matter. He will fit his ideas into whatever notion of Romanticism he may have, usually without specifying what it might be, but very rarely, at least in public and in print, will he use a considered theory of Romanticism as a starting point for his investigations. It is a discouraging situation, but my purpose is to suggest that it is not so discouraging as it appears.

In the last few years there have been signs that some scholars at least are moving toward a common concept of Romanticism. In 1943, Jacques Barzun spoke of Romanticism as a biological revolution;[1] and in 1949, he defined it as part of "the great revolution which drew the intellect of Europe . . . from the expectation and desire of fixity into desire and expectation of change."[2] Stallknecht, in his fascinating book on Wordsworth, *Strange Seas of Thought* (1945), spoke of how Romanticism established the sentiment of being in England and then, reversing his statement, suggested that the sentiment of being established Romanticism. In his admirable introduction to his edition of *Sartor Resartus* (1937), C. Frederick Harrold—whose death has deprived us of one of the most valuable of contemporary students of Victorian literature—wrote of Carlyle's ideas about organicism and dynamism. And in his and Templeman's excellent anthology of Victorian prose (1938), there is an appendix "illustrative of nineteenth-century conceptions of growth, development, evolution." But the most recent attempt to tackle the problem, the best yet, though I think not entirely satisfactory, has been René Wellek's two-part article "The Concept of Romanticism," published in 1949 in the first two issues of *Comparative Literature*. There he offered three criteria of Romanticism: imagination for the view of poetry, an organic concept of nature for the view of the world, and symbol and myth for poetic style.

Wellek does establish to my mind three things in his article: first, that there *was* a European intellectual and artistic movement with certain intellectual and artistic characteristics, a movement properly known as Romanticism; second, that the participators in that movement were quite conscious of their historic and revolutionary significance; and third, that the chief reason for the current skepticism in America about a theory of Romanticism was the publication in 1924 of Arthur O. Lovejoy's

---

[1] *Romanticism and the Modern Ego* (New York, 1943).

[2] "Romanticism: Definition of a Period," *Magazine of Art*, XLII (Nov., 1949), 243.

famous article, "On the Discrimination of Romanticisms."[3] In this article Lovejoy pointed out that the term is used in a fearful variety of ways, and that no common concept can include them all. Indeed, the growth of skepticism about any solid conclusions on Romanticism does seem to begin—or at least start to become very powerful and eventually dominant—with the publication of that article. Wellek decries what he calls Lovejoy's excessive nominalism and skepticism, and refuses to be satisfied with it. He also puts in the same category of nominalism and skepticism Lovejoy's 1941 article, "The Meaning of Romanticism for the Historian of Ideas."[4] Here Lovejoy offered three criteria of Romanticism, or rather the three basic ideas of Romanticism, "heterogeneous, logically independent, and sometimes essentially antithetic to one another in their implications." These ideas are organicism, dynamism, and diversitarianism. Now in discussing Lovejoy's 1941 paper, Wellek has made, I think, an error. He seems to have confused the nature of the two articles, because, apparently, he has forgotten about the last three chapters of *The Great Chain of Being* (1936).[5]

Lovejoy's great book is a landmark of scholarship, and also for scholarship. It is a book on which some of the most useful scholarship of our times has been based, and it is as useful to the teacher who uses it with intelligence as it is to the scholar. Twenty-five years from now, scholars of literature will look back on the publication of *The Great Chain of Being* as a turning point in the development of literary scholarship; for it has been of astonishing value in opening up to our understanding in quite unexpected ways the literature of the sixteenth, seventeenth, and eighteenth

[3] *PMLA*, XXXIX, 229–53; republished in his *Essays in the History of Ideas* (Baltimore, 1948).

[4] *JHI*, II, 237–78.

[5] Wellek's confusion, or apparent confusion, lies in his implication that the "Romanticisms" Lovejoy discussed in 1924 are the same as the "Romantic ideas" which in 1941 he called "heterogeneous, logically independent, and sometimes essentially antithetic to one another in their implications." As I read the 1941 article, I interpret the latter as these three: organicism, dynamism, and diversitarianism. (See below, Section II of this essay.) These are not the "Romanticisms" of 1924. (See the first paragraph of Wellek's article, "The Concept of 'Romanticism' in Literary History," *CL*, I, 1.)

centuries. But, so far as I know, almost no use has been made of the last three chapters, especially of the last two, in explaining Romanticism and Romantic works. It is a curious situation; for these chapters contain the foundations for a theory of Romanticism which will do everything that such a theory must be able to do—place works and authors in relation to each other and illuminate individual works of art as they ought to be illuminated.

By ignoring (at least in his two papers) *The Great Chain of Being*, Wellek concluded that the same kind of skepticism was present in both Lovejoy's 1924 and 1941 articles. Actually *The Great Chain of Being* is an answer to Lovejoy's 1924 article. Without emphasizing the fact, Lovejoy *did* in 1933 and 1934, when he delivered the lectures on which the book is based, what in 1924 he said could not be done. To be brief, in 1936 he stated simply that literary Romanticism was the manifestation of a change in the way of thinking of European man, that since Plato European man had been thinking according to one system of thought—based on the attempted reconciliation of two profoundly different ideas about the nature of reality, both stemming from Plato—and that in the late eighteenth and early nineteenth centuries occidental thought took an entirely different direction, as did occidental art. Furthermore, he says that the change in the way the mind works was the most profound change in the history of occidental thinking, and by implication it involved a similar profound change in the methods and objects of European art.

I

What I wish to do here is, first, to explain what these new ideas of the late eighteenth century involved, to reconcile Wellek and Lovejoy, and Lovejoy with himself, and to show the relevance of certain other ideas about Romanticism I have mentioned; and second, to make one addition to the theories of Lovejoy and Wellek, an addition which I hope goes far toward clearing up an essential problem which Lovejoy scarcely faced and with which Wellek is unable to come to terms.

It is scarcely necessary to outline what *The Great Chain of Being* implied. Yet I should like to reduce the concepts involved to what I think to be their essentials. Briefly, the shift in European thought was a shift from conceiving the cosmos as a static mechanism to conceiving it as a dynamic organism: static—in that all the possibilities of reality were realized from the beginning of things or were implicit from the beginning, and that these possibilities were arranged in a complete series, a hierarchy from God down to nothingness—including the literary possibilities from epic to Horatian ode, or lyric; a mechanism—in that the universe is a perfectly running machine, a watch usually. (A machine is the most common metaphor of this metaphysic.) Almost as important as these concepts was that of uniformitarianism, implicit both in staticism and in mechanism, whenever these two are separated, as frequently happens. That is, everything that change produces was to be conceived as a part to fit into the already perfectly running machine; for all things conformed to ideal patterns in the mind of God or in the nonmaterial ground of phenomena.

If, in short, you conceive of the universe as a perfectly ordered machine, you will assume that any imperfections you may notice are really things you do not understand. You will think of everything in the universe as fitting perfectly into that machine. You will think that immutable laws govern the formation of every new part of that machine to ensure that it fits the machine's requirements. And, although with delightful inconsistency—as Pope made his *Essay on Man* the basis of his satires[6]—you will judge the success of any individual thing according to its ability to fit into the workings of the machine, your inconsistency will be concealed, for a time, by the influence of either original sin, if you are an orthodox Christian, or the corruptions of civilization, if you are a deist or a sentimentalist—not that there is much difference. Your values will be perfection, changelessness, uniformity, rationalism.

Now this mighty, static metaphysic, which had governed perilously the thoughts of men since the time of Plato, collapsed of its own internal inconsistencies in the late eighteenth century —or collapsed for some people. For most people it still remains

---

[6] See n. 12, below.

nrealized base for most of their values—intellectual, moral, social, aesthetic, and religious. But to the finer minds of the eighteenth and nineteenth centuries it was no longer tenable. There are a number of reasons why this should have been so. The principal cause was that all its implications had been worked out; they stood forth in all their naked inconsistency. It became impossible to accept a theodicy based upon it. More and more, thinkers began searching for a new system of explaining the nature of reality and the duties of men.

I shall omit the development of the new idea. The grand outlines have been magnificently sketched by Lovejoy, and the details are steadily being filled in. Rather, I shall present the new idea in its most radical form. Let us begin with the new metaphor. The new metaphor is not a machine; it is an organism. It is a tree, for example; and a tree is a good example, for a study of nineteenth-century literature reveals the continual recurrence of that image. Hence the new thought is organicism. Now the first quality of an organism is that it is not something made, it is something *being* made or growing. We have a philosophy of becoming, not a philosophy of being. Furthermore, the relation of its component parts is not that of the parts of a machine which have been made separately, i.e., separate entities in the mind of the deity, but the relation of leaves to stem to trunk to root to earth. Entities are an organic part of that which produced them. The existence of each part is made possible only by the existence of every other part. Relationships, not entities, are the object of contemplation and study.

Moreover, an organism has the quality of life. It does not develop additively; it grows organically. The universe is alive. It is not something made, a perfect machine; it grows. Therefore change becomes a positive value, not a negative value; change is not man's punishment, it is his opportunity. Anything that continues to grow, or change qualitatively, is not perfect, can, perhaps, never be perfect. Perfection ceases to be a positive value. Imperfection becomes a positive value. Since the universe is changing and growing, there is consequently a positive and radical intrusion of novelty into the world. That is, with the intrusion of each novelty, the fundamental character of the universe itself changes. We have a universe of emergents. If all these things be true, it therefore follows that there are no pre-existent patterns. Every work of art, for instance, creates a new pattern; each one has its own aesthetic law. It may have resemblances even in principle to previous works of art, but fundamentally it is unique. Hence come two derivative ideas. First, diversitarianism, not uniformitarianism, becomes the principle of both creation and criticism. The Romantics, for example, have been accused of confusing the genres of poetry. Why shouldn't they? The whole metaphysical foundation of the genres had been abandoned, or for some authors had simply disappeared. The second derivative is the idea of creative originality. True, the idea of originality had existed before, but in a different sense. Now the artist is original because he is the instrument whereby a genuine novelty, an emergent, is introduced into the world, not because he has come with the aid of genius a little closer to previously existent pattern, natural and divine.

In its radical form, dynamic organicism results in the idea that the history of the universe is the history of God creating himself. Evil is at last accounted for, since the history of the universe—God being imperfect to begin with—is the history of God, whether transcendent or immanent, ridding himself, by the evolutionary process, of evil. Of course, from both the old and the new philosophy, God could be omitted. Either can become a materialism.

In a metaphysical nutshell, the older philosophy grounded itself on the principle that nothing can come from nothing. The newer philosophy grounded itself on the principle that something *can* come from nothing, that an excess can come from a deficiency, that nothing succeeds like excess.

II

I have presented these ideas in a radical form to make them as clear as I can and to bring out in the strongest possible colors the contrast between the old and new methods of thought. Now I should like to apply them to Lovejoy and Wellek. Lovejoy stated that the three new ideas of Romantic thought and art were organicism, dynamism, and diversitarianism. He says that they are three separate and inconsistent ideas. I agree that they often appear separately, but I am convinced that they are all related to and derived from a basic or root metaphor, the organic metaphor of the structure of the universe.[7] Strictly speaking, organicism includes dynamism, for an organism must grow or change qualitatively, but I prefer to use the term "dynamic organicism" in order to emphasize the importance of imperfection and change. Diversitarianism, of course, is in these terms a positive value; for the diversity of things and their uniqueness are proof of the constant intrusion of novelty in the past, the present, and the future.

Turning to Wellek and his three criteria, I have already included one, organicism; the other two are imagination and symbolism. Wellek means the creative imagination, and a little thought will show that the idea of the creative imagination is derived from dynamic organicism. If the universe is constantly in the process of creating itself, the mind of man, his imaginative power, is radically creative. The artist is that man with the power of bringing new artistic concepts into reality, just as the philosopher brings new ideas into reality. And the greatest man is the philosopher-poet, who, supremely gifted, simultaneously does both. Furthermore, the artist is the man who creates a symbol of truth. He can think metaphorically, and if the world is an organic structure only a statement with the organic complexity of the work of art can create an adequate symbol of it. And is this not the method of symbolism? In allegory, a symbolic unit preserves its meaning when taken from its context. The Cave of Error *is* the Cave of Error. There is a direct one-to-one relationship between any unit in the world of phenomena and any unit in the world of ideas. But in symbolism, a symbolic unit has power only because of its relationships to everything else in the work of art. Ahab has symbolical value because of the whale, and the whale because of Ahab. In symbolism the interrelationships of the symbolic units involved are equated with the interrelation-

[7] I am alarmed at finding myself in disagreement with Lovejoy. Although I think his three ideas are not heterogeneous, but homogeneous or at least derived from a common root metaphor, the possibility that they really *are* heterogeneous does not deprive them in the least of their value in understanding Romanticism, nor does their possible heterogeneity have any effect on my proposal which follows.

ships of a group of concepts. Let a series of 1, 2, 3, 4, etc., stand for a series of ideas in the mind, and a similar series of a, b, c, d, etc., stand for a series of things in the real world or in the world of the concretizing imagination. Now in allegory, if "a" is a symbolic unit, it stands for "1," "b" for "2," and so on. Thus the Dragon in the *Faerie Queene*, Canto i of Book I, stands for Error, whether the Red Cross Knight is there or not, and the Knight, on one level of interpretation, stands for Holiness, whether the Dragon is there or not. But in symbolism, "a" or "b" or "c" has no direct relation to "1" or "2" or "3". Rather, the interrelationships among the first three have symbolic reference to the interrelationships among the second group of three. Moby-Dick has symbolic power only because Ahab is hunting him; in fact, he has symbolic power only because almost everything else in the book has symbolic power as well.

The now current though probably not widely accepted critical principle that a symbolic system is capable of an indefinite number of equally valid interpretations is itself a Romantic idea, in the sense that the work of art has no fixed or static meaning but changes with the observer in a relationship between the two which is both dialectical, or dynamic, and organic.

Thus we may conclude that Wellek's three criteria—organicism, imagination, and symbolism—are all derivable from the basic metaphor or concept of dynamic organicism.

There is yet another profoundly important idea which I have not so far mentioned, the idea of the unconscious mind, which appears in Wordsworth, in Coleridge, in Carlyle, and indeed all through the nineteenth and twentieth centuries. In 1830, in his magnificent essay "Characteristics," Carlyle says that the two big ideas of the century are dynamism and the unconscious mind. The idea of the unconscious mind goes back to Hartley, to Kant, to Leibniz, and is implicit in Locke. Indeed, it goes back to any poet who seriously talks about a muse. But it appears in full force only with the appearance of dynamic organicism. Best known to the English Romantics in the mechanistic associationism of Hartley, it became a central part of their thought when they made the mind radically creative. Heretofore the divine had communicated with man either directly through revelation or indirectly through the evidence of his perfect universe. But with God creating himself, with an imperfect but growing universe, with the constant intrusion of novelty into the world, how can there be any apprehension of truth? If reason is inadequate—because it is fixed and because historically it has failed—the truth can only be apprehended intuitively, imaginatively, spontaneously, with the whole personality, from the deep sources of the fountains that are within. The unconscious is really a postulate to the creative imagination, and as such continues today without the divine sanction as part of present-day critical theory. It is that part of the mind through which novelty enters into the personality and hence into the world in the form of art and ideas. We today conceive of the unconscious spatially as inside and beneath; the earlier Romantics conceived of it as outside and above. We descend into the imagination; they rose into it. The last method, of course, is the method of Transcendentalism.

Furthermore, as I shall shortly show, not only was the unconscious taken over from Locke and Kant and Hartley and converted into something radically creative, it also became an integral part of dynamic organicism because a number of the early Romantics proved it, as it were, empirically, by their own personal experience. It became to them proof of the validity of the new way of thinking. Hence also Romantic subjectivism, the artist watching his powers develop and novelty emerging from his unconscious mind.

What then is Romanticism? Whether philosophic, theologic, or aesthetic, it is the revolution in the European mind against thinking in terms of static mechanism and the redirection of the mind to thinking in terms of dynamic organicism. Its values are change, imperfection, growth, diversity, the creative imagination, the unconscious.

III

Perhaps the result of my remarks so far is to make a much larger group of determined skeptics on the subject of Romanticism. The proof of the Martini is in the drinking, and in the rest of what I have to say I hope to show not only that a group of literary works can be related in terms of the ideas I have given but also that particular literary works can be genuinely illuminated by these ideas, can be given richer content, can be more readily understood. And in addition I wish also to advance one more concept, the only one indeed to which I lay any claim of originality, for what I have already said is only an attempt to reconcile various ideas about Romanticism which seemed to be fairly close together and to develop them into some consistent whole, on the basis of Lovejoy's statement that the coming of Romanticism marked a great turn in the direction of European thought. For instance, Barzun's "desire and expectation of change" is an important part of my proposal; Stallknecht's "sentiment of being," i.e., of a living universe, is right at the heart of it; Harrold's ideas of growth are equally central.[8] Nevertheless, the theory is still incomplete.

Dynamic organicism, manifested in literature in its fully developed form, with all its main derivative ideas, I have called "Radical Romanticism." To this term I should now like to add "Positive Romanticism," as a term useful in describing men and ideas and works of art in which dynamic organicism appears, whether it be incomplete or fully developed. But by itself "Positive Romanticism" for the purposes of understanding the Romantic movement is not only frequently useless; it is often worse than useless. It is often harmful. If some of my readers have been muttering, "What about Byron?" they are quite right in doing so. Positive Romanticism cannot explain Byron; Positive Romanticism is not enough. To it must be added the term "Negative Romanticism," and to that I now turn.[9]

[8] An extremely interesting parallel, although later in time than the period I am immediately concerned with, is Wiener's demonstration that American pragmatism came out of the union of Mill's diversitarian and dynamic dialectic with Darwin's theory of evolution. See Philip P. Wiener, *Evolution and the Founders of Pragmatism* (Cambridge, Mass., 1949).

[9] Wellek, for instance, says that Byron "does not share the romantic conception of imagination," or does so "only fitfully." He quotes *Childe Harold*, Canto III, written and published in 1816, when Byron was temporarily under Wordsworth's influence through Shelley. Byron's Romantic view of nature as an organism with which man is unified organically by the imagination is equally fitful and limited to the period of Shelleyan influence. Wellek's suggestion that Byron is a symbolist, depending as it does on Wilson Knight's *The Burning Oracle*, is not very convincing. Knight strikes me as a weak reed to lean upon, and Wellek himself calls Knight "ex-

It may at first seem that I am here denying my basic aim of reducing the multiplicity of theories of Romanticism to a single theory, but this is not really so. Negative Romanticism is a necessary complement to Positive Romanticism, not a parallel or alternative to it, with which it must be reconciled. Briefly, Negative Romanticism is the expression of the attitudes, the feelings, and the ideas of a man who has left static mechanism but has not yet arrived at a reintegration of his thought and art in terms of dynamic organicism. I am here, of course, using a method of analysis which is now so common that one inhales it with the dust of our libraries, the method of analyzing the works of a man in terms of his personal development. Before we study any artist, we begin by establishing his canon and chronology. We *begin*, that is, by *assuming* that there is a development in his art. I hope I am not being merely tedious in pointing out that this method is in itself a particular application of one of the main ideas derived from dynamic organicism, or Positive Romanticism—the idea of evolution in the nineteenth-century sense. But to show what I mean by Negative Romanticism, therefore, and how it fits in with positive Romanticism, and to show how the theory works in practice, I shall discuss very briefly three works from the earlier years of the Romantic movement: "The Rime of the Ancient Mariner," *The Prelude*, and *Sartor Resartus*.[10]

Briefly, all three works are about spiritual death and rebirth, or secular conversion. In its baldest form, such an experience amounts to this: A man moves from a trust in the universe to a

---

travagant," certainly an understatement. In short, I think Wellek's three categories of Romanticism are useless, or only very rarely useful, when they are applied to Byron. So are Lovejoy's three Romantic ideas, for the same reasons, of course. (See Wellek's second article, *CL*, I, 165 and 168.) To be sure, Byron uses symbols; but he uses them compulsively, as everyone else does, not as a conscious principle of literary organization and creation.

[10] In what follows I shall offer an interpretation of "The Ancient Mariner" which I worked out some years ago, but which is substantially that developed from different points of view by Stallknecht, Maud Bodkin, and various other critics. I shall also suggest that all three works are about the same subjective experience. Stallknecht, so far as I know, is the only commentator who has pointed out—in his *Strange Seas of Thought*—that *The Prelude* and "The Ancient Mariner" are about the same thing; and so far as I know, no one has suggested that *Sartor Resartus* is concerned with the same subject.

period of doubt and despair of any meaning in the universe, and then to a reaffirmation of faith in cosmic meaning and goodness, or at least meaning. The transition from the first stage to the second we may call spiritual death; that from the second to the third we may call spiritual rebirth.

Let us first consider *The Prelude*. The subtitle, not Words-worth's, is *The Growth of a Poet's Mind*. After Wordsworth had started *The Recluse*, he found that in order to explain his ideas he must first explain how he came to have them. This decision is in itself a sign of Positive Romanticism. If you think in static terms, you will, as Pope did in *The Essay on Man*, present the result of a process of thought and experience. But if you find that you cannot explain your ideas except in terms of the process of how you have arrived at them, your mind is working in a different way, according to the principles of development and growth. The central experience which Wordsworth describes is spiritual death and rebirth. He began by having a complete faith in the principles of the French Revolution as the deistic *philosophes* and constitutionalists explained it. Their basic political principle was that we have only to restore to man his originally pure but now corrupt political organization and social contract, and a perfect society will necessarily result. Wordsworth accepted this as he also accepted the sentimentality, most notably and fully expressed by Shaftesbury, which was the eighteenth-century emotional expression of faith in the perfection and goodness of the universe, a sentimentalism which became more strident and absurd as its basic theodicy became increasingly less acceptable. Any man who is defending an idea in which he is emotionally involved will become more emotional and passionate in its defense as his opponent shows with increasing clarity that the idea is untenable.

The French Revolution, to Wordsworth, failed. It made men worse instead of better, and from the creation of political and intellectual freedom it turned to tyranny, slaughter, and imperialist expansion. He saw that he had been misled by his emotions into too facile an acceptance. It was then that he rejected sentimentalism and brought all values before the bar of reason, so that reason might sit in judgment. But reason also was not enough. The boasted reason of the Enlightenment could neither explain the failure of the French Revolution nor provide a means of acceptance. Then occurred his spiritual death. He had invested heavily in emotion and in reason. Each had betrayed him. He was spiritually bankrupt. Where was a means of acceptance? Moving to Racedown, rejoining Dorothy, coming to know Coleridge, and going to live near him at Nether Stowey, he reorganized all his ideas, with Coleridge's and Dorothy's intellectual and emotional help, and reaffirmed in new terms his faith in the goodness and significance of the universe. He stood, he said, "in Nature's presence a sensitive being, a *creative* soul"; that is, his creative power was a "power like one of Nature's." Nature and the creative soul maintain, he believed, an ennobling and enkindling interchange of action. The voice of nature is a living voice. And there are moods when that living voice can be heard, when "We see into the life of things," when we feel "a sense sublime / Of something far more deeply interfused; . . . / A motion and a spirit, that impels / All thinking things, all objects of all thought, / And rolls through all things."

The universe is alive, not dead; living and growing, not a perfect machine; it speaks to us directly through the creative mind and its senses. Its truth cannot be perceived from the "evidences of nature," but only through the unconscious and creative mind. And this is the point of the famous description of the ascent of Mt. Snowdon, in the last book of *The Prelude*. Climbing through the mist, Wordsworth comes to the top of the mountain. Around and below him is a sea of clouds, with the moon shining over all, clear, beautiful, and bright. But through a gap in the clouds comes the roar of the waters in the valleys around the mountains. Thus in the moon he beholds the emblem of a mind "That feeds upon infinity, that broods / Over the dark abyss, intent to hear / Its voices issuing forth to silent light / In one continuous stream." This is his symbol of the unconscious mind, both of man and of the universe, ultimately identical, both striving to become as well as to be. He has by a profound experience proved to himself the existence and the trustworthiness and the power of the unconscious mind, of the life of the universe, of the continuous creative activity of the cosmos.

Let me add that he also, unfortunately I think, retained within his new attitudes a nostalgia for permanence, an ideal of eternal perfection. Thus early do we have the compromise called Victorian. And this inconsistency was to prove his eventual undoing, to cause his loss of creative power, comparatively speaking, and to effect his return to a kind of revised Toryism, to a concept of an organic society without dynamic power. But that is another story, and I cannot go into it here.

Leaving chronological order aside, I turn now to *Sartor Resartus*. The central chapters of Carlyle's work are "The Everlasting No," "The Centre of Indifference," and "The Everlasting Yea." They obviously present a pattern of spiritual death and rebirth. Carlyle, speaking of himself under the guise of Professor Teufelsdröckh, tells us how he lost his religious belief. "The loss of his religious faith was the loss of everything." "It is all a grim Desert, this once-fair world of his." "Invisible yet impenetrable walls divided me from all living; was there in the wide world, any true bosom I could press trustfully to mine? No, there was none. . . . It was a strange isolation I then lived in. The universe was all void of Life, of Purpose, of Volition, even of Hostility; it was one huge dead immeasurable Steam-engine, rolling on, in its dead indifference, to grind me limb from limb." "The Universe had pealed its Everlasting No authoritatively through all the recesses of his being." But in the moment of Baphometic fire-baptism he stood up and cried out that he would not accept that answer. This was not yet the moment of rebirth, but it was the first step, the step of defiance and rebellion.

There follows the Centre of Indifference, of wandering grimly across the face of Europe, of observing the absurdities and cruelty and wickedness of mankind; he is a wanderer, a pilgrim without any shrine to go to. And then one day, surrounded by a beautiful landscape, in the midst of nature and the tenderness of the natural piety of human beings, came a change. "The heavy dreams rolled gradually away, and I awoke to a new Heaven and a new Earth. . . . What is nature? Ha! Why do I not name thee GOD? Are not thou the 'Living Garment of God'? The universe is not dead and demoniacal, a charnel-house with spectres, but godlike and my Father's." It is alive. Nature—as he tells us later in the book, in the chapter called "Organic Filaments"—nature "is not completed, but ever completing. . . . Mankind is a living movement, in progress faster or slower." Here indeed is a Positive Romanticism so complete that it is almost a Radical Romanticism, though Carlyle, like Wordsworth, retained an inconsistent static principle in his thought. Like Wordsworth's, his nostalgia for a static principle or static ground to the evolving universe was to prove his undoing, but that again is another story.

In "The Ancient Mariner" Coleridge tells us of an experience which is the same as that given by Wordsworth and Carlyle. The mariner, on his journey around the world, or through life, violates the faith of his fellow man by shooting the albatross, the one thing alive in the world of ice and snow, always symbols of spiritual coldness and death. His fellow mariners reject him, marking him with the sign of his own guilt. From the world of ice and snow they come to the world of fire and heat, again symbols of spiritual death, alienation, and suffering. The soul of the mariner is won by Life-in-Death. He alone remains alive while his fellow sailors, silently and with reproachful eyes, die around him. As Carlyle put it, "it was a strange isolation I lived in then." And Carlyle also uses the symbols of ice and fire to describe his condition. Isolation, alienation, and guilt possess the soul of the mariner. He is alone, in a burning and evil universe. "The very deep did rot," and the slimy and evil water-snakes surround his ship. And as he watches them in the moonlight he is suddenly taken with their beauty, and "I blessed them unaware." From the depths of the unconscious rose an impulse of affirmation, of love, of acceptance. The albatross drops from his neck into the sea. The symbol of guilt and alienation and despair vanishes. The universe comes alive. It rains, and the rain is the water of life. The wind blows; the breath of a living universe wafts the ship across the ocean. The air is filled with voices and the sky is filled with living light. The spirit of the land of ice and snow comes to his aid. (As Carlyle put it, even in his most despairful moments there was within him, unconsciously, a principle of faith and affirmation.) Angels come into the bodies of the dead sailors and work the ship. The whole universe comes to the mariner's aid, and he completes his journey.

And thereafter, though he has been forgiven and reaccepted

into man's life by the act of confession, there comes an impulse
to tell his story, the creative impulse of the poet rising powerfully from his unconscious mind. Poetry is conceived of as a
compulsive but creative act. In a sense Coleridge is more profound than either Wordsworth or Carlyle. He knows that, for a
Romantic, once alienated means always alienated. He cannot
join the wedding feast. Edwin Markham put it well:

> He drew a circle that shut me out—
> Heretic, rebel, a thing to flout:
> But Love and I had the wit to win:
> We drew a circle that took him in!

Though a man may create a synthesis that includes the ideas
of his fellow men, to those very men he will always be outside
the circle of accepted beliefs, even though he blesses all things
great and small.

At any rate we see here a highly radical Positive Romanticism.
It is the record of a process; it affirms the unconscious mind and
the creative imagination; it affirms the principle of the living universe; it affirms diversitarianism; and it is a fully developed symbolism, an organic symbolism in which the shooting of the albatross is without symbolic power unless it is thought of in terms
of the power and the interrelations of the various symbolic units.

These interpretations, to me at least, demonstrate the excellence of Lovejoy's three principles of Romanticism—organicism,
dynamism, and diversitarianism—to get us inside various works
of Romantic art and to show us the relationships that tie them
together into a single literary movement. And again to me, they
show that these ideas are not heterogeneous, independent ideas,
but closely associated ideas, all related to a central concept or
world metaphor.

And now to define Negative Romanticism. I have, of course,
taken the term from Carlyle's Everlasting No. As various individuals, according to their natures, and their emotional and
intellectual depths, went through the transition from affirming
the meaning of the cosmos in terms of static mechanism to affirming it in terms of dynamic organicism, they went through a

period of doubt, of despair, of religious and social isolation, of the separation of reason and creative power. It was a period during which they saw neither beauty nor goodness in the universe, nor any significance, nor any rationality, nor indeed any order at all, not even an evil order. This is Negative Romanticism, the preliminary to Positive Romanticism, the period of *Sturm und Drang*. As the nineteenth century rolled on, the transition became much easier, for the new ideas were much more widely available. But for the early Romantics the new ideas had to be learned through personal and painful experience. The typical symbols of Negative Romanticism are individuals who are filled with guilt, despair, and cosmic and social alienation. They are often presented, for instance, as having committed some horrible and unmentionable and unmentioned crime in the past. They are often outcasts from men and God, and they are almost always wanderers over the face of the earth. They are Harolds, they are Manfreds, they are Cains. They are heroes of such poems as *Alastor*. But when they begin to get a little more insight into their position, as they are forced to develop historical consciousness, as they begin to seek the sources for their negation and guilt and alienation, they become Don Juans. That is, in *Don Juan* Byron sought objectivity by means of satire, and set out to trace in his poem the development of those attitudes that had resulted in himself. As I said earlier, Positive Romanticism cannot explain Byron, but Negative Romanticism can. Byron spent his life in the situation of Wordsworth after the rejection of Godwin and before his move to Racedown and Nether Stowey, of the Mariner alone on the wide, wide sea, of Teufelsdröckh subject to the Everlasting No and wandering through the Centre of Indifference.

It is the lack of this concept that involves Wellek's second article and much of Barzun's book, for all their admirable insights, in certain difficulties, in such a foredoomed attempt to find in figures who express Negative Romanticism and figures who express Positive Romanticism a common and unifying element.[11] Theirs is the same difficulty as that with which Auden gets involved in *The Enchafèd Flood*. It is true that both Positive

[11] See, for example, n. 9, above.

and Negative Romanticism often cause isolation of the personality, but, as Coleridge of these three men alone realized, Negative Romanticism causes isolation and despair because it offers no cosmic explanations, while Positive Romanticism offers cosmic explanations which are not shared by the society of which one is a part. To Arnold, "Not a having and a resting, but a growing and a becoming, is the character of perfection as culture conceives it." His ideas isolated him from Barbarians, Philistines, and Populace; they were impressed but they did not follow; for they could not comprehend, so far were his fundamental attitudes separated from theirs. Picasso has in his painting expressed profoundly the results of the freedom that Romanticism has given to the creative imagination, but he is detested by most people who have seen his Cubist or post-Cubist paintings—as well as by a great many who have not. He is at home in the universe, but not in his society.[12]

[12] This is perhaps the place to insert a word about pre-Romanticism, a term which I would wholly abandon. Apparently it arose in the first place from a naïve application of Darwinian evolution to literary history. If the great Romantics liked nature, any eighteenth-century enjoyment or praise of nature became pre-Romanticism, in spite of the Horatian tradition of neoclassicism. If the Romanticists liked emotion, any praise of emotion in the eighteenth century was pre-Romantic, as if any age, including "The Age of Reason," could be without emotional expression. In their youth Wordsworth and Coleridge were sentimentalists; therefore sentimentalism is Romantic. And so on. James R. Foster, in his recent *History of the Pre-Romantic Novel in England* (New York, 1949), has shown that sensibility was the emotional expression of Deism, just as Lovejoy has demonstrated in various books and articles that deism and neoclassicism were parallel. If it seems odd that sentimentalism, "cosmic Toryism," and Deism are all expressions of the same basic attitudes, it must be remembered that the eighteenth century was the period when the mechanistic and static theodicy broke down from its own inconsistencies. Romanticism did not destroy its predecessor. It came into existence to fill a void. As an example of the difficulties eighteenth-century figures experienced in trying to hold their world together, consider the problem of understanding how Pope's *Essay on Man* could possibly be the foundation for his satires. Yet he was working on both at the same time and apparently thought the *Essay* gave him exactly the foundation and justification for satire that he needed. But if whatever is is right, why is it wrong that there should be such people and such behavior as Pope satirizes in the *Moral Essays*, the imitated and original satires, and *The Dunciad*? It is the old problem of accounting for evil in a world created by a perfect, omnipotent, and benevolent deity. I would recommend the total abandonment of the term "pre-Romantic," and the

IV

My proposal is now complete. This theory does, I firmly believe, what such a theory must do. It gets us inside of various works of art, and it shows the relevance of one work of art to another. Consider Beethoven's Fifth Symphony. It builds to a triumphant close. Unlike the symphonies of Haydn and most of those of Mozart, its last movement, not its first or second, is the most important and the most fully developed, for it is an affirmation which is the result of a tremendous struggle. Between the third and fourth movements is a bridge passage which repeats the rhythm and the harmonies of the opening theme, and the whole work is developed from germinal themes, ideas from which are derived the themes of subsequent movements. It is a symphony developmental and organic in construction. It is the record of a process, of an experience. It is a symbol of the cosmos conceived of as dynamic organism.

The same insights can be extended to painting, to impressionism, for example, with its evocation and record of a particular moment; or to modern architecture, especially to the work of Wright, with his lifelong search for an "organic architecture" of

---

substitution for it of some term such as "neo-classic disintegration." For instance, to refer to Wellek once more, on the first page of his second article he has this to say: "There was the 'Storm and Stress' movement in the seventies which exactly parallels what today is elsewhere called 'pre-romanticism.' " In a widely used anthology, *The Literature of England,* by G. B. Woods, H. A. Watt, and G. K. Anderson, first published in 1936, the section called "The Approach to Romanticism" includes Thomson, Gray, Collins, Cowper, Burns, and Blake; and in Ernest Bernbaum's *Guide through the Romantic Movement,* another widely known and used work (I refer to the first edition, published in 1930), the "Pre-Romantic Movement" includes the following, among others: Shaftesbury, Winchilsea, Dyer, Thomson, Richardson, Young, Blair, Akenside, Collins, the Wartons, Hartley, Gray, Goldsmith, MacKenzie, Burns, Darwin, Blake, Godwin, and Radcliffe. Some of these are "Storm and Stress"; others are quite plainly not. To lump all of them together, as a great many teachers and writers do, is to obliterate many highly important distinctions. To my mind, for *some* individuals neo-classicism disintegrated; thereupon what I call "Negative Romanticism," of which "Storm and Stress" is a very important expression, for *some* individuals ensued. Then *some* individuals, initially a very few, moved into the attitudes which I call "Positive Romanticism." As it is now used, "pre-Romanticism" confuses the first two of these three stages, just as "Romanticism" as it is now generally used confuses the second two and often all three.

houses that are part of their sites, with living rooms and gardens which interpenetrate. But I cannot here offer a full history of the development of modern culture. Rather, I wish to make one final suggestion, to issue a warning to anyone who may be taken with these ideas enough to try to employ them.

Although Negative and then Positive Romanticism developed by reaction out of the static-mechanistic-uniformitarian complex, with its cosmic Toryism, its sentimentalism, and its Deism, they were also superimposed upon it. At any point in nineteenth- or twentieth-century culture it is possible to take a cross section and find all three actively at work. The past 150 years or so must be conceived as a dramatic struggle, sometimes directly between Positive Romanticism and static, mechanistic thought, sometimes three-cornered. It is a struggle between minds and within minds. It is seen today in the profound disparity between what is sometimes called high art and popular art; it is expressed in the typical modern cultural phenomena of the avant-garde, which is as modern as Wordsworth and Coleridge. It appeared in the struggle over the "packing" of the Supreme Court and in the wearisome but still vital quarrels about progressive education. It appears in the antagonism between our relativistic critics and our absolutistic critics. It appears in the theological struggle between the theology of such a man as Charles Raven[13] and the proponents of the "theology of crisis." A very pure Positive Romanticism is at the heart of Ruth Benedict's *Patterns of Culture*; her ideal of a good society is organic, dynamic, and diversitarian. In short, the history of ideas and the arts in the nineteenth and twentieth centuries is the history of the dramatic struggle among three opposing forces: static mechanism, Negative Romanticism, and Positive Romanticism. In this drama, to me the hero is dynamic and diversitarian organicism, and I think Goethe and Beethoven and Coleridge and the other founders of the still vital Romantic tradition—a tradition often repudiated by those who are at the very heart of it, and understandably—have still much to say to us, are not mere intellectual and aesthetic curiosities. Nevertheless, I am aware that to many scholars and thinkers, Positive Roman-

[13] Raven is both biologist and theologian. See his *Science, Religion, and the Future* (Cambridge, England, and N. Y., 1943).

ticism is the villain, responsible for all the ills of our century. The drama may indeed turn out to be a tragedy, but if it does, it is because static mechanism persists in staying alive.[14]

Of course, the fact that my attitude towards the continuing and future usefulness of Positive Romanticism may not after all be justified is not essential to my argument, or even germane to it. I ask only that my readers take under serious consideration, and test in their studies, in their reading, and in their classrooms the theories about Romanticism which I have outlined. I trust that many of them will find these ideas useful, even though they withhold final assent.

[14] The Romantic metaphysic does not *necessarily* involve optimism. That is, although the world is growing in a better direction, the sum of evil may still outweigh the sum of good. Nor does it *necessarily* involve progressivism. That is, the development from the simple to the complex may mean development toward the better, or it may mean development toward the worse, or it may simply mean development without either improvement or degeneration. However, in the early part of the nineteenth century and generally since then, it usually implies both optimism and progressivism. There have been exceptions, however, of whom Eduard von Hartmann is one of the most thoroughgoing, both in his pessimism and in his Positive Romanticism. It must be noted that he has a technique of acceptance in the sense that he discerns cosmic order and meaning, though he doesn't like it.

2

TOWARD A THEORY OF

ROMANTICISM: II. RECONSIDERATIONS

[1960*]

In March, 1951, I published in *PMLA* "Toward a Theory of Romanticism."[1] I am glad that I called it "*Toward* a Theory." To summarize, Romanticism is a sharp break with the rationalizing and sentimentalizing Enlightenment, expressed in a number of works dramatizing spiritual death and rebirth. I distinguished between Negative Romanticism—a stage in which the individual was isolated by the loss of a meaningful relation to the universe provided by a metaphysic of static mechanism of the Enlightenment and was thus alienated from his society—and Positive Romanticism—a stage in which the individual was once more related to the universe by acquiring a metaphysic of dynamic organicism, but was still alienated from his society, which con-

---

* Delivered at the annual meeting of the Modern Language Association, December, 1960. Reprinted by permission from *Studies in Romanticism*, I (Autumn, 1961), pp. 1–8. Copyright 1962 by the Trustees of Boston University.
[1] LXVI, 3–23; see pp. 3–26 of this volume.

tinued to live on Enlightenment and pre-Enlightenment principles. I explained Romantic symbolism in organic terms. I rejected the concept of pre-Romanticism. I asserted that the cultural development of the nineteenth and twentieth centuries is properly to be regarded as a development of Romanticism, the specific values of which I classified as "change, imperfection, growth, diversity, the creative imagination, the unconscious."

Several years later, when I had arrived at the point of thinking the whole thing purest nonsense, I set out to reconstruct the theory. I felt that much was sound and worth salvaging, and to an exposition of my current notions on this maddening subject I shall now turn, only begging the reader to prefix mentally to each sentence, "At the moment I find it useful to employ the following proposition in thinking about Romanticism."

If order is perceived as structured into the empirical world—natural and social—value (i.e., what is variously referred to as "meaning" or "purpose") and identity are also thus seen. Consequently, the perception of order is felt to be interchangeable with the perception of value, and the perception of both is accompanied by the emergence of identity, perceived in terms of a socially structured role. Nevertheless, because of the disparity between an orientation and the data it is called upon to organize, the individual, if he is to adapt successfully to his environment, *must* perceive a disparity between the order affirmed by orientation and his actual experience of randomness. In the Western tradition there have been two primary pseudo-explanations for this disparity. The first is the myth of paradise and the Fall. That it is an emotionally and pragmatically satisfactory resolution is evidenced by its continuing vitality. An environment such that the orientation corresponds exactly with the experienced world would be paradise, a place of pure order, pure value, and never-threatened identity, that is, salvation. From this point of view the reason for the Fall is of no importance. The possibilities for explaining it are infinite. The important element is the contrast between the prelapsarian state and the postlapsarian, between perfect orientation and the world as we experience it. The Platonic solution, at least after the Neo-Platonists had their way with it, exhibits the same pattern, nonhistorically. A real world of pure order and value is set against the experienced, shadowy, imitated world, of disorder and little or no value. Thus the myth of the Fall and the Neoplatonic epistemological myth can be perfectly synthesized by containing time in eternity. The Middle Ages were founded on a world hypothesis according to which the world of space and time is disordered and of only partial and occasional value, in which even perceived order can be used as a temptation by Satan, the spirit that denies value; the moral task is to maintain as much order and value as possible until death, or the last judgment, when the individual would either re-enter paradise, a world of total order, value, and salvation, or identity, or be forever plunged into its opposite. Since such a scheme embraced orientation and perception, order and disorder, good and evil, in an all-embracing orientation, it exhibited remarkable stability, and continues to do so.

However, the Renaissance brought out a different attitude; in the older scheme the source of the order was revelation and the means of its transmission was the Church, through its redemptive power. The progressive organization and accumulation of knowledge in medieval science and philosophy led to a situation in which some individuals began to believe that it was possible to arrive at the vision of order outside of the Church, and even outside of religion. The human mind, it was decided by a few, could achieve the truth of revelation without the instrumentality of ecclesiastical transmission and sanction. A revival of Neo-Platonism was the consequence, or rather the separation of Neo-Platonism from its Judeo-Christian twin. Recent investigations have shown the Neo-Platonic background of both Galileo and Newton; and Descartes's decision to think through the world, since order was thought of as discovered and not ascribed, and value and identity as given, led, with the aid of Galileo and Newton, to a wholly new orientation. The sensational results have been admirably described and the roots investigated in the remarkable contributions to the history of science made in the past ten years, and for the literary scholar in Marjorie Nicolson's

Mountain Gloom and Mountain Glory: The Development of the Aesthetics of the Infinite[2] and particularly in Ernest Tuveson's *The Imagination as a Means of Grace: Locke and the Aesthetics of Romanticism.*[3] The new orientation was that this is not a fallen world, nor a shadowy world, but that order and value are structured into the perceived world, and that identity is given with the existence of each biological human entity. Society is a natural emergent, not the result of divine fiat. The disparity between the orientation and the experience lies in the fact of our ignorance—a notion easily demonstrated—not in the fact that we are faced with a corrupt world. Man is naturally part of that order; the moral task is to restore his originally perfect adaptation by exploiting his civilization and knowledge. Since the natural order grants perfect adaptation, what has been lost through ignorance can be regained through knowledge. Or—and here was the rub —since man is the product of nature, he is not in fact maladapted at the present time. His task is to adapt himself morally and emotionally to the order in which we now find ourselves. In either case observable order assures that value is structured into the universe. However, in the long run neither perspective offers any means to make moral discriminations. Down one can be seen Soame Jenyns, down the other, Robespierre. Rigorously interpreted, whatever moral decision you make, you cannot be wrong; you can only be ignorant. If you wish to persuade people that they are in a perfect world, you are quite justified in your choice of means, since by definition the ends, which will be arrived at by a natural process, have order and value structured in them; and De Sade's frustration emerges: it is impossible to peform an unnatural act. Recent studies in Enlightenment pessimism have shown that as the eighteenth century wore on, more and more Enlightenment figures became aware of the difficulty. An important consequence for students of literature was the steady development in intensity and quantity of sentimentalism. Its original source was the necessity to discharge the tension consequent upon the affirmation that the world is radiant with order and value which any mind free from superstition, tyranny, and

[2] (Ithaca, 1959).
[3] (Berkeley, 1960).

priestcraft could arrive at for itself, and the inconsistent perception that it is not. An aesthetic stimulus came to be valued for its power to discharge that tension in tears and enthusiasm. Further, the more the basic instability became apparent, the more necessity there was to fall back upon an emotional affirmation of order, value, and identity as qualities structured into the real world. From this point of view Ossian was a typical late Enlightenment phenomenon. The enthusiastic poet and the man of feeling dominated the scene. As Professor Tuveson has so well demonstrated, Nature, through the exercise of the imagination, redeemed man. If you wish, as many do, to use the term "Romanticism" to refer to this Enlightenment and enthusiasm and sentimentalism and natural redemption, I have no objection. One long tradition has always called it Romanticism. But nothing could be more different from what I am talking about when I use that word. When the crash came, when a tiny minority of Enlightenment personalities, themselves a cultural minority, saw through Enlightenment pretensions and saw that it is impossible to maintain them, and when the Enlightenment was put to the test in the French Revolution and its superficiality revealed, a major cultural break occurred.

The logical possibilities of identifying Nature with order and value had been exhausted. If it is not true that order and value once were in this world and no longer are, or that they are outside the world, if it is not true that order and value are in the world, where are they? They do not exist at all, cries in anguish the Negative Romantic. But it is impossible for people at a high level of culture and civilization to endure for long such total disorientation. In such a situation was (and still is) any individual who enters the Negative Romantic stage, unless he can turn back to a pre-Enlightenment orientation or successfully repress his doubts about the Enlightenment construct. If he can do neither, he turns the world inside out.

Long ago George Herbert Mead said that Romanticism is marked by the separation of the role from the self. With the collapse of the Enlightenment there also collapses the natural social structure, and with it the possibility of playing a role. Hence the social alienation which accompanies the cosmic isolation, or loss of relatedness to the perceived world. The first step at reconstituting value, then, is to strip bare the self, or, more accurately, to invent the self, to conceptualize the sense of identity. To survive, one asserts pure identity as the basic datum. As two recent studies have pointed out, Schelling and Wordsworth attempted to assert the self as real and the world as a symbol of value.[4] Wordsworth eventually regressed, for such a position is a compromise. To be sure, there is all the difference between perceiving the world as evidence of divine order and perceiving it as a symbol of divine value, and finding order in the act of perception itself, but the latter, or symbolic, perception is extremely unstable, since it really asserts the existence of two sources of value and order, the self and the world. Rather, the more stable solution is to perceive the world as symbol of the self, and order and value as projected upon the world by the self. I think Professor Tuveson is in error, therefore, when he thinks of eighteenth-century Enlightenment and enthusiastic "early Romanticism" as the predecessor of "high Romanticism" (*my* Romanticism), which is its fulfillment. Rather, *my* Romantics used the same words, but sang them to a different tune. Imagination is a means of grace, to be sure, but Nature does not redeem man. Rather, man, through the exercise of the imagination, redeems Nature. Value enters the world through the self, which is not supported by any perceptible social or cosmic order, and the self projects upon the world an order which serves to symbolize that self-generated value. To be sure, for a time, and for some, the self was seen as the portal of the divine, a mythological symbolization for the sense of value. This was the transcendental stage of Romanticism; but side by side, and eventually superseding it, was a nonmetaphysical realization that the only conceivable source of value was the necessity for the individual self to create it in order to maintain itself. In short, the self does not emerge through the perception of order and value in the world; rather, order and value emerge from the perception of the self. Nature is not the source of value, but the occasion for projecting it.

Man therefore redeems the world; and since in the poet the imagination is predominant, the poet is the primary source of

---

[4] David Ferry, *The Limits of Mortality* (Middletown, Conn., 1960) and E. D. Hirsch, Jr., *Wordsworth and Schelling* (New Haven, 1960).

value—in traditional language, redemption. The Romantic poet thus takes upon himself the role of Christ; he becomes Christ, and he is himself his own redeemer and the model for the redemption of mankind. Eventually this task of the artist is extended to every human being. Further, if man is to redeem the world, it is only this world which can be redeemed. After yielding up moral questions in despair, because they are ultimately unsolvable by the Enlightenment orientation, Wordsworth grasped both horns of his dilemma. Nature is the source of both disturbance and equilibrium, of disorientation and orientation. To see what a gulf has here been crossed it is sufficient to call to mind that, to the Enlightenment, Nature was the source of orientation only. Hence the frequent marriages of heaven and hell in the Romantic tradition. Kubla Khan's garden includes both. Here or nowhere we find our home. Since it is this world which must be redeemed, the first task of the Romantic is to face fully the horror, the brutality, and the evil which before had been either thought away or dismissed or regarded as either temporary or ultimately unreal. The flower of value must be plucked not on the sunny mountaintop, but in the very abyss. The worship of *sorrow* is divine. The world must be redeemed, in its absurdity and ugliness, as well as in its order and beauty. Hence Romanticism leads directly to the realism of Dickens and Balzac and so down to the present. It is the Romantic's tradition that is really tough-minded. To him nothing is so beautiful as fact, nor does anything offer such sweet bones to gnaw on as the empirical world itself, the only world we can know, for the self can only be symbolized, not known. And hence the profoundest way to symbolize it is to recognize and assert its existence in another; and this empathic assertion is the basis of Romantic social morality.

From this fundamental percept of the self as the source of order flows Romanticism's essentially antimetaphysical character. With and without the aid of Kant, an orientation is now seen not as a discovery but as a projection. Thus a metaphysical theory is thought of as an instrument, not as a reality, not as something in Nature, but as something imposed upon it. On the one hand it is conceived as an instrument for symbolizing the self or value; on the other it is thought of as an epistemological instrument.

Further consequences flow from this. If an orientation is only instrumentally, not constitutively, valid, it is useful only temporarily. But then value, identity, and order can be experienced only temporarily, in moments of illumination, spots of time. Further, the Romantic knows from history, his own and man's, that the great human temptation is to regard an orientation as final and that succumbing leads to disaster, for Christianity and the Enlightenment had ultimately collapsed. Consequently his moral task is to break down an orientation once it has been fully realized. His only means is self-disorientation. Hence the judgment often made that the Romantic values emotional disturbance for its own sake. Not at all; he values it as a means to break down an orientation which, as a human being, he is tempted to preserve but, as a Romantic human being, he knows by definition is inadequate. As Browning implied, the only failure is success. Hence throughout the nineteenth century the use of drugs, alcohol, sex, and Asiatic theologies as means of deliberately dislocating the senses so that new worlds may emerge. Only with the breakthrough into modern art did the Romantic artist and thinker learn how to break down an orientation without partially disintegrating his personality.

From this perspective it is possible to develop a more adequate explanation of the presence of dynamic organicism in the Romantic tradition than the one I proposed several years ago. To begin with, it is now apparent—and perhaps was then, though not to me—that organicism is a product of the Enlightenment, that the increasing dependence on the natural world was bound to lead to conceiving the cosmos on the model of an organism rather than of a machine, and did. Further, the values of diversity, change, growth, and uniqueness, derived from organicism, are mainly late Enlightenment values, though, to be sure, relatively rare. From this point of view Herder, for example, appears as an Enlightenment figure, not a Romantic one. The organic episode in the development of Romanticism occurred partly because it was in the culture and could be used to symbolize the subjective experience of the Romantic personality, the emergence of the self, partly because it was a novelty to many Romantics, who did not realize its Enlightenment origins. Nevertheless, to the Romantic it is always an instrument, while to nineteenth-century Enlightenment thinking it is constitutive. Although it was the most important metaphysical episode in the history of Romanticism, it was abandoned, as all Romantic world hypotheses are abandoned, for by definition they are inadequate; and this process continues until Romanticism learns that it can do entirely without constitutive metaphysics and can use any metaphysic or world hypothesis as a supreme fiction.

To conclude with a phrase from Wallace Stevens is, I think, appropriate, for I still believe what I said years ago and what is now, in fact, becoming almost a platitude, that modern art is the triumph of Romanticism, that modern culture, in its vital areas, is a Romantic culture, and that nothing has yet replaced it. Since the logic of Romanticism is that contradictions must be included in a single orientation, but without pseudo-reconciliations, Romanticism is a remarkably stable and fruitful orientation. For the past 175 years the Romantic has been the tough-minded man, determined to create value and project order to make feasible the pure assertion of identity, determined to assert identity in order to engage with reality simply because it is there and because there is nothing else, and knowing eventually that his orientations are adaptive instruments and that no orientation is or can be final. The Romantic artist does not escape from reality; he escapes into it. We may expect that the present revival of interest in nineteenth-century Romanticism among younger scholars and artists will continue, for, as a consequence of the current widespread breakdown of the Enlightenment tradition, Romanticism is at last beginning to receive an adequate response.

3

THE DILEMMA OF A CENTURY:

THE FOUR STAGES OF ROMANTICISM

[1964*]

When does the nineteenth century begin? It is much easier to say than it used to be. The cultural leaders of the time certainly knew when it had begun and what marked that beginning. It was only in the later nineteenth century and the first half of the twentieth that the question became obscured by the quarrel over the meaning of the term "Romanticism." That maddening and confusing word still has a fearful variety of meanings, and always will; but there is a growing agreement among cultural historians to limit its historical sense to a period that began in the late eighteenth century, when a small number of cultural leaders throughout Europe almost simultaneously, but at first quite independently, began to feel that they had arrived at a way of viewing the world which was profoundly different from any world view that had ever appeared before. And they also felt that this new

* Reprinted by permission from *Romanticism: The Culture of the Nineteenth Century,* ed. Morse Peckham, George Braziller, New York, 1965. Copyright © 1965 by Morse Peckham.

Weltanschauung (the Germans had to coin a new term to express what they were experiencing) forced them to see everything— philosophy, religion, the arts, history, politics, society—down an entirely new perspective.

Men have always had world views, or metaphysics; it is impossible to cross a crack in the sidewalk without a metaphysic. But such metaphysics had been unconscious; that is, there had been no language in which to discuss them. There were arguments about this or that view of the world as it affected some aspect of human behavior; but these were arguments about metaphysics as truths which described the character and structure of the world. But the new way of thinking, the Romantic way, looked at itself from right angles, saw itself creating a world view because the very character of the mind's relation to the world required it to have a metaphysic. At the same time, however, there was a conviction, at first but faint though deeply disturbing, that any world view told the mind nothing about the world, but merely told it something about the mind. Any metaphysic was seen not as derived from the nature of the world but rather as derived from the nature of the mind and projected onto the world. A single step was taken, and all the world was changed. All previous world views had assumed that the mind had access, whether through revelation from God or from study of the world, to the real nature and character, the true essence, of what was not the mind; and this assumption was unconscious. Or, more precisely, the assumptiveness of this assumption was not verbalized or, apparently, experienced. The new attitude was not a simple assertion that we cannot know the world. Rather, it realized that we cannot know whether we know it or not. For all we know, a metaphysic may be a reliable description of the world; but there is no way to know that we know. For we are always inside a metaphysical system; we can get outside of one system only by gliding, whether we are aware of it or not, into another.

But the same position was arrived at in various ways, whether it was put in philosophical terms or not. One of the best indications of a profound cultural change is the emergence of new social roles. From this point of view, the fact that Romanticism developed a genuinely new social role is in itself almost sufficient evidence that the nineteenth century was experiencing a cultural earthquake, a convulsion at the profoundest levels of being. By itself, the new role, in all of its varieties, is enough to suggest that no profounder change had occurred in human life since the development of urbanism or "civilization" in the fourth millennium B.C. The essence of the new role is that it was an anti-role and that it was designed to symbolize the difference between role and self. To play a role is to act according to the cultural conventions of a particular category of situations. For men before Romanticism, when one played a role there was, so to speak, nothing of the personality left over. To be sure, there was "self-consciousness," but it consisted merely of role rehearsal and criticism of how well one had played or was playing the role. For the vast majority of human beings in our cultural tradition, and so far as I can tell, in all others, this is still the ongoing state of affairs. But to the original tiny group of Romantics and to a steadily growing portion of the population ever since, role-playing did leave something over. So true was this that these men played roles only for the sake of isolating what they called the self, the sense of identity, the only subjectively perceived quality of experience common to the playing of all roles. And this was precisely analogous to the new attitude toward metaphysics. Roles were seen not as modes of behavior derived from the natural world, or dictated by a divine being, or inherent in man's relation to his world, but as something that man imposes on the world, something that serves only to carry out a given human intention, something, therefore, with the character of a mask. Masks and metaphysics—ultimately, they are identical. Man cannot live without such masks, but the vital, the essential, quality of experience came to be the realization of what the mask concealed. But since that hidden element was inaccessible, it was necessary to create an anti-role, a role that was different from all other roles in that it could not be integrated into the social structure of interlocking roles.

Today most people, even at the higher levels of culture, live according to the metaphysics of the Enlightenment, which reached its first climax of attempted realization in what a recent historian has called the Age of Revolutions. The American and the French revolutions were simply the most conspicuous and sensational examples of revolutionary attempts all over western Europe. The Enlightenment can be reduced to one principle—the adaptation of the organism to the environment is properly the basis of all scientific and moral decisions; the aim was to make every scientific decision a moral one, and every moral decision a scientific one. Thus, it was thought, moral decisions can be grounded upon the real structure of nature, and this of course implied a metaphysic that asserted that the structure of the mind was identical with the structure of nature. Because, however, of man's ignorance and stupidity and his religious and political tyranny, the structure of society was out of line. The revolutionary effort of the late eighteenth century was designed to correct that fault, to line up mind, society, and nature into one unitary system.

But at the same time there was a conservative Enlightenment, best represented by Edmund Burke. He saw mind, society, and nature as an organic system that had gradually developed, and thus he saw the revolutionary effort as something that was bound to damage and even destroy the exquisitely complex and delicate interdependence of the three elements of reality. Reform, not revolution, was the answer to the social difficulties of the times. From the same metaphysic and with the same values of adaptational effort two diametrically opposed positions emerged; one justified the slaughter of the rich and powerful; the other, the suppression of the poor and weak. To a few men of the day (Wordsworth, the English poet, for one), it became apparent that some other force was at work in the mind. Not an unconscious force—Burke's organicism included that—but some force, some character of the human mind which called into doubt the fundamental assumption of the Enlightenment: the isomorphism, or structural identity, of mind and nature. No matter how cunningly fitted together mind and nature might be, they were nevertheless utterly different in their character. The structure of one was not identical with the structure of the other. The mind could not know nature. Society, then, was but an extension or instrument of the mind, a means of adaptation. But that adaptation could not be perfect, must always be, perhaps, very imperfect indeed. It was an adjustment of mind to nature, but it violated, for that very reason, both. The role was a violation of the self.

What, then, was the self? How could it be defined? How could it be talked about? What was the evidence for its existence? Since the basic human desire was for structure, for order, or, to put it in other terms, for meaning and the sense of value, the essence of the self was precisely that desire. Meaning was not immanent in nature, was not something that the mind found in the world; it was something the mind imposed on the world. And for this notion there was, in the experience of the pioneer Romantics, felt evidence. For many of them the failure of the Enlightenment metaphysic was revealed by the course of the French Revolution, which shifted from Utopian liberation to tyrannous oppression, *without shifting its ground*, without changing its metaphysic. Ultimately there was no difference between the revolutionary and the reactionary. This perception was like a new Fall of Man. The world suddenly lost its value; life lost its meaning; the individual no longer had a source for his sense of identity and a ground for his desire for order and structure. Even before the French Revolution, a few individuals had had this experience. The nineteenth century may almost be said to have begun with Goethe's *Sorrows of Young Werther*.

Werther committed suicide, and his creator, Goethe, thought he would lose his sanity. Rebirth, restoration, rediscovery of value for these men came from within, came from, they felt, the ultimate depths of the mind itself, from its very nature and structure. At a stroke, mind was sundered from nature, subject from object, the self from the role, which was seen at best as the means of realizing the self and, at worst, as the instrument whereby nature violated the self. The Romantic experienced a sense of profound isolation within the world and an equally terrifying alienation from society. These two experiences, metaphysical isolation and social alienation—they are of course two different modes of the same perception—were the distinguishing signs of the Romantic, and they are to this day. To symbolize that isolation and alienation, and simultaneously to assert the self as the source of order, meaning, value, and identity, became one task of the Romantic personality. To find a ground for value, identity, meaning, order became the other task. I believe that there were four basic stages in the development of this second task. But it will help to glance first at some of the solutions to the social symbolization of this task in what I have called the various kinds of Romantic anti-role.

The first, though it is initially found in *Werther*, is generally called the Byronic Hero. It is a way of symbolizing precisely that utter loss of meaning and value which so many people experienced—and continue to experience—when the Enlightenment collapsed. The Byronic hero appears in numerous forms—the wanderer, the outcast, the Wandering Jew, the mysterious criminal whose crime is never explained. The normal development for the emerging Romantic type in the nineteenth century was from pre-Enlightenment Christianity to Enlightenment, and then to the stage of the Byronic hero, a stage which can well be called Negative Romanticism, for it negates all value and all meaning, both within the bounds of the individual and outside of it. The tremendous appeal of Byron's poems throughout Europe and America shows how widespread was the feeling, even though few understood the sources of the malaise which was responsible for it. Jack London's Wolf Larsen is an early twentieth-century instance.

The first stage of recovery and the first true or positive Romantic anti-role is that of the Poet-Visionary. The word often used at the time was "mystic," but what it represents is so profoundly different from traditional mysticism that it is evident that the term was employed simply because no other word was available. Indeed, it was hard to understand at the time that "mystic" meant not much more than "incomprehensible." Actually it referred to an effort to bridge the gap between subject and object, between self and world, by a peculiar mode of perception which enables one to, as Wordsworth put it, "see into the life of things." Even Kant, in his aesthetic, had suggested that there is a mode of perception which enables us to experience the *Ding-an-sich*, the world-in-itself. It expresses the conviction that there is an order and meaning immanent in the natural universe, even though the understanding cannot reach it, even though we cannot say anything about it. It is the pure experience of value which arises from so intense an observation of the natural world that all roles, all mental categories, disappear. It is the pure revelation of truth, though what that truth is cannot be stated. And it was felt to be the peculiar task and privilege of the poet, the artist, to communicate that experience in the work of art. This is the source of the tremendous valuation given to art in the Romantic tradition, of the redemptive character of art; for in the act of creating the work of art, the artist both repeats and embodies, and also makes possible for himself and others, the act of seeing through and past, of dissolving, all purely human or role-playing perceptions which mask the world, as the rational part of the mind does, so that the value immanent in the self reaches out and touches the value immanent in the world. This tradition still survives, though in an extraordinarily desiccated form, in the most modern aesthetics, and more vitally in such painters as Malevich and Klee.

But even while this Visionary Artist was developing, another anti-role was emerging, perhaps the most important of the various Romantic anti-roles: the Bohemian. Even today it is probably impossible, and certainly very difficult, to become a genuinely modern man—a Romantic of the twentieth century—without going through Bohemianism. Paris is the classic locale of Bohemianism, but it actually started in Germany, or even, in a mild sort of way, in England, with the experiments in living of Wordsworth and Coleridge in the last decade of the eighteenth century. All the essential ingredients of Bohemianism were as visible in the first decade of that century as they are today. Perhaps the key lies in the Bohemian's fascination with alcohol and drugs, for these are the means of shifting and changing consciousness, of putting the mind through permutations of perceptions which for the square, who is always boxed in by his social role, are impossible. Similar is the interest in sexual experimentation, in nonbourgeois modes of living, in indifference to middle-class standards of dress, furnishings, cleanliness; W. H. Auden warns against people who bathe too often. And this interest in the deliberate distortion of the senses and of the ways of relating to society is closely related to the aims of the Visionary Artist. Hence the Bohemian invariably makes art the center of his life, and the excuse for his deliberate offensiveness. And so he is constantly involved in unstable anti-institutions which reveal a new and, of course, at last the *true* nature or task of painting or poetry or music or philosophy. He publishes his manifestoes, his little magazine; he starts his ephemeral publishing house. And then he wanders off to a new little group or emerges as the dedicated artist who cannot be bothered with even a minimal Bohemian role.

The 1820's and the 1830's saw the emergence of two more anti-roles: the Virtuoso and the Dandy. It was Baudelaire who first saw the true significance of the Dandy. But even so, the full meaning of this anti-role has rarely been realized. And less comprehended is the anti-role of the Virtuoso. Yet the two greatest painters of the twentieth century have realized magnificently the essence of these two roles. Matisse gave the Dandy his full freedom; and Picasso did the same great task for the Virtuoso. Wallace Stevens has gone beyond them, for he is at once Dandy and Virtuoso. Some light on the related nature of these two roles can be gained from the realization that Stevens was both poet and successful businessman, while Matisse and Picasso exploited the business of being painters with a success that can make the most hardheaded middle-class anti-Romantic businessman, with his devotion to Enlightenment laissez-faire and free trade, blush with shame and envy.

The Visionary Artist avoided role-playing; the Bohemian defied it; but the Virtuoso and the Dandy transcended it, the one by fantastic mastery, the other by irony. Paganini was the first great Virtuoso, and for decades the anti-role model and the ideal. That he took something from the Byronic hero appears in the legend that he had gained his mastery of the violin by selling his soul to the devil, a Virtuoso theme that Thomas Mann uses in his *Doktor Faustus*, a study of a great twentieth-century Virtuoso composer. The Virtuoso explodes the role, then, from within. He symbolizes the uniqueness of the self as the source of value by transforming the role into a source of unimagined splendor, order, power, and beauty. One such role exploded and transformed by the Romantic type was that of traveler. The great English Romantic Virtuoso traveler was Richard Burton, the translator of the

Arabian Nights, who also extended the Virtuoso anti-role into sexual experience. From the Virtuoso traveler emerged that most remarkable Romantic manifestation, the mountain climber, whose superhuman effort finally culminated in the conquest of Mt. Everest. The essence of the Virtuoso, then, is the symbolization of the inadequacy of society to meet the demands of the self, and this inadequacy the Virtuoso reveals by a superhuman control and release of energy in an activity which, to the socially adapted, can only be pointless. "Why did you climb Everest?" "Because it was there." The word for the Virtuoso is "sublime."

The Dandy, on the other hand, transforms the role not by excess but by irony. The role of the highest status in European society is that of the aristocratic gentleman of leisure. By willfully playing this role better than those born and trained to it, the Dandy reveals the pointlessness of the socially adapted. He makes a mode of life designed to symbolize social status into a work of art designed to symbolize nothing at all, or nothing that the society values. It is an anti-role because it is purely gratuitous, because, indeed, it is pure, utterly free from self-interest. He erects play into a creed. But this, of course, ironically reveals the triviality of society: the social type with the highest status spends his life in play and pettiness. The Dandy, then, offers perfection and elegance without content, without social function. By stealing the clothes of society, he reveals its nakedness. But at the same time he symbolizes his own demands for a greater exquisiteness and order and perfection than society can achieve. And this explains the irritation of society with the dandy, its efforts to deprive him of his value and his ironic authority, the moral nastiness with which England relished the downfall of Oscar Wilde.

One of the most perplexing qualities of the Romantic tradition is its historicism, which is most obvious in its architecture. But an examination of that reveals the historian as a final Romantic anti-role. The capacity to respond to nineteenth-century architecture, to penetrate through our modern notions of taste, is perhaps the ultimate test of whether one has truly grasped the spirit of Romantic culture. It is by no means enough to say that nineteenth-century architects imitated historical styles; for, in the first place, they did not imitate them. Rather, they manipulated the historical styles with an extraordinary freedom and architectural imagination. Even when, toward the end of the century, they were less concerned with free fantasies on historical styles than with designing according to the principles of those styles, they were not imitating. Far from it. In an odd way, the buildings of the late nineteenth and early twentieth centuries are better examples of particular styles than the originals from which they were derived. Thus Ralph Cram's nave in St. John the Divine in New York City is one of the greatest Gothic naves ever designed, more beautiful, in some ways, than any nave designed or built during the Middle Ages, though it seems like blasphemy to say so. Such men designed according to a conscious theory of Gothic or Renaissance or Enlightenment architecture; they built according to a construct that attempted to formulize the essence of the Gothic or Renaissance architectural spirit. To deny the exquisite perfection of the Morgan Library is aesthetic pedantry. Free manipulation and conscious perfecting of immanent principles, then, are the forms of the spirit of Romantic architecture; and its sources are highly similar to those of the Virtuoso and the Dandy. On the one hand, it is a studied reference to the superiority of the past. It is a nostalgia which symbolizes alienation. On the other hand, it is a completely personal manipulation of a social tradition. The Romantic architect, at least for a long time, could not create a Romantic nonhistorical style, for to do so would have been to serve his society, which his alienation prevented. He could serve it only by providing for its bourgeois, Enlightenment, adaptational functions a completely inappropriate setting—cathedrals for railroad stations, aristocratic palaces for the new rich, classic temples for Christian services.

But historicism pervaded all aspects of Romantic culture. The great period of literary history, as opposed to modern scholarly history, was the nineteenth century, and the histories of Michelet, of Ranke, of Carlyle, of Froude, are still the best historical reading in the world. What the Historian symbolized was, in fact, the Romantic historical consciousness. For this consciousness there were two sources. Anyone who had gone through the profoundly disorienting transition of experiencing the failure of the great hopes of the Enlightenment, of experiencing also the consequent total loss of meaning and value and identity, and then of arriving at the new Romantic vision, saw his own life as history. Psychology became history; personality became history; the manifestation of the self became history. But there was another way of arriving at the same result, a way of which Hegel is the great exemplar. Once the subject and the object, the mind and nature, have been sundered, once an unbridgeable gap has been placed between them, once the *strangeness* of human existence has been experienced without any falling back on Original Sin, then one concludes that the only way the subject can know itself is through what it does to the object, and the only way the object can be known is through what it does with the subject. What can we talk about? The interaction between the two, the interpretational tension between mind and world. For mind cannot know reality, it can only interpret it, dictated by its profoundest interests, which are in fact unknowable. Neither the self nor the world can be known, that is, talked about; they can only be experienced, the one in terms of the other. Reality, then, is what mind has done to world and what world has done to mind. Reality is history, the history of how, in its dealings with the phenomenal world, the interests of the mind, the will, as Schopenhauer called it, have been revealed; that is, the will to creation, to order, to meaning, to value, to identity. Just as the early Romantic could understand himself only in terms of what had happened to him, so man can be understood only in terms of his history, and reality can be understood only in terms of the history of man's dealings with the world. "Spirit" is the term many Romantics used for the interpretational tension from subject to object, and reality, therefore, is the history of Spirit. Thus, in understanding Picasso, it is the history of his style which provides the clue for the individual painting. The Enlightenment placed perceptions by putting them into the frame of unchanging nature; Romanticism places them by putting them into the frame of historical process. Reality is neither space nor time; it is the process of history.

These, then—Byronic Hero, Visionary Artist, Bohemian, Virtuoso, Dandy, Historian—are the novel roles that mark the emergence of Romanticism, and are sufficient proof that Romanticism is the profoundest cultural transformation in human history since the invention of the city. I do not insist that it is an exhaustive list, but these are the only novel roles which I have been able to discover. And they are roles, in Romantic culture; but to non-Romantic culture they were and still are anti-roles. Existentialism centers upon the problem of alienation, which is the necessary preliminary to the act of commitment, the creation and realization and symbolization of the self. But this modern position could not have been arrived at without intermediate stages. It is post-Nietzschean, for it depends upon and derives from Nietzsche's solution to the problem of the ground of value, its authority, its metaphysical meaningfulness. To the discovery of that ground there can be discerned, I believe, four stages.

The first of these is Analogism. This was the initial stage of positive Romanticism, the first result of the attempt to find a ground for value. Its essence we have already seen in examining the Visionary Artist, the Romantic Mystic. It depended upon a particular mode of perceiving or, more properly, of interpreting the world, particularly the natural world. Nature worship, which is often identified as the hallmark of Romanticism, is actually in origin an Enlightenment idea. Its source lay in the great Enlightenment notion of adaptation; psychological or emotional adaptation to the natural world was felt to be a necessary preliminary, a kind of rehearsal, for the adaptation of the total organism and of society to the structure of nature. It had two aspects, the sentimental and the sublime. The first Romantics made use of this idea, but deprived it of its metaphysical assumptions, or rather changed them. Instead of being the model for all other experience, it became a unique, superior, transcendent mode of experience, to be achieved only after long preparation, great difficulty, and profound introspection. Instead of leading to successful role-playing, Romantic nature worship was designed to lead away from any role-playing at all. And, in fact, it was not, strictly speaking, nature worship; rather it was the use of the natural world—free from human social enterprise—as a screen against which to project that sense of value which is also the sense of the self. Yet at the same time, because the experience was not yet fully understood, it was interpreted as both projective and revelatory. In such heightened moods one became aware, it was thought, of the immanent in the natural world. One saw *through* the phenomenon of nature into the divine noumenon (or ultimate reality) that lay behind it. And at the same time, one released the noumenal self from the bondage of the phenomenal self, the personality and the world of social roles. Both the natural noumenon and the noumenon of personality derived from God. This mode of perception, then, was like the closing of an electrical circuit. The ultimate union in the divine of the thing-in-itself of nature, and of the self of the human being, gave a ground of value both to nature and to the purely human. This was the vision of which Wordsworth in poetry and Caspar David Friedrich in painting are the purest examples. Goethe, however, felt the difficulties, and in *Faust* proposed a solution: the eternal postponement of value, the acceptance of the inadequacy of human beings to meet the demands of experience.

For Analogism had real difficulties. One was that nothing could be done with such an experience. No morality could be derived from it; no metaphysic which could be used as a guide to action could be deduced from it. It was pure contentless experience. So a second difficulty was that it failed to solve the problem of reality, that is, of the relation of subject to object. It deprived the object of all substance, turning it into a mere transparency. This was unsatisfactory, for one of the basic determinations of Romanticism was to meet reality head on, that determination arising from the realization that all metaphysical systems were derivations from the needs of the individual, and that those needs could be met only by the encounter with experience itself. To the Romantic, nothing is sweeter than the white bone of a pure fact. Since Analogism offered no basis for action, it was reduced to the status of a mere psychological experience, of a value state, not of a value ground, which was what was needed. Hence its third difficulty; it was static. The Negative Romantic, finding no ground for value, found no imperative to action. The best that Kant could do was to prate about conscience and duty; but he could give no reason for action, no imperative to act. Even Goethe, asserting that the act was the essential character of man, shows Faust surrendering over and over again to the illusion of a final action. Analogism offered a ground for value, but no imperative to act. And without action, reality could not be encountered and the self could not be realized. Finally, by its staticism it denied history; and to the Romantic, history—at least his own history—was reality.

Schopenhauer was the first to see that the way out lay through the denial of the Analogistic symmetry between self and thing-in-itself, which threatened to abolish or reduce to meaninglessness everything in between. Or, as with Hegel, to return to a conservative Enlightenment position which asserted that whatever is, is right; for Hegel attempted to solve the difficulty by converting history into the noumenal, into the divine. He attempted to fill up the gap between subject and object and to preserve both by erecting "Spirit," as defined above, into value. But this threatened to deny freedom of choice, and therefore the basis for action, which comes into existence only when choice is offered. It was obvious that an asymmetrical position was the only solution. To Analogism succeeded Transcendentalism. This deprived the world wholly of value, turned it once again into a meaningless chaos, but preserved the self and gave the self's drive for meaning, order, value, and identity a divine authority. This is the heroic, world-redemptive stage of Romanticism. It has survived in numerous forms: German Fascism was one; Marxist Communism is another. It is evident that Transcendentalism was filled with numerous dangers. Its success at the highest cultural levels for several decades lay in its solution to the problem of action. The Transcendental hero was to redeem the self in the act of redeeming the world. The Visionary Artist and the Bohemian, both products of Analogism, denied the value of society, but the Transcendental Virtuoso, as we have seen, adopted a social role and pushed it beyond the point that existent society could achieve. He imagined himself, then, as creating a model, or paradigm, for the future action of mankind. The literature of the time is filled with schemes to save the world, schemes so powerful that the mind of Western man is still haunted by them. Marx was a Virtuoso of economics. Taking the assumptions of the English political economists, Ricardo, Bentham, and the elder Mill, he developed them by a Transcendental, Virtuoso manipulation into a breathtaking vision of world redemption, just as Liszt took piano technique and developed it into something nobody would have thought possible.

But Transcendentalism also ran into difficulties. It had placed value in the human being; it had found authority for that value in the divine or in the material (Marx's metaphysic) or in history (the other post-Hegelians); and it had provided an imperative for action. But it also placed the Transcendental hero in the position of imposing his will upon other human beings. Contemporary accounts of responses to Paganini and Liszt and Carlyle and Turner and Chopin emphasize the sense of being swept away, of being dominated, of being violated. This is what people meant when they gossiped that Paganini had sold his soul to the devil. But the Romantic cannot violate another person. If he does so, he violates himself. This is the morality of Wagner's *The Ring of the Nibelung*. The basis of Romantic morality is, and must be, empathy. If one consists of self and personality and role, then so do other human beings. Schopenhauer saw this very clearly, as did all the really perceptive Romantics. One can assert the existence of the self only by affirming the self of others through empathy. One can assert one's own value only by asserting and affirming and recognizing the value of others. Therefore, to impose one's will upon others, even for the sake of redeeming them and the world, even for the sake of revealing value to them, is to treat them as mere instruments for realizing the will, to treat them as objects, to treat them, in short, as society treats the alienated Romantic. It means that either their humanity is denied or the humanity of the Transcendental hero is denied. It cries out against the fact of the situation, which is that all human beings belong to the same category. Each has a self to be revealed; to insist that one way and one way only is proper for the revealing of that self is to deny the ultimate conviction of Romanticism, that a metaphysic with its derived value system cannot be an absolute, that the only absolute, at best, is the *drive* to a metaphysic, the *drive* to order and value, never to a particular order or a particular set of values. Morality is something in and of this world, of the world between subject and object, which is the only reality we can know with the understanding. If the Transcendental hero sets up a morality and imposes it upon others for the sake of revealing and realizing the self, it makes no difference, really, what that morality is; it can perfectly well be an evil and tyrannous morality, if it does the job for him. This is what Browning's hero Sordello realizes, and the realization kills him: Browning's way of stating the impossibility of the morality of the Transcendental hero.

The solution to this difficulty lay in withdrawing any suprahuman or supra-individual authority for the ground of value. There followed the Objectist stage of Romantic development. It is a new symmetry, like Analogism, but it differs from Analogism in that the noumenal is denied both to the self and to the thing-in-itself. There is left only the phenomenal. The theme of this stage is "illusion." All metaphysics, all moral systems, are not even human instruments for realizing value; they are at best human instruments for dealing with the world, for staying alive, but in themselves they provide no imperative to action, no imperative to duty, no imperative to morality, no imperative to world redemption, for the world cannot be redeemed: any scheme for redemption is but another illusion. The result was a new wave of alienation, an alienation that was profounder than anything that had occurred before. The conclusion to *The Ring* revealed all action as an illusion. The drive to create order creates society, freedom, and love; but it also destroys what it creates, for each of these insists on its total adequacy; each creates the illusion that it alone is the ground of value; each fancies that the world is redeemable. The full terror of human behavior always justifies itself by an appeal to society or freedom or love. Each fancies that the world is redeemable, can be penetrated in its entirety with value. Each can offer only an illusion, for the world is unredeemable. Yet *The Ring*, which appears to be tragic, is really triumphant. It is the realization of what Goethe had adumbrated: man's inadequacy lies in his illusion that he can be adequate, in the illusion that the drive to order and value can be finally gratified. No, the Objectist says, the only perfect order is death. Life and value, then, lie in the pure encounter of self and object, of subject and reality, without illusions. Society and personality are seen to be natural products, and therefore unredeemable, because inaccessible to man. Alienation has now extended to everything man can understand, including his personality, including eventually, as Freud was to show (but as many Romantics knew long before Freud made it scientifically acceptable), his unconscious mind, which hitherto had been identified with the divine.

But what of the self? If it can no longer be identified with the unconscious, as Wordsworth, for example, had identified it, how can it be experienced? The answer to that question was that the self, and therefore value, can be experienced only by facing, unflinchingly, the unredeemable character of experience, in saying only what is, in talking only about the phenomenal world. Nature and society and personality are meaningless; therefore, they are hell. Value flowed from the confrontation of that hell. It was an antiheroic heroism; such as Baudelaire's. It was a scientific heroism; such as Zola's and Manet's. It was the exaltation of the nakedly human, without the traditional consolations of religion, or metaphysics, or idealisms. The peculiar exaltation of the objective scientist of today derives from this stage of Romanticism. Its Bible was Darwin's *On the Origin of Species*, published in 1859, just when it was badly needed by the cultural pioneers of Objectism.

But Objectism also had its difficulties. One was that, like Analogism, it deprived the individual of any imperative to action. The only action possible was description, and that was done in heroic despair. Further, there was no way to symbolize the experience of value which flowed from the naked encounter with unredeemable reality. For this reason, there was no defense against the hell of existence. It required a tough-mindedness which even the tough-minded could not endure, for it provided no mode of existence, of getting from day to day. The next, and in the nineteenth century the final, stage of Romanticism solved all but the first of these problems. It was the stage traditionally called Aestheticism, but which I prefer to call Stylism. It was successful in that it symbolized the experience of value and offered a defense against the hell of existence. And, in a peculiar way, it even provided an imperative to action, though not to political or social moral action. But it at least provided an imperative to live without illusion, the problem Ibsen exposed in *The Wild Duck*, though he did not there solve it.

Style, which is so often identified with art, partly because of the success of Stylism, is in fact a universal quality of human behavior. For every situation which a society recognizes and categorizes and institutionalizes either in language or in behavior, there is a culturally transmitted pattern of action. But the rules or pattern of action are applicable only to categories of situations. Each actual situation requires the individual to improvise, to innovate, in order to fill in the gap between the learned pattern and the actual unique situation. In each category of situation, then, each individual creates for himself a special set of rules or a special pattern of behavior which is unique to himself. It is an energy-conserving device, which saves him from having to innovate in every situation. This individually created pattern of behavior is style. It is his unique mode of arming himself against the surprises every actual situation offers; it keeps him going when the social pattern does not work. It maintains his sense of identity while he summons his resources to meet the contingent. It narrows the gap between behavioral pattern and situational demand. This universal characteristic of human behavior, then, the Stylist seized upon. It permitted him, first of all, to symbolize the continuity of identity from situation to situation, from hell to hell. But it also provided him a defense against that hell, because style precisely was pattern, an individual's unique pattern; it was, therefore, the perfect way of symbolizing the sense of order and value and meaning without tempting him to impose that pattern upon reality. It even to a certain extent permitted him to solve the problem of the imperative to action, for it gave him an imperative, if not to act upon the world, at least to create a unique style which, as it was perfected, offered him a new and richer gratification of the drive to order and value, and therefore a promise of greater gratification. Further, it was at once a universal human characteristic, not only possible to everyone but even required of everyone, and one that required no authority for its existence other than the necessities of the human condition. It could do without authority derived from metaphysics, or religion, or history, or science. It was the most complete and satisfactory solution to the problem of freedom humanity had yet found. Nor was it morally irresponsible, because with an alienation even deeper than that of the Objectist, the Stylist could look at the world and face its heaven as well as its hell. So defended, he could say things about human behavior with an objectivity that even the Objectist could not summon, because the Stylist was free from pain, while the Objectist was necessarily involved in suffering. It was not heroic but it was debonair. The Dandy had been created before, but Stylism is the fullest possible realization of the possibilities of dandyism.

The writing and the life—and the death—of Ernest Hemingway provide a perfect twentieth-century example of Stylism, though culturally belated and old-fashioned even in the 1920's. Hemingway and his friends lived by a code, not because it was a code of right and wrong but simply because it was a code, that is, a style. And the older he got, the more he was involved with the style of everything; of hunting, of fishing, of writing. The Old Fisherman in *The Old Man and the Sea* is a redemptive or Christ figure simply because he knows how to fish, and in knowing how to fish he knows how to endure, and how to die. Hemingway's suicide was not a betrayal of his life but a fulfillment of it. And in that lies the weakness of Stylism.

For Stylism ultimately revealed that it too had a weakness; it too, though it solved problems, created new ones. For one thing, it had not solved the problem of the imperative to action, only to living. It provided no basis for moral responsibility, except its freedom from moral commitment and suffering. But most of all, it degenerated, with all the great Stylists, into mannerism, from Swinburne to Hemingway himself. For mannerism, in this sense, is the consequence of devoting oneself to the creation of a unique personal style. And the more successful one is at this task, the more that style becomes a role, so that Swinburne and Debussy ended up playing the roles of "Swinburne" and "Debussy," which they had invented, and Hemingway ended up playing the role of "Hemingway." He *had* to commit suicide, in order to play the role of facing the ultimate horror, death, with style, just as in the Second World War he was more interested in playing

Hemingway-as-War-Correspondent than in being a war correspondent. In short, the great Romantic problem of re-entry, of commitment, of solving the paradox of entering into social action without betraying one's own selfhood or the selfhood of others —this central problem of Romanticism remained unsolved, for the problem of the ground of value remained unsolved. Stylism had found its ground in one aspect of human behavior, but it left the rest of human behavior unaccounted for. It could symbolize the self. But how was one to *be* the self? It had separated itself from history, for it had separated itself from all but one aspect of human life, but to the Romantic, sooner or later, history must be encountered, for history is reality.

It was Friedrich Nietzsche, whose achievement is only now being understood, who solved the problem and returned the Stylist to history. Each of the stages of Romanticism had been threatened by the static. It was Nietzsche who saw that the answer lay in the various metamorphoses of Romanticism. The fault was in the very search for a ground of value, a resting place from which the rest of the world might be moved. It was that primitive desire for a ground, a finality, an answer, that led to the debacle of Analogism, Transcendentalism, Objectism, and Stylism, though Nietzsche also saw that Stylism, with its dandyism, its insouciance, its armor, had made an astounding contribution. The answer, therefore, lay in reversing this system, in the transvaluation of all values, and in the continuous transvaluation. The sorrow of the nineteenth century rose from its continuous failure to find a ground for value that would not give beneath the pressures put upon it. Nietzsche saw that to search for such a ground was to involve mankind in an infinite regress, a regress that took it farther and farther from the world, the only reality there is. If, therefore, one accepted the fact that there was no ground, that there was no justification for the search for order and meaning and value, that the world was quite meaningless, quite without value, in both subject and object—for subject and object are one—then sorrow could be converted to joy. Eternal recurrence was the answer, continuous renewal of identity by continuous transformation and transvaluation of style in art, in thought, and in individuality. Nietzsche realized that this is neither a world which once held value nor a world which holds value now or a world which ever will hold it. It is without value, without order, without meaning. The world is nothing. Value and identity are the ultimate illusions. We emerge from nothingness and encounter the nothingness of the world, and in so doing we create being. But being can be renewed only if we recognize that being is illusion. With that recognition as our ultimate weapon we can re-create it, not from sorrow but from joy. From the desire for value we create ourselves, but to renew that value we must destroy ourselves. The profoundest satisfaction of the human mind is the creation of the world—out of nothingness. From that act of creation emerges the *sense* of value, the *sense* of identity, which are sources of joy only if we recognize them as illusions. The sense of order, the sense of meaning, and the sense of identity are but instruments for the act of creation. Thus the Romantic once more enters into history and human life, for to create is to choose, without ever knowing whether or not the choice is the right choice, for the act of choice changes the world. And so we can never know, even by hindsight, whether or not we chose rightly, for the situation in which we performed the act of creation and choice no longer exists. And this solves the problem of re-entry, for it is clear that alienation is the illusion of the Romantic.

And so Nietzsche's work is the triumph of Romanticism, for he solved its problem of value and returned the Romantic to history, by showing that there is no ground to value and that there is no escape from history. As the Romantic had always known but had never, until Nietzsche, been able to believe, reality is history, and only the experience of reality has value, an experience to be achieved by creating illusions so that we may live and by destroying them so that we may recover our freedom. Value is process, a perpetual weaving and unweaving of our own identities. Sorrow is a sentimental lust for finality; joy is the penetration beyond that sentimentality into the valuelessness of reality, into its freedom, the achievement of which is inevitably its loss. Joy is the eternal recurrence of the same problem, forever solved and forever unsolvable. Nietzsche found what the Romantic had sought for a hundred years, a way of encompassing, without loss of tension, the contrarieties and paradoxes of human experience. The *feel* of reality, in the subject, is tension and the sense of contradiction. As for violating others, that is the ultimate moral responsibility, for to maintain the tension of human experience, which is to achieve and destroy and re-achieve value, we must violate others—as we must violate ourselves.

4

ROMANTICISM:

THE PRESENT STATE OF THEORY

[1965*]

Romanticism is still the most vexing problem in literary history, even more irritating than the problem of the Renaissance. And it is still true, as I wrote fifteen years ago, that if we cannot solve this problem we can hope to solve no problem of literary periodization. Or even cultural periodization, for Romanticism is a term used in the historiography and criticism not only of the arts but also of philosophy and political thinking. I have never come across the phrase "Romantic economics," but I am sure somebody has used it. The question I wish to raise here is whether or not there has been enough progress in the past fifteen years to justify any optimism at all.

Why fifteen years? Well, it has been about that length of time since I first presented in public my "Toward a Theory of Ro-

* Delivered at the annual meeting of the Pennsylvania Council of Teachers of English, October, 1965. Reprinted by permission from *The PCTE Bulletin*, No. 12 (December, 1965), pp. 31–53.

manticism,"[1] an essay which has not been without influence, which has been publicly cited as one of the three most important articles in the field ever published in *PMLA*, which has been reprinted several times, and is about to be reprinted again, which has, indeed, been referred to as a classic, and most of which I myself publicly repudiated in 1960.[2] I suppose that I have been invited to address you because of these two papers and my book, *Beyond the Tragic Vision*.[3] And by "progress" I mean, "Has there been any convergence of opinion on the nature of Romanticism?" I believe that there has been, but first I should like to inquire why there has not been more.

This, I think, is an important question to ask, because it really asks a question about the nature of the investigation. If we know how we are proceeding, now that we are making some progress, we may be able to proceed a little more rapidly and successfully toward a notion on which there will be sufficient agreement to be useful. I shall begin as far back from the problem as I can. Initially I shall play the devil's advocate and assume a stance which in fact many people, quietly as well as loudly, do assume.

What do we need a definition of Romanticism for? Of what value can it possibly be? The attempt to categorize that which is in fact a steady flow of literary and cultural activity is a vain and useless effort. Of what possible advantage is there in deciding that Burns was or was not a Romantic? There is the poetry; let us read it. The game of deciding where to draw the line between Romantic and Enlightenment is pure scholarly buffism. At best such efforts serve only to keep pedantic academics off the streets, and if this is what they are going to busy themselves with, they had better be on the streets than in the library or the scholarly journal or the classroom. The only possible use of the term is to tell our readers what group of writers we are currently talking about. If it is not clear whether or not we mean Burns, it is certainly clear that we mean the great five, and if we do mean Burns,

<hr>

[1] *PMLA*, LXVI (1951), 5–23.
[2] "Toward a Theory of Romanticism: II. Reconsiderations," *Studies in Romanticism*, I (1961), 108; see pp. 27–35 of this volume.
[3] (New York, 1962).

it is a simple enough matter to say so. Why, then, should we want to define Romanticism?

This is not only a powerful argument; it is exceedingly tempting. But there is a reason, a very strong reason, for wanting an agreement on the term, and it is possible to explain why we need it.

The following passage comes from Plato's *Protagoras*. Socrates has been demonstrating most ingeniously that an apparent logical inconsistency in a poem by Simonides is in fact what we might call a dramatic consistency. And he goes on to say:

I would rather have done with poems and odes. . . . The talk about the poets seems to me like a commonplace entertainment to which a vulgar company have recourse; who, because they are not able to converse or amuse one another, while they are drinking, with the sound of their own voices and conversation, by reason of their stupidity, raise the price of flute-girls in the market, hiring for a great sum the voice of a flute instead of their own breath, to be the medium of intercourse among them: but where the company are real gentlemen and men of education, you will see no flute-girls, nor dancing-girls, nor harp-girls; and they have no nonsense or games, but are contented with one another's conversation, of which their own voices are the medium, and which they carry on by turns and in an orderly manner, even though they are very liberal in their potations. And a company like this of ours, and men such as we profess to be, do not require the help of another's voice, or of the poets whom you cannot interrogate about the meaning of what they are saying; people who cite them declaring, some that the poet has one meaning, and others that he has another, and the point which is in dispute can never be decided. This sort of entertainment they decline, and prefer to talk with one another, and put one another to the proof in conversation. And these are the models which I desire that you and I should imitate.[4]

I should like to see this passage printed as the foreword to every scholarly and critical journal printed anywhere in the world, and in every issue. Perhaps it should be repeated as the introduction to every article. For the point that Socrates makes is crucial and, to us, unspeakably embarrassing. According to Socrates we are ignorant and ungentlemanly drunks who inflate the

---

[4] *Protagoras*, 347, Jowett's translation.

price of flute-players, who inflate the value of poets. And why? Because it is only in a face-to-face encounter with another man that it is possible to discover what he means, what you mean, what you both are trying to say, what your semantic intention really is; possible, but as the marvelous dialogues show, exceedingly difficult. As for discovering the meaning and true intention of someone whom you cannot interrogate, that, clearly, is impossible, an idle drunken entertainment. If Plato is correct, we have no moral right to continue in our chosen profession.

Do not imagine that I am here supporting the position called the intentional fallacy, as presented in the famous and, to my mind, disastrous article of that title by Beardsley and Wimsatt, first published in 1946 and reprinted frequently ever since.[5] I believe that essay to be quite wrong. And I believe Plato to be in error. The fact is that we do interpret correctly statements made by people whom we cannot interrogate. Nevertheless, he is clearly correct about one part of his statement: we can confirm our interpretation only by interrogating the original utterer of the statement. Socrates' basic technique is to ask, "Is *this* what you mean?" An interpretation, then, is a prediction that some action or some statement on our part will win the assent of the original speaker. It is a prediction that our judgment of the speaker's intention can be confirmed. And it is also clear that when the speaker is unavailable, our predictions enter the world of unconfirmable probabilities. Our problem, as interpreters of literature, is to confirm unconfirmable probabilities. A less attractive task it would be difficult to imagine.

To bring the nature of the problem out more sharply, I shall turn again to the Beardsley-Wimsatt essay. Had I the time, I should like to show just how confused that essay is, and it is almost worth the trouble. A couple of sentences must suffice. "Poetry succeeds because all or most of what is said or implied is relevant; . . . In this respect poetry differs from practical messages, which are successful if and only if we correctly infer the intention. They are more abstract than poetry." I cannot imagine what is meant by this last statement. If I am told that my child has just been run over by a truck, I would consider it, certainly,

[5] *The Sewanee Review*, LIV (1946).

as a practical message, but I cannot understand in what way it is abstract. Even if everything "irrelevant has been excluded" from poetry, I cannot see that such exclusion is a defining characteristic. The statement, "Your child has just been run over by a truck," strikes me as admirably concise. I can see no irrelevancies. But the real tangle here is the assertion that "poetry differs from practical messages" in any respect. All these authors' sentences rest on the assumption that poetry *does* differ from practical messages. But this is something which, though constantly asserted, remains to be demonstrated. At least I have seen no demonstration which can stand up under analysis. Nor is it possible at the present time to contrive such a demonstration that will be sound.

The reason is this. We cannot know whether or not poetry presents interpretational problems unique to itself until we have a general theory of interpretation in ordinary verbal behavior. What happens when you ask me to go to the movies and I say that I would rather not? What happens between your utterance and my response? At the moment we haven't the faintest idea, although we have been trying to talk about it for more than two thousand years. Clearly, I have interpreted your remark; or rather, the word "interpretation" refers to what happens inside of me that results in my response. It may be that the linguists will one day give us a respectable theory of interpretation. Though they have barely begun to move in the direction of semantics—and one understands very well their hesitancy—Noam Chomsky has made a start. Ludwig Wittgenstein also, in his *Philosophical Investigations*, pointed the way, but he did no more than point. In the meantime, we must operate as well as we can. We must—and most sensible scholars and critics do—act as if there were no difference between the problem of interpreting poetic and nonpoetic language. We must assume that there is no special problem to interpreting poetry except that it involves making predictions about the intentions of an inaccessible speaker, and this is by no means a defining problem. Our solid ground is that in ordinary life we do this all the time quite successfully. But it is also absolutely vital to remember that very frequently we fail.

In facing this fact there are certain considerations to be kept constantly in mind. The first is that when in ordinary situations

we interpret the statement a speaker makes to us, we do not, oddly, merely interpret the statement. Rather, we interpret the entire situation. That is, we limit the possible interpretations of the
statement by our interpretation of the total situation in which the
statement appears. The basic reason for this is that the semantic
function of words is not immanent but conventional. We need the
situation to determine which conventions are operant.

The next reason is that all terms are categorical. No term names
a thing; it refers to a category of objects, or, preferably, perceptual phenomena. The range of that category, therefore, since
semantic functions are conventional, and the set of the attributes
of that category—let us call these the denotation and connotation
of the term—are functions of the situation in which the term occurs. Hence the denotation and connotation of terms change from
slightly to grossly as we move them from one situation to another.

Finally, since semantic function is conventional and unstable,
all terms are polysemous, that is, capable of an indefinably large
number of semantic functions. When we interpret a statement,
we make, therefore, certain decisions about the semantic functions of the terms in the statement, and these decisions are dependent upon the situation and have to do with what we judge
to be the semantic intention of the speaker. Nor is that all. These
decisions are also dependent upon our own intention. This is
why there is always slight disagreement about the meaning of
any but the most common statements firmly embedded in the
most frequent situations.

But in all this there is a ray of hope. Since terms are conventional, it is possible to locate the same category of phenomena by
means of an indefinitely large number of terms and statements.
Thus, often, when we appear to be in disagreement, we are actually agreeing with each other. Further, we are always talking
about something, even though we do not know what—and for the
most part it is quite unnecessary to know—and even though our
statement may be negative predictions rather than confirmed or
confirmable positive predictions. Thus even when we make unconfirmable interpretations, which, as we have seen, are predictions, it does not follow that they are necessarily negative predictions just because they are not confirmable. Clearly, in the

absence of the original speaker, we infer his intention from our interpretation of the situation from which the utterance emerged; and we are part of that situation simply because we are engaged in the act of interpretational predictions; that is, if the situation is not present, we construct a situation which will enable us to infer the intention. Beardsley and Wimsatt, then, are wrong in implying that we infer the intention from the message. We do not; we infer it from our construction of the situation. Finally, because our own intentions are at work in the interpretational act, even when the situation of the utterance is still directly before us, we still infer intention from a constructed situation, because the situation is not self-explanatory; its meaning is not immanent, but interpreted by us. To construct a situation, then, means to set up limits to the possibilities and probabilities of semantic function.

The act of interpretation, then, involves the deriving of a speaker's intention from the constructed situation in which the speaker's statement occurs. As interpreters of literature, intention is all we ever talk about; it is all we ever will talk about; it is all we ever can talk about.

From this it is possible to understand why we need such terms as Romanticism, why we must have them. When we say, for example, that *The Prelude* is a Romantic document, we are asserting that it was uttered in a particular situation which limits the semantic functions of the statements Wordsworth made. To construct a theory of Romanticism is not to attempt to say what Romanticism is, or was. We cannot say what Romanticism is. We cannot say what anything is. When we try to say what a tree is, we can only say that a tree is a manifestation of treeiness. This looks like metaphysics, but is not. It is only language. It merely means that we are placing this particular perceptual configuration in the category "tree" because we perceive within its bounds the attributes which conventionally mark it as belonging to that category. And so with Romanticism, except that currently there is little agreement about the attributes or connotation of this category and therefore little agreement about the range of literary and other cultural documents to which it refers, or should refer, or can refer—its denotation. We cannot say what Romanticism is, then. We can only hope to establish a conventionally determined category of documents and artifacts, and our purpose in doing so, our intention, will be to limit the probabilities of the semantic functions of the words and other signs in those documents and artifacts.

How shall we do this? It is important to remember that the aim will not be to create a definition of Romanticism, at least a definition that can take the form, "Romanticism is————." Rather, we want to be able to say, "The Romantic situation was ————." For our proper intention is not to have a definition of Romanticism, to know what Romanticism is or was. That would be pure scholarly buffism. Our proper intention is to construct a situation which will enable us to set up limits to the possibilities and the probabilities of semantic functions in Romantic documents. Nor is this a special scholarly or historical kind of problem. A lumberman refers to one category of trees when he uses the word "tree." A proper tree is one big enough to cut down and turn into lumber. But a landscape artist has an entirely different intention when he uses the word, and he refers to quite a different category of trees. And the botanist, with a different intention, uses the word with still another category in mind. Our intention is to interpret, it is to construct a situation from which we may infer the intention of a group of writers. If the semantic intentions of Burns are not the same as those of Wordsworth, then it follows that if Wordsworth is Romantic, Burns is not, in spite of the superficial similarity of many of their statements—in spite of the fact that they both say they like daisies.

From this point of view it is useful to ask what procedures for establishing Romanticism as a category have been employed in the past. Two methods have been used. One has been to examine a number of literary works, usually poems, and by interpreting various statements in those poems to establish a set of attributes for the term "Romanticism." The error here is obvious. The initial selection of the works to be examined has no basis other than a highly unstable scholarly and critical semantic tradition for the range of the term "Romanticism," together with the intuition and feeling for what properly belongs in the category. Further, such a procedure begins with what it should end with: a notion of what properly constitutes the Romantic situation, which is used for the interpretation of the poems and the selection of the attributes. But since on the whole that situational construction is highly uncontrolled, there is little defense against the treachery of polysemy.

The other method is to select a set of attributes, to assert on grounds which are rarely examined and again are principally a matter of unstable scholarly and critical tradition that these are indeed the attributes of Romanticism, and then to select those works in which such attributes may be located and to call them Romantic works. This in fact is the more popular method. There are for almost any word far fewer attributes than there are perceptual configurations in the categorial range of that word.

Now obviously this is the way we proceed in the ordinary affairs of life, but because the situations of ordinary life are highly repetitive and relatively stable it works well enough. The situation of a lumberman can be easily established and his intention readily determined, at least when he is examining trees. And though all situations are constructed by the interpreter, in the ordinary situations of life, as we have seen, an interpretational prediction can usually be confirmed. But this way out is closed to us. To show the difficulties and necessary failure of the pre-establishment of attributes, let me first examine a most interesting, though ultimately unsatisfactory work that appeared four years ago, *The Romantic Syndrome*, by W. T. Jones, Professor of Philosophy at Pomona College.[6] It is with some regret that I find myself ultimately in disagreement with Jones, for many of our fundamental assumptions are identical, particularly epistemological assumptions and very probably also ontological attitudes. Certain expressions and even whole sentences in Jones are identical with words of my own in *Beyond the Tragic Vision*. Further, when he talks about a syndrome he is talking about a metaphysical attitude which governs interpretation and other behavior. He believes that modern metaphysics is functionally identical with ancient mythology, and he also believes that it is impossible to do anything without a metaphysic, including science. By "orientation" I mean substantially what he means by syndrome, and what

[6] (The Hague, 1961).

Harold Bloom, for example, means by "myth."[7] The approach of both Jones and myself is cultural, anthropological, sociological, psychological. But from this point on we part company.

A syndrome, he proposes, is an attitude toward experience consisting of biases, that is, a prior basis for judgments. Each of these biases may be metaphorically imagined as an axis, with polar extremes, although a particular individual may hold a position at any point from one pole to the other. He distinguishes seven axes of bias, which might as well be named, to give some notion of what he is proposing. These are the Static/Dynamic, the Continuity/Discreteness, the Inner/Outer, the Sharp-Focus/Soft-Focus, the This-World/Other-World, the Order/Disorder, and the Spontaneity/Process axes. If these terms are not very clear, it is for our purposes of little importance. The Romantic syndrome he defines as cutting across the axes quite near the polar extremities of the Dynamic, Disorder, Soft-Focus, Inner, Other-World axes, even farther toward the pole of the Continuity axis, and ambivalent across the axis of Spontaneity/Process. The presentation of the Romantic syndrome is preceded by the Medieval, Renaissance, and Enlightenment syndromes. As might be expected, the last is exactly the reverse of the Romantic syndrome. In short, Jones examines Romanticism as a test case for his theory of determining periods in cultural history. Romanticism is examined in some detail, at least compared with the other three. He takes his evidence from poetry, metaphysics, and political theory. He introduces the section on the Romantic syndrome with the following statement.

We have chosen "romanticism" for study because this seems to be both an important concept and also a singularly vague one as it is currently employed. It is therefore a good test case for our purposes. I propose to try to show (1) that the seven biases leave distinguishable traces in the culture of the period, marking different types of theoretical behavior in characteristically different ways, and (2) that it is possible to reach substantial agreement among observers regarding the presence or the absence of these marks in specific poems, philosophical writings, and other cultural products. Thus (it is my contention) an analysis in

[7] *The Visionary Company* (New York, 1961). This work has some splendid *aperçus*, but is of little theoretical interest.

terms of our several axes has the following advantage: a very vague
and loose notion of romanticism is replaced by a relatively precise and
relatively operational definition—a definition that first specifies each
of a number of "romantic characteristics," or "marks," by designating
a certain range of positions on a given axis, and then formulates instructions for ascertaining whether a particular poem or other work of
art, has or lacks, the marks in question.[8]

It is apparent that Jones's claims are very large indeed. Let us
discover, if we can, what he has actually proposed. To begin with,
there is very serious difficulty in the expression, "the seven biases
leave distinguishable traces." In the introduction to his work he
has warned us that he does not intend that the syndromes and
the biases should be hypostatized, that, so to speak, they have
any phenomenal existence. Yet in spite of this warning, the language throughout the book on the relation of the syndromes and
axes to the documents and artifacts is a causal language. He constantly implies, in spite of his self-awareness, that his syndromes
and biases and axes do cause certain behavior which leaves its
traces in various documents and artifacts. But actually a syndrome, or orientation, is a mere construct of sentences which
interpret and derive attributes from a set of documents or other
events which have already been placed in a particular category.
If he means that such a construct has predictive power, can get
at least a probabilistic confirmation, I entirely agree, but he certainly does not say so.

As for the latter part of the passage quoted, this impressive
rhetoric amounts to a mere truism: if people agree on the attributes of a category, they will tend to agree on what items are properly included in its range. From the point of view offered here,
it is apparent that he has done nothing more, so far, than what
every traditional investigator into Romanticism has done. He has
established a set of attributes. Anyone can do that, and almost
everyone has. But the getting other people to agree is quite a
different matter. Jones implies that his predecessors have been
arbitrary and intuitive in setting up their set of attributes, but
that he, on the contrary, has been operational and provides satis-

---

[8] *The Romantic Syndrome*, 118.

factory reasons for selecting this set of attributes rather than some other set. Let us examine this.

He proposes seven axes of bias. Why seven? Why these particular seven? He gives no reason. But seven is such an anciently magical number that one is suspicious. Ruskin tells us in *Fors Clavigera* what a great deal of trouble he had to go to in order to get his discussion of architecture organized under *seven* lamps; it could have been eight or nine just as well. With Jones one feels that the number of axes could be indefinitely large. For my own part I think that all of them may be subsumed under his Order/Disorder axis, or, better yet, under the simple rubric of the drive for order, a term which he uses and which I also use. In *Beyond the Tragic Vision* I speak of the orientative drive, and in my new book, *Man's Rage for Chaos: Biology, Behavior, and the Arts,*[9] I discuss the drive to order in some detail, and I offer reasons for believing that it is explicable physiologically and is probably genetically transmitted.

Jones offers, then, no reason for limiting his axes to seven or any explanation as to why he selected these seven. I suppose it was all he could think of, but there is no way of telling. But even if we accept his proposal so far, we must ask if he offers any reason for constructing the Romantic syndrome as he does. And here again, I fear the answer is that he does not. It is reasonably evident that he has acted as everyone else has done. He has selected his particular axial segments on the basis of tradition, intuition, feeling for what makes sense in this situation. But everybody does that. That is the whole source of the difficulty. And as for his evidence, I can, or anybody can, find passages in the works he cites which would support just as well the notion that Sharp-Focus is as characteristically Romantic as Soft-Focus, or that an interest in the Outer world, is as Romantic as one in the Inner world, or that This-worldliness is as Romantic as Other-worldliness, and so on. *The Romantic Syndrome* has been apparently neglected, and I cannot believe that it deserves very much attention. Analysis discloses that Jones has not offered, as he claims, a radically new methodology. It is, unfortunately,

---

[9] (Philadelphia, 1965).

merely another theory of cultural history, a little more hard-headed than most.

I should now like to turn to a figure whose reputation, if not his work, is considerably more formidable than Professor Jones's. I refer to Professor René Wellek, who has recently offered a survey of the past twenty-odd years of Romantic theorizing. This paper was originally given at the 1962 meeting of the English Institute and has since been printed twice.[10] He begins by taking credit for reopening in 1949 the problem of the unity of European Romanticism and of Romanticism in general after it had been closed by the extreme nihilism of Arthur O. Lovejoy. This claim is fanciful. By no means all American scholars had accepted Lovejoy's proposition that the term "Romantic" meant nothing, or "had given up such questions in despair." Certainly however, Wellek deserves credit for challenging Lovejoy in his articles in *Comparative Literature*, which made it difficult to believe that Romanticism was not a European cultural movement.[11] However, he then proceeded in the usual fashion, to set up *his* set of attributes: imagination, symbol, myth, and organic nature. He now claims that "students of the issue agree with my general view or have arrived independently at the same or similar results." This is simply not true. My own first article, which I wisely called "Toward a Theory of Romanticism" was in response to Wellek, and in it I did the same thing that he had done. I set up *my* set of attributes. As I have already stated, in 1961 I publicly repudiated that aspect of my original theory, though there was a saving grace in that essay to which I shall return. In his English Institute paper Wellek has attacked me, has indeed trounced me thoroughly. Fair enough; or it would be fair enough if he had reported my position with any accuracy. But he has not. Indeed, I have rarely seen so inaccurate an instance of scholarly reporting. He is also almost as inaccurate about some of the other writers whose work he discusses. At least I am in good company.

I should like, therefore, to take this opportunity to reply to

[10] "Romanticism Re-examined," in Northrop Frye (ed.), *Romanticism Reconsidered* (New York and London, 1963); and in René Wellek, *Concepts in Criticism* (New Haven, 1963).
[11] I, 1023 (1949), 147–72.

Wellek, since his reputation is infinitely greater than mine, and since he has published his paper twice in the same year, thus insuring it considerable attention.

"Peckham," he says, "now calls Romanticism Enlightenment."[12] I do nothing of the sort. I have devoted twenty years to trying to establish as sharp a division between Enlightenment and Romanticism as I possibly can, and I have grown increasingly assertive in insisting that Romanticism came into existence because of the failure of the Enlightenment, and because when the Enlightenment failed, two thousand years of European metaphysics collapsed. What I actually said was this:

If you wish, as many do, to use the term "Romanticism" to refer to this Enlightenment and enthusiasm and sentimentalism and natural redemption, I have no objection. One long tradition has always called it Romanticism. But nothing could be more different from what I am talking about when I use that word. When the crash came, when a tiny minority of Enlightenment personalities, themselves a cultural minority, saw through Enlightenment pretensions and saw that it is impossible to maintain them, and when the Enlightenment was put to the test in the French Revolution and its superficiality revealed, a major cultural break occurred.[13]

To say that this passage means that I now identify Romanticism with Enlightenment is almost inconceivably irresponsible in a respectable scholar.

Let us take another instance of Wellek's reliability. "Peckham," he asserts, "takes a quite unjustified view of Kant as a kind of pragmatist. 'Romanticism learns from Kant,' he says, 'that it can do entirely without constitutive metaphysics and can use any metaphysic or world hypothesis as supreme fiction.' "[14] What I actually wrote was this: "Although it [dynamic organicism] was the most important metaphysical episode in the history of Romanticism, it was abandoned, as all Romantic world hypotheses are abandoned, for by definition they are inadequate; and this process continues until Romanticism learns that it can do en-

---

[12] *Romanticism Reconsidered*, 110.
[13] *Studies in Romanticism*, I (1961), 4.
[14] *Romanticism Reconsidered*, 111.

tirely without constitutive metaphysics and can use any meta-physic or world hypothesis as a supreme fiction."[15] There is no mention of Kant in this sentence. However, on the previous page I do say: "With and without the aid of Kant, an orientation is now seen not as a discovery but as a projection. Thus a meta-physical theory is thought of as an instrument, not as reality, not as something in nature, but as something imposed upon it."[16] It is not I who say that Kant was a pragmatist, but John Herman Randall, a name not without authority. But I do not think that Kant was a pragmatist, and I have not said so, though I do believe —and I am anything but alone in this belief—that pragmatism must necessarily result, sooner or later, from the Kantian po-sition, and did.

As for *Beyond the Tragic Vision*, there is nothing that indicates that Wellek has read anything but the jacket copy, and that care-lessly. "Peckham," he says, "now believes the essence of Roman-ticism to be the imposition of order on chaos." I do not say this, and I do not believe it. I do believe that a striking characteristic of human behavior is the imposition of order on chaos. And my whole argument amounts, one way or another, to the assertion that the Romantics discovered such imposition to be the center of the human position, and that modern perceptual theory has confirmed their discovery over and over again, as well as much modern philosophy. Previous metaphysical revolutions had sub-stituted a new metaphysics for an old, had been constitutive meta-physics. It was the Romantics who discovered that one of the things human beings do is to construct such systems. It was a century before Nietzsche worked out the real significance of this discovery, and we are still exploring its implications and en-deavoring to explain it. Originally, the first couple of generations of Romantics offered a number of explanations and justifications for metaphysical behavior, all of which proved failures, and *Be-yond the Tragic Vision* is an attempt to chart the four principal nineteenth-century stages of the attempt to explain and justify metaphysical behavior, and the failure of each. I assert that

[15] *Studies in Romanticism*, I, 7.
[16] *Ibid.*, 6.

throughout the century, and even at the present time, one form in which the problem was tackled was the hypostatization of the "self." The Romantics saw metaphysical construction as intimately related to the problem of the value of human experience, which constituted by the self, as the result of the Enlightenment collapse, could be seen as the source of all value. To establish and symbolize the self, therefore, is to establish the sense of value and to explain metaphysical activity. But it was a century before the implications of this position could be seen with anything like clarity.

Now all this is plainly presented in my book, as well as briefly stated in my 1961 paper. But Wellek completely ignores it, denies the value of my work, and then praises what he calls the Geneva school—Albert Béguin, Georges Poulet, and Albert Gérard—for asserting, in one way or another, that the essence of Romanticism lies in the establishment of the self as the point from which it was now necessary to begin all speculation and poetic activity and creation of human meaning and value. To be sure, his exposition of what they said, particularly in the case of Gérard, is almost as unsatisfactory, in accuracy of reporting, as what he says about me. It is evident either that he has not read my book, or that he completely forgot what he had read, or that he depended upon someone else to give him an account of my position. In any case it is not agreeable to be called an incompetent fool and then to read of others being praised for making almost precisely the same point.

Wellek also attacks me for my notion of "Negative Romanticism." This notion asserts that between the collapse of the Enlightenment position and the emergence of the Romantic position, there occurred a period of despair, of perceiving the world drained of value with no way to reconstitute it, since all the traditional ways were now revealed as dead ends. I constructed this notion specifically to take care of Byron and people like him, and it was based upon the autobiographical record of such men as Wordsworth, Coleridge, Shelley, and Carlyle. Particularly, I found in it the source of Romantic alienation, which by now is almost universally accepted, and which continued into Positive Romanticism, for it led to the discovery of the self, or the creation of the self as the central myth of the nineteenth and twentieth centuries. I asserted that such a concept was necessary to account for Byron, whom Wellek's Romantic attributes could not take care of, for it seemed absurd to me and still seems absurd to me to dismiss Byron from the Romantic problem. To this Wellek replies in his English Institute paper thus:

The argument runs that positive romanticism does not fit Byron, but that "negative romanticism" does. I am supposed to be unable "to come to terms" with this phenomenon. Still, it seems to me that little has been accomplished by calling familiar states of mind—*Weltschmerz, mal du siècle*, pessimism—"negative" romanticism. It is a purely verbal solution; as if we should call naturalism "negative symbolism," or symbolism "negative naturalism." By showing the coherence of the point of view which other writers as well as I have called "Romanticism"—its organicism, its use of the creative imagination, its symbolic and mythic procedures—we have excluded nihilism, "alienation," from our definition. A man who considers nature dead and inimical to man, who considers imagination merely a combinatory associative power, and who does not use symbolic and mythic devices is not a Romanticist in the sense in which Wordsworth, Novalis, and Hugo are Romantic.[17]

Well, in the first place, this is exactly what I had said, though in *Beyond the Tragic Vision* I find that Byron, in *Don Juan*, had made the first step toward Positive Romanticism, the establishment of the self and the acceptance of alienation as the necessary foundation for any solution to the problem of creating value. But this, of course, Wellek ignores, since he seems not to be familiar with that book. Wellek, in replying to my argument, has simply asserted that since his attributes for Romanticism do not reveal Byron as a Romantic, Byron is therefore not a Romantic "in the sense in which Wordsworth, Novalis, and Hugo are Romantic." I cannot see that a restatement of my charge is an answer to it. No theory of Romanticism is worth its salt unless it can explain why Byron has always been considered the arch-Romantic. But Wellek, of course, leaves a loophole for himself in the phrase "not a Romantic in the sense." Does this mean that in some other

[17] *Romanticism Reconsidered*, 109.

sense, equally valid, Byron *was* a Romantic? If so, what other sense? But Wellek does not tell us. Instead of replying to my argument, he offers mere verbal weaseling.

Now the notion of "Negative Romanticism" is very important to me, if to no one else, and to my position, for it was precisely this point that in 1961 I wished to preserve from my 1951 article. The weakness of the latter essay lay in the logical incompatibility between the procedure by which I proposed to establish the notion of Negative Romanticism and that by which I assigned attributes to the term "Positive Romanticism." It is the latter procedure that I now repudiate, and it is the former from which my new position has been derived. When I talked in 1951 about the attributes of Positive Romanticism I was merely doing what everybody else, including Wellek, had done, assigning attributes to the category of Romanticism on the basis of tradition, feeling, intuition, and essentially uncontrolled interpretation. But when I proposed the notion "Negative Romanticism" I was doing something else; I was making the first step, though I did not know it, toward constructing a theory of the Romantic situation. I was moving away from the form of the statement, "Romanticism is ————," toward the statement, "The Romantic situation was ————." To understand the significance of this, it is necessary to go back to the point at which we left the examination of situation construction. I have said that "our intention is to interpret, it is to construct a situation from which we may infer the intention of a group of writers." How, in ordinary interpretational behavior, do we do this? Clearly we do do it, and we do it successfully, in spite of Plato.

It is clear that at this point what we need is some very general statement, some universal, it may be, about human behavior. A good many such universals are quite possible, but what is needed here is one that will provide a general explanation of the dynamics of behavior, some reason for speakers to have intentions. Let us look again at the lumberman saying that he has found a real tree. From our general construction of the situation we make a prediction that upon interrogating him we would find that he is talking about a tree that can be turned into lumber of excellent quality. Assuming that our interrogation has confirmed our prediction, we need to know a little more about what kind of activity his statement was a part of. It seems evident that he is engaged in search behavior. He is looking for trees he can put into his category of "real tree." But search behavior is designed to solve a problem. His problem is to find such trees, so that he can cut them down, turn them into lumber, and sell them for a profit. It appears to be promising to consider human activity as essentially problem-solving activity. Indeed, this may very well be a more precise way of talking about the ordinarily hypostatized "motive." It is at least possible that when we use that word we are really talking about problem-solving, and that when we ask, "What is his motive?" we are really asking, "What problem is he seeking to solve?"

Fortunately, a considerable amount of work has recently been done in examining human behavior from this point of view. Some account of the perceptual and cognitive theory necessary for this way of looking at human behavior is to be found in my recent *Man's Rage for Chaos*, but a more authoritative discussion can be found in *Plans and the Structure of Behavior*, by G. A. Miller, E. Galanter, and K. H. Pribram.[18] All we need here is to recognize that when we make interpretative predictions about semantic intention—or motive—we are in fact making predictions about what problem the speaker is trying to solve and what attitudes, or orientations, he is using to do so. Thus, when we are puzzled by someone's behavior, our tendency is often to ask, "What is he trying to do?" "What problem is he trying to solve and what is he using to solve it with?" In the case of the lumberman, our prediction is that he is using the attitudes, the values, and the knowledge normally found in the behavior of a successful lumberman. This explanation of what is meant by semantic intention seems to me to clarify a good deal the problem of what we do when we infer from our construction of a situation the semantic intention of the speaker, which we can then use to set boundaries to the semantic probabilities of his statement, to control polysemy. We make in fact a two-pronged prediction, aimed at the problem the speaker is attempting to solve and the orientation, or syndrome, or directive state, as the psychologist Jerome Bruner

18 (New York, 1960).

calls it, or the myth, which is, so to speak, his set of conceptual tools. But it must always be remembered that such predictions are always, like the situation itself and like the orientation and the problems, constructed, to be confirmed or disconfirmed by future inquiry.

If we use this model of what goes on when we interpret statements, it is evident that the traditional ways of asking "What is Romanticism?" are inadequate. The movement from attributes to range, or from range to attributes, must necessarily be unsatisfactory. At worst, it is a mere random casting about for what the lumberman is referring to with his category of "real tree." At best, it might hit upon some attribute of the problem itself, as I believe I did when I proposed the term "Negative Romanticism." If there is any validity to my proposal, it is mostly a matter of luck. I didn't know what I was doing, but what in fact I did was to begin to construct the situation by noting that each of the major Romantic authors went through a similar stage before arriving at a way out of his nihilistic despair.

What I did not see then was why there should be both resemblances and differences among the various solutions they offered; but what my work did make apparent, though I was not yet capable of formulating it, was that each of these men faced a similar problem, the problem of spiritual death—doubt and despair of any meaning in the universe. What was implied, though I did not yet know it, was that each must have had similar tools with which to solve his problem, because each had used and then rejected the attitudes of the Enlightenment. Their problem, to continue the metaphor, was that the Enlightenment tools had broken in their hands. Those tools could not construct a solution to the problem—the perfect adaptation of man to society and nature—they were designed to construct. *Beyond the Tragic Vision* is a theoretical construction of the successive situations of Romantic development from *The Sorrows of Young Werther* to *Also Sprach Zarathustra*. Its thesis is that the basic problem of the Romantics was, What is the ground of value? It develops by showing how each stage ensued upon the failure of the previous attempt to solve that problem, for each stage developed more precise and adequate tools than had hitherto been available.

Today, four years later, I would put it somewhat differently, or at least more concisely. What the first couple of generations had in common was the realization that the thing to be explained was not the nature of the world but rather that the most important thing men do is to create explanations of the world. The answer to the problem of value, it gradually came to be realized, lay not in constructing yet another metaphysic, but in understanding the metaphysical process, in comprehending and explaining metaphysical behavior. Instead of merely offering another metaphysic, as I had originally thought, what marks the Romantic situation is that the Romantic attempted to get outside of metaphysical behavior, to look at himself, so to speak, from right angles, to understand what he was doing when he attempted to explain experience in such a way that it became impregnated with value. When the Romantic talks about Imagination, this is what he is talking about.

But instead of discussing my own position further, I should like to conclude by commenting on the work of Professor Earl Wasserman, of Johns Hopkins. His first important contribution to Romantic theory is the first chapter of his book *The Subtler Language*.[19] It pleases me that the conclusions of this notable scholar and my own conclusions should show a considerable convergence, though I am not at all sure it will please Professor Wasserman. To begin with, I find this chapter a far from satisfactory performance. It is an almost inextricable tangle of unsound assumptions and extremely fancy language, filled with unconscious metaphors and conscious metaphors over which he seems to have very little control. I quote a few sentences from his second paragraph.

One of the most valuable commonplaces of modern critical theory ascribes to a poem the formulation of its own reality. . . . This conception of the poem as somehow a self-constituting and self-sustaining reality has been adumbrated by a series of metaphors ranging from Coleridge's image of organic growth and subsistence . . . . the principle that a poem is an organic unity and therefore a kind of cosmos of its own making has proved so profitable and accurate a premise for ap-

[19] (Baltimore, 1959).

propriating poems of all types and times as to suggest that it derives from the true character of any artistic manipulation of language, no matter what the poet's own critical assumptions.[20]

This, of course, is merely a restatement of the Beardsley-Wimsatt position discussed above. It asserts that poetry presents unique semantic functions and, therefore, unique interpretational problems. I have yet to see any attribute of this peculiar poetic language which cannot be located with perfect ease in language which is not poetic. The notion that poetry is a unique kind of language remains to be proved, and depends upon a general theory of interpretation, something we do not yet have. Now what Wasserman wants to talk about is not at all the autonomy of the poem. Far from it. He wants to talk about the metaphysical creativity of the Romantics, particularly Shelley. Consequently he has to wiggle quite hard to get out of his autonomous position and into his metaphysical position. The way he does it is to assert that " 'serious' poetry—that is, poetry of sufficient seriousness and scope as to touch on ontological concerns—has always been an effort to call into valid being a particular ordering of reality."[21]

What this amounts to is an assertion that metaphysical creativity is uniquely a poetic task, or perhaps uniquely suited to the poet's task, whatever that might be. Actually, what he wants to do is to take seriously the Romantic poet's assertion that Imagination, as defined, is uniquely the task of the poet. Rather, sometimes they made that assertion, and sometimes they said something quite different, merely asserting that in their situation it was the only thing that a poet could do. But insofar as they did make it, they can be forgiven; they were just at the edge of locating, let alone solving, an enormously difficult problem, a problem that can scarcely be said to be solved even yet. That is why we are still in the Romantic age, at least at the higher and more advanced levels of culture. They were forced into metaphysics not because they were poets but because preceding metaphysics were no longer viable. In this they behaved just like philosophers, and painters, and political scientists, and everybody else who

[20] *The Subtler Language,* 3.
[21] *Ibid.,* 10.

felt the problem. In this Wellek and even W. T. Jones are right and Wasserman is wrong. But the Romantic poets, recognizing that they were approaching metaphysics from a new perspective, and identifying that right-angle perspective, as I have called it, with the Imagination, traditionally the primary faculty of the poet, often, though not always, felt that in their attempt there was something uniquely poetic. Their error is understandable, but it is no longer necessary for us to make it.

Wasserman then goes on to discuss how the eighteenth-century poets could use existing world pictures, which they shared with others. (How they could do this and still be poets, by Wasserman's own definition, is mysterious; but elsewhere he implies that they really weren't poets anyway, or at least not very good ones. I find them quite delightful.) But, he continues,

By the nineteenth century these world-pictures had passed from consciousness for the purpose of public poetry, and no longer did men share in any significant degree a sense of cosmic design. The change from a mimetic to a creative conception of poetry is not merely a critical or philosophic phenomenon; the mimetic theory was no longer tenable when men ceased to share the cosmic designs that made mimesis meaningful. Now, therefore, an additional formulative act was required of the poet, for he must simultaneously employ the syntactical features of poetry to shape an order that has no assumed prototype outside the creative act, and with this internally contained order create the poem. Within itself the modern poem must both formulate its own cosmic syntax and shape the autonomous poetic reality that cosmic syntax permits; "nature," which once was prior to the poem and available for imitation, now shares with the poem a common origin in the poet's creativity.[22]

Much of this is nonsense and much is false. It is not true that "no longer did men share in any significant degree a sense of cosmic design." On the contrary, most men did, even at all but the most advanced cultural levels. Only a tiny handful, initially, lost the traditional "sense of cosmic design." To this day only a small minority of human beings have felt the problem with any intensity. Most people in America today live in terms of Medieval

[22] *Ibid.*, 11.

or Enlightenment world pictures. The rest of the passage, except for the last sentence, is simply a result of Wasserman's impossible effort to synthesize into one intellectual system the New Criticism and Lovejoy's History of Ideas. It cannot be done.[23]

With the last sentence, however, Wasserman makes an important point. Nature, or cosmic design, "now shares with the poem a common origin in the poet's creativity." That is, if a poet wants to write "serious" metaphysical poetry, he must make up his own metaphysics, and the way he puts his poem together has to be derived from the metaphysics the poem is presenting. This is not actually logically or empirically necessary, but they thought it was. Wasserman agrees with them, but it is not necessary to do so.

In a very clumsy way Wasserman has made some important points, but the most important thing he has done is to see that the Romantic situation offered, because of the contingencies of cultural history, a unique problem, and that we must understand that problem if we are to have any boundaries for the possibilities of interpreting Romantic literature.

In a subsequent paper, presented at the Romantic Achievement Conference held at Ohio State University in April, 1963, Wasserman made a considerable advance over the position proposed in *A Subtler Language*.[24] Not the least of the improvements is that his language has cleared up a remarkable degree. It is now much easier to understand what he is talking about. His new position is clearly stated.

What Wordsworth, Coleridge, Keats, and Shelley chose to confront more centrally and to a degree unprecedented in English literature is a nagging problem in their literary culture: How do subject and object meet in a meaningful relationship? By what means do we have a *significant* awareness of the world? Each of these poets offers a different answer, and each is unique as poet in proportion as his answer

---

[23] The statement about the change from a mimetic theory to a creative theory is presumably a reference to M. H. Abrams' *The Mirror and the Lamp* (New York, 1963). Certainly Abrams offers all the evidence necessary to establish that change; unfortunately he offers no explanation as to why it took place.

[24] "The English Romantics; The Grounds of Knowledge," *Studies in Romanticism*, IV (1964).

is special; but all share the necessity to resolve the question their predecessors had made so pressing through philosophic and aesthetic concern and poetic neglect or incompetence. . . . Of course epistemologies involve ontologies and can, and do, interconnect with theologies; but the epistemological problem is radical to this poetry as poetry, since it determines the role the poet will assign his raw material, how he will confront them, and how he will mold them into a poem.[25]

In the rest of the paper he shows how the self emerges as an important element in the solutions the various poets offered.

It is clear that he is in profound disagreement with Wellek, who has asserted that most students agree with him that, among other things, Romanticism is the great endeavor to overcome the split between subject and object.[26] And it is also clear that he is talking not so much about epistemology but rather about, to use a phrase I once applied to Wallace Stevens, the emotion of cognition, what it *feels* like to know something, and what that feeling does in creating the sense of value, of a "meaningful relationship," of a "*significant* awareness of the world." The Romantics, then, are concerned with epistemological problems because in the problem of knowledge lies concealed the answer to the problem of meaning and value. This, of course, sounds very much like the sort of thing I have said, but the real importance of Wasserman's paper lies elsewhere. The following comes from his concluding paragraph.

The four Romantics, it is clear, are sharply at odds with each other, in the terms I have been concerned with. But the very fact that their positions do clash so directly on these terms, instead of being merely unrelated, confirms that they all face the central need to find a significant relationship between the subjective and objective worlds.[27]

These are perhaps the most important sentences ever written, I submit, on the theory of Romanticism. To be sure, Wasserman does not offer any explanation as to why the eighteenth century did not face the problem, though the materials, Wasserman asserts, (I do not entirely agree) were available. He simply asserts

[25] *Ibid.,* 22.
[26] *Romanticism Reconsidered,* 123.
[27] *Studies in Romanticism,* IV, 33.

that the eighteenth-century poets were neglectful and incompetent, which is not an explanation at all. Nevertheless, what makes these sentences important is that Wasserman has broken through the method of asking, "What was Romanticism," to the method of asking, "What was the problem of the Romantics and how did they solve it?" He has shown that with much the same equipment, or set of tools, and precisely the same problem, four individuals could arrive at very different solutions. This means that they do not share certain attributes, but it also means that the sharing of attributes is not the proper way to decide whether particular poets belong in the same period. The old methods of assigning or discovering categories he distinctly repudiates in his introductory remarks. By demonstrating that it is the problem and the intellectual tools which mark a period, not categorical attributes, he has made an immense advance toward constructing the Romantic situation and thus setting up limits to semantic probabilities. It is a major contribution.

I have attempted in this paper to show that the problem of Romanticism is a problem of interpretation, of what used to be called hermeneutics. I have suggested that in this problem all that we are concerned with is the semantic intention of the writer, and that by semantic intention we very well may mean the inference from situation to problem and to orientation, or, if you prefer, intellectual or mental tools. And I have endeavored to find a model or paradigm for literary interpretation in the interpretative aspect of ordinary verbal behavior. On these grounds I have endeavored to show that the traditional way of solving the question of Romanticism, by categorial attribution and range assignment, is bound to fail, and I have offered several examples of exactly how it does fail. I have, finally, endeavored to justify my own recent procedures and to pay tribute to the only other effort I know of to advance in what I consider to be a correct and fruitful direction, the construction of the Romantic situation. But we must always remember, first, that such a construction is necessarily historical, with all the ill-understood limitations of historiography, and second, that we cannot be on really solid ground until we have a general theory of verbal interpretation, and that such a theory is still far in the future. I do not expect to live to see it.

II APPLICATIONS

5

THE PROBLEM OF

THE NINETEENTH CENTURY

[1955*]

The Philomathean Society is to be congratulated for choosing as its topic for this year's lectures so stimulating a subject as the nineteenth century, or rather—to be more precise in indicating its intentions—the survival of the nineteenth century into the twentieth. That it does survive there is no question. We live in one of the ugliest cities in the world, and it is largely the product of the nineteenth century. I do not refer merely to the architecture. Although the row house was not a nineteenth-century idea but comes from an earlier time and continues in the present—as the wretched wastes of the new Northeast Philadelphia make so hideously clear—what was done in Philadelphia with the row house is the responsibility of the nineteenth century alone. When 250

* Delivered in the Philomathean Lecture Series of the Philomathean Society, University of Pennsylvania, November, 1955. Reprinted by permission from *The Cultural Heritage of 20th Century Man,* Pennsylvania Literary Review and The Philomathean Society, Phil., 1956. Copyright 1956 by the Penna. Lit. Review.

years ago Philadelphia was planned and began to grow, its builders had in mind the ancient notion of the City, the *Urbs*, the
concentration within a limited area of the energies which make
civilization possible. To be civilized is to be the product of a city,
a place one can walk around in a couple of hours or less, a place
like Athens or Rome or London in the time of Shakespeare, or
better still of an earlier age.

> Forget six counties overhung with smoke,
> Forget the snorting steam and piston stroke,
> Forget the spreading of the hideous town;
> Think rather of the pack-horse on the down,
> And dream of London, small, and white, and clean,
> The clear Thames bordered by its gardens green;
> Think, that below bridge the green lapping waves
> Smite some few keels that bear Levantine staves,
> Cut from the yew wood on the burnt-up hill,
> And pointed jars that Greek hands toiled to fill,
> And treasured scanty spice from some far sea,
> Florence gold cloth, and Ypres napery,
> And cloth of Bruges, and hogsheads of Guienne;
> While nigh the throned wharf Geoffrey Chaucer's pen
> Moves over bills of lading—

So William Morris, "the idle singer of an empty day," opening his
vast work *The Earthly Paradise*, written, observe, in the 1860's.
Such a city did the planners of Philadelphia have in mind. Quiet
streets, red and white, green squares, churches, buildings of civic
dignity, markets, schools, small manufacturing concerns, great
wharves, and in the background the Schuylkill, clean and wild,
with farms and country houses, radiant in the clean air. A clean
country, new, rich, and in the center of it the city, small, energetic,
civilized, the ideal of the European civic imagination.

What happened to it? Even in 1886 Matthew Arnold could say,
"We drove out to Germantown after my lecture at the University
(quite a success) yesterday; it might have been England, the country was so green, so fenced and cultivated." Out Germantown
Avenue through North Philadelphia! A simple idea, the row
house, and a good idea, when, as the eighteenth century planned,

the houses were built around squares, or near them, and with the open country only two or three miles away. But in the nineteenth century the squares were forgotten, the nearness of the country was forgotten, the necessary limits of a proper city were forgotten. Monotonously, block after block, mile after mile, pushing the country farther and farther away, blocks, miles of big houses, blocks, miles of little houses, endlessly stretching along drearily straight streets, no surprises, no relief, appallingly alike, differing only in the increasing ugliness as the century wore on—50 houses alike, 100 houses just alike, 1000 houses exactly the same—out of the mill-yards trundling a million tuscan columns—out of the metal-working shops pouring an endless belt of abominable ornaments—out of the glass companies acres of leaded glass, uniformly ugly, revolting, repellent—a vast city, more aesthetically arid than the arctic in mid-winter. We look in awe. Was there some vast conspiracy to make Philadelphia the dreariest city in the world? Was some diabolic force at work? What happened to three centuries of the Renaissance culminating in the peerless eighteenth century? What happened to the hundreds of years of Gothic work, the few forlorn fragments of which are so cherished in Europe and America, centuries so masterly that four square yards of worm-eaten oak panelling are treasured in a museum and pored over with reverence and awe?

This city is the legacy of the nineteenth century. Is it any wonder that we think of it as a symbol of that century, and turn from all of its achievements with a shudder? Is it conceivable that a century guilty—not just in Philadelphia, but in New York, in Boston, in Chicago, in London, in Paris, all over Europe and America—guilty of the mindless repetition of a few simple and uninteresting architectural elements reiterated like the chattering of an idiot—only less stimulating—a century that has condemned most European and American men and women to live and work in an atmosphere which forces them to abandon man's natural joy in his immediate surroundings—which brutalizes the sensitivities that in the most primitive people find joyous expresson—is it conceivable that such a century could have had any mind at all?

Perhaps it is useful to the Sociology department that our University should have a skid row virtually on the campus, but it is not exhilarating. Yet the nineteenth century forced our University to its present position. None too attractive in itself, it is surrounded by a graveyard, a hospital, an open sewer, and a slum. And of these the home of the dead gives the strongest impression of life. What conceivably could have happened that tempted the nineteenth century to pervert man's most wonderful invention, the city, a place to which everyone wanted to come, into a place from which everyone wants to flee?

It would be pleasant to think of nineteenth-century Philadelphia as the result of blind economic forces, or of uncontrollable population pressures, as it would be reassuring to think of nineteenth-century London in the same way, a city improved by the German bombing. But it is impossible to do so. The older parts of the town were still attractive hardly more than 100 years ago, and London was building in the eighteenth-century manner as late as 1820. The planners and builders of what we have to live in today were surrounded by the evidences of an infinitely superior ideal of city life, evolved from definite and obvious values. All that was not merely abandoned. It was furiously denied. Such a denial could only have come from an opposing set of values, a concept of human life to which the earlier ideal was deliberately sacrificed, together with its products and manifestations. And so powerful was the new concept that less than a generation after the new city began taking form, there was a rebellion by men like Ruskin and Morris, and in this country Greenough and Olmstead; and yet that rebellion is hardly more powerful today, though far more widespread, than it was 50 years ago. Indeed, as early as 1820 Robert Southey saw what was coming, as did his friend William Wordsworth, but their warnings were judged the ravings of poetic idealists. After the new pattern was established similar warnings by Ruskin were likened to the preachings of a mad governess. Indeed, this new concept of human life which emerged over 100 years ago is still at work today; only it is no longer the creation of individual builders. We cannot blame it on the uncontrolled raging of laissez-faire individualism. Today it is the creation of the City, the State, and the Nation. Art commissions can maneuver helplessly, and Lewis Mumford can write brilliant essays in the *New Yorker*, but Robert Moses piles up enormous heaps of brick, doubling and tripling the population density, and the Uris brothers, with the money of corporations publicly controlled for the public benefit, build on the most valuable piece of empty land in any American city today buildings that make you wish you were blind and almost persuade you that you are, fearful perversions of the achievements of nearly 100 years of modern architecture.

I wish I could tell you what caused this revolution so deadly to human happiness, so destructive of values passionately worked out over more than 5,000 years. But I cannot tell you. I don't know. I have been studying the nineteenth century for years, and the more I study it the more perplexed I am. Was it an enormous access of energy? Was it the immense growth of population? I am sure it was an infinitely greater force than a little thing like classical economic theory. That was at best a feeble rationalization of what people were doing because they had no choice. Was it simply the Decline of the Western World? But the Eastern World is not in any too good shape either, and hasn't been for a long time, especially in its cities. I cannot tell you why it happened. I can only say that it appears to me that man turned upon his achievements, the world that took 5,000 years to create, a natural world even more beautiful than it was when he started cultivating it, a world to which he had added thousands of cities—in China, in India, in Africa, in South America, in North America, throughout Europe—cities small and yet centers of proud cultures, cities so charming that old prints fill us with a terrible nostalgia—man turned on this world and began, deliberately and consciously, to destroy it, and that at this very day all over the world from Russia to Indonesia, from Canada to the Argentine, he continues to destroy it, more rapidly each year.

I cannot tell you why we have done this. But I can tell you that a few great men rebelled. To them the nineteenth century was not sentimental, but violent, bitter, tragic. They hated it more than we do, because they had to live in it. And they lived in agony. Mockingly, and with a terrible irony, Marx lived in poverty which he made more frightful by his dirtiness, his emotional disorders, his brutality, and his hate. Darwin became a saint of science by protecting himself behind a solidly built wall of hypochondria.

Freud, finding his soul sick from the terrible wounds of the nineteenth century on the psyche of man, had to invent psychoanalysis and climb an intellectual mountain to escape, and even there he was pursued by a revenge which is turning his indictment into a parable for the nursery. And the artists, sick, pursued, self-torturing, nourishing from a million wounds their flowers of evil, fleeing to the South Seas, cutting off their ears, trailing the pageants of their bleeding hearts across Europe, deliberately deranging their sensibilities, coldly, brutally, and permanently taking European art apart and putting it together in ways that are still anathema to most people—except those willing to accept the emasculations of the universities and the perversions of Madison Avenue—these artists, huddled in their depraved Bohemias, abused when they were not neglected, issuing their powerful plain manifestoes, which the winds swept into the gutters of dirty streets—these artists, what of them, who hated the nineteenth century so?

These men, Darwin and Freud and Marx and Baudelaire and the rest of them, who felt in their bones what was coming, the cataclysms of our century—these men, what shall we say of them? We can say that out of their struggles and their wounds, recorded in *The Origin of Species*, in *Das Kapital*, in *The Psychopathology of Everyday Life* (terrible title), stretched on the walls of museums, played by thousands of orchestras, felt whenever we dare to look seriously at the savage pages of *Little Dorrit* and *Our Mutual Friend*, out of their universe of horror has emerged an idea, frail, not yet fully trustworthy, denied by most people, unused by those who accept it, an idea, a vision born of their struggle with the nineteenth century, a notion, an idea of human life which perhaps may redeem us, the people of the twentieth century, that century which is the child of the nineteenth and more terrible than its parent, more terrible, not because it is violent, bitter, and tragic, but because it is quiet, and clean, and liberal, and socially conscious, and tired, and a bore, and probably, if Erich Fromm is right, quite insane.

In 1850 Alfred Tennyson, a 41-year-old semi-Bohemian who had spent the preceding 15 years skulking in melancholy about the coffeehouses and pubs of Victorian London, published a long poem about himself. He called it *In Memoriam*, and a great many people thought it was a poem of faith in the immortality of Tennyson's friend who had died so young, Arthur Henry Hallam. But they were mistaken. It was a poem more like Baudelaire's than almost anything else in English.

> I held it truth, with him who sings
>   To one clear harp in divers tones,
>   That men may rise on stepping stones
> Of their dead selves to higher things.
>
> But who shall so forecast the years
>   And find in loss a gain to match?
>   Or reach a hand thro' time to catch
> The far off interest of tears?
>
> Let Love clasp Grief lest both be drown'd,
>   Let Darkness keep her raven gloss:
>   Ah, sweeter to be drunk with loss,
> To dance with Death, to beat the ground,
>
> Than that the victor Hours should scorn
>   The long result of love, and boast,
>   'Behold the man that loved and lost,
> But all he was is overworn.'

This poem is so frequently misunderstood that I should like to dwell on it a moment, for its central position in the century and the very fact that it was misunderstood make it marvelously pertinent to our considerations. I have asked a great many people, colleagues as well as students, to tell me what this poem means. And invariably I am told that the lesson of the stanzas is that we should and can transcend ourselves, learn from our mistakes, and so rise to higher things. But this is not at all what Tennyson says. Rather, he questions this notion. He denies it. Once, he tells us, he held this self-transformation to be a truth, but he does so no longer. To behave in such a way toward the past is to betray it, and to betray the human beings who have inspired us. It is to act toward an emotion as if it were a financial investment. It is to calculate the dividends to be gained from a capital put out in interest. It is to exploit both ourselves and those whom we love. It is better, he tells us, to embrace grief, to indulge it fully, to be intoxicated by it, than so to misuse our emotions that in the future we are forced to realize that our lives have been without continuity or honor or self-respect.

Now I am not concerned with whether or not Tennyson is right. Rather, I am concerned with the particular kind of problem presented in these lines, for it is central to the century. It puts very poignantly its particular problem. Baldly, to what extent is self-transcendence self-betrayal? Observe the things rejected here and the terms in which they are rejected. He rejects calculating exploitation. And calculating exploitation he identifies with an attitude toward experience which regards all activity as necessarily and properly modeled on money transactions. Better than to handle life in such a manner, he says, is to handle it in a way everyone condemns, a luxuriating and self-indulgent intoxication with emotional abandonment. Better to dance with death than to deny our selves, even for the purposes of self-improvement. Freud may have been wrong when he stated that the death wish is universal; it is hard to think that he was mistaken when he found it in the nineteenth century, or at least in the nineteenth-century artist and intellectual. Tennyson is recommending most improper behavior, the violation of some of the most sacred of Victorian shibboleths. He recommends a deliberate cultivation of the flowers, not of evil, for that is an inadequate translation, but of the flowers of illness, of disgust. He is recommending the emotion so brilliantly explored by an American, Tennessee Williams, in his *Cat on a Hot Tin Roof*, which is also for the hero a kind of *In Memoriam*, the intoxicated lament for a dead friend and the exploration of the terrible feeling that any action will result in a self-betrayal. Tennyson, in this poem, like Williams' hero is, in the phrase of Delmore Schwartz, one who would not take his life in his hands. Not an admirable attitude. Yet, as Williams shows, both men are faced with the problem that the only terms on which one can take one's life in one's own hands are the terms which one's society offers, a money morality. Of what value is a self-transcendence which involves simply a recasting of oneself in the mould which society so complacently offers? Better to withdraw completely. Or as Tennyson puts it later in *In Memoriam*:

Sleep, kinsman thou to death and trance
   And madness, thou hast forged at last
   A night-long Present of the Past
In which we went through summer France.

Hast thou such credit with the soul?
   Then bring an opiate trebly strong,
   Drug down the blindfold sense of wrong,
That so my pleasure may be whole.

Here in Tennyson, of all people, usually thought of as the perfect complacent and sentimental Victorian, is exactly that same desire for death, that same cultivated derangement of the senses, that same denial of society's values which we find in Baudelaire, in Rimbaud, in Marx, and still today in Williams' Brick. It is a terrible position to be backed into, and yet it is possible to see how it can happen.

Darwin's life lets us see most clearly what the purpose of this derangement actually is. He used illness as a defense. He used it to protect himself from his overwhelming father, from his delightful but demanding wife and children, and especially from a society which he knew would crush him if it knew what he was up to. Huxley was the bulldog of Darwin, simply because Darwin was intelligent enough to see that to engage with his society over the issue of evolution would destroy that delicate emotional balance so essential to the scientist, that poise which he needs if he is to maintain his role with consistency, and to employ himself in destroying the lies on which society fancies itself to be based. Neurosis, then, as a defense. We can see this in Wordsworth and in Williams, in Tennyson and in Auden. And can the careful division of his life into poet and businessman which Wallace Stevens so brilliantly effected—can such a strategy be called really a success, really healthy? Stevens was a successful insurance executive; he once wrote me that he saw nothing strange in being both poet and vice-president of an insurance company. Perhaps he saw nothing strange, but the rest of us can be permitted to do so. One might say that he didn't dare see anything strange. And not to dare to look at something is not to be strong.

Illness, derangement, brutality, hate, self-division, Bohemian depravity as defenses, then. But psychiatry instructs us that the neurotic's defenses are after all erected against something unreal, or at least something that no longer exists. But if Philadelphia is a symbol of the nineteenth century, surely it can scarcely be said that these men were building defenses against something that wasn't there. It all too obviously was there, just as it is here, now, today, present everywhere, in the continuous corruption and degradation of our art, our language, and our culture, in advertising, in mass communication media, in housing developments, in Johnny's inability to read. Nor can we blame business any more now than it could be blamed then. Such men were forgiven, over 19 centuries ago, on the grounds that they didn't know what they were doing. We may dismiss them. For we scarcely know any better than they do what they were doing. Or rather, both of us know *what* was being done. The question is, *why* was it being done. And the answer to that question, as I have already admitted, I cannot tell you.

I should like to give an example of the sort of thing I am talking about. A few years ago I was asked to set up a program of humanistic education for junior business executives. The general idea was that if such men could have some experience in such matters as literature and logic, art, music, anthropology, history, philosophy, and so on, they would be better prepared to deal imaginatively and intelligently with the crisis which a few farsighted business leaders believe is soon going to face the great business corporation. In sympathy with such a program, I set out to create the best course of a year's training I could. The only test for the success of my efforts which I could respect was, I think, passed. My colleagues admired it enough to be willing to teach in it and even be enthusiastic. Last spring a man high in the upper and misty realms of adult education asked me what my real aim was. "To make better executives, of course." He refused to be taken in. He kept at me until I surrendered. "Very well, I'll tell you the truth, although I have never publicly admitted it. I saw this was the one chance I would ever have to strike even a feeble blow, for it is a very feeble blow, at the whole character of American civilization. And I set about making it as powerful and violent a blow as I could." "I thought so," said he, this former general sales manager of a huge corporation, "I thought so. Congratulations!"

Now I should like to draw attention to the significance of this little story, the pattern of it. Whether I was right or wrong in my attitude is not the question. The point is that, given this particular opportunity, I reacted with the violence which has been characteristic of the intellectual and artist for the past 150 years. Observe how I phrased my attitude. "I wanted," I said, "to strike a blow." How often, in the course of nineteenth-century studies, have I met that phrase! Even Matthew Arnold, who tried to be as urbane as possible, speaks of dissolving the powers of his own time which were inimical to sweetness and light. And he was capable of referring to the "brutal licentiousness" of evangelical theology. To Arnold, the only saving remnant of his society were the aliens, those whose stance or assumed position in relation to their society was that of an enemy, to be sure, an enemy whose whole desire was to save society from itself, but still an enemy. Erich Fromm, who calls our society insane, takes the same position. The greatest amount of mental illness and alcoholism, he says, is to be found exactly in those countries which by nineteenth-century standards have been most successful, America, England, and the Scandinavian countries. Nearly 100 years ago Ruskin, with terrible accuracy, saw what Erich Fromm sees. In "The Mystery of Life and Its Arts" he described the same madness, and found it quite inexplicable.

It is perhaps immodest of me to compare myself with such great figures, and it would be immodest if I suggested any such comparison. No, I wish only to show how widely that pattern of rebellion has spread. It was not I but a former general sales manager of a great corporation who said, "Congratulations." To be sure, if he hadn't been the *former* general sales manager, perhaps he would have felt differently. But the fascinating thing is that somehow or other he had come to the point where he shared my attitude, a point at which he could approve my violence. We were both participating in, and this is the real significance of the incident, what has ceased to be an isolated position. Because if two people with such disparate backgrounds as his and mine could arrive at the same position, there must be a great many people who have traveled the same road. And that road was the one carved out by the heroes of the nineteenth century in the jungle which was their world. Like all jungle paths, it is always threatened with overgrowth, every now and then it seems to be once again swallowed up in the jungle, but in spite of everything people are still traveling it.

But does this jungle road lead anywhere? Or does it exist only to provide a relief from the jungle and easier going? Perhaps it simply leads deeper and deeper into the jungle, winds around, crosses itself, retraces itself, goes north, south, east, and west, gets no place, and finally ends in a cul-de-sac, a lost world, a pit for the bones of the lost traveler. To this problem we must now turn.

Let me indicate again, so that there may be no confusion, exactly what the problem was. Given what was happening to European culture, the artist and intellectual could only become alienated, isolated within their society. But someone who tends the mad is still called in our courts an alienist. To them it was the only way they could become the saving remnant, and thus defend what was being destroyed. Yet an attitude of permanent defense is not adequate. It involves the perilous position of the reactionary. You may be defending what has lost its function and never again will have any function. Edmund Burke was perhaps the first to realize this dilemma in its full intensity when he attacked the French Revolution with all his powers and ended with, "Perhaps, after all, I am wrong." The alienated intellectual, if he simply adopts a position of defense, is threatened with certain weaknesses, treason within his walls.

There is the treason of conservatism; the strategy adopted was one that often appears during the century. Wordsworth and Coleridge tried it. So did Carlyle and Ruskin. It is the position of radical conservatism, a strangely ambiguous and paradoxical position. It implies rehabilitating society, re-creating society, in the radical manner, while at the same time preserving the order which, one fancies, at one time existed, though it probably never did, and also setting up institutions which will foster those values and that beauty of the world which is so horribly threatened. But it is founded on a sentimentality. There never was a time when man's social institutions were an adequate adaptation of man to his world, and the emphasis upon an imaginary order which we can never know can lead to real difficulties, and a world more terrible than the one the alien is trying to destroy. Such an attitude, many people maintain, led to fascism, and they may be right. At any rate, the position of radical conservatism opens a gate to the enemy without the walls, because it opens a way to dealing with the enemy on the basis of what is to be conserved. The trouble is that the real radicalism which destroyed eighteenth-century Philadelphia masked itself, through its use of classical economics, as conservatism. Just as today the world created through the distribution methods of advertising is more radically revolutionary and destructive than anything the most violently alienated revolutionaries ever imagined.

Another form of treason within the alien's walls is madness. That this is a real threat, the pitiful experience of Ruskin and so many others fully demonstrates. The strategy against this treason is something like radical conservatism. It is the adoption of madness, or, to use a more modern and milder term, neurosis, as a defense. People like Rimbaud and Baudelaire and Browning, at least in his style, and Joyce feigned neurosis in order to protect themselves against it. Baudelaire was, in that delightful phrase, crazy like a fox. The strategy was a kind of willed paranoia. The results are often magnificent, but the strategy has one weakness, as the history of the reputation and public reception of modern art only too painfully shows; it is easy to dismiss the work of such men as the work of real madmen. They depart so far from the expected norms of creation that they are incomprehensible. Or they depart so far from the accepted standards of behavior that their work is dismissed as necessarily useless to society. And again, their life style is so easily imitated by lazy and untalented Bohemian depravity that it is discredited. The public simply makes fun of it and passes on. Nor do I mean just the half-educated public. Do not forget that there are plenty of men, respected scholars and philosophers and critics, to whom *Ulysses* is simply the irresponsible ravings of a disturbed and perverted maniac. Such men are to be found not only on the second page of the Sunday *New York*

Times Book Review. They also have occupied and still occupy some of the most respected and powerful positions in the academic world.

A third enemy within the walls is the mask of conformity. The alien, sufficiently protected, he thinks, by his values, which he is sure are the basic values of mankind, thinks he can be most effective by a kind of controlled schizophrenia. Externally he achieves acceptance by conforming to the expected aesthetic, intellectual, and behavioral patterns of a world which he detests. But this is hypocrisy, and the penalty of hypocrisy, even of honest hypocrisy, is that we become what we pretend to be. Max Beerbohm pointed this out in his *Happy Hypocrite,* and he said it so well that it is foolish to try to say it again. This was the strategy of Tennyson and Browning. It was also the strategy of Thomas Mann. But the older men, with less of a tradition behind them, often failed, and perhaps Tennyson always failed. But Mann, diabolically clever, continued the masquerade to the end, and in his last work, the incomparable *Felix Krull,* with an irresistible irony, presented the artist as a confidence man. Melville, too, wrote a *Confidence Man*—and then gave up.

In short, all of these strategies have their possibilities, but all are open to grave dangers. What the alien needs is some means of self-transformation without self-betrayal, some way that will not involve him in stupidity, or madness, or hypocrisy, with their various dangers. For stupidity, madness, and hypocrisy are dangerous devices. They can destroy you unless you use them with eternal vigilance, and perhaps even if you do. But worse, they are exhausting, they use up energy, they distract you from the real problem. And each strategy, for that reason, can become an end itself. Designed to preserve independence, they can and must inhibit growth.

And the failure of artist after artist, thinker after thinker, in the nineteenth century is that same failure to grow. And yet no artists or intellectuals in history strove so hard to maintain and continue growth. Because in the concept of growth lies not only what they were trying to do, but the way out of their intolerable dilemma. Up to the nineteenth century man's problem was to fulfill the patterns which already existed, perhaps to clarify the pattern, as Milton and Pope did, perhaps to complete it up to its logically necessary contours, as did the philosophers, but essentially the notion was that there is a pattern for human behavior which has but to be discovered, and of which we can already trace the general outlines. But with the close of the eighteenth century arose new problems, problems of energy, of population, of communication, of clarified reason, problems such as men had never faced before. Perhaps instead of condemning the mass of nineteenth-century men, we should praise them. To be sure, they failed, but they faced problems for which there were no known solutions. Their social institutions were hopelessly inadequate for the functions which they had to try to fulfill. From this point of view, the city itself, which they destroyed, was simply a human institution which was hopelessly inadequate, inappropriate, for the world which was developing. This was indeed their failure. This perhaps is the cause for the disaster of the nineteenth century which perplexes me so. In using the row house in a way and for a purpose for which it was simply not designed, they merely applied an already existing pattern to an entirely new situation. And indeed, let us not condemn them too bitterly; the problem of decent mass housing has not yet been solved, even in principle, nor do I see any signs of an adequate solution. And wherever we look in the nineteenth century we can see the same thing happening. The classical economics of Smith, which was only a part of his total thought and which was a kind of construction developed to see what kind of results you would get if you looked at human affairs only from an economic point of view, an economics developed from an examination of economic behavior which was on the verge of being totally transformed—this classical economics was applied as an explanation and justification for a wholly new kind of economic world, characterized by necessary behavior for which there was no precedent. We can look back now and see how terribly inadequate it was. Only Carlyle and Ruskin and a few others saw this truth at the time. Or we can look at the history of architecture: Gothic for religious buildings, classical for public and financial buildings. For the home, either, according to your taste. Only Ruskin saw that both were inadequate. It was another example of applying ready-made formulas to a new situation.

Or in art, the vast mass of painters were still choiring sweetly about chiaroscuro and the glories of Poussin. But Turner and the Impressionists, in the face of public hatred, perceived that a new world had come into being, and that it must be looked at in a new way. Or in poetry, most English and American poets continued to write in the style of Milton, or Shakespeare, or Chaucer, or Pope, or Thomson. Only Coleridge, out of his agony, created in "Kubla Khan" a new poetic vision, which Tennyson tried to handle and then gave up. And Whitman, the greatest and most self-conscious poseur of them all—for which I admire him—was experimentalist enough to attempt, clumsily, and brutally, a new prosodic instrument.

This then is what our heroic rebels perceived. The forms with which man had organized his experience, the very structure of his thinking, would have to be changed. It was not a matter of adaptation. That wouldn't work. They had only to look at what was happening around them to see that it wouldn't. What was needed was something else, some new principle, some way whereby our culture as a whole could transform itself without betraying itself; some way of re-creation which would involve at once defense and abandon, preservation and destruction; some way in which the desperate act, by achieving a goal, could at once convert the goal from an end into a means.

To this purpose it was first of all necessary to make certain decisions. And the first decision was the basic one, from which all others would flow. Growth, they felt, was the way that was desirable. This would be the path through the jungle that led someplace and not merely to a whited sepulcher filled with the bones of the dead. But growth must first found itself on some foundation. To live a life of growth through developing a life style of experimentation—the ambition and solution of men as various as Thoreau and Walter Pater—was to require some justification, some sanction. And they found it. Man, they said, is inadequate. He can never achieve the adjustment and adaptation he wishes. Nor, they maintained, is this a matter of original sin. It is not the fault of something that happened only a few thousand years ago to an entirely mythical human pair; it is endemic to man's situation; it is not unnatural but natural. Mankind's moral failures,

Darwin implied, come not from some metaphysical sin but from his organic character. Instead of being so perfectly adapted to his environment that the only conceivable explanation of his failure is some moral malevolence, his failure arises from the fact that he is imperfectly, inadequately, badly adapted to his environment. If there is a God, said Mill, he is not very good at creation and he certainly is not very interested in mankind. But this very inadequacy is the source of the principle of growth, of self-transformation. This then is the paradox of the nineteenth-century failure. Success is to be founded on a necessary and eternal failure. It is for this reason that I have referred to them as heroes, for I take this to be an heroic position.

Marx and Darwin and Freud and the artists have one theme in common. The nineteenth century has deeply wounded the soul of man because it has not grasped the fact that the forms of its culture and its thought have suddenly become hopelessly inappropriate. Yet in that very failure lies the one hope for success. For if we realize that failure, we can act. Hence the single task of the nineteenth-century hero—to hurl at Western civilization as powerfully as he could, over and over again, the terrible indictment, "You have failed. And you always will fail. And yet from that failure, from the very fact of that necessary and eternal failure can, if you realize it, arise your one hope of success."

Darwin, Freud, Marx, the artists. What unites them? This one hope of growth from failure, of self-transformation without self-betrayal. Darwin looked at the biological world, pushed it back millions of years, and said, "See, man struggles for his existence, by cooperation as well as competition, for he is part of nature, and so all nature does. But self-transformation through adaptive failure is also part of the natural process." Marx turned knock-kneed Hegel on his head and said, "See, man has created society, and has created it badly, but if he understands how and why his very limitations led him to create the society that he did they can teach him to refashion it." Freud looked at man's soul and said, "See, you are wounded, and those wounds interfere with man's capacities for spiritual growth. But the capacity is there, and the wounds can, if rightly understood, become not the chains of a prison but the windows of a palace." And the artists said, "Look! Look at the world! See what it is, and see how the artist transforms it. The artist is free, not tied to the world. Within himself he has the power of the symbols which can re-create man's vision."

Near the end of *Dr. Faustus*, Thomas Mann's great novel, Serenus Zeitblow, the narrator, describes the last great work of the musical genius Adrian Leverkühn, the symphonic cantata *The Lamentation of Dr. Faustus*.

At the end of this work of endless lamentation, softly above the reason and with the speaking unspokenness given to music alone, it touches the feelings. . . . This dark tone-poem permits up to the very end no consolation, appeasement, transfiguration. But take our artist paradox: grant that expressiveness—expression as lament—is the issue of the whole construction: then may we not parallel with it another, a religious one, and say too (though only in the lowest whisper) that out of the sheerly irremediable, hope might germinate? It would be but a hope beyond hopelessness, the transcendence of despair—not betrayal to her, but the miracle that passes belief. For listen to the end, listen with me: one group of instruments after another retires, and what remains, as the work fades on the air, is the high G of cello, the last word, the last fainting sound, slowly dying in a pianissimo-fermata. Then nothing more: silence, and night. But that tone which vibrates in the silence, which is no longer there, to which only the spirit hearkens, and which was the voice of mourning, is so no more. It changes its meaning; it abides as a light in the night.[1]

[1] Thomas Mann, *Doctor Faustus*, trans. H. T. Lowe-Porter (New York), 490–91.

6

CONSTABLE

AND WORDSWORTH

[1952*]

Obvious resemblances between Constable and Wordsworth have been noted often enough: devotion to the natural world and to humble life, accurate observation, a vague pantheistic feeling. But recently an even more striking connection has been suggested. In 1950 Kurt Badt offered a new explanation for Constable's extraordinary oil sketches, which he began to do in 1808, by pointing to Wordsworth's theory of the creative imagination, as it appears in the Preface to the *Lyrical Ballads*, first published in 1800, and reprinted in 1802 and in 1805.[1] Badt disclaims any attempt to prove that Constable knew Wordsworth's theories,[2] but he has raised a problem which has teased me for years. Are there any reasons for thinking that Constable consciously ap-

* Delivered at the annual meeting of the College Art Association of America, January, 1952. Reprinted by permission from *College Art Journal*, XII (Spring, 1953), pp. 196–209.
[1] Kurt Badt, *John Constable's Clouds* (London, 1950), Chap. IX.
[2] Badt, 81.

plied Wordsworth's ideas about writing poetry to his own creative activity, painting? A positive answer would be of the greatest interest to the student of nineteenth-century culture as well as to the student of the relations between poetry and painting, not less interesting to the literary historian than to the historian of art. For more may be involved than an influence of Wordsworth on Constable. If we accept the idea, as Andrew Shirley puts it in his introduction to his edition of Leslie's *Life of Constable*,[3] that modern art goes back to Constable, through the Impressionists, the Realists, the Barbizon school, and the painters who saw the Constables at Paris in 1824 and after, does it not follow that modern art goes back to Wordsworth, providing of course that what Constable gained from Wordsworth he passed on to his French successors? In what follows, I shall suggest two answers: first, Constable was almost certainly conscious of Wordsworth's ideas; and second, the characteristics of art which he derived from Wordsworth's precepts and practice were taken up by later painters.

The crucial year in Constable's life is 1808, when he began to do the amazing oil sketches which still are fresh and modern. Only a look at his work in chronological order tells that these sketches were entirely new, a deliberate experiment, a complete break with what had gone before, new because, as Shirley puts it, of the "quality of their light or by the violence of the transitory effect presented,"[4] and that their unique character was not realized in his large "finished" paintings until the mid-1820's, if ever. That Constable was conscious of his daring and his novelty appears in a remark he made that spring to Benjamin Robert Haydon. Joseph Farington, painter, student of Richard Wilson's, diarist, friend of Constable's since 1798, records for May 19, 1808, the following: "Constable called.—Haydon asked him 'Why He was anxious abt. what he was doing in art?—'Think, sd. He, what I am doing,' meaning how much greater the object and the effort."[5]

[3] Charles R. Leslie, *Memoirs of the Life of John Constable*, ed. Hon. Andrew Shirley (London, 1937), lvii.

[4] Leslie, lxii.

[5] Joseph Farington, *Diary*, ed. James Gleig (London, 1924), V, 65.

Certainly up to 1808 Constable's originality had shown itself only in a conscious effort to be truthful to nature. On May 29, 1802, he wrote to his old friend Thomas Dunthorne that he was determined to be a "natural painter." He felt there was "room enough," judging by the current academy. "Nature is the fountain's head, the source from whence all originality must spring."[6] There is nothing really new here. Such an idea could have come from Wordsworth, but it could have come from innumerable sources, some of which are suggested by Leslie and his editor, Shirley. The most probable source is simply the current Natural Theology of England. Another 1802 passage is more significant. "For the last two years I have been running after pictures, and seeking the truth at second hand. I have not endeavored to represent nature with the same elevation of mind with which I set out, but have rather tried to make my performances look like the work of other men."[7] His problem was this; it is all very well to be true to nature, but to what in nature should one be true, and how? He had the consciousness of the great Romantics that his mission was to found a new mode of art, but no painter then living could have told him what to do. It was, I think, Wordsworth who pointed the way.

There is one obvious connection between Wordsworth and Constable. From East Bergholt, where Constable's family lived, it is only a short walk to Dedham, where Golding Constable owned a mill. In Dedham lived the Dowager Lady Beaumont, and at her house, sometime before 1795, Constable was introduced to her son, Sir George Beaumont, born in 1753, painter, connoisseur, collector, quasi artistic dictator of London. Beaumont had perceived Constable's talent and thus the introduction was effected. The two men were intimate, more or less, as much as two men of different ages and different levels of society could be, until Beaumont's death in 1827.[8] In Leslie's *Life* there are frequent references to visits to Beaumont, to favors conferred by Beaumont upon Constable, to Beaumont's directions to Constable to take care of his health, when, between the ages of 35 and 40, he came

[6] Leslie, 20. See also Farington for Feb. 10, 1804 (III, 189).
[7] Leslie, 21.
[8] Leslie, 5–6.

close to a breakdown. In 1823, when Constable visited Beaumont at Coleorton, which Beaumont, after 1809, preferred to his ancestral estates at Dunmow, in Essex, Beaumont read parts of Wordsworth's *The Excursion* to him, and Constable was most impressed. It is plain, from Farington's diary, that not long after Constable came to London more or less permanently, around 1800, he became a part of the circle of artists around Beaumont, a group which included, among others, Haydon and Wilkie.[9]

One of the most important events in Beaumont's life occurred in August, 1803. In the spring, he had met Coleridge at the poet Sotheby's, and had disliked him at once. When he went to the Lake District in August of that year, he was at first distressed that, having taken lodgings at Jackson's, in Keswick, he was a neighbor of Coleridge's, who leased Greta Hall, practically next door. But on August 6, 1803, Coleridge wrote to Wordsworth at Grasmere that the Beaumonts, Sir George and the sensitive, sentimental, easily excited, and slightly absurd Lady Beaumont, "are half mad to see you."[10] Apparently they did not meet at that time, but within a few weeks Beaumont had bought a plot of land where Wordsworth and Coleridge could build together, though Wordsworth, knowing his S.T.C., never did. Well within a year William and Dorothy Wordsworth were carrying on an active correspondence with Sir George and Lady Beaumont. It is unnecessary to enter into the details of these letters, except to note that they are frequent to 1808 and sporadic thereafter.[11] Occasionally the Beaumonts summered at the Lakes, and in the winter and spring of 1806 and 1807 the entire Wordsworth family spent the winter at Coleorton, where the new house, for which Wordsworth designed a winter garden, had not yet been built. When Wordsworth was in London he often stayed at Beaumont's. In April and May, 1806, he stayed with them. In 1807, April and

[9] Farington, V, 94; Leslie, 152.

[10] Samuel Taylor Coleridge, *Unpublished Letters*, ed. E. L. Griggs (London, 1932), I, 266.

[11] See Ernest de Selincourt's edition of the Wordsworth family letters: *Early Letters of William and Dorothy Wordsworth (1787–1805)* (Oxford, 1935); *The Letters of William and Dorothy Wordsworth: The Middle Years (1806–1820)* (Oxford, 1937).

May, he was again in London; at this time his *Poems in Two Volumes* was published. Though he did not stay with his aristocratic friends, the three of them called on Farington.[12] In March, 1808, again in London, to take care of Coleridge, he spent part of his visit at Dunmow.

Constable first met Wordsworth in 1806. At the suggestion of his Uncle, David Pike Watts, and perhaps with the approval of Sir George, he had gone on a sketching trip to the Lake Country. Farington records: "Constable remarked upon the high opinion Wordsworth obtains of himself; . . . He also desired a Lady, Mrs. Loyd, near Windermere when Constable was present to notice the singular conformation of his Skull.—Coleridge remarked that this was the effect of intense thinking."[13] When he was in London, Constable called frequently on Farington, once or twice a month at least; and he was in London during Wordsworth's 1806 and 1807 visits, though perhaps not during the visit of March, 1808, when Beaumont was not in town. Wordsworth was again in London at Beaumont's in May, 1812, and visited London in 1815 and in 1820. This is important, for these are two bits of information from another source that indicate that at least once Constable met Wordsworth at Beaumont's house in Grosvenor Square.

In August, 1824, Henry Crabb Robinson, diarist and friend of most of the major Romantics, was at Brighton on a holiday. Part of his entry for August 26 reads as follows: "of the party Mr. Constable, a landscape painter of great merit, Masquerier says: he knew Wordsworth formerly, took an interest in his conversa-

[12] Farington, April 28, 1807, IV, 129. Wordsworth called on Farington again on April 26, 1808 (Farington, III, 206). I have determined Beaumont's movements from Farington's diary, the Wordsworth letters, and the Coleridge letters, including both the Griggs edition and *Letters*, ed. E. H. Coleridge (London, 1895). I have also consulted *Memorials of Coleorton: being Letters from Coleridge, Wordsworth and his Sister, Southey, and Sir Walter Scott to Sir George and Lady Beaumont of Coleorton, Leicestershire, 1803–1834*, ed. W. Knight (Edinburgh, 1887). Leslie is also of some value for this purpose.

[13] Farington, IV, 239. "Mrs. Loyd" was presumably the wife of Charles Lloyd, friend of Wordsworth, Coleridge, Lamb, and DeQuincey. Christopher Wordsworth, William's brother, married Priscilla Lloyd, Charles's sister.

tion, and preserved some memorials of his composition when they met at Sir George Beaumont's."[14] On the following December 13, he wrote to Dorothy Wordsworth: "At Brighton I met with a painter who had met Mr. W: at Sir Geo: Beaumonts Mr. Constable—It was some years ago. He seemed to have retained just impressions of your brothers personal distinction among the poets, tho' too passionately & exclusively attached to his own art to allow himself leisure for the study of any other."[15]

The reference to "some years ago" could refer to any of Wordsworth's visits to London. A vague phrase, it cannot be pressed too hard. On the other hand, the diary entry, written down when the meeting with Constable was still fresh in Robinson's mind, seems to indicate more than just one dinner meeting at Beaumont's; that meeting probably took place in 1812 or in 1815, since, with one exception, all of Wordsworth's poems to Beaumont were published in 1815. The important thing is that Constable, who "when young, was extremely fond of reading poetry," was impressed by Wordsworth, and took the trouble to "preserve some memorials of his composition." In his published letters he mentions only Cowper, Wordsworth, and Coleridge of contemporary poets, and of Wordsworth quotes only the "Thanksgiving Ode."[16]

It is not, fortunately, necessary to depend solely upon the meager evidence of a few meetings to get a better idea of what Constable may have picked up from Wordsworth. The poet kept Beaumont thoroughly informed about what he was doing in

[14] *Henry Crabb Robinson on Books and their Writers*, ed. Edith J. Morley (London, 1938), I, 312. Wordsworth wrote a number of poems referring to Beaumont or dedicated to him: "Elegiac Stanzas suggested by a picture of Peele Castle in a Storm, painted by Sir George Beaumont" (wr. 1805, pub. 1807); "Inscriptions in the Grounds of Coleorton," etc. (wr. 1808, pub. 1815); "Written at the Request of . . . Beaumont . . . and in his name, for an Urn . . . in the Same Grounds" (wr. 1808, pub. 1815)—this is the monument in the painting finished by Constable in 1836 (Leslie, 341); "Epistle to . . . Beaumont" (wr. 1811, pub. 1842); "Upon the Sight of a Beautiful Picture Painted by . . . Beaumont" (wr. 1811, pub. 1815); "In a Garden of . . . Beaumont" (wr. 1811, pub. 1815); "For a Seat in the Groves of Coleorton" (wr. 1811, pub. 1815.)

[15] H. C. Robinson, *Correspondence with the Wordsworth Circle*, ed. Edith J. Morley (Oxford, 1927), I, 134.

[16] Leslie, 361, 141.

poetry. Especially he told him about *The Prelude*, as it was later called, the poem about the growth of his own mind. He finished it in 1805, at least the first version, though it was not published until 1850, and the fact that Beaumont knew of it in 1804 and had read it by 1808 is of the greatest importance, for in *The Prelude* are to be found the most important expositions of Wordsworth's ideas. Farington, who met Wordsworth at Beaumont's in 1806, reveals how the Beaumonts broadcast Wordsworth's fame from 1803 to 1809. On November 29, 1803, Beaumont told Farington about the greatness of Coleridge and Wordsworth at Keswick the previous August. On March 21, 1804, he told him all over again and added information about *The Recluse*, as *The Prelude* was then known. He read "Tintern Abbey" to him, a poem which, Beaumont said, he had read a hundred times. Again at dinner at Beaumont's on November 7, 1806, Farington heard more about *The Prelude*, and in 1809 Lady Beaumont praised the great Preface to the *Lyrical Ballads*.[17] Beaumont, in these years when Constable was forming his style, knew more about Wordsworth's work than almost anyone outside of the immediate Wordsworth-Coleridge circle. Coleridge had shown him parts of *The Excursion* by May, 1804, probably when he was staying at Dunmow before going to Malta in late March, 1804. Wordsworth wrote to him about *The Prelude* in December, 1804. By May, 1805, both the Beaumonts had seen "some books" of it. In June, 1805, Wordsworth sent Beaumont the first 61 lines of Book VIII. In 1805 Dorothy expected that he would read him the whole work. Most important of all, the Beaumonts were entrusted to take care of the binding of the copy of the work destined for Coleridge, on his return from Malta, and this bound copy was received at Grasmere, along with other books and presents from the Wordsworth children, in June, 1806. It is not surprising, therefore, that Beaumont told Farington more about the poem in the following November; by that time he had read it. It was planned that he should; apparently, not wishing to make Beaumont wait for the return of the dilatory Coleridge from Malta and no doubt anxious to have a reaction from a man for whom he had great affection and respect,

[17] Farington, II, 172, 207; IV, 42; V, 132.

Wordsworth sent him the poem so that he could read it, and have the MS bound for Coleridge.[18]

From these facts it is quite permissible to conclude that Beaumont told Constable about *The Prelude*, and persuaded him to read the Preface as well as Wordsworth's poetry, of which two important volumes appeared in 1807. It will also be remembered that the Preface became available easily with the republication of *Lyrical Ballads* in 1805. When he was fifty years old, Beaumont became the patron of the two greatest creative artists in England, Wordsworth and Coleridge. If he and Lady Beaumont told an old but apparently never intimate friend like Farington about them and their writings, they undoubtedly told a great many other people, especially since they lionized Wordsworth when he came to London. Would Constable, who was in and out of their house when they were in London for the season, whom Beaumont always regarded as a kind of pupil and protégé, who probably visited them at Dunmow and certainly in later years visited at Coleorton, whom Beaumont knew intimately and constantly advised for over thirty years—would Constable have been kept in the dark? It seems most unlikely. I think we can assume with considerable confidence that Constable knew Wordsworth's poetry, published and unpublished, his principal essay on poetry, and Coleridge's "The Rime of the Ancient Mariner," which was to be read only in the *Lyrical Ballads* until it reappeared, revised, in 1817 in *Sibylline Leaves*. And this poem, in 1824, Constable called the best modern poem. Presumably he knew others. The next step is to ascertain what Constable might have learned from Wordsworth; to this problem I now turn.

The following analysis is based upon a concept of early nineteenth-century Romanticism of which I have published elsewhere a more detailed account.[19] The fundamental assumption of Romanticism is that the cosmos, or external reality, is a living organism, and that the psycho-physical personality is also a living organism. From this idea are derived others. Change is a positive value; the artist's task is to reveal a world in which "reality" lies in the process of change, not in forms which underlie illusions of

---

[18] Wordsworth, *Early Letters*, 392, 424, 495, 517, 561; *Middle Years*, I, 36.
[19] "Toward a Theory of Romanticism."

mutability. In the same way he reveals the processes of the internal world of mind and emotion, or spirit. The poet and the musician can show the process itself, but the painter must reveal the unique moment of change, both external and internal. Change depends upon imperfection, another positive Romantic value; hence lack of "finish" is desirable in a painting. Change and imperfection involve novelty; the artist can bring something new into the world, create something out of nothing. His instrument is the creative imagination, the source of which is in the unconscious mind. Both poet and artist, therefore, turn from the imitation of the real or ideal worlds in traditional genres to unique and original insights expressed in unique forms; here is the source of the all-important break with the subject. Form and matter become identified. The meaning of the work of art lies not in what is represented but in how the work is presented. As Pater put it, "It is the art of music which most completely realises this . . . perfect identification of matter and form." "In art's consummate moments the end is not distinct from the means, the form from the matter, the subject from the expression;—and to it therefore . . . all the arts may be supposed constantly to tend and aspire." The formal qualities of a work of art, more than the subject matter or even rather than the subject matter, have an emotional effect. Contemplation of a work is in itself a form of creation. The observer's imagination creates a moment of intense perception and self-revelation from the "unfinished" materials the artist has assembled for him. To quote Pater again, "Not the fruit of experience, but experience itself, is the end." To the Romantic poet and artist, the dignity of a work of art does not depend on the subject but on the way it is used in pure creative activity. A poem—and a painting—can be made about anything.[20]

Now all of this is in Wordsworth, though sometimes confused with and overlaid by eighteenth-century thinking. And the great places to find it are "Tintern Abbey" (1798), the Preface to the *Lyrical Ballads* (1800), and *The Prelude*, finished in 1805 and known to Beaumont by June, 1806, and through Beaumont available by report to Constable. The acceptance of change is the point

[20] See also my essay on modern art, "The Triumph of Romanticism," *The Magazine of Art*, XLV (1952), 291–99.

of *The Prelude*, which Wordsworth often referred to as the poem about the growth of a poet's mind. "Tintern Abbey" is concerned with the differences between Wordsworth's feelings at two different times in his life. *The Prelude* is built around "spots of time," moments of unique self-realization inspired by certain aspects of the visible world, specific places at specific times, under the influence of specific conditions of weather. He repeatedly emphasizes that the world itself is a living thing, and his connection with it he characterizes as standing "in Nature's presence a sensitive being, a creative soul," with a "power like one of Nature's," just as in "Tintern Abbey" he speaks "of all the mighty world of eye and ear,—both what they half create,/ And what perceive." Stylistically, the concept of imperfection appears in the alternation between a neutral style, neither prose nor poetry, and a heightened or poetic style. To Wordsworth the sources of creative activity are in the unconscious mind. Furthermore, Wordsworth threw off the tyranny of the genres when he treated pastoral subjects in an epic, or lofty and dignified, manner. Although he arrived at the idea by the way of eighteenth-century sentimental humanitarianism, the important thing about his choice of insignificant subjects, both in the human and in the natural worlds, is that style "will entirely separate the composition from the vulgarity and meanness of ordinary life"; this is a profoundly different concept of style from that of his predecessors, who searched for a style appropriate to the subject matter. And in fact, he regarded himself not as a poet of nature, but as a poet of psychology. Hence he was interested in the growth of the mind and in the nature of creation as a process. Hence "poetry takes its origin from emotion recollected in tranquillity; the emotion is contemplated till, by a species of re-action, the tranquillity gradually disappears, and an emotion, kindred to that which was before the subject of contemplation, is gradually produced, and does itself actually exist in the mind." The initial shock of illumination sinks into the conscious and unconscious mind, becomes an organic part of the artist's psycho-physical personality, gradually rises to the surface in a "spontaneous overflow of powerful feelings," and takes poetic form. Thus, instead of being imitation, poetry is creation, the emergence of novelty in the world, the creation of something out of nothing. The excellence of the work of art does not depend upon what is represented, but upon the style, which is an expression of the organic and intellectual superiority of the poet; hence the rejection of poetic diction, which is the expression of the distinction between form and matter. Poetic diction, like the genres, was externally applied to give charm to the idea. Wordsworth, however, emphasized rhythm, to which "the Poet and Reader both willingly submit"; aesthetic creation and aesthetic contemplation are different functions of the same power, imagination, the faculty which gives the experience of unity with the outer world, the experience of simultaneously creating and perceiving.

Again and again the Preface has profoundly stimulated the minds of young poets. Imagine what even an imperfect notion of the character and possibilities of these ideas might have meant to an artist who felt himself a dedicated spirit, but who had arrived at his thirtieth year without yet knowing how to go about fulfilling his mission. Constable spent most of 1804 and 1805 in Suffolk, but in 1806 he went to the Lakes and met Wordsworth, and thereafter he was often in London, in contact with Beaumont and his circle, including Farington, and in a position to hear about Wordsworth from Beaumont and discuss him with Beaumont and his friends. In 1807 he tells Farington that he thinks that he is on the track of "something original," and in 1808, in May, shortly after the first of his wonderful oil sketches, he expresses to Haydon his agitation over what he is trying to do, his sense of what is at stake both for himself and for the future of his art.

Now it is necessary to show how many of these ideas of Wordsworth's are expressed in Constable's painting, especially in the great sketches of the years following 1808 and occasionally in his later works, and also how they are expressed in his letters and recorded remarks. First of all, consider the acceptance of change. If an artist wishes to symbolize the idea that reality lies in change, both internal and external, and if he wishes to paint landscapes, he must focus on a unique aspect of landscape, a particular spot at a particular time, and on a moment of unique response, for he must paint in terms of the most transitory qualities he observes, light and weather. To quote Shirley again, Constable meant by chiaroscuro "that the world is comprehended by the eye in terms of light and shade, that in fact one never sees line but only coloured light and dark." Hence he uses the palette knife and blots of color. Again, these sketches are "typical of the later Constable either by the quality of their light or by the violence of the transitory effect presented." "In these sketches Constable shows for the first time complete mastery of his new method for expressing light in motion." Gradually he began to get this quality in his paintings. Shirley points out that in 1811–13 his pictures began to have an air of impending change in the sky.[21]

Yet his problem was not fully solved. Badt's first point is that the landscape and sky were not yet perfectly organized into aesthetic unity. According to him, the release came with Constable's study of Luke Howard's *Climate of London*, published in London from 1818 to 1820, which included Howard's classification of clouds and their place in the levels of the atmosphere. From 1821 to 1822 Constable was absorbed in huge cloud studies, oil on paper, based on Howard's classifications. The studies enabled him to bring together the appearance of the landscape with the appearance of the sky and get the quality of unity he had so far missed. Badt feels that only after these paintings did Constable realize his ambition to catch the particular moment. And indeed, such was his ambition. "Yet, in reality, what are the most sublime productions of the pencil but selections of some of the forms of nature, and copies of a few of her evanescent effects."[22]

[21] Leslie, lxv, 47.

[22] See Leslie, Chapter XVIII, Lecture V, June 16, 1836, next-to-last paragraph. He also said, "Painting is a science, and should be pursued as an inquiry into the laws of nature. Why, then, may not landscape painting be considered as a branch of natural philosophy, of which pictures are but the experiments." The contrast between this remark and such statements as that quoted below on the comparison of his own work to Coleridge's "Ancient Mariner" is striking. Any attempt to discuss this inconsistency would take me far beyond the limits of my subject. However, it may be said (1) that the notions which I have called "Romantic" are also to be found in nineteenth and twentieth-century science and philosophy; and (2) the attempt to justify art, especially to the Philistine, by putting it on a level with science, was common in the nineteenth century and is far too common today. Those who try to make science and art rivals do not know what either is. Constable's intellectual background of Natural Theology (see Leslie, 10) is one of the most common sources of the confusion of art and science in nineteenth-century England. It got Ruskin into even more trouble than Constable.

Now according to Wordsworth, the sensitive soul before nature also created in a state of aroused emotion. And this is also apparent in Constable's work, especially in the sketches.
Shirley notes the "violence of the transitory effect presented,"
and Badt's second main point is that the Constable sketch bears
exactly the same relation to the final picture as Wordsworth's
original emotion does to the spontaneous overflow of powerful
emotions which find themselves expression in poetic language. I
think Badt is quite correct, and I shall say nothing more about it,
except to emphasize the creative activity of the artist.

In 1824 Constable wrote: "It is the business of a painter not
to contend with nature, and put such a scene, a valley filled with
imagery fifty miles long, on a canvas of a few inches; but to make
something out of nothing, in attempting which, he must almost
of necessity become poetical."[23] From this important passage I
would first point out the phrase, "make something out of nothing." Here is the concept of radical creative activity, alike in both
poetry and painting. The neoclassic idea was that the resemblance
of painting and poetry lay in the subject, but Constable finds the
relation in the making of something out of nothing, that is in the
making, or style. "Chiaroscuro," he once said in later years,
"colour, and composition, are all poetic qualities."[24] Later in 1824,
the year his paintings appeared at the Salon in Paris, he wrote:
"My wife is translating for me some of the French criticisms.
They are very amusing and acute, but very shallow and feeble.
This one—after saying 'it is but justice to admire the *truth*, the
color, and *general vivacity* and richness.'—Yet they want the
objects more formed and defined—etc., etc., and say that they are
like the rich preludes in musick, and the full harmonies of the
Eolian Lyre—which *mean* no thing and they call them orations,
and harangues, and highflown conversations affecting a careless
ease—etc., etc., etc., . . . Is not some of this *blame* the highest
praise? What is poetry? What is Coleridge's *Ancient Mariner*—
(the best Modern poem) but something like this."[25]

[23] Leslie, 173. This letter, dated Aug. 29, 1824, was written three days
after he met Robinson and talked about Wordsworth.
[24] Lecture III, June 9, 1836, last paragraph. Leslie, Chap. XVIII.
[25] Leslie, 180. Note the interesting anticipation of Pater.

This leads us to subject matter. The typical eighteenth-century attitude was expressed by J. T. Smith, one of Constable's early mentors, in his introduction to a series of etchings of cottages published in 1797. "I am content," he says, "that rural and cottage-scenery shall be considered as no more than a *low-comedy* landscape."[26] Badt points out the Wordsworthian nature of Constable's devotion to humble landscape.[27] "The ordinary things," wrote Wordsworth in his Preface, "should be presented to the mind in an unusual aspect." But Badt does not realize the full significance of this in Constable's work. True enough, subjects can be found everywhere, "under every hedge," as Constable put it once, but the important thing was the break from the tyranny of the subject. Sentimental humanitarianism could lead to humble subjects, and did, but in Constable the dignity of the painting did not lie in the subject. Two passages are important here. The first again comes from 1824, in November. "I have to combat from high quarters even from Lawrence, the plausible argument that *subject* makes the picture."[28] The second comes from a letter of March 12, 1831. "The painter [meaning himself] is totally unpopular, and ever will be on this side the grave; *the subjects nothing but the art*, and the buyers wholly ignorant of that."[29] This is to Lucas, the engraver for the book of plates from Constable's paintings, a project which brought him immense trouble and little profit.

We come finally to the concept of the positive value of imperfection, which lies at the very heart of Romanticism. Badt and others have pointed out that Constable's sketches, even more than his paintings, lack the traditional qualities of composition, yet somehow hang together. I have mentioned the importance of rhythm to Wordsworth. It seems to me that these early sketches are given their special excitement by exactly that quality. The large rough brush strokes, dashed on in heat of inspiration, or moment of imaginative shock, the patches of paint smeared on with a palette knife, directly express the psycho-

[26] Shirley's addition to Leslie, 7.
[27] Badt, Chapter IX.
[28] Leslie, 175.
[29] Leslie, 260. Cf. Farington's complaint to Constable that his paintings were "unfinished." (July 23, 1814, VI, 152).

physical relation of the painter's organism to the work in hand. One can feel the movement of the painter's hand and arm; the swing of his body is recorded in the application of the paint; the observer reconstructs the moment of creative inspiration. Again, especially in the cloud studies, the unity, the felt organization, comes from the rhythmic repetition of elements presented spatially with just enough regularity to be noticeable. The technique of these sketches, then, necessarily leads to lack of finish, or to imperfection.

That imperfection *is* a positive value, indicating capacity for growth, symbolizing the world, inner and outer, caught in the moment of mutation, is one of the central ideas of Romanticism. Farington and others were always telling Constable that he lacked "finish," by which they meant that if you look at his paintings close up you find that they lack the representational quality. Yet Constable persisted in his ways, and his loose, roughly impressionistic technique gradually became more and more conspicuous in his Academy paintings, especially, according to Shirley, after 1829.[30] Such a technique, regularized by the French Impressionists, has its well-known representational advantages, but I should like to emphasize its expressive quality, that is, its symbolization of a growing inner and outer world by, according to traditional standards, its very incompleteness. But even more, it brings the observer into the aesthetic situation. From blobs and spots and loose strokes of paint assembled from his point of view by the artist, the observer creates a painting. He is not a passive observer; he half creates and half perceives. He also experiences the workings of the creative imagination, the experience of unity with the outer world. It is not surprising that Pater was able to adapt Wordsworth's ideas about nature to the world of painting.

I am convinced, then, that Constable had the opportunity through Sir George Beaumont to become acquainted with the ideas of Wordsworth, as expressed in conversation, in letters, in published prose, and in poetry, published and unpublished, and that he did actually become acquainted with them, that he was profoundly affected by them, and that the sudden redirection of his art worked out in the sketches beginning in 1808 was the

[30] Leslie, lxxiii.

result of that impact upon his mind and sensibility. If all this is true, and if Constable is one of the major sources of modern art, through the several dozen pictures and sketches in Paris beginning in 1824,[31] and through the study of Constable made by Monet and Pissarro on their visit to London, we are presented with a fascinating possibility.

For those terms in which I have described the similarities of Wordsworth and Constable can be just as successfully applied to the Impressionists. The first category, the acceptance of change, is even more strikingly worked out in the work of the Impressionists than in Constable's. Monet's famous haystacks, painted under an immense range of light and weather conditions are perhaps the most perfect example, while the Impressionists' technique is, of course, even more "unfinished" than that of Constable. The principal difference is, of course, that the Impressionists methodized their technique by the study of color, but the impulse behind that effort is the same as Constable's, the determination to catch the changing aspect of the world.[32] Further, the ultimate success of Constable in getting unity of sky and landscape was carried further and fully consummated by the Impressionists' technique. Light, the most evanescent quality of observable nature, becomes the means of organizing the whole painting into an aesthetic structure. Each painting catches, literally, one of Wordsworth's "moments of illumination."

This principle of seizing the moment can even be extended to their treatment of space. They paint, as it were, a spatial moment. The observer is aware that the landscape or the interior extends beyond the frame of the picture; there is no particular reason why

[31] In his edition of Leslie, Shirley included a large amount of new material about Constable's pictures in France and about his art dealers there. See especially p. 205 for the number of Constable's pictures on exhibition or in collections in and near Paris from 1824 to 1838.

[32] Another obvious relation between the two is the attempt of both Constable and the Impressionists to base their work on scientific observation. (See Note 22, above.) I do not, however, think this is particularly important. For one thing, presumably the Impressionists did not know about Constable's scientific interests, and for another, the attempt to have the arts rival the sciences by placing them on a "scientific" basis was so common in the nineteenth century, in all schools of art and criticism, that it would probably be impossible to find a source.

it should stop where it does. There is something deliberately arbitrary about the selection of both the spatial and the temporal limitations of the picture. That the will, or creative power, of the painter is arbitrarily imposed upon the landscape is forced to our attention. Thus our attention is directed to the painter rather than to the objects. Consequently, he is pretty indifferent to what he paints.

Although the sociological and moral critic can find something extremely significant in the fact that the Impressionists painted "vacation scenes" or scenes, as Degas and Renoir did, of bourgeois amusement—pretty flowers, the "Townsman's landscape," boating trips, picnics, race meetings, the ballet—from the point of view of the aesthetic critic, the important thing is that the Impressionists constantly indicate their lordly indifference to the subject, their deliberate refusal to get an emotional response by choosing subjects which have a sentimental lure. The radical creativeness of the artist is the important thing. He paints a picture; he doesn't make a representation of an object. Perhaps this radical break with the subject matter is the most important thing which Constable contributed to the French tradition.

Finally, to these categories of growth, of change, of the moment of illumination, of radical creativity, may be added "imperfection." Even more than in Constable, the technique of the Impressionists forces the observer to experience the moment of internal illumination, of union of the inner and outer worlds, forces him to create the painting. So that the value of painting becomes the opportunity it offers painter and observer to experience the creative act. "Not the fruit of experience, but experience itself, is the end," said Pater in the 1860's, in the decade when the Impressionists were beginning to formulate their theory. "The moment of illumination," objective and subjective, allies Wordsworth, Constable, and the Impressionists—"the moment of illumination" with all its associated and supporting ideas of change, organicism, imperfection, growth, radical creativity.

A fascinating vista—Wordsworth to the Impressionists—but when we think of how the work of the latter has led to the astonishing achievements of painting in this century, the possibility that Constable's accomplishments can be traced to Wordsworth's ideas and poetry becomes immensely important. To me the line from Wordsworth to the moderns through Constable and the Impressionists is irresistible. It will not be to everyone, of course, but at the very least it is a possibility that requires examination and consideration. If art historians think I have asked a serious question about the sources and continuity of the art of the past century and a half, I shall be satisfied.

7

THE PLACE OF

ARCHITECTURE IN NINETEENTH-CENTURY

ROMANTIC CULTURE

[1966*]

The architecture of the nineteenth century presents two different but equally vexing problems. The first is the question of its value as art. Through almost the entire twentieth century, advanced taste has uniformly rejected it. The second problem is to account for its peculiar character, the fact that architects seem to have been incapable of designing in anything but revivalistic styles, or of originating a style of their own; and their efforts are usually seen, in the rare instances in which any sympathy at all is manifested, as efforts to create a modern style. On the other hand, the proponents of the now triumphant "modern" style, or styles, have found the sources of that style in the "functional" building of engineers. That the two problems are associated is becoming clear in the currently growing awareness that it is possible to look at nineteenth-century architecture with something

* Reprinted by permission from *Yearbook of Comparative and General Literature*, No. 15, 1956, pp. 36–49. Copyright 1966 by the Comparative Literature Committee, Indiana University, Bloomington, Ind.

other than a feeling of revulsion, that the use of historical modes does not necessarily damn a building, and in the concurrent realization that modern architecture has not been so functional as has been thought. Certainly, we begin to realize that many of the functional ideas of modern architecture can be found in Victorian buildings; and a few skeptics even begin to suspect that modern functionalism is one of the least functional manners of building ever devised by the human mind.

Above all, the change in value attitudes toward even the most horrendous examples of the architecture of the last century is a phenomenon of the 1960's, and during the same period certain contemporary architects have begun to build in a modality which, if one ignores the historical sources of the decorative forms of mid-nineteenth-century buildings, looks, in its deep plasticity and its increasing elaboration of wall surface and profile, remarkably like the High Victorian buildings, such as the Philadelphia City Hall, or the old State, War, and Navy building in Washington, which have traditionally been the most rejected of their period. For example, the recent work of Paul Rudolph at Yale and especially of John M. Johansen, if one forgets about the superficialities of historicism and dismisses symmetry, displays the most extraordinary similarities to this violent nineteenth-century style known as Napoleon III, or, in this country, as General Grant.

Again, the cornice has been studiously avoided in modern architecture, but about five years ago it suddenly made a massive reappearance, usually in the form of two or three stories successively cantilevered outward over bearing walls and columns. Even the elegant Mies van der Rohe has been designing what in the past would have been called a cornice. Indeed, he may have started the whole fashion. The effect, however, is again one of deep plasticity as opposed to the smooth and unarticulated walls, whether of concrete, stone, glass, or any combination of these three, which have reigned for decades. Le Corbusier, of course, really started the whole new trend in the postwar years.

At any rate, this new development in contemporary architecture has created a cultural climate in which nineteenth-century buildings can be looked at without derision or, what is worse, as occasions for displaying High Camp tastes. Since it is now possible to see these older buildings as successful in their own terms, we are in a position to inquire what those terms were, and what were the cultural forces in response to which the architects of the nineteenth century made the artistic decisions they did. It is, one must admit, peculiarly difficult to understand the history and character of any artistic style to which it is impossible to ascribe artistic value. The long eclipse of the Baroque, which many people still detest, is a case in point. In what follows I shall make use of the theoretical construct of nineteenth-century Romantic culture offered in my *Beyond the Tragic Vision* (New York, 1962) and of the explanation of artistic behavior and the methods of artistic analysis offered in *Man's Rage for Chaos: Biology, Behavior, and the Arts* (Philadelphia, 1965). For illustrative material I shall for the most part refer to the plates in Henry-Russell Hitchcock's *Architecture: Nineteenth and Twentieth Centuries* (The Pelican History of Art, Z15, Baltimore, 1958), partly because it is a recent work, and partly because it is the first account of nineteenth-century architecture as a whole which has any real value. (This work incorporates the very valuable findings in Hitchcock's *Early Victorian in Britain*, New Haven, 1954). I shall attempt to define the problem of Romantic architecture and to account for its functionalism and historicism.

I

To begin with, it is necessary to have a somewhat clearer concept of the term "style" than is usually found in architectural criticism and history. We may speak, for example, of Baroque architectural style in two quite distinct senses. One sense refers to a theoretical construct of the history of European style from, let us say, about 1600 to about 1730. Although it continued to be built after that, the emergent style was Rococo. Thus it is usually said that Baroque style ended with the emergence of Rococo; but this statement, of course, is not true. In ordinary usage, then, the "style" of a period refers to the style dominant during a certain time span at the highest and most modern cultural level. The other sense refers to a particular style of ornament, of planning, of decor, of manipulating and articulating the surfaces and profiles of a building. That these are two quite different and often

confused semantic functions appears in arguments about whether
Versailles, for example, or Blenheim Palace is Baroque. From
the point of view of "style" as an historical construct, it is usually
claimed that they are; but if mid-seventeenth-century Italian
church architecture is taken as the paradigm of Baroque style in
the second sense of the word, it can and for decades has been
argued that these two buildings are not Baroque. The point comes
out more clearly if we ask, for example, "How many styles did
medieval Gothic style have?" Or if we assert that nineteenth-
century architectural "style" is distinguished by its use of the
historical "styles." Clearly, in this proposition the word has two
sharply different semantic functions. Indeed, the problem of
nineteenth-century architecture clarifies these functions in a
striking and unique way. Versailles and Blenheim Palace are close
enough to some Italian mid-seventeenth-century paradigm or
norm to be genuinely puzzling. The most obvious reason is that
the source of the means for manipulating and articulating the
building surfaces and profiles was in all three instances Renaissance Classicism. The grammar of their ornament, to use an old-
fashioned phrase, was ultimately Vitruvian. The manipulatory
decisions of all architects, with a few and trifling exceptions of
Gothic survival and revival, were determined by their obedience
to the current pre-eminent cultural valuation of the Classical tradition. All differed from Gothic architects in that choice was possible but was ignored in the overwhelming majority of instances.
In the nineteenth century, however, there was evidently no such
cultural demand to which architects could and would respond.
The decision did involve choice; and consequently there was an
enormous amount of public and private argument about what
choice should be made. The style of architectural decision in the
nineteenth century was characterized by the necessity to make a
choice about which of the available styles for manipulating and
articulating was to be used for a particular building or for all
buildings. Hence the enormous amount of propaganda in favor
of one style or another. To distinguish between these two semantic functions, I shall use "style" to refer to the theoretical construct which relates buildings within an historical epoch by tracing the decisions of the architect to the demands and values of his

culture, and "modality" to refer to the various devices, historically determined, selected, or entirely emergent or original, which he employs to manipulate and articulate the surfaces and profiles of his buildings.

Since this use of "modality" implies a distinction between "architecture" and "building" which is not widely accepted at the present time, it seems wise to offer some justification for it. To put the distinction in a purposely trivial way, I would say that architecture is building covered inside and out, or inside or out, with a lot of attractive decoration. This is Ruskin's position. I would distinguish, then, between two semiotic aspects of a building. Both aspects are matters of cultural convention, in that they have to be learned. The one aspect informs the perceiver what the building is for, how it is to be used, whether as a church or as a chicken coop. On the other hand, the building also informs the perceiver what attitudes, whether intellectual, valuational, or emotional, he should take toward the behavior for which the building is designed to serve as setting or stage. This second kind of sign may also be divided into two classes, configurational and primary. By "configurational" I refer to such signs as trophies, animal and vegetable carvings, and so forth; in short, the kind of signs found in representational (or iconic) sculpture and painting. By "primary" signs I refer to such architectural features as verticality, solidity, horizontality, hollowness, light, rectangularity, shadow, closed solids, open pavilions, the continuum from deep to shallow plasticity, axiality, whether deep or shallow, the sequences of screens (or walls), panels, and profiles, the subdivisions within screens, panels, and profiles, and openings through screens.

I shall not attempt to justify my position that such architectural features are signs. It derives from a philosophical and psychological position that we live in an interpreted world, that a recognized perceptual configuration is a sign, that all signs, including verbal signs, are categorial, and that the ultimate function of such signs is behavioral control. Rather, I shall simply quote from my recent book. "Our lives are bathed in a continuous flow of signs which we interpret to catch the world in an ever-shifting network of categories. The condition of human life is continuous categorial metamorphosis. We are forever engaged in constructing around us an architecture of categories as fluid and yielding to our interests as the air" (*Man's Rage for Chaos*, pp. 92–93).

A much more philosophically adequate and in every way superior defense of virtually the same position is to be found in Colin Murray Turbayne's *The Myth of Metaphor* (New Haven, 1962). To Turbayne, building on Berkeley's theory of vision, "language is the model for vision," and indeed all sensory perception.

The psychological basis for the special category of signs I call "primary" or "nonsituational" is the following. Any stimulus is responded to in two ways. The one is the interpretative response, the response of the "mind," to use a most unsatisfactory term which refers, to my way of thinking, to the phenomenon of interpretational variability. The stimulus, then, elicits a semiotic response. But at the same time there is a response of quite a different sort, a physiological response, of which butterflies-in-the-stomach is a very obvious example. It is evident that this physiological response is a consequence of the interpretative activity, but the important thing here is that this physiological response is also interpreted. Two considerations are of vital importance at this point. The first is that our statements about what happens inside the skin have no greater authority than do our statements about what happens outside of it. The second is that the interpretation of the physiological response—now itself, of course, a stimulus—can be, and usually is, perceived as part of the total perceptual situation, and so interpreted. Thus perceived, it is often referred to as the "emotional coloring" of a situation. But interpretation can also separate it from the situation, just as the external stimulus can be separated from the internal stimulus. This is possible first because perception is selective and because such selectivity can be controlled; and second, because any perceptual configuration which serves as a sign can itself be referred to by a sign, either natural or artificial. Thus, to take an extreme instance, a scientist may interpret an experimental situation as being full of anxiety but still may manipulate the signs in that situation as well as the signs of those signs without including in his manipulations his interpretations of the internal signs, although these are, as we have seen, also part of the total or global situation. Further—

and this is a factor most confusing in human affairs—there is no necessary link, in the sense of a fully conventionalized one, between the external signs and the internal signs. That is, to put it more precisely, the internal signs and the external signs vary independently, although the individual may have conventionalized such links idiosyncratically. Finally, just as the external signs can be perceived and signified without reference to the internal signs, so these latter can be perceived and signified without reference to the external signs. Signs of internal signs, perceived without reference to the external situation, I call nonsituational or primary signs. Professor Irvin L. Child of Yale University calls them "exemplary" signs in an essay, "Aesthetics," currently being prepared for the revised edition of *The Handbook of Social Psychology*, ed. G. Lindzey and E. Aronson. He does not find my terms fully satisfactory, nor, I must admit, do I; but for various reasons I am not prepared to adopt his terms, principally because in my theory of artistic behavior I wish to use "exemplary" for another semantic function. My original notion in calling them primary signs was that they take precedence over situational signs and the signs of those signs in cases of semantic ambiguity. But of this I am no longer convinced.

Such signs are to be found both in and out of nature: a mountain and a pyramid, a tall tree and a steeple, natural darkness and artificial architectural darkness, and so on. They are, then, both natural and artificial; and to my mind music, insofar as it is not emblematic, that is, situationally defined, as a hunting call, consists of such signs. After music they have, in Western culture, been traditionally more important, or at least more conspicuous, in architecture than in any other art. That they are also extremely important in painting has been made evident by the emergence in this century of nonobjective painting. Such a theory accounts for statements that architecture is frozen music and that nonobjective painting is visual music, as Wyndham Lewis has put it. There is no settled terminology for such signs, even in psychology. People who attempt to talk about them generally improvise terminology. In *Man's Rage for Chaos*, I have proposed a terminology, but more as an example of what a conventionalized terminology might look like than as a claim that this is what they "really mean," if one uses the arbitrary signs of verbal behavior. In any case, for what follows, it is unnecessary to use any such terminology. One need only accept the proposition that internal responses are interpreted as signs and that in architecture, external signs of such internal signs are the architectural features (verticality, horizontality, etc.) listed above.

From this point of view it is possible to understand the purpose or function of architectural style in the second sense of architectural modality. The Gothic, or Classic, or Arabian, or Chinese modalities are fundamentally no more than means to present and manipulate signs of internal signs. All architectural modalities are capable of presenting and manipulating all such signs. The cultural variations which we refer to by such terms as Gothic, Classic, etc., are ultimately arbitrary, settled upon over a long course of time in response to a thousand cultural demands, and, like all patterned behavior, assuming the pattern they have solely to eliminate the necessity for choosing and to create a more predictable world, as in the choice of food and the order or pattern in which it is presented at a meal, or, very probably, in the choice of one kinship system rather than another. Thus, in the shift from Gothic modalities to Renaissance-Classic modalities, it is possible to find extra-architectural and cultural reasons for the shift; but the new modality having been established, it was continued for no other reason than the fact that it had been established by the cultural levels responsible for deciding what modality should be used.

II

By the end of the eighteenth century, however, the situation had changed. Modalities other than the Vitruvian had become available and were in use. There had been a revival of Gothic modalities; archaeologically determined rather than traditionally determined Classic modalities had appeared, and there were mild outbreaks of various Oriental and even Egyptian modalities, notably in theater scenery. However, two important points must be made. First, the modality was linked to the situation. The "historical style" or modality became, in one sense of the word, a "symbol." I prefer for this semantic function the term "emblem."

Picturesque situations called for the Gothic modality and occasionally the Oriental, but sublime and beautiful situations, courtly and ecclesiastical or other social power situations, still required a Vitruvian modality occasionally slightly modified by archaeology. In situations in which the behavior was primarily private or immediately interpersonal, Gothic modalities were acceptable; but public situations still called for Classic modality, for the most part Vitruvian. Even archaeologically inspired Classicism was for the most part confined to private situations. What frequently passes for archaeological Classicism was actually motivated by a quite different cultural force, though it played an important part in the separation of the categories of sublime, beautiful, and picturesque, not merely in architecture but in landscaping, painting, and, of course, literature.

That cultural force was the Enlightenment ideal of perfect adaptation of organism to environment, which found its expression in an ideal of psychological and physical comfort. It is no accident that Enlightenment domestic architecture and furniture are still the model for comfortable domestic life. An increasing simplification of formal configuration is characteristic of all the arts from 1725 or thereabouts to the end of the century. The Thomsonian style of *The Seasons* is one very early important manifestation of it and the beginning of the French Rococo in the second decade of the century is another. The various formal decisions of the artist were in response to the demand for greater immediacy and adaptation of the perceiver to the work. The particular attributes of the categories of the sublime and the beautiful were well worked out and even in part established by Burke. There remained the Picturesque, which was developed later. What this last category provided was the possibility for "irregularity," which neither of the other two took care of, for both moved steadily in the direction of the regular, that is, of perceptual fields which could be grasped with the minimum of ambiguity and hesitation. In both of these categories, particularly in that of the sublime, architecture in fact, at the end of the century, moved toward an abandonment of all traditional modalities, and in the work of Bouleé, Ledoux, and, in England, Soane resulted in the presentation of pure solid geometry, with no surface manipulation. The possibilities for primary signification, were, therefore, sharply reduced. Architecture could be increasingly sublime or beautiful, but it could signify less and less.

As this tendency became dominant, the Picturesque became more important, for only the Picturesque could still manipulate the primary signs at will, subject only to very loose rules. For this the Gothic was ideal, for nobody knew very much about the rules of Gothic or the distinctions between the various Gothic modalities, and it made no difference how one manhandled the Oriental styles. There was no one to care. Further, the Picturesque modalities, confined as they were to intimate social situations, were peculiarly fitted for such situations, for in intimacy the internal signs can be given an importance and attention impossible in public situations. Hence, the Picturesque was strongly associated with sentimentality; indeed, it was the architectural and landscape and pictorial name for sentimentality. The explanation is that eighteenth-century sentimentality was devoted to the psychological comfort of openly displaying and turning one's attention to the internal signs and their interpretation and external signification. The sentimental situation, like the Picturesque situation, was selected for the opportunity it gave for adapting the organism to the environment by openly exhibiting, manipulating, and caressing internal responses interpreted as signs and signified by external primary signs. The sentimentalist and the hunter of the Picturesque alike devoted themselves to seeking out such situational opportunities.

III

The new Romantic architect now found himself confronting a difficult and perplexing cultural problem. In this, of course, he was no different from the Romantic painter, or poet, or composer, or philosopher; but his problem had special dimensions. The explanation of the basic Romantic problem can be put in several ways. The essence was the breakdown of the Enlightenment metaphysic, either through its own internal contradictions or through what some perceived as the proof of the invalidity and inviability of Enlightenment value in the failure of the French Revolution. The efforts of various individuals to meet this problem can be put variously. Metaphysically, it was the decision not to create a new metaphysic without first understanding the nature of metaphysical activity, without looking at oneself from right angles. The metaphysical solution lay in founding a new metaphysic by placing the subject and object in irresolvable tension, so that neither could be conceived as existing without the other, but also that neither could be collapsed into the other, in the sense that the one could exhaustively explain the attributes of the other. The transcendence of phenomena became, therefore, an indivisible aspect of the encounter with phenomena. Emotionally, Romanticism was the decision to seek the sense of value in the psychological fact that men can and must create a sense of value. Socially, it was the internal division of the personality by distinguishing and separating the self from the role, so that the individual could have freedom in manipulating roles. Personally, it was the acceptance of social and metaphysical alienation, which was the consequence of the collapse of the Enlightenment into what for some years I have called Negative Romanticism. Epistemologically, perception and cognition were seen as under the control of the will; or in modern terms, perception began to be understood as instrumental, determined by interests, culture, and language. As Coleridge put it, everything was seen to begin with and depend upon the problem of perception. However the architect put it to himself—and this list is by no means exhaustive—he was faced with the problem of how to govern his architectural decisions by these novel and, on the whole and even by the most penetrating, ill-understood cultural demands.

All of these ways of conceiving the problem can be summed up in the notion that the human organism can never perfectly adapt itself to its environment, that there always will be an adaptational gap between his interest and the potentialities of his environment for satisfying those interests, and that this gap is at once the peculiar horror of the human condition and man's enormous opportunity. This was, in a sense, a naturalistic mode of conceiving or explaining the notion of original sin. This meant that the task of the artist was to create a perceptual field which would be problematic, rather than one easily adapted to, ambiguous rather than clear, and disorienting or even confused. Such an interest was, of course, exactly the reverse of the direction in which the most advanced Enlightenment architecture had been tending. An excellent example can be seen in the house Sir John Soane created for himself (1812); it is full of problematic spaces, light sources, mirrors, and volumetric interpenetrations. (See Plate 174 in John Summerson, *Architecture in Britain: 1530–1830*, The Pelican History of Art, Z3, Baltimore, 1954.) Particularly, a good many Baroque devices were revived, for Baroque was the most recent architectural period in which the problematic had been a dominant architectural concern, even though for quite different reasons. Now obviously the one architectural category which had retained a considerable degree of the problematic, the "irregular," was the Picturesque mode, which was closely, though not entirely, identified with the Gothic. It is not surprising, therefore, that the Gothic modality should have been picked up and developed from the Picturesque tradition. Indeed, so obvious was this development that for a long time Gothic modality was identified with Romantic architecture. But such an attitude is no longer tenable, thanks in particular to Henry-Russell Hitchcock, who has clearly demonstrated the correctness of such terminology as Romantic Classicism (*Architecture: Nineteenth and Twentieth Centuries*, Chapters 1–5). Indeed, he has demonstrated unequivocally that the Romantic architects used the Classic modality far more than they did the Gothic. In the early part of his life, when he had few commissions, Schinkel, for example, designed marvelous Gothic fantasies for cathedrals and tombs, but when he began to get commissions, for the most part he employed the Classic modality. The fact is that, in spite of the availability of Gothic and Oriental modalities, the authority of the Classic was still very great. But that fact is by no means confined to architecture. Literature and painting, as in Ingres, saw an intense revival of both ancient and Renaissance Classicism. (It is instructive, also, to remember that at one time literary Romanticism was identified with Gothicism and Medievalism.) Further, as far as the presentation of problematic perceptual fields is concerned, Baroque architects had clearly demonstrated that such fields can be presented in the Classic modality at least as well as in the Gothic. Indeed, any architectural modality can be manipulated equally well for this purpose.

As with primary signs, no modality has an edge over another. From this point of view, it is the increasingly frequent use of Gothic modalities that needs to be explained, not the revivification of Classic ones. After all, Sir John Soane, who more than any other English architect had participated in the reductionism of the Enlightenment, was one of the first and most imaginative to turn back to Classic modalities when it became obvious to him that the problematic, not the simplistic, was the new proper aim of the architect. He did not turn to the Gothic.

But there was still another reason for picking up the Gothic modality from the Picturesque tradition, which, to be sure, continued in a minor way for some time, just as did late Enlightenment Simplistic Classicism, particularly in France, in what Hitchcock calls the "Doctrine of J.-N.-L. Durand." It is, after all, always to be remembered that quantitatively the most important cultural event in nineteenth-century Europe was the spread of Enlightenment values; only a very small minority of highly cultured individuals as yet found them invalid, and they were penetrating steadily into the lower cultural levels. That other reason lay in the fact that the Picturesque had continued the tradition of using architecture for the presentation of primary signs much more powerfully than had the other categories. It is for this reason that Hitchcock makes what I believe to be an error in his belief that Romantic architecture, in one strand, particularly the Gothic, continued the Picturesque tradition (*Architecture: Nineteenth and Twentieth Centuries*, Chapter 6). Actually, both Romantic Classicism, as opposed to the Durand tradition—and even that was touched by it—and Romantic Gothicism are marked by a heavy increase in the manipulation of the surfaces, the screens, and the outlines of profiles. It becomes more deeply plastic, though mildly so compared with what was to happen in the 1850's. The Romantic, in his concern to distinguish self from role, is necessarily interested in those responses and signs which he can most easily identify with himself, internal signs and their external signification in primary signs. This can be seen easily in comparing Wordsworth's mature style with Goldsmith's, Cowper's, and even Blake's. Syntactically, for example, it is considerably more problematic, and the shifts from one rhetorical mode to another are continuous and striking. It is obviously quite a different matter from the sentimental-Picturesque category of *The Task*; while Blake's prophetic books are, in these terms, distressingly and boringly close to Ossian. Blake's proper names and his subject matter (but not his syntax) are problematic and, of course, esoteric; nor does he show much variety in the syntactical phonic and semantic overdeterminations of his rhetoric. Coleridge, in "The Rime of the Ancient Mariner" and "Kubla Khan," invented a whole new rhetorical mode both to indicate the control of perception by will and to increase the incidence of primary signs. (These signs are often referred to as his "music.")

But it was not merely the increase in the incidence of primary signs that marked the Romantic architect and enables us to distinguish him from his Picturesque predecessor. More important is the kind of situation in which he employed that incidence, especially when he employed the Gothic modalities or that late sixteenth- and early seventeenth-century modality known as the Jacobethan, in which a Mannerist modality was strangely mixed with Gothic survivals. It was, by all European standards of the eighteenth and nineteenth centuries, an aberrant Classicism, if a Classicism at all. The Picturesque architect was interested in the intimate situation, but the Romantic architect used the Gothic modality for public purposes. He designed churches, and wanted to design cathedrals. Increasingly, as the century wore on, he was able to persuade his clients to use the Gothic modality, and even, in the 1830's and 1840's, Egyptian and Oriental modalities. From this point of view, the Picturesque tradition was so profoundly transformed that it is, I believe, an error to think that Picturesque values determined the decisions of Romantic architects. The transformation of the Picturesque was, further, exactly parallel to the transformation of Enlightenment Classicism. And the same impulse can be found in Wordsworth and Goethe, among many others, both of whom took vast public and social literary forms, the epic and the tragedy, and used them to display the problems of the Romantic self and its struggle to separate itself from the role. Enlightenment types, of course, thought there was a certain madness in such a public display.

Still another impulse marked the use of both of these modalities and separated the Romantic Gothic from the Enlightenment Picturesque—the use of archaeologically justified details in both modalities, and eventually in the other modalities as well. I have suggested that to the Romantic the transcendence of phenomena became an indivisible aspect of the encounter with phenomena. In literature this problem was solved by simultaneously presenting a deep concern with the self and its unique attributes together with an enormous increase in verifiable factuality. In this sense, as I have indicated (see my *Beyond the Tragic Vision*), Romanticism and Realism are not antithetical but complementary, or rather, Realism is one mode of Romanticism. One must, for example, enter fully into the orientation of this stage of Romanticism to enjoy and respond properly to Wordsworth's intense concern with exact statement of fact, a concern so tedious to those capable of responding only to the transcendental and visionary aspect of Romanticism. Ingres shows the same drive toward iconicity, the equivalent in configurational signs of predictability in verbal, or arbitrary, signs. In his painting of Thetis pleading with Zeus, the fold of flesh down and partly over Zeus's navel is the kind of highly iconic detail inconceivable in earlier painting of the nude, not to speak of the extraordinarily awkward position of Thetis, a genuine novelty in the repertoire of European figure-painting, and the disturbing way her breast is squeezed upward against Zeus' body. At the same time, the transcendent, the self, is apparent in the rigid frontality and symmetry, as in so many paintings of Caspar David Friedrich, and the almost hallucinatory precision of both men serves the same purpose. One is, as with Wordsworth, utterly, almost distressingly, aware of the intermediation of the artist between perceiver and scene. Further, this drive towards the phenomenal is another way of solving the self-role problem; the role determines both artistic presentation and perceptual interpretation in the arts before the nineteenth century. To present what the role had ignored was, then, to violate and undermine the role. The architect had no such recourse, but he did have one way of meeting the same problem: an enormous increase in archaeological accuracy, which was a way of asserting that Vitruvian Classicism was inauthentic. At the same time it gave him a knowledge which was unique to himself. Each architect could distinguish himself from other Romantic architects as well as Vitruvian architects by his selection and command of archaeologically justified detail. Again, the later style of Soane is to the point; for he made absolutely novel investigations into Mannerist Classicism and hitherto neglected aspects of ancient Classicism.

Furthermore, the drive towards reality explains how functionalism is a part of Romantic architecture as well as of the surviving and spreading Enlightenment tradition. Here the determination of which is at work is a problem for the future. And the decision will often be difficult to make as to whether the architect and landscape designer were influenced by Enlightenment or Romantic values and problems. It seems to be one of those rare instances in which the two traditions reinforced each other, instead of being at opposite poles. The usual current explanation is that one kind of functionalism, that of the specifically architectural tradition, can be traced to the teachings of Durand and beyond him to Ledoux. Hitchcock here certainly makes a most convincing case. It seems also possible that the functionalism of engineering building can be traced back to eighteenth-century engineering and factory-building dictated by the effort to solve problems posed by Enlightenment values. However, certain points are not clear.

First is the fact that the way the engineers raised their sights may have been influenced by the deliberate Romantic search for the problematic. Second, attempts to trace the "functionalism"— a bad misnomer—of twentieth-century architecture back to the Enlightenment tradition of the engineers and of such architects as Bouleé and Ledoux seem to me quite unconvincing. Rather, I suspect that the modern kind of functionalism comes directly from the Romantic architectural tradition and particularly from Pugin, Butterfield, and Ruskin. Certainly, Pugin was not merely a Romantic architect in his passionate enthusiasm for the Gothic modality; he was a high transcendental architect in his conviction that the architect's task was to redeem society, a charming illusion that still enflames architects and city-planners today. At the same time, few architectural propagandists—and Pugin was one of the greatest—have so thoroughly based their thinking on justification of form by function. The error of connecting modern functionalism with the engineers' functionalism—if error it is—

lies in examining the superficial similarities of certain structures instead of studying closely the cultural situation and the tradition and surviving documents of those architects who first enunciated the doctrine of modern functionalism. A study, for example, of the house-planning of those architects who on other grounds obviously belong to the Romantic tradition of nineteenth-century architecture clearly shows a functionalism based on thinking through the life of the family and seeing aspects of family roles hitherto neglected. In reading critiques of nineteenth-century architecture by professional architectural historians and by professional architects, one often comes across admiring testimony to the brilliant planning of nineteenth-century architects, particularly in domestic architecture, and especially in those great houses in which wealth made possible the most extreme and elaborate responses to Romantic cultural demands. The famous twentieth-century dictum that "form should follow function" is hardly more than an explicit enunciation of the tradition which developed in domestic architecture and reached a climax of freedom in the planning of Frank Lloyd Wright.

Again, the first volume of Ruskin's *Stones of Venice* is very possibly the most brilliant and sustained functionalistic justification ever written of almost every detail of a structural system. Finally, it is, I think, an error to imply, as Hitchcock does, that the irregularity of mass that results from Romantic functionalism is a consequence of the Picturesque tradition. At most that irregularity was picked up from Picturesque, but it was transformed by being functionally and realistically adjusted to actual environmental situations, while most of the Picturesque architecture of the eighteenth century belongs to the folly tradition, and in that tradition alone does it, to my mind, survive well into the nineteenth century. It is worth noting that engineers' architecture retains the regular disposition and strict symmetry—as in the Crystal Palace and in the early railroad stations and sheds—so characteristic of late eighteenth-century reductionist Classicism. There is little so formally rigid as a nineteenth-century factory. Only in this century have engineers somewhat timidly begun to use the asymmetry made available by architects since the 1830's at the very latest; the only suspension bridge I am aware of in

which one tower is higher than the other was designed by Wright
for the unexecuted Pittsburgh triangle project.

IV

With these considerations presented, it is now possible to
attack frontally the problem of the historicism of nineteenth-
century architecture, of which the most famous instance is the
Battle of the Styles. Two important errors have been made in all
discussions of this problem I have encountered. The first is that
the historicism of nineteenth-century architecture was culturally
unique; the second is that it was really historicism. If the first
error is corrected, it is easy to correct the second.

To begin with, a relatively minor point needs to be made. I have
insisted above that insofar as Enlightenment modalities survived,
the Romantic architect strikingly transformed them, both as modalities and in terms of the situations for which the Picturesque, at
least, was employed. For a contemporary literary student of the
problem of Romanticism, this kind of distinction is fairly easy to
make. His instrumental hypothesis is that there must have been
some kind of significant break in the cultural continuity, for in the
last twenty years, in spite of considerable disagreement on the
exact nature and consequences of the break, there has come to be
pretty general agreement that the movement from Enlightenment
to Romanticism was a revolutionary consequence of a cultural
crisis. Architectural historians, however, as well as art historians,
still use the term "Romanticism" to refer to much that happened
in the second half of the eighteenth century, just as political historians refer to Enlightenment political thinking as "Romantic."
Terminology, after all, controls our behavior by controlling what
we look for, by directing our attention and perceptions. Consequently the use of the same term to refer to what, to the literary
historian, are two quite different and antithetical metaphysical
evaluative, literary, and artistic systems, is bound to produce a
neglect of what is of great importance; and in architectural history, this neglect is compounded by the failure to observe the
distinction between the two semantic functions of "style." Here
Hitchcock's work is very much to the point, for he slides over this
cultural crisis, although his divisions of nineteenth-century style

are almost exactly where I make them, approaching the problem from quite a different point of view.

His first period corresponds to my "Analogistic" stage, his "Early Victorian" to my "Transcendentalism," his "High Victorian Gothic" and "Second Empire and Cognate Modes" to my "Objectism," and his "reaction" against these two to my "Stylism." Our principal difference is that he thinks of Art Nouveau as the first stage of Modern, but to my mind it belongs to the same stylistic period as the "reaction" against High Victorian and Second Empire by Shaw, Webb, and later Richardson, McKim, Mead, and White, Voysey, and the early Wright. I believe our difference rises from his failure to distinguish between "style" and "modality," as I have defined those terms here. Thus, to me, Art Nouveau is a new modality of the Shaw-Richardson, etc., style, which preceded it. Thus he sees, in much the same way, early Romantic architecture as a continuation of the Enlightenment, where I discern a revolutionary transformation; and he sees nineteenth-century architecture as ending before I do.

As far as historicism is concerned, it is true in one way that Romantic culture was responsible for the historicization of European culture, but from another point of view such a proposition is not acceptable at all. Obviously, the Enlightenment itself was profoundly interested in history. But the two interests stemmed from concern with quite different problems. The Enlightenment historian was primarily interested in examining history for positive and negative models of political and social behavior. Since, as an Enlightenment man, he was concerned with devising means to adapt the human organism to its society and society to the physical environment, he studied history to find instances of successful and unsuccessful adaptation.

The Romantic historian, however, was faced with quite a different problem. For one thing, all advanced Romantic thinkers tended to adopt an historical orientation toward any event, including the events of their own day. As the Goncourts put it, a realistic novel is an historical novel about the present; *Madame Bovary* is as much an historical novel as *Salammbô*. And of this historicism two trends may be observed, both stemming from an encounter with the same problems, scientific history and, for want of better terms, literary or imaginative history. The latter is the easier to understand. It is necessary here to see the role of the nineteenth-century historian, and of historicism as it was employed by musicians, writers, painters, and architects, as an anti-role, just as the Visionary Poet, the Bohemian, the Virtuoso, and the Dandy were Romantic anti-roles. The self can, after all, achieve social embodiment only by playing a role. The alienated self, therefore, can achieve this end and still maintain its alienation only by innovating and playing anti-roles. But there was a still more fundamental reason. "Anyone who had gone through the profoundly disorienting transition of experiencing the failure of the great hopes of the Enlightenment, of experiencing also the total loss of meaning and value and identity, and then of arriving at the new Romantic vision, saw his own life as history. Psychology became history; personality became history; the manifestation of the self became history" (see my "The Dilemma of a Century," reprinted on pp. 36–57 of this book). Historicism, then, accomplishes several strategies. It separates the self from the role, the individual from society. It provides an orientation in which alienation can be successfully maintained. To see a situation from an historical perspective is to separate oneself from those who see it as a value situation because they are unself-consciously sunk in the present. Historicism thus separates the individual from his social values. A further Romantic strategy is put into practice as a result. The individual is now in a position to criticize and undermine the values of his society; his knowledge of the determining historical facts of the matter undermines the adequacy of the decisions of those ignorant of those facts. We have already seen an instance of the function of this in the Romantic architects' use of archaeological accuracy; they thus undermined the traditional and prevailing Vitruvian tradition, which purported to be Classically correct but was not. These two strategies are certainly at work in the "scientific historiography" of the nineteenth century. I daresay even Ranke knew that the ideal of finding out "how it really was" was at best heuristic; but the real advantage of this slogan was the implication that current conceptions of how it was are not notions of how it really was, or is, but illusions. The presence of this strategy explains not only the objectivity but the aggressiveness, often quite disagreeable, of the "scientific" historian.

To these two strategies the "literary" or "imaginative" historian added a third, which links the historian proper to the omnipresence of historicism throughout Romantic culture. He showed in his work a tendency toward iconicity and factuality which we have already seen in Ingres and Wordsworth. Historiography gave such an historian the opportunity to place in extreme and unresolved tension the subjectivity of the self and the objectivity of the phenomenal world, a problem which, as we have seen, was a major one of the period. Hence the, to our minds, perplexing character of Carlyle as historian, for example. All this is the source of the current notion that historiography is both science and "art." On the one hand Carlyle is very obviously manipulating history as a means of manifesting the transcendence of the self over the historical-phenomenal world. And at the same time even Ranke went to no greater trouble to discover how one of Frederick's battles, for instance, unfolded on its unique terrain, under unique climatic conditions. The word "art" was used to refer to the transcendent aspect of the historian's work because the Romantic conceived as the unique attribute of "art" its power to "symbolize" the self and its unique orientations.

In this third strategy, therefore, lay the appeal of the historical modalities for the Romantic architect. Hence the two pulls of that historicism, one in the direction of archaeological accuracy and functionalism, the other in the direction of manipulating freely that modality so as to manifest the unique creativity of the architect as Visionary Poet, the transcendence of the self, or subject. Thus it appears correct to say that the historicism of nineteenth-century architecture was not really historicism. Ultimately, there is no better way to indicate one's alienation from one's culture and freedom from its values than to manipulate with free and extravagant invention and innovation the behavioral patterns of that culture, and this is what the Romantic architect did to the historical modalities, whether Gothic or Classic or non-European. It may be argued that later in the century, in the work, for example, of Ralph Adams Cram and other late nineteenth- and early twentieth-century architects called "traditional," by Hitchcock, that principle was denied; but this, to my mind, would be an error. The point of Cram's work is not that it was archaeologically accurate—as it certainly was to a degree hitherto scarcely known in the Romantic use of the Gothic modality—but rather that he designed a purer Gothic than the Middle Ages ever did. His Gothic, like the eighteenth-century Classicism of the Morgan Library, obeys rules derived from the Gothic "style" in its first sense, style in its semantic function as intellectual and theoretical construct.

Such men worked not in the tradition of a modality but rather in a purified modality; hence their work shows a consistency of architectural modality rarely, if ever, found in any actual building of the historical modality they were employing as the basis for their design. As with all Romantic art, one is intensely aware of the presence of the artist as intermediary between the perceiver and the tradition in which he is working or the subject matter he is presenting. Thus it is that even the most careful and archaeologically correct restorations done in the later nineteenth century have a subtly wrong look. In short, for these various reasons, architects, like all nineteenth-century artists, transformed the modalities, plans, and formal devices which had originated and been established before the nineteenth century, and which that century inherited. That the nineteenth-century is historicist is true of all nineteenth-century Romantic culture and its arts, and true of none, including architecture.

8

CAN "VICTORIAN"

HAVE A USEFUL MEANING?

[1967*]

This is a miscellany of lectures, BBC broadcasts, reviews, an introduction or two, and a few brief essays and more formal papers. Perhaps half the material, at a generous estimate, is worth reprinting. For the most part we are instructed in the Tillotsons' literary taste, which I do not find interesting. Geoffrey Tillotson, for example, tells us that he has been stupid about Browning, and then, with a self-satisfaction not easily justified, informs us that he has become more intelligent and that he can now see that some faults are not indeed faults but virtues. This sort of thing has its uses in the classroom, but in a book addressed to advanced students of Victorian literature it is irritating. Kathleen Tillotson begins a lecture, "Matthew Arnold and Carlyle," with, "the conjunction of these two names may seem surprising." To whom? Not to anyone who has read both of them. But an extraordinary

* Reprinted by permission from *Victorian Studies*, X (March, 1967), pp. 273–77. A review of *Mid-Victorian Studies*, by Geoffrey and Kathleen Tillotson, London and New York, 1965.

amount of this book seems to be addressed to readers who have never read in Victorian literature by individuals who are just beginning to and are, with a decorous excitement, reporting on their discoveries.

To be sure, there are a few essays of value. Critically, the best thing is "The Tale and the Teller," by Kathleen Tillotson, which offers an agreeable and welcome attack on the notion that a novel should contain no trace of the "intrusive author." Unfortunately, the explanation of why and how that doctrine emerged and became widely accepted is shallow. Her lecture on *The Idylls of the King* is of some use, as is her "Donne's Poetry in the Nineteenth Century"; and her "Rugby 1850: Arnold, Clough, Walrond and *In Memoriam*" is at least a pleasant piece of literary gossip, but as with so many pieces in this volume it stops just as it is about to begin to get interesting. Perhaps the best thing by Geoffrey Tillotson is his polite objection to Walter Houghton's *The Victorian Frame of Mind*, but even this is a review of fewer than three pages reprinted from *Victorian Studies* for December, 1957. The value of republishing something so readily accessible is only to remind one that for some students that study has been excessively admired.

On the whole this book can be safely neglected by advanced students of Victorian literature. It might make agreeable reading for undergraduates and even beginning graduate students, and it would be perhaps of most interest to students of Victorian culture who are not concerned, except indirectly, with Victorian literature. In the Preface is the statement: "Another common concern of the authors is a related 'work in progress,' the writing of the mid-nineteenth-century volume of the *Oxford History of English Literature*. The pieces in the present volume are in no sense samples of that history, but rather mile-stones or halting-places, in the several ways that lead towards it." I confess that *Mid-Victorian Studies* does not make me look forward to that volume with any eagerness. Rather, I suspect that it is going to be a fairly depressing intellectual experience, perhaps mostly a handing out of gold stars to some authors and works, but for others the equivalent of a sharp note to the parents, in the hope that the student authors may be stimulated to improve. So many volumes of that series are of that character that one wonders if it were not best to abandon the whole project right now.

Taste, gossip, superficiality—is there something fraudulent in the whole enterprise, as it is currently practiced, of studying and writing about literature? I know few serious scholars who are not haunted by that possibility, and the ghost is always present for the student of Victorian literature. The Tillotsons are, indeed, in a dilemma which is not of their own making, though they could well do more to get out of it. The difficulty lies in the word "Victorian" itself. What does it mean? To use it as the editors of this journal do, if I understand them, is to take it to refer to anything and everything that happened in the last three-quarters, roughly, of the century, though even those limits are not entirely binding. Yet it is doubtful if such a usage can ever be standardized, except for one or two journals. The difficulty is that the word unavoidably ascribes certain attributes to all works and artifacts and events which it subsumes. It is only recently, for example, that a few people are beginning to see Hopkins as a "Victorian" and not a "modern" or "early modern" or "proto-modern." But what have we done when we decide to call him Victorian? In a footnote Geoffrey Tillotson asserts that "Hopkins received vital help from Browning," and it is refreshing to hear it, though it seems strange that it needs to be said. The reason that such a view of Hopkins is still relatively novel (I have known graduate students and colleagues to become enraged at the suggestion that Hopkins learned much of his technique from Swinburne) is that he did not seem "Victorian" as the word was used in the 1920's and as late as the 1950's or even, for some, today. In that period it was easy to ignore the fact that the major Victorian figures hated the Victorian period even more than the moderns; after all, they had to live in it. As our comprehension of Browning and Tennyson and Carlyle and Swinburne and Ruskin and the rest of the big figures improves, they begin to appear, in the old sense of the word, not Victorian, but anti-Victorian. To call them Victorian is beginning to seem a little quaint. Hence the usage of "Victorian" as the editors of this journal practice. Yet such a practice does not meet the problem; it merely avoids it.

Actually, I suspect that the tone of surprise and discovery

which is so dominant in the volume under review does the Tillotsons far less justice than occasional evidence of scholarship and learning indicates. They appear to have a notion of the attributes which the term "Mid-Victorian" subsumes. This is the purport of the objections to *The Victorian Frame of Mind*; Houghton neglected certain Victorian attributes—the comic, the sense of beauty, and so on. "I cannot discern," Geoffrey Tillotson says, "enough connection between the 'frame' here offered and the teeming literature and art and music of the age." He calls for "a deeper book behind this one." And he goes on, "It is usually assumed—and Mr. Houghton quotes Alfred North Whitehead to this effect—that the whole literature of an age preserves the fullest record of its 'inmost thoughts.'" Houghton appears to use Whitehead to justify his position that "I cannot doubt there was a common culture for which the term Victorianism, though in a wider sense than it usually bears, is appropriate." But Tillotson complains that his "wider sense" is not nearly wide enough.

Actually Whitehead's remark is so vague as to be quite useless; indeed, it is tautological. We cannot know whether the "literature of an age preserves the fullest record of its 'inmost thoughts'" because the only evidence for the inmost thoughts is the literature. Our problem is to explain and relate the statements and implications in the literature and the problems the writers were seeking to deal with, and perhaps solve, in the works themselves. Nothing is accomplished by calling the works the "record of inmost thoughts" except to ascribe spurious dignity to one's undertaking.

Behind Whitehead, Houghton, and Tillotson alike lurks the unquestioned assumption that the "culture of an age," the "common culture," is continuous and coherent, that all aspects of it are properly subsumed under a single categorical term for reasons other than mere convenience. It assumes that when you have called a poem by Hopkins, say, "Victorian," you have actually said something both true and useful. Houghton growls, "In fact, it is now smart to say that of course there is no such thing as Victorianism," and he goes on to assert that the "same fundamental attitudes" were to be found "among High Churchmen and liberals, agnostics and Tories." Of course, but what of it? Undoubtedly these groups—but why *these*?—shared certain attitudes, but there is no reason to think they were fundamental simply because they were shared. It is not merely that the notion of "shared assumptions" may very well result from the phenomenon that the language in which those attitudes are defined may be remote and abstract from the text. Even more at fault is the assumption that the attitudes, the orientations, the personalities of individual High Churchmen, liberals, and so on, were coherent and structured, and that assumption is concealed in and carried by the metaphor "fundamental."

Houghton has in fact proposed three categorical modes: (1) the culture; (2) High Churchmen, liberals, agnostics, Tories, etc. (presumably); and (3) individuals. But the data for these categories are precisely the same: the literature, widely interpreted—though, as Tillotson points out, a great deal of pertinent data has been left out, probably most of it. But the omission is not the difficulty. Rather, assertions about the relations among the three categorical modes are in fact assertions about, at best, relations between ways of organizing, interpreting, and building constructs of the same data.

To give an example from the twentieth century, the recently published letters of Wallace Stevens show that some of his attitudes were those of typical American businessmen, that is, they are categorized as "business-man attitudes." But other of his attitudes can be categorized as "Pennsylvania-Dutch attitudes," as "Harvard-undergraduate attitudes," as "Romantic-poetics attitudes," as "modern-philosophy attitudes," and so on. The task of cultural, and literary, history is to discover and classify these attitudes, to locate their historical origins and emergence, to establish their strategical functions, and to attempt to find out whether or not there is a relation among them; it is not to assume that because they were all held by Wallace Stevens they all had something in common. Nor is it to assume that because these attitudes existed simultaneously in the twentieth century they must necessarily have something in common, or that one set is more fundamental than another. What is there in common between my admiration and love for the poetry of Wallace Stevens and the fact that I faithfully stop for red lights when I am driving?

What is there in common between the paintings of Picasso and Norman Rockwell? What is there in common between the chronologically concurrent beliefs of the Jehovah's Witnesses and the position of Wittgenstein's *Tractatus*?

Houghton and the Tillotsons are right in thinking that the terms "Victorian," "Victorianism," and "Mid-Victorian" do direct our attention to something, but not to what they think. The object of reference, to speak very loosely, is not Victorian culture but a construct of Victorian culture. The culture itself we cannot know or talk about; we can only talk about the construct and the verbal and nonverbal phenomenal data which are or are not accounted for and explained by the construct. The only desirable quality of that construct at the present time is its actual fluidity and instability, but most scholars seem to regret that and manfully, at least for themselves, try to fix and stabilize their notion of the Victorian. The most encouraging thing about the work of the Tillotsons, as opposed to that of Houghton, is their frequent air of innocent surprise at the consequences of just a little poking about among the enormous mass of Victorian documents. The value of such a construct, as of any construct, is heuristic. It serves as a hypothesis which directs our searches, our observations, our interpretations, and which is valuable to the degree to which it is corrigible and to which in fact we do correct it. Clearly, its efficacy depends upon its richness, its complexity, and its articulation. What we need first of all, in short, is a general model of a culture, any culture, further refined by notions of what is possible and probable in any European culture.

I can hardly offer such a complete model here, even if it were possible at the present time to construct one, and perhaps it is not, though that does not mean that a beginning cannot be made. Any such model must at the outset be exceedingly crude. To begin with, it must have several dimensions. The first obvious lines of cleavage are the well-used low-, middle-, and high-level culture. Thus the poetry of Wallace Stevens, and much of his philosophical thinking, is at the highest level of the culture of his lifetime. It had, further, one of the most significant marks of high-level culture; it was emergent, innovative, shared by very few people at his time, in response to problems which only a limited number of individuals felt. The Jehovah's Witnesses, on the other hand, have quite different marks. They have scarcely an idea which postdates the seventeenth century, at the most recent. What was a middle-level culture then, and a high-level culture in the sixteenth century, is now at a low cultural level, and has the mark of a low-level culture: it is singularly resistant to change and, as a construct, to correction. Stevens' business ideas, however, were at a middle level; the business model was not, as a construct, changed very much in his lifetime, but in its empirical deductions was quite adaptable and innovative; otherwise neither he nor his insurance company would have been so successful, a matter about which he was quite proud, and, naturally, he was more confident of that success than he was of his success as a poet, simply because as a poet his behavior was so much more emergent and innovative and problem-laden. To the low-middle-high dimensions, then, must be added the dimension of the historical emergence of an attitude and its subsequent cultural vicissitudes and positions.

In the nineteenth century the highest cultural level was, to my mind, the Romantic tradition. In *Beyond the Tragic Vision* (1962) I have proposed, *as a construct*, four stages of Romanticism in the nineteenth century, each defined by an attempt and a failure to solve the basic problem posed by the cultural crisis to which the first stage of Romanticism (Romanticism proper, as it is known in official literary history) was a response. If such a notion is used, it must be recognized that each stage continued after the subsequent stage emerged, and frequently, perhaps always, continued in the work of the same man. Thus even a single work must not be regarded as culturally coherent, as reflecting one and only one aspect of a constructed model. Rather it will always contain traces of other levels within the highest cultural level and often attitudes of lower cultural levels. The reason is that since the data for a cultural construct are identical with the data for a personality construct, one kind of construct serves equally well for the other kind. That is, we should speak of a personality-cultural construct, taking "personality" to include and indeed consist of attitudes, just as "culture" does. The difference is not the difference of constructs but the differences of the purposes for which we use the same construct or model.

Such might be the first requirements for a theory of Victorian culture which could both control and improve our present efforts to deal meaningfully with this material. The most important thing always to have in mind and to be fully conscious of is that "Victorianism" is merely an historical-cultural construct or model which is to be used, not constitutively asserted. At best its value is heuristic, but at the same time it must be recognized that in the nature of things it is inadequate and is vital only so long as it is continuously corrected. If we think that there once actually existed "Victorian culture" we shall forever be hopelessly confused; if we recognize that "Victorian culture" refers to a model and a construct and an operational fiction, we can use the term "Victorian" with hope, though never with impunity.

9

HAWTHORNE AND

MELVILLE AS EUROPEAN AUTHORS

[1966*]

I

The problem of the culture of the United States is so perplexing, and the place in it of the artist and intellectual so baffling, that anyone who attempts to discuss Melville and Hawthorne, if he is not an Americanist, must commit himself to unequivocal statements of his position. That there is an American culture in the sense that there is a European culture and that the problem is one of the interrelation between two independent cultures is to me untenable. Perhaps it is held by no one, yet I have gathered a different impression. The culture of the United States, then, is neither more nor less than a geographical extension of European culture, and is thus similar to the other cultures of this

* Delivered at the Hawthorne-Melville Conference, Williamstown, Mass., September, 1966. Reprinted by permission from *Melville & Hawthorne in the Berkshires*, Kent State U.P., 1968, pp. 42–62. Copyright © 1968 by the Kent State University Press.

hemisphere and of the geographical borders of Europe itself, Russia, for example, and Norway.

But I find equally untenable the notion that ours is a provincial culture. Modern Denmark and Sweden, modern Ireland and Spain, are truly provincial; but it is clear to me that though the term "provincial" may properly be applied to Irving and Cooper, it is hopelessly inadequate for Emerson, Hawthorne, Melville, or Emily Dickinson, or Whitman. For such figures some other term is necessary, and we do not have one. Or it may be perfectly accurate to class them as European writers. Nevertheless, they did not live in or write from or for a truly European situation, though they came to live at the highest level of European culture. They were in a situation novel in recent European cultural history. It was the frontier of a geographical extension of an old and highly developed culture of many levels. For the moment let us accept the judgment of the highest cultural level of Europe and assert that the Americanization of European culture is a vulgarization. But let no European assume airs of superiority. It cannot be too strongly asserted that Americanized Europe is more vulgar—a term I hope to give a somewhat more exact meaning to—than the United States. Miami Beach may be a vulgarization of the aristocratic resort of nineteenth-century Europe, but Torremolinos is a more vulgar Miami Beach. In this circumstance lies, I propose, a clue to the problem of the artist and intellectual in the United States.

I should like to call anthropology and psychology to my aid. Everyone knows that when a higher culture encounters a less-developed one, the effect on the latter is disastrous. Yet I have never seen it proposed that when a higher culture is extended to a geographical environment different from that to which its behavioral patterns are adapted, and when, at the same time, it is exposed to less-developed cultures, a deterioration of its higher cultural levels may, and perhaps must, follow. Yet such I believe to be the case.

The history of the United States is the history of the progressive westward movement of European culture into alien physical environments and in constant contact with less-developed cultures, both Indian and Negro. Thus European culture was transformed into a frontier culture. Frontier patterns are still the basic cultural patterns of the United States, and the frontier values are still our fundamental values. These are scarcely novel propositions, but it seems to me that what a frontier culture involves has not been adequately considered. The highest level of any culture is marked, first, by extreme richness; it contains in solution innumerable ambiguities and ambivalences and puzzles and problems. Anyone who lives at that level is as much involved in discovering and creating problems as he is in solving them. Second, therefore, the life of the members of that highest cultural level requires psychic insulation, for only that makes problem-exposure tolerable. Third, that level maintains itself by alliance with political power, social status, and wealth. These are the economic and social defenses for its psychic insulation. The American academic tenure system is an example, though perhaps a rather crude one. Yet it brings out a fourth character of high-level culture; it is exceedingly wasteful in every possible way, from economic to psychic. It must be; the human capacity for problem-exposure and controlled innovation is so limited that a tremendous loss is involved in any genuinely high-culture creative breakthrough. Parsons College is a financial success because it has eliminated the waste of high culture.

Of course there is no such thing as a culture or a society. There is only the behavior of an infinitude of human beings, none of whom can learn perfectly any cultural pattern. Few have the capacity for high-level problem tolerance, even fewer have the capacity for significant creativity, and far fewer have the opportunity for either. It must always be remembered that the highest cultural level exists only because a few people need it in order to adapt to their physical and social environments. The need is mysterious, but a crude explanation is possible.

To me the most significant and useful current theory of cognition is the perceptual or cognitive model theory, sometimes called set theory, or expectancy theory. It is the basis of my recent study of artistic behavior, *Man's Rage for Chaos*. Briefly, it amounts to this: To every situation we bring, by picking up clues from the situation, a perceptual, or cognitive, model, or orientation. But since this model is prepared to deal only with a category of situations, but with no existential situation, there is a necessary disparity between the model and the data fed into the brain by the sensorium. That disparity is reality. Our general tendency is to suppress as much of it as possible, because any awareness of it is cognitively disorienting and emotionally disturbing. The safer, the more protected, the human organism, the more it can afford to be aware of disparities, to search for problems, to account for the disparity, to solve those problems, and to correct the original cognitive model by feedback. If the organism does not have to act for its own defense and survival, it can thus become aware both of the disparity between model and sensory data and of difficulties, ambiguities, ambivalences, and puzzles in the cognitive models themselves. In a crisis situation, one which it interprets as requiring action, it cannot afford such luxuries. Behavior in crisis situations is, thus, invariably simplistic. A life history which involves continuous exposure to crisis situations effects an increasing simplification of behavior and a continuous reinforcement of increasingly simplified cognitive models.

A frontier is a crisis situation. Although there are exceptions, all of them technological, the tendency of Europeans on the American frontier, whether North or South America, was necessarily to apply European cognitive models by simplification, reductionism, and reinforcement, rather than by feedback and correction. Instances are easy to come by. In Europe violence, though certainly present, tended to be ritualized, at least in those areas of violence, such as war, under some control by higher cultural levels. But violence on the frontier is the response of the individual who cannot afford the luxury of correcting his adaptational models, but can only apply them by eliminating any disparity from the environment, not by understanding it. Hence our Civil War was the bloodiest war in the history of European culture. Grant's determination to destroy the enemy army and his indifference to elegant maneuver and the ritualistic capture of the enemy capital is an instance of frontier, or crisis, behavior, the de-ritualization and hence simplification of cultural patterns. Thus unritualized violence has become endemic to American culture. Whether or not President Kennedy was assassinated by a plot, every American is quite ready to believe that it was the work of an unaided individual; this country is full of trigger-happy crackpots. But the European is convinced that there must have been a plot, an elaborate behavioral pattern. In the same way, although Enlightenment thinking at its best was very rich, the founding documents of this Republic are almost parodic simplifications of Enlightenment philosophy. Again, as a total behavior pattern, Jackson Pollock's version of European abstract painting was a striking simplification, involving a minimally corrected, rapid, and violent attack upon ever larger canvasses.

But this simplification, reductionism, and reinforcement of behavioral patterns, which to the man at the highest cultural level constitutes vulgarity, has two further consequences, one flowing from the other. The first is that the process was necessarily seen as good. Since it was necessary for survival on the frontier, it was, as values always are, universalized. It was interpreted as an ennoblement, a redemption of European culture. Here is the source of the myth of America as a Paradise, in spite of all evidence to the contrary, and of the absurd myth of the American as the new Adam. The result was a culture in which behavioral simplification became the ideal. Here is the source of the anti-intellectualism of American life. But the second consequence, flowing from the first, has meant a peculiar American helplessness before the enormous social problems industrialization and uncorrected exploitation of natural and human resources have brought into being. The automobile has destroyed the old semirural American culture from which I learned that the only significant human distinction is that of the philosopher, the scientist, and the artist; it has stabbed our cities to the bone; it has polluted our air; and it is killing us at a greater rate than all our wars, just as murder is. We are helpless before it. And we are helpless before the problem of the Negro. It is evident that the efforts of the past ten years have only made the problem worse. Every year fewer white Americans are sympathetic with the Negro's cause, and, as an American of almost as many Anglo-Saxon generations in this country as possible, I feel in my bones that millions of my fellow citizens are getting ready to act out what they dream of, the elimination of the problem by the bloody elimination of the Negro.

Nevertheless, as I suggested earlier, let no European feel superior. All this—simplification, idealization of that simplification, helplessness before modern problems—has been exported to Europe and has found there a welcome and an intensification. World War I imitated the American Civil War; the ritualization of European war disintegrated and led to a military process which the Europeans were quite unable to stop, although previously there had been effective patterns for stopping wars. The English have been even more helpless than we in the face of a far less severe Negro problem. Apparently Europeans are incapable of learning from American failures. Experiencing for the first time the onslaught of the automobile, they are proving even more helpless than we have been, for they have far more to be destroyed. If Jackson Pollock made a parodic simplification of Picasso, European artists have made a parodic simplification of Jackson Pollock. If we have pointless riots in Watts and Berkeley, the Europeans have more pointless riots in Amsterdam and West Berlin, simplifications of their consciously imitated American models. But enough; anyone, once alerted, can think of a thousand instances.

Why should this be so? Here it is useful to introduce the notion of the internal frontier. I mean by this the exposure of lower cultural levels to higher. When a man from the middle or lowest cultural level encounters a higher cultural level, he has several strategies at his disposal. He can see that the high level offers what he needs, and, if the social situation permits it, he can earn his place there and achieve acceptance. In this sense, European culture has generally been democratic. Or he can retreat back to his own culture, realizing that there is where he properly belongs. Or he can resent his exclusion and demand simplification, reduction, and reinforcement, insisting that the high culture be transformed downward to meet his needs, or what he feels to be his needs. If he has enough political, social, and economic power, he can make his demands felt and acted upon. He can dismantle the high culture. It need only be remembered that exactly the same cognitive forces are at work on the internal frontier as on the external. In the past couple of hundred years those forces have become not only effective in Europe but predominant.

The first factor in the situation was the Enlightenment itself, which was a simplification of European culture at the highest level. It was, to be sure, soon followed by Romanticism, which made that level of culture richer than ever—more ambiguous, ambivalent, self-conscious, and problem and reality oriented. However, in the nineteenth century the most important cultural phenomenon quantitatively was the spread of Enlightenment ideas. But those ideas suffered a further simplification as a consequence of the communications revolution and the enormous increase in literacy and education. For the first time, the whole middle level of culture developed an extremely sensitive awareness of the existence of high culture, and much of this awareness penetrated to the lower levels. Simplification, idealization of simplification, violence, and helplessness were the result. Further, the economic rewards for culture businesses in vulgarizing high culture, particularly publishing, proved to be infinitely greater than in serving it. Inferior culture began to drive superior culture out of the marketplace, making high culture even more dependent on political and economic power. Moreover, one of the direct consequences of Enlightenment thinking was that for members of the high cultural level to vulgarize their own culture was not only safe but a moral imperative. A social environment was created, therefore, in which exposure to American cultural simplifications met not merely acceptance but intensification. This is what I mean, then, when I propose that geographical extension and contact with less-developed societies bring about the deterioration of the high culture of the more developed society. On the internal frontier there is always a demand and a market for the vulgarizations necessarily developed on the external frontier. The deterioration of social support for high culture follows.

From this point of view it is possible to understand the peculiar difficulty of the artist and intellectual in the United States. Since he was one of those people who turned to the highest level of culture because he needed it, he had to turn to the highest level of European culture. There was no other possibility. Any cultural pattern, however, is learned by imitation of a behavioral paradigm. I mean by this that the learning of the behavior patterns of a high culture is not merely learning what can be absorbed from books. It is a matter of learning elaborate behavioral patterns of which published verbal behavior is only a part. In particular, the various techniques for achieving psychic insulation can be learned only paradigmatically. The difficulties of Hawthorne and Melville in learning the necessity for psychic insulation and in improvising insulatory techniques are too well known to need comment. Such behavior paradigms were by no means absent, but they seem to have been more common in the eighteenth century than in the nineteenth. The carriers of the paradigms had come directly from Europe, and the frontier simplification had not yet much affected them. For instance, as a relatively trivial example, it is known that the exquisite plasterwork in eighteenth-century Philadelphia houses was done by Irish craftsmen who had learned their trade in Dublin.

But the greatest difficulty for the nineteenth-century artist and intellectual, not to speak of the twentieth, was that he was attempting cultural complexity in a situation in which cultural simplification had become the ideal. And so seductive is such an idealization, as in the earlier books of Melville, that it was easy for him to think that somehow there was something wrong about his desire to enter into a world of ambiguity, ambivalence, and exposure to the problems and recalcitrance of reality. Romanticism involves alienation and social isolation, but these were doubled when the American Romantic found himself in a social environment increasingly dominated by the values emerging from the cognitive crisis of the frontier. This is why today's European artist and intellectual believes that some Americans preceded him in the Existential experience. He is partly mistaken, of course. The Existential vision develops out of his own Romantic tradition; it is the modern form of it. But he is right in thinking that the American artist somehow felt its full intensity before the European. That intensity, however, comes not from the character of Existential thinking but rather from the fact that Romanticism historically coincided with the American deterioration of European high-level culture. I should say that, generally speaking, the European scarcely yet knows that the same thing is happening to him. And it needs to be pointed out that he too is feeling the seductiveness of frontier simplification and reinforcement and the consequent helplessness and violence.

For the American intellectual and artist, the only counterattraction to that simplistic seduction has been Europe itself. Not only was it the source of that high culture which he needed, but it was there that social support for that culture was present. Paradigms existed in numbers enough to make a difference, and they were protected by power, status, and wealth. Hence the climactic experience for the American has been the first visit to Europe. To be sure, actual contact with European high-level culture has usually been a disappointment. The principal reason, perhaps, is that he has not entered the high culture by the paths ritualized in Europe, nor is he familiar by living example with the paradigms. To the European, therefore, he does not properly belong and his pretensions to belong are usually not taken very seriously. For this attitude of the European there is some justification. What American intellectual has not felt bitterly the inadequacies and unnecessarily slow pace of his formal education? Nevertheless, the American learns something of great value, particularly because of his exclusion from the circles he wishes to enter, but also because of the barriers of the most trivial, as well as the most important, language and behavior differentia. He learns that to be what he is, he has to be a foreigner in his own country. Whether he lives the rest of his life abroad or at home, the American intellectual who has been to Europe is an expatriate. For even at home he is a foreigner in a country all of the values of which are aimed in a direction diametrically opposite to the values he desires. For these reasons, therefore, I think it is useful, and perhaps correct, to think of Hawthorne and Melville as European writers.

II

In what follows I should like to propose that these two writers can best be understood as European Romantics. That is, although they often concerned themselves with problems of the United States, the instruments or cognitive models they employed were the same as those of European Romanticism. Further, I wish to propose that their intellectual and artistic development can be understood, and best understood, as recapitulations, more or less independent, of the development of the cognitive models of European Romanticism. To explain this I fear it is first necessary to present here as briefly as I can the main outlines of a theory of Romanticism I have presented elsewhere, though I shall offer some novel propositions. (See my *Beyond the Tragic Vision*, 1962, and *Romanticism: The Culture of the Nineteenth Century*.)

Using again the theory of the cognitive model, one may say that human organisms experience two difficulties with it. One, insufficient feedback, I have already touched in suggesting that frontier culture is a crisis culture. The other may be called cognitive overload; that is, feedback is too great for the individual to endure. The cognitive model, instead of being corrected, collapses. Studies of creativity have shown that a major creative breakthrough is usually preceded by a disorientation so severe that it resembles psychosis, and is likewise frequently followed by something very like it. My notion of Negative Romanticism is supported by this discovery. That is, the breakdown of Enlightenment thinking through its own internal contradictions and its empirical failure led, in some people at least, to a severe dislocation, or disorientation. This was signified by guilt, alienation, isolation, and wandering; the disappearance of goals and the breakdown of goal-directed activity. The sense of the value of human existence appears only when the individual's cognitive models are instrumentally functional in goal-directed behavior.

The creative breakthrough into Positive Romanticism, or Romanticism proper, was made possible by a new metaphysical insight, quite different from anything that had happened in Europe before. Instead of striving to create a new constitutive metaphysic, or regnant cognitive model, the Romantic created a metaphysic the heart of which was an explanation for the necessity for metaphysics. He looked at himself from right angles, and his fundamental postulate became the self, or the subject. Instead of creating a new metaphysic from which the soul might be derived, he created the self, the sense of identity, of value, of goal-directed behavior in the service of which any metaphysic exists. But he was not solipsistic. For the object was as real as the subject; the categories of neither could exhaust the attributes of the other. Romantic reality thus became the tension, forever unresolvable, between the subject and the object. Hegel called that tension the Idea, and in this mode of thinking reality is the Idea.

In the course of the nineteenth century, I believe, there emerged four main stages in Romantic development. The first I have called Analogism. It is the stage of Wordsworth and Emerson's *Nature*. The structure and the value of subject and object are conceived of as analogous, not identical. Thus the subject can know that the object has structure and value, but the nature of that structure and value he cannot know. This solution, however, proved unviable, because it provided no basis either for action or decision. The next stage, which I have called Transcendentalism, solves that problem by conceiving the object as without structure and value and the task of the subject as the redemption of the object. Divinity, which Analogism had found both in subject and object, was perceived as only in the subject. But this position led to difficulties because there was no way of controlling or setting moral limits to the redemptive activities of the subject. The temptation was to violate other subjects in the exercise of a redemptive enterprise, but to do that is to violate the self, for it exists only by the assertion of other selves.

From this it followed that the subject did not have a divine authority; it was not the instrument through which divinity entered the phenomenal world. Stripped of that divine authority, there is left nothing but the naked subject nakedly exposed to the naked object. This is the stage I have called Objectism. Its great theme is illusion, the notion that all metaphysics or cognitive models are illusions, that none have transcendental authority. But this situation, as Wagner's *Ring* and Tennyson's *Idylls* demonstrate, suffers, for a different reason, from the deficiency of Analogism. The weakness of that is that it offered nothing but passive acceptance; the weakness of Objectism is that it offered nothing but passive suffering. Value arose only from the endurance of an appalled vision. Cognitive overload is the peculiar experience of the Objectist. It was necessary, therefore, to create a citadel, a strategy of both offense and defense, a means of holding the self together and of preventing cognitive overload. Yet it had to be a means that was metaphysically indifferent. The next and final stage of nineteenth-century Romanticism, first appearing in the late 1850's and the 1860's, I have called Stylism, rather than the more common term Aestheticism. Style is a universal of human behavior. Yet it is arbitrary and metaphysically indifferent. Thus the creation of a style became the way out of the impasse of Objectism. It gave the individual a goal—looking at the metaphysical emptiness of the object—but did not commit him to any specific ethical direction or morality. At the same time he could adopt or improvise a metaphysic or a morality for whatever purpose he might have, dropping it when it had done its job. The instrumentalism or pragmatism implicit in Romanticism came to the fore. Both William and Henry James are Stylists.

III

Coming to Hawthorne once again after an interval of twenty years, I was struck by two features. First is the extraordinary quality of Hawthorne at his best. Even *Fanshawe* showed at once that here was a man of astounding literary gifts, and *The Scarlet Letter* is the only novel to which I would ascribe the word "perfect." The second thing was that I encountered no themes with which European Romanticism had not made me familiar. This does not mean that Hawthorne was a mere imitator, or that his version of Romanticism was not unique. But that uniqueness does not make him peculiarly American. The great European Romantics were as different from each other as he was different from them. Each major author—and almost every minor one—discovers, examines, and proposes solutions to the Romantic problems in his own manner.

In his early short stories and sketches Hawthorne was particularly concerned with three Romantic themes, guilt, alienation, and historicism. These three are so intimately intertwined in his work, as in most Romantics, that it is extremely difficult to separate them. In terms of cultural development, Hawthorne, with Byron, is the great exponent of Negative Romanticism, and his efforts to understand the nature of guilt and to devise a strategy to be free from it while preserving its advantages is a central Romantic problem. It can be done only—or at least has been done only—by postulating a self independent from social role. Once this has been done, the guilt can then be seen as a strategy for achieving the self; and alienation can be interpreted not as the punishment for guilt but as the opportunity for achieving an independent self, one which can morally transcend the society and the culture. Guilt and alienation, therefore, are something to be exploited, and one of the most important techniques for that exploitation is historicism. For the Enlightenment moralistic historian, the past was something to be ransacked for good and bad behavioral paradigms, but the Romantic historicist used the past for a double, interconnected purpose. On the one hand it was a means for separating oneself from society. As such it has often been criticized as emotionally regressive, as mere nostalgia, and perhaps it would be were it not for the use the Romantic made of that historical separation or alienation. In any institution the individual who knows its history has an instrument for analysis and a means of defense against mindless surrender to its current values. He can be aware of the failure of the institution to fulfill its avowed intentions and its social function. So we find in Hawthorne two kinds of guilt, that of the individual and that of New England society. His first notable exploration of the latter is to be found in "My Kinsman, Major Molineux." The strategy of the alienated by which he relieves his own guilt of alienation by locating guilt in the society is by now a relatively standardized device, but at the time of Hawthorne it was reasonably innovative, particularly in this country. It is a self-justifying strategy in a special sense, for it postulates and confirms the self in opposition to the social role. Romantic historicism, therefore, is never an end in itself but a strategy for placing the current social conditions in an ironic perspective, and Hawthorne's historicism, though it has its particular character, is a standard Romantic variety.

Once the self has been redeemed from society it can be explored in its own terms, and for this purpose Hawthorne developed his peculiar use of emblematic allegory, which reaches its perfection in *The Scarlet Letter*. This technique, though Hawthorne's is different from that of European writers, creates analogies between self and not-self, between personality and the world. It has much in common with E. T. A. Hoffmann's work; *The Golden Pot* is thematically and technically Hawthornian. Henceforth Hawthorne's theme is the redemption of the self through the acceptance and exploitation of what society terms the guilt of the individual but which to the Romantic is society's guilt. The two themes can be seen in their relation to one another if one juxtaposes the virtually contemporaneous "The Maypole of Merry Mount" and "The Minister's Black Veil." Nevertheless, the Romantic self cannot be established until it has found a relationship with others, and the normal Romantic relationship of this sort is empathy. The self has no real existence unless it affirms the existence of other selves, and that affirmation is the basis of Romantic morality. The most thoroughgoing exploration of this theme in early Romanticism is to be found in Schopenhauer's *The World as Will and Representation*, published when Hawthorne was fifteen, but not known in the United States for some time. Whether Hawthorne arrived at the perception of empathy by himself or derived it from earlier Romantics is irrelevant. Certainly, it is one of the central themes of *The Scarlet Letter*. Chillingworth is evil because he used, in his comfortless old age, Hester as an object. Thereafter—one of Hawthorne's most subtle points—he is emotionally dependent upon the woman whose self he has violated. Dimmesdale also has violated both Hester and himself by his failure to acknowledge publicly his guilt and his love. Pearl, however, who has grown up in antisocial innocence and is therefore not human, becomes human and eventually, we are assured, a splendid woman by her sudden experience of empathy for her dying father. Hester, in proper Romantic fashion, accepts her guilt, locates the source of that guilt in society, embroiders her A with great splendor, and becomes a free and self-substantiating self, transcending the moral limitations of her world. But at the end of the book, in her return to her hut, Hawthorne touches, rather gingerly, the next stage of Romantic development, Transcendentalism, the attempt of the free Romantic self to re-enter society and to redeem it. That problem was to baffle him for the rest of his life.

In *The House of the Seven Gables*, one of the most magical and exquisitely accomplished works in European fiction, he attempts to deal with the problem with the utmost delicacy. But perhaps that word does him a little too much credit. Perhaps the apparent delicacy is really a gingerliness, as if he were a little afraid to engage too seriously with the theme of social redemption. The house itself and its inhabitants have certain resemblances to Tennyson's "Lady of Shalott" and "Marianna," which are both, particularly the latter, very Hawthornesque works, with something of Hawthorne's odd use of emblems. In the "Lady of Shalott" Tennyson is directly engaged with the relation of alienated Romantic to society, of tower to city. And the house is such a tower. We even have in Holgrave the wandering Transcendentalist artist who redeems the past, the guilt of the social order, and releases the imprisoned, although this was more than the Lady-of-Shalott-as-artist could do. Nevertheless, if this is the theme, those who have been freed from the past and social guilt move not from the tower into the city, but merely into another tower, delightfully modern, to be sure, but also built by Judge Pyncheon on a foundation of social guilt. Are we supposed to be aware of this? I think not. Rather I suspect that Hawthorne got a little more started than he could quite manage.

Hence, perhaps, the element of savagery in *The Blithedale Romance*, in which the theme of social redemption is directly in the foreground, and is thoroughly mauled, and yet regretfully, too. It appears that Hawthorne has so far entered into the second stage of Romanticism—*The House of the Seven Gables* having as one of its central themes decision and action—that the world is no longer seen as having an analogical value but rather as having no value at all. "More and more I feel that we had struck upon what ought to be a truth. Posterity may dig it up, and profit by it." It is typical of many Transcendentalist statements. The artist and the thinker can present models of world redemption, but that redemption can actually take place only in the future. At any rate, the possibility of world redemption is the only basis for re-entry into society, as Hawthorne indicates in his perhaps too self-consciously amusing remarks about Kossuth.

But another theme begins to appear, a matter which now involved Hawthorne in the gravest difficulties, the theme of American simplification, that notion that was so common among American Romantic Transcendentalists; not only is world redemption possible, but America is the predestined place for it to happen. Hawthorne has now emerged sufficiently into the world to encounter directly the peculiar problem of the American artist I have already discussed, the desire for the complexity of high-level culture in an environment turned in the direction of simplification and reductionism. The problem had first appeared faintly in the personality of Holgrave, the photographer, the new man. Further, Hawthorne was by now no longer a provincial. He had been exploring the Romantic themes which had been explored in Europe in the first quarter of the century. Emerging on the European stage, he was, in the 1850's, and in Europe, out of phase. The most advanced Romantics had already gone beyond a stage he was just beginning to struggle with. But his further progress was blocked by the confusion between the absurdities of American frontierism, of *"Amerika, du hast es besser,"* and Romantic Transcendental world redemption. It was not, of course, a confusion from which he alone suffered. On the contrary, he was aware that some baffling snarl was before him. He made four attempts to understand the problem. Three of them proved abortive, and the fourth probably would have failed had he not died. It is not surprising that after his first attempt he should have carried to completion *The Marble Faun*. Here was the theme, or a theme, of *The Scarlet Letter* all over again, in a new setting and in some ways more richly developed, the humanizing power of guilt and empathy. The faun is a kind of fusion of Hester and Pearl. But at the end of the book he is in prison. There is scarcely a hint of Hester's re-entry into society from above. That is, so long as he did not attempt that Transcendentalist theme, Hawthorne could finish a novel.

His difficulty was that he could not locate his problem. The four abortive efforts, therefore, consist of four permutations of the same factors: the footstep, or the guilt of society; the spider, the guilt of the individual; the elixir of life, the self; and the inheritance. The first three he could handle easily, but the last was too much for him, for in that emblem was adumbrated two inextricably confused themes, the relation of the United States to England, of America to Europe, and the redemption of society by freeing it from the past. On the one hand he was politically too sophisticated as well as far too alienated to imagine that the self-conception of his proper fellow citizens as representations of the new Adam was anything but self-inflationary illusion. On the other hand, he was intellectually and culturally too sophisticated, too modern, to be able to enter fully into the Transcendentalist vision, which was already an outmoded stage of Romanticism, at least for the advanced. Moreover, he was apparently unwilling or unable to take the essential step in moving from Transcendentalism to Objectism, the stripping away of divine authority from the self, the naked exposure of subject to object, though, again in a gingerly fashion, he moved in that direction. When Hilda shrinks from Kenyon's daring move that way, is it Hawthorne who shrinks, or is Hawthorne deferring to his public? One of the marks of Transcendentalism is a fantastic extravagance of style, as in *Sartor Resartus* or the music of Liszt. By setting the work in Rome, with its churches and catacombs, and in Tuscany, with its old castles and pagan traditions, Hawthorne achieves the equivalent of stylistic extravagance. I would suggest then that Hawthorne's difficulty with the four efforts to write the same novel lay in the fact that he could neither get to the ultimate weakness of the Transcendentalist position nor move out of it into full abandonment of soul for self because in his way was the confusion between Transcendentalism and Americanism. The heart of the problem lay in the frightful paradox of the artist and intellectual in America, which has made it so difficult for the American artist to understand himself as either American or artist, the fact that there seems to be every reason that this country should be a place of magnificent opportunity but is, as one lives in it, so terribly constricting to the kind of man who needs desperately to live at the highest cultural level. Did Hawthorne's illness deprive him of his energy to solve his problem, or did the problem and his failure to solve it make him ill? Or was his real problem his incipient movement into Objectism? Melville's fate was different. He stayed alive, but his later years were grim.

IV

Melville began his writing career at a much earlier cultural stage than Hawthorne did. At first he was controlled by an almost total surrender to the seductiveness of American frontier and crisis values. The theme of *"Amerika, du hast es besser,"* in an increasingly pure Enlightenment mode reaches from *Typee* to a climax in *White-Jacket*. Indeed, these works are classic instances both of American simplification and reductionism and of the spread of Enlightenment ideas in the nineteenth century, just as *Mardi* is a splendid instance of the Enlightenment allegorical fantasy, of which *Candide* is the best example and *Peter Wilkins* the one closest to *Mardi* itself. These works have also another characteristic which indicates that Melville had not yet felt the Romantic problems. They are grab-bag books, like Rabelais, Montaigne, *Don Quixote*, *Tristram Shandy*, and the grab-bag way of organizing a work is still to be found in *Moby-Dick*. *Pierre*, however, moves in the direction in which Romantic art invariably moves, toward a tightly controlled plan. I would not maintain that one is better than another; it is merely that this change in the way of putting a book together is itself an indication that Melville had entered the world of Romantic consciousness, for the Romantic must control every detail from a single point of view in order to create a symbol of the self-justifying self. Organizationally, then, *Moby-Dick* is a transitional work, like *Mardi* and *White-Jacket* in that much could be omitted without damage to the exploration of Melville's central problem, but like *Pierre* in that what appear to be several layers of rewriting move the book in the direction of total thematic control.

This is as it should be, for to my mind *Moby-Dick* is directly concerned with the initial Romantic problems, identity and the immanence of value in the universe, or its transcendence. Who knows what precipitated Melville into the Romantic problems? By 1850 it was too late for a man who had read at all in Romantic literature, as Melville had, to experience the breakdown of the Enlightenment entirely independently and to arrive at Romantic conceptions unaided. Wherever he turned in what was to him modern literature he was bound to encounter them, and he turned, I am convinced, particularly to "The Rime of the Ancient Mariner" and to *Sartor Resartus*. Yet just as it is possible today to read those works without any understanding, it certainly was even more possible in Melville's day. Somehow he had already thought himself to the position where he could use the Romantic tradition.

It is typical of him that he went to the heart of the matter and began at the beginning. He presents in their initial form the great Romantic themes: Ishmael, the wanderer, the loss of goal-direction; the opposition of land and sea, or the sundering of self from role; the pool of Narcissus, the Romantic rejection of so-lipsism, whence flows the hardheaded realism and factuality of Romanticism; the enormous amount of exact information, an-other instance of Romantic factuality; the loss of identity at the masthead, a perfect Romantic assertion that looking up through nature to nature's God, the melting together of subject and object, is a loss of identity; the survival on the coffin, the Romantic in-sight that the acceptance of death is the confirmation of the self; the Romantic rejection of soul in favor of self; and finally Ahab, the almost perfect Negative Romantic, who loses his connection with reality by rejecting his role but who has not gained a self. Probably because he came to Romanticism so late, and, as an American, so freshly, Melville used for Ahab the theme of il-lusion, which was not used in Europe in the early Romantic stages, except for Schopenhauer, and does not appear generally until Objectivism, that is, until the 1840's at the earliest. Ahab, then, having lost the Enlightenment sense of value immanent in the universe determines either to prove the universe has no mean-ing or to give the universe meaning by an act, whether that mean-ing be good or bad. But Ahab is also like a Wordsworth who wants to prove his Analogism, to link, beyond breaking, the analogies of the self and the not-self, and to do this empirically. So, though Ahab has not discovered his self, it is, we are in-formed, nevertheless at work within him. Ahab's actions may be condemned but not his motives. But Ahab is also something of an Emersonian Transcendentalist; he is engaged on a hunt which, if successful, would be world-redeeming.

In short, it is as if Melville had absorbed all at once all stages of Romanticism up to his own time, and had presented them in *Moby-Dick* in inextricable confusion. I am inclined to believe that this is why the interpretation of *Moby-Dick* is so difficult and why in all probability it will never be understood with clarity or agreement. It represents Melville's thrashing about in a tangle of culturally emerging ideas, the relationships of which he did not understand. The style of *Moby-Dick* is as confused as the analysis of Ahab, and as improvisatory. Nor do I wish to condemn or in the slightest devalue the book on this account. My point has nothing to do with literary quality. It is rather that the various styles are derived from various stages of Romanticism, just as the ideas are; and that much of the later portions of the book are written in a high Transcendentalist style strongly influenced by Carlyle.

Pierre is a work of a wholly different character. It has nothing of the grab-bag plan of *Moby-Dick* and is stylistically consistent. Melville has now more deeply entered into Romantic culture, for the book shows that rigid planning and stylistic overdetermination by which the Romantic both symbolized the self and held it together. Furthermore, it is a style in the high Transcendentalist manner. Today it is not to most people's taste, but then neither is the prose of Carlyle, the poetry of Mrs. Browning, or the music of Liszt. It is the style of Transcendentalist virtuoso extravagance, and, different as it is, it derives from the same cultural values as Emerson's *Essays* and Whitman's *Leaves of Grass*. The purest model of this style has always been Paganini, both as man and artist. It is not inappropriate to the theme of *Pierre*. The style of the narrator separates him entirely from the protagonists and their environment. It symbolizes a self which has transcended that world. It is therefore intended to be of redemptive value to the reader. But I suspect that Melville's relative failure with it as opposed to its success in certain passages in *Moby-Dick* results from the fact that he had already passed the position for which such a style is the proper symbol. Already in the brief appearance of Plinlimmon appears the icy detachment of the Objectist, such as one finds in Baudelaire, which is one of the strategies by which the Objectist naked self keeps itself intact. This was to be the Melville of the future, the position which he had already sighted, which even in *Moby-Dick* he had dimly glimpsed.

That new vision was to find both its style and its metaphor in *The Encantadas*, the horrible world with the seductive and illusory name, and in *Benito Cereno*, in which the good captain is entirely deceived by the illusions deliberately thrown about him, and in which the truth of the matter is revealed in the form of legal depositions. Illusion is likewise, mildly and amusingly, the theme of *Israel Potter*, and pitilessly of *The Confidence-Man*. The theme of the first half of that work is that we con other people by digging at them until we reach a personality factor which desires illusion; the theme of the second half is that we can do this so well because our principle activity is conning ourselves. Everything cancels out everything. One is reminded of Swinburne's *Atalanta in Calydon*, in which the positions that we should not trust in the world and those that we should cancel each other out. But *Atalanta* is a work of the Stylist period of Romanticism. The reader as well as the author is protected by a functionless style and a setting remote in time and place. *Pierre*, *The Encantadas*, *Benito Cereno*, and *The Confidence-Man* are about America. They are and always have been repugnant to those who have accepted the American simplistic and reductivist myth, which has made Americans so helpless before their major problems, as Melville cruelly points out in *Benito Cereno*.

For these are cruel and bitter works, and they are above all novels about the American problem. Melville, who had now traveled in Europe and shortly was to go again, took the step which Hawthorne could not bring himself to take, the rejection of the American illusion, a step which always costs an American terrible suffering. Few Americans have won their way to the highest level of European culture so rapidly and with such metaphysical grasp, although there were necessarily, because of his timing, confusions on the way. He had now, with *The Confidence-Man*, arrived at a position comparable to Wagner's *Ring* or Tennyson's *Idylls*, or Baudelaire, or the painting of Manet and the first stage of Impressionism. He was now absolutely exposed, with no transcendental authority whatsoever. At the time few Europeans had gone so far. But, as with all Americans, the price for such rapid and isolated development was premature exhaustion, as it had been, one suspects, with Hawthorne, and as it was to be with so many great Americans who were yet to appear.

To the terrible strain of being a foreigner in his own country was added the almost equal strain of the Objectist position. Melville, therefore, turned to the strategy of Stylism. He did exactly the opposite of what Arnold, his slightly younger contemporary, did at almost the same time. Arnold turned from an Objectist poetry to a Stylist prose. His famous disinterestedness, which he accomplished and celebrated in a delightful prose, is the attitude of the Stylist, detached, observing, not noncommittal but rarely recommending action for anyone but himself. Melville, who had been writing prose, turned with remarkable symmetry to poetry, for poetry, far more overdetermined phonically and syntactically than nineteenth-century prose, provided the protection, the citadel which Melville needed, just as Swinburne enormously increased poetic overdeterminations to create his Stylist manner. It is not surprising, therefore, that Melville should have turned for his first major poetic effort to the Civil War, nor that next he should turn to a consideration of the great religious, metaphysical, and scientific questions of the day. Of the quality of *Clarel* as a poem I wish only to say that I find it something of a scandal that it has never been admitted to its proper place in the canon of major American poems. I found it a delightful work to read, written with great prosodic deftness and imagination, and consistently interesting. To my mind it is Melville's finest achievement after *Moby-Dick*, and it makes considerably more sense. I suppose that what troubles readers, aside from the fact that very few readers, even professional critics and scholars, are well disciplined in reading long poems, is the discussion of what seem to be long-forgotten issues. I rather suspect, therefore, that it is more interesting to someone who comes to it from a background in English literature of the period, for there is hardly anything, including the diatribes of Ungar against democracy, which is not thoroughly familiar to him. But perhaps to most readers the most baffling thing about it is that none of the issues are resolved. Everything cancels out everything. In this it is remarkably similar to Pater's *Marius the Epicurean*, published nine years later, or

Fifine at the Fair, by Browning, published four years before, or Morris' Prologue to *The Earthly Paradise*, published eight years earlier. It is even more like Browning's *Parleyings*, published eleven years later, which is an exploration of the various semantic functions of the word "truth," with no conclusions about what truth really is. I rather fancy that the difficulties Melville interpreters have had with *Billy Budd* arise from an insufficient knowledge of *Clarel* and a failure to understand it. The story is an exemplum of the discursive *Clarel*; it shows how, in a critical situation, in which everything should come clear and be focused, nothing is clear. It is a story deliberately constructed to defy interpretation. It links Melville with Joyce. By revealing the gritty recalcitrance of reality to the desires of man it offers an unbounded appeal to the twentieth-century mind. When Melville died, and for decades before that, he was at the forward edge of European thought.

10

DARWINISM

AND DARWINISTICISM

[1959*]

Everyone knows that the impact of the *Origin of Species* was immense and that it has had a profound influence upon the literature of England and of the West ever since that late November day in 1859. But when one tries to tally up the writers affected and to list the books and make an inventory of passages showing Darwinian influence and Darwinian assumptions in novels, poems, and essays, a fog seems to arise in one's mind, through which are discernible twinkles of what may or may not be bits of genuine Darwinism.

Indeed, here is the first problem. What is Darwinism? Or at least, what is the Darwinism found in the *Origin*, for that alone is the Darwinism with which I am here concerned. The name of Darwin has magnetized to itself a thousand bits and pieces of

*Reprinted by permission from *Victorian Studies*, III (September, 1956), pp. 19–40.

ideas which are certainly not to be found in the book itself, and
some of which Darwin, had he been able to understand them,
would certainly have repudiated. For example, it has been said
a million times and will be said a million times more that for
Darwin competition between species and members of species is
the only mechanism of directive and progressive evolution. Thus
he has been adulated for having revealed that in capitalism and
its related and derived values was to be found the natural system
of social and economic organization which assures the progress
of man; and execrated for having led men to disbelieve the seemingly obvious truth that man's proper, natural, and normal mode
of behavior is cooperation, harmony, and love. Again, it is always
being rediscovered that in natural selection there are cooperative
as well as competitive mechanisms at work. Alternatively, it is
frequently stated that Darwin failed to perceive the element of
cooperation because he was himself the product of a laissez-faire
society: Marxists are particularly grand and imposing on the
subject.

In this one example are to be found the typical confusions observable in many discussions of Darwinism carried on by non-
scientists and even by scientists when they are not scientizing.
First, there is by the very use of the terms an introduction of
values into a descriptive construct, or the misinterpretation of
descriptive terms by ascribing to the words a moral significance
and to the author a moral intention. The roots of this error are
to be found in the ancient exhortation that nature should be our
basic model for right behavior. Not surprisingly it is constantly
assumed that the *Origin* rests on moral assumptions: that a value
statement may be verified in the same way that an empirical or
predictive statement is verified is an attitude that only a small
fraction of human beings have yet outgrown, and that in only a
small part of their behavior. The difficulty arose because Darwin
did not have the word "ecology." He was in fact an ecological
thinker, and in ecology words like "competition" and "cooperation" are too inexact, too value-weighted, too metaphorical, and
too anthropomorphic to be used at all.

Second, scientific statements are continuously subjected not only to moral interpretations but also, and more subtly, to metaphysical interpretations. Hence, the unconscious ascription to the *Origin* of a metaphysic. Darwin is said to have discovered the law of evolution, according to which the universe is characterized by a steady growth in richness and complexity and excellence. Now Herbert Spencer formulated a law of evolution, but there is no such law in the *Origin*. In fact, in the fourth edition there is a brief but profoundly important passage at the beginning of Chapter Four in which Darwin specifically disclaims any knowledge of and any statements about laws of nature, which he clearly labels mental conveniences, or constructs. He is a scientist, not a moralist and not a metaphysician, and he knows it. Unfortunately, most humanists then and now have little notion of what a scientist is and does. They are interested in metaphysics and morals, and when a science seems to have a metaphysical and moral implication, or when a scientist assumes another role and makes metaphysical and moral statements, then only do they evince interest and subject themselves to what they think are scientific influences.[1]

It will be apparent from what I have said so far that the problem of the impact of the *Origin* upon the culture of the last 100 years is a complex one. It involves, above all, the question, what is the difference between "Darwinian" and "Darwinistic" (that is, between those propositions and implied assumptions which may be properly ascribed to a source in the *Origin* and those propositions and derived assumptions which are not properly so ascribed). I shall attempt to clear the way for future studies of the *Origin* and literature, using "literature" generally and loosely.

[1] The question of the influence of the *Origin* hangs on not merely, what is Darwinism? or, what is the Darwinism of the *Origin*? but also on what is the Darwinism to be found in which edition of the *Origin*? In my recent variorum text of the work are to be found between 15 and 20 thousand individual variants, or well over seven thousand sentence variants, a sentence variant ranging from the exclusion or addition of a sentence to a minor and apparently nonsemantic change in punctuation. The majority of these are probably of not very great importance, but there are thousands of sentence variants of crucial significance. The collation of these variants reveals how difficult the question of Darwinian influence really is, but at least in the future it will be possible to find out if Darwin really made a statement ascribed to him.

The question to be answered, then, is, what was the Darwinian and Darwinistic impact of the *Origin* upon Western culture? But even this is much too vague. How is the culture of the past available and what do we mean by "culture"? It is said that historical investigation is concerned with the events of the past. But of course past events are not observable, and so we are left with the question as to what in fact the historian observes. The problem may be tackled somewhat crudely, though I think not naïvely, by observing what the historian actually does. He is engaged in the manipulation (with all that the word implies) of documents and artifacts. These are his data, not past events. The empirical referent of his "History," that is, his construct which purports to refer to the events of the past, or "history," is his own operations with those documents and artifacts which he assumes to have had an existence prior to the moment he began examining them. His History is a linguistic construct, characterized by what he hopes is at least an intuitive consistency, designed to justify his work. Since internal inconsistencies are always discoverable in his construct, and since his collection of documents and artifacts is never complete, nor its degree of completeness ever known, History, like any science, is characterized by instability. (Like physics, it is always being reconstructed.) Thus the process of historiography is the consequence of a continuous interaction, manipulated by historians, between construct and data.

One particular problem remains:[2] what is the model of the historian's construct? Such models certainly are now, and perhaps

---

[2] Another question is more easily answered and is less important to the problem of this essay, for the historian derives from his construct certain propositions which purport to predict where certain documents and artifacts may be found and what will characterize them when they are found. Thus a construct led me once to predict that certain unidentified watercolor illustrations to Milton would be found to have been prepared between 1790 and 1810 for copper engravings to illustrate an edition of *Paradise Lost*. An examination of such editions led to the discovery of one with such engravings and with the name of the artist. An intuitive construct of stylistic history had led me to predict that they had been done about 1800, and according to bibliographical information derived from the engravings themselves they could be dated in 1797 and 1798. Finally an intuitive model of the behavior of artists and publishers led me to conclude that the watercolors had not been done more than three or four years before the date of first publication.

always will be, intuitive. At least I know of no mathematical or logical model for a historical narrative. But though models for battles, parliamentary debates, and assassinations are probably pretty reliable, those for cultural history are probably not. In cultural history we are involved with matters of extraordinary difficulty and subtlety. Whereas the assassination of Lincoln was eminently observable at one time (there were witnesses; a reasonably consistent construct may be created of his murder and death), a priest may lose his religious belief and nobody be the wiser (Pater thought he could have a successful career as an Anglican clergyman with no religious belief whatsoever, and he was probably right). The difficulty lies in the fact that the locus of cultural history is covert behavior. When we realize that there is no such entity as "culture" but only human beings doing something, or behaving covertly, and that such behavior may or may not leave traces in documents and artifacts, the general problem of the inaccessibility of the past is twice compounded; for cultural behavior is not necessarily observable even when it is going on in a human being who is right before the observer's eyes or even, at times, when it is going on inside the observer. When we talk about "culture" in the old-fashioned way, or "high-level culture" in the modern way, we are referring somewhat vaguely to two kinds of data—first, recorded verbal behavior, sufficiently complex and highly valued to be called literature, philosophy, or science, and recorded sign systems of a parallel complexity which we call the visual and auditory arts; and, second, unrecorded and covert linguistic and aesthetic semiotic behavior. On the model of our own behavior, insofar as we can train ourselves to observe it and have done so, aided by various admittedly inadequate personality or psychological theories, we try to write cultural history. Now, we know very little about cultural transmission and cultural innovation at any level, let alone complex high-level transmission and innovation. It is not surprising that when we undertake to write cultural history we finish feeling a bit baffled and inadequate.

At least, however, we can now see our basic problem somewhat more precisely. On the one hand there are the Darwinian and Darwinistic documents, on the other, documents and artifacts which show Darwinian and Darwinistic influences, and in between, causally, we hope or assume for constructive purposes, connecting the two categories, a doubly inaccessible process of cultural history of which we wish to make a construct. But, alas! each part of the problem consists of a set of variables. For instance, a single Darwinistic sentence might have had a profoundly revolutionary impact upon the covert behavior of an individual, with the consequence that he wrote a single poem profoundly different from anything he had written before. (Did this happen in the case of Swinburne's "Hertha"?) Or a reading of the entire *Origin* might have had a slight impact which resulted, for the moment at least, in a fairly brief document. (Was this the case of Kingsley's famous letter which Darwin was so happy to quote in later editions in order to avert the theological lightning?) Or a very thorough reading of Darwinian and Darwinistic material might so confirm the already existing attitudes of an individual that he perceived nothing innovative. (Was this the case with Browning, whose post-*Origin* work indicates that he not only read Darwin but read him with such extreme care that frequent rereading is implied?) To analyze this range of variables is the next task.

I have already given one example of a fairly notorious confusion between Darwinism and Darwinisticism. I wish now to treat this problem more extensively, and particularly to indicate how the two came to be confused. I shall begin with one of the biggest questions, evolution itself. Evolution may be considered as a fairly straightforward metaphysical theory with a long history which was not so much confirmed by the theory of natural selection as embarrassed by it. The difference between the two is indicated by the fact that Darwin himself did not use the word until the fifth edition of the *Origin* (1869), and then he appears to have used it with some hesitation, almost as if he did not quite know what he was talking about. And no wonder. I have called it a metaphysical term, because it purports to make certain descriptive propositions about the structure of the universe. One way to indicate its significance is to employ a metaphysical distinction between appearance and reality and their relation to permanence and change. According to a nonevolutionary metaphysic the changes which we observe are only apparent; the reality of things lies in their permanence. The exalted status of Platonism in the Western tradition, both in theology and out of it, was one of the principal reinforcements of a nonevolutionary metaphysic. In his recent intellectual autobiography, *My Philosophical Development*, Bertrand Russell has related how his early interest in mathematics was stimulated by a desire to penetrate a world of ideal permanence and perfection, and he admits that he still has a certain regret that Wittgenstein persuaded him that mathematics and logic are tautological and do not refer to any such ideal realm. But Yeats, Russell's contemporary, and the hardheaded and profoundly antimetaphysical Nietzsche toyed with eternal recurrence, though how seriously they wished us to take them presents an apparently unresolved problem for their commentators. All of these men were post-*Origin*, and they all evince the distress which resulted from the apparent confirmation of metaphysical evolutionism by the scientific construct of natural selection.

For according to a metaphysic of evolution, the appearance lies in permanence, the reality lies in change. The permanence of things, whether houses or social institutions, is only a function of the fact that they change more slowly than we the observers do. But the difference between evolution and a Heraclitean doctrine that all things are a flowing lies in the proposition that evolution is directive. As I have indicated above, the claim that natural selection works in an orthogenetic or teleological fashion is an application to Darwinism of the already existent and widespread notion that the laws of nature direct the course of events to move toward a higher, purer, better state of affairs. I have encountered in recent years a theology which claims that the history of the universe is the history of God ridding himself and his creation of evil, and that the purpose of man's existence is to help God in this sublime task.

Hegel is, of course, the figure whom everyone thinks of in connection with metaphysical evolution, and "One far-off, divine event/Towards which the whole creation moves," the lines that everyone quotes. But the concept is ubiquitous in the earlier nine-

teenth century. It seems, at first glance, almost impossible that
Browning could have written Paracelsus' great final speech a
quarter of a century before the *Origin*. In the canceled stanzas of
the "Palace of Art,"[3] written even earlier, Tennyson applied metaphysical evolutionism to the data of science, specifically astronomy and geology. It is implicit in Carlyle's theory of history,
in which each inorganic period is less inorganic than the preceding
one, and each organic period more thoroughly organized than
its corresponding predecessor—an idea which seems to inform
The Idylls of the King, the first installment of which came out in
the same year as the *Origin*. Newman has both the notion of
progressive revelation and, of course, of the growth of doctrine.

The two essential ideas of metaphysical evolutionism are that
the world is an emergent world, with novelty continually being
introduced from outside or coming into existence by the nature
of the evolutionary process, and that it is an irreversible and a
nonrepetitive world; evolution has direction.

Even before Darwin, as Tennyson's stanzas suggest, there had
been apparently scientific substantiations of the evolutionary
metaphysic. Ever since 1839, J.P. Nichol, the astronomer, had
been writing and rewriting a whole series of books popularizing
astronomy. Over and over again, basing his conclusions on the
nebular observations of the younger William Herschel, he had
painted a picture of a universe in the process of creation and in
1855 had used the word "evolution" to describe it. It is hardly
necessary to point out how Lyell gave apparent confirmation to
the notion at the geological level. Yet the evolutionary metaphysic
is not necessarily or logically connected with scientific constructs
about the biologic past. The term "the development hypothesis,"
which was employed throughout the century until in the 1860's
"evolution" took its place, is considerably more descriptive and

[3] Hither, when all the deep unsounded skies
    Shuddered with silent stars, she clomb,
And as with optic glasses her keen eyes
    Pierced through the mystic dome.

Regions of lucid matter taking forms,
    Brushes of fire, hazy gleams,
Clusters and beds of worlds, and bee-like swarms
    Of suns, and starry streams.

relatively free from the metaphysical implications of "evolution."

To understand what happened, it is necessary to keep the distinction between the two quite clear. The development hypothesis was a scientific hypothesis concerned with the problem of how biological species originate. Are they specially created by God, or do they somehow or other develop out of already existent species? As early as 1827 Lyell wrote in a private letter that he believed the latter, but since he had no explanation of how it could have happened, he had to use, in his great *Geology*, the theory of special creation. The scientists were of course perfectly aware of the implications, for contemporary theologians, of denying the theory of special creation, and they had no desire to get into trouble unless for a good scientific cause. Hence their lack of interest in Chambers' *Vestiges of Creation*, and even annoyance with it, for it aroused theological fury to no good scientific purpose, simply substituting one metaphysic for another. What was above all necessary was a scientific explanation of what a great many scientists were quite prepared to accept, the origin of species from pre-existing species.

The crux of the matter is revealed by comparing Spencer's essays and books with the *Origin*. In his introduction to the *General Principles* Spencer complained that Darwin had received credit for establishing biologic evolution, although, in fact, he had already revealed the truth several years before. And of course a great many people, particularly in the United States, believed him. Yet Spencer had all but disappeared from contemporary culture while the current scientific theory of biologic evolution still has a firm, if partial, place for Darwin's theory of natural selection and admits and insists that the *Origin* was the foundation for all subsequent work. Scientifically, Spencer's theories on the subject were of no importance; they were entirely metaphysical, more complicated than Chambers' but not less naïve. Spencer uttered a law of evolution; Darwin proposed a theory of the origin of species from pre-existent species.

In the later chapters of his *Great Chain of Being*, A. O. Lovejoy has shown how metaphysical evolutionism emerged from a kind of static, Platonic thinking which had dominated the Western mind for over two millennia. In my "Toward a Theory of Romanticism," I attempted to show some of the cultural forces responsible for that shift in metaphysics. Using the argument of that essay, and developing it further, I should like here to suggest how the evolutionary metaphysic, although it had an unimportant previous existence, was accepted and developed in the early nineteenth century.

To use the terminology of that article, the "Negative Romantic" was left without any metaphysic and without any theoretic basis for morality. In his isolated state he was thrown back upon himself. But since it is extremely difficult to maintain a total spiritual death for a very long period, some of the Negative Romantics simply returned to former beliefs. But others turned to a new metaphysic, which in its many forms can be generally subsumed under the rubric of evolutionism as I have defined it above. In this process of recovery there were usually two stages. First came the stripping bare of the self, the discovery of the ego as the basic datum of experience. That revelation is one of the principle themes of works as various as *The Prelude*, the "Ancient Mariner," *Sartor Resartus*, the paintings of Constable after 1808, of Caspar David Friedrich beginning about the same time, and of Turner after 1827. It is the subject of Berlioz's *Harold in Italy* and of Schumann's piano cycles of the 1830's. It is the theme of *The Red and the Black* and even, faintly enough, *Rob Roy*. This discovery of a basic datum, however, was not sufficient. It had to be connected with the rest of the world; the problem of how to get from the self to the world remained to be solved. For its solution there was only the data of the self and its experiences, of which now the most important event was the recovery or rebirth consequent upon the discovery of the self. If the self is the model of the world, and if the process of the self in moving from negation to affirmation is its essential character, it then followed that the character of the world is not merely process but process directed toward a goal.

The weakness of this position was precisely in assuming that the self was a model of the world; but that assumption could be and was easily overlooked, for Western culture was filled with all sorts of notions which would provide the bridge between self and world. Hence the mental construct by which the processes of the personality were organized under the terms "self" or "ego" or "Ich" or "I" was projected upon the experienced world, and, as Coleridge put it, the act was substituted for the fact. The tremendous emotional force behind this projection made it easy to find its confirmation, first, in already existent evolutionary metaphysics, and second, in apparent scientific confirmations of evolutionary metaphysics. The total development is perhaps most clearly outlined in *Paracelsus*, which reveals Browning as a man who grasped the Romantic culture of his century with astonishing profundity. Hence it is no accident that the conclusion of the poem sounds like an anticipation of Darwin[4]—to one who has not really understood the *Origin*.

In 1859 a metaphysic of goal-directed organic growth was dominant in the higher levels of Western culture. Canon Raven has pointed out that the agitation produced by Darwin cannot be understood without reference to the *Essays and Reviews*, which appeared only a few months after, or to Colenso's work, which appeared in 1862. The academic difficulties of Max Müller and of Benjamin Jowett are equally inseparable from the total situation. Today it is somewhat difficult to understand why all of these books and events should have been interconnected in the covert culture of the day. But a reading of *Essays and Reviews* shows the deep penetration of metaphysical evolutionism into the minds of its authors. That was their offense: they were addressing a world of a lower cultural level which still lived by a static metaphysic. I have referred to Newman's speculation about the possibility of applying his ideas of development to the biological world, and he

---

[4] Paracelsus describes the formation of the surface of the earth, then the coming of vegetation, insects, birds, land-animals, and he continues:

> Thus he [God] dwells in all,
> From life's minute beginnings, up at last
> To man—the consummation of this scheme
> Of being, the completion of this sphere
> Of life: whose attributes had here and there
> Been scattered o'er the visible world before,
> Asking to be combined, dim fragments meant
> To be united in some wondrous whole,
> Imperfect qualities throughout creation,
> Suggesting some one creature yet to make,
> Some point where all those scattered rays should meet
> Convergent in the faculties of man.

has been praised for his profundity in thus anticipating and understanding Darwin. But the praise has come from individuals who did not themselves understand Darwin, for in fact the *Origin* was an embarrassment to the metaphysical evolutionists.

The evolutionists were already used to having their metaphysic apparently confirmed by scientific developments. Lyell and Herschel and Nichol seemed to support them, and they took the *Vestiges of Creation* to be a scientific work. Consequently, there is no indication that the *Origin* disturbed Tennyson, for example, or Newman, or George Eliot. "Hertha," again, is a good example. Written in the latter half of the 1860's, it appears to be a perfect instance of the impact of Darwin. Yet it can just as well be thought of as a humanistic and antireligious interpretation of the concluding speech of *Paracelsus*. It could have been written had the *Origin* never been published. That it was written as a consequence of the *Origin* seems highly probable, but as a consequence of a misunderstanding of the *Origin*. For the biologic world that Darwin revealed, if you do not read him with the assumptions of metaphysical evolutionism as instruments for understanding the book, is a world totally lacking in the organized and teleological process characteristic of evolutionary metaphysics. New species come into existence by a process which can only be described as accidental. If a species has a range of variations among its individuals such that when the environment of the species changes, hitherto nonadaptive variations are selected as means of survival, a new species will in the course of time emerge, provided that the change in environment is not so great as to cause the total extinction of the species and provided that the population of the species is sufficient to maintain itself during the period of the development of the new species out of the old. No organism, Darwin said, is as perfectly adapted as it might be. That is, it includes within its population instincts and organs which are not instrumental to its environmental adaptation, although in its ancestry at some time or other such organs and instincts were adaptive. (To be sure, Darwin was not very certain about this and proposed other reasons, particularly morphology, for nonadaptive organs.) Further, there are numerous instances not only of extinction but of total or partial regression, or regression at some stage of an organism's life cycle. Nor is there any reason to believe that natural selection operates in a morally or metaphysically progressive fashion. Indeed, from the *Origin* it is very easy to conclude that the more complex an organism the less its chances to survive. It is impossible to find in the *Origin* a basis in the biological world for any kind of orthogenesis or goal-directed process. Consequently it has been misread or simply not read at all, though discussed by all varieties of metaphysical evolutionists from Newman to Gerald Heard and current Catholic theologians.

Thus the grand thesis of metaphysical evolutionism—from simple to complex means from good to better, infinitely or finitely, as your metaphysical taste determines—not only received no support from the *Origin* but, if the book were properly understood and if the individual involved felt that a metaphysic should and could have scientific support, was positively demolished. Hence the curious spectacle, to be found so often, of orthodox fundamentalist Christians and anti-Christian or quasi-Christian metaphysical evolutionists ranged side by side in opposition to Darwin. And hence the equally curious spectacle of other metaphysical and Christian evolutionists swallowing the book without even a catch in the throat.

But the book presented an even deeper problem of which very few were apparently aware, although it was implied in the early editions and was clearly spelled out in the fourth. In the middle of the century most scientists characteristically conceived their task as discovering the laws of nature. Newton's law of gravity was held to be unrepealable, and for 150 years law had been gradually replacing Providence at the higher cultural levels. To be sure there were exceptions. Newman preferred to believe that the weather was controlled by angels, and he has several very pretty passages on the subject. But for the most part advanced thinkers felt like Nichol, who in 1839 hailed the advent of the comprehension of nature through discoverable laws and rejoiced at the disappearance of the capricious ways of Providence. He felt it added greatly to the dignity of God to think that He governed the world through laws and not through unpredictable willfulness. It is hard not to see the influence here of political liberalism. Or perhaps it is the other way around. Certainly the two seem to be connected, for the idea of the subjection of the Crown to the rational laws of elected representatives, the progress away from capricious tyranny, is remarkably like Nichol's conception. An Enlightenment idea, it was a basic ingredient of most Romantic metaphysics and fundamental to evolutionary metaphysics. The metaphor unconsciously used seems too transparent to be missed, and yet it was missed. The notion was that just as it is possible to study the political behavior of a people and hence deduce its laws, so it is possible to study the behavior of nature and arrive at the laws which govern it. It was a notion particularly appealing to Englishmen, who, because of the peculiar and highly admired nature of the English Constitution, were in part governed by written laws and in part by laws not spelled out in a written constitution in the style of the infidel Bentham and the misguided Americans but implicit in the political structure of the nation. In nature the laws are there, they are immanent in the natural world, and it is the will of God that in our enlightened progress we should discover them. Constant reference to such economic ideas as the law of supply and demand continually reinforced such concepts; and it is typical that Ruskin's aesthetic and socio-economic writings are filled with laws of this and laws of that.

The *Origin* did not fit into this conception at all. Not only was an apparently accidental world revealed, but even if one insisted upon discovering an order in the apparent chaos of the biological world, the incredible intricacy of ecological relations was such that Darwin himself felt that a full comprehension was beyond him or any human being. When biology can be studied mathematically—and biologists are making progress in that direction, particularly in genetics—perhaps a few people will comprehend the biologic world, but it is too much for mathematically unorganized descriptive language.

Thus at the time there were frequent complaints that Darwin did not really reveal the laws of nature. The culture was still penetrated by the Baconian notion that the laws of nature not only were immanent, because they had been put there by God, but also were few in number and essentially simple, because God had so designed them that the human mind might understand them. The culture accepted the Baconian notion that if one assembled all the data pertinent to a line of inquiry, the true relations between the separate bits of data and the laws that governed them would reveal themselves. Again we find, metaphysically, the desire to penetrate into a world of pure order.

But Darwin's notion of scientific law was empiricistic and extraordinarily modern. He implies it in his superb discussion of the term "species" and its related words. He demonstrates that to the term there is no corresponding reality or entity in the biologic world. It is essential to his argument that species should not be regarded as fixed, and he disproves their fixity not so much by aligning data as by analyzing the term to demonstrate that the attempt to find distinct species in nature is necessarily fruitless, since the term is only of convenience in creating hypotheses, or, as we should say today, constructs. Further, he spelled his notion out in additions made to the opening of Chapter Four in the fourth edition. To him a scientific law was a mental convenience. The mind organized the data into meaningful structures; it did not discover the principles of organization immanent within the data. To a certain extent his public was at least intuitively aware of this position and responded to it negatively. Nevertheless for the most part the legalists of nature simply derived from the *Origin* further proof of their arguments. It is yet another example of how Darwinism was converted into Darwinisticism and is comparable and related to the similar absorption of the *Origin* and natural selection into metaphysical evolutionism.

There are further variables in this part of the basic question, such as adaptation, economy, and morality. Huxley, in his Romanes lecture, and Mill, earlier, in *Three Essays on Religion*, concluded that the ancient "Follow nature" as a basis for morality was in error, and that if a genuine morality were to be developed it must be on a purely human basis, indifferent to and even opposed to the workings of evolution. The economists, as we have seen, followed a different course, and with the aid of Spencer found in the *Origin* a basis for their own morality. And in the matter of adaptation, the final basis of British empirical theology, the notion of perfect adaptation of organism to environment was washed away by the *Origin*. Consequently, as might have been expected, Darwinisticism in the field of moralized psychology has used Darwin as a basis for attempting to make perfect adaptation of the individual personality to its social environment into the criterion of psychological health. There can be located still other variables, but I have attempted to go into at least two of the problems involved in the impact of the *Origin* in order to show the profound difference between Darwinism and Darwinisticism. Darwinism is a scientific theory about the origin of biologic species from pre-existent species, the mechanism of that process being an extraordinarily complex ecology which can be observed only in fairly small and artificially isolated instances. It reveals a world not of accident precisely but rather one in which "accident" becomes a meaningless problem. Darwinisticism can be an evolutionary metaphysic about the nature of reality and the universe. It can be a metaphysical and simplicistic notion of natural law. It can be an economic theory, or a moral theory, or an aesthetic theory, or a psychological theory. It can be anything which claims to have support from the *Origin*, or conversely anything which claims to have really understood what Darwin inadequately and partially presented. Once one is aware of the distinction, much which is ascribed to Darwin and much which appears to be Darwinian in the cultural documents of the past 100 years turns out not to be Darwinian at all but Darwinistic. Is it true that what Darwin said had very little impact, but that what people thought he said, that is, what they already believed and believed to have been confirmed by Darwin, had an enormous impact?

We appear to be faced with a curious problem, not with the impact of Darwinism but with the absence of impact. The answer, or at least some insight into the possible structure of an answer, lies in the area which I have called covert culture. We need, to begin with, a formula or model which will do something to explain not the rejection of the *Origin*, which is not too difficult to understand, but the perverting and self-deluding acceptance of the work. The following formulation will serve, I think, as a start.

When a human being encounters a stimulus which cannot be fitted into an existent orientation, the fundamental tendency is either to negate the value and importance of the stimulus or to inhibit its effect, either by denying its existence or by misinterpreting it. Beyond this range at one end we have dying of fright and at the other the highly sophisticated effort not to do away with the stimulus but to restructure the disturbed orientation without misinterpreting the stimulus. The two extremes are fairly rare, and perhaps, if we include the entire human race, equally rare. The arrival at a new high-level orientation requires high intelligence, a personality strong enough to endure considerable disturbance and frustration without collapsing or putting up defenses, a high-level culture, and—very probably the most important factor—willingness to endure considerable loss of energy. For maintaining a pattern involves loss of energy, but creating and maintaining a novel pattern, particularly one not reinforced by the environment, involves even greater loss. It is easy now to range the responses to the *Origin* in a kind of order: those who totally rejected it; those who completely misunderstood it; those who incorporated it into their existing set of attitudes by misinterpreting it; and finally those who understood it and subjected their personal cultures to a complete restructuring.

The history of high-level culture is the history of complex and richly structured orientations. Considering the rarity of thoroughgoing re-orientations, it is by no means surprising, it is indeed to be expected, that the history of the impact of Darwinism should principally have been a history of rejection or misinterpretation.

By talking of "kinds" of orientation I refer to their function in the culture of the time. At any time a stimulus which conflicts with an existent orientation is disturbing, and Darwin is still capable of being very disturbing. It is difficult to absorb the fact, but for the most part our total culture has still been only very superficially affected by Darwinism. In May, 1959, I was interviewed over a Philadelphia radio station on the *Origin*; it was a program in which the listeners are encouraged to telephone in questions and comments. The first call was from a woman to whom Darwin was a vicious man, ideas about biological evolution worthless, and I an ignorant and evil person for encouraging the young even to be aware of such notions. I must confess to having been a bit startled that the cultural conditions responsible for the Scopes monkey trial were still so active. The promptness and vehemence of her message were interesting, and equally interesting was her refusal not only to consider reading the *Origin* but even to say why Darwin and I were so utterly wrong and bad. Similarly, a recent book by Gertrude Himmelfarb, written at a higher cultural level, attempts to dismiss Darwin by raising evolutionary problems long since out of date and, most significantly, by appealing to the authority of Kierkegaard and Bergson and by ridiculing Darwin's metaphysical knowledge and abilities. In both instances one has a feeling that the anger and, in the second case, the sophisticated contempt conceal fear. Certainly, the *Origin* has always displayed an extraordinary capacity for arousing anger and fear.

The reason for the fear is to be found in the fact that between any orientation and a reorientation comes a stage of disorientation. An orientation functions as a means of reinforcing the sense of identity, and it would seem that another way of referring to the sense of identity is to speak of the sense of value. (I mean the conviction that life is worth the trouble it takes to live it, as irrational a proposition as one could well arrive at.) For instance, the denial of the adequacy of a religion or a metaphysic, since it implies a denial of the system of values apparently derived from it and dependent upon it, involves guilt as well as fear. Anger, fear, guilt, the loss of value and values, and the loss of identity were therefore the great themes of what I have called the literature of Negative Romanticism. In Coleridge and in Byron, for example, the whole nexus of emotions is symbolized by the inability to love, inversely expressed in Wagner's *Flying Dutchman* by the inability to be loved.

This may seem a long way from Darwin, and yet I think it is not. Reading from bottom to top, it is possible to discern a limited range of religious and metaphysical orientations current in 1859. The lowest level of higher culture was occupied by the believers in Providence. Such a "metaphysic" is perhaps the most primitive way of maintaining stability of personality and the sense of value in the face of the unpredicted and the accidental. It simply states that accidents are not accidents; they are willed by a Deity who controls, from behind the scenes, the sparrow's fall. Next comes the notion of transcendent order, of which the observed world is only the dark and confused shadow. A step higher, at least historically, is immanent order, natural law or cause-effect determinism. Both were often enough the underpinning of an evolutionism. Next came what was perhaps the most modern, confined, I think, to a very few individuals (or at least to very few who left documents), of whom Browning was, or was to be after 1859, the most important. I would call it Radical Romanticism. It assumed, as Browning put it as early as *Sordello*, that great and wickedly neglected poem, that any metaphysic is only temporary, that as soon as we arrive at a solution to a metaphysical problem, or any problem, that very solution immediately gives birth to a new problem and is incorporated within it. This is essentially a psychological and skeptical metaphysic, not to be confused with Hegel's, which is both less subtle and more rigid. Its classic statement was given by Rimbaud with his realization that a new orientation could only be arrived at by a willed disorientation totally devoid of any expectancy, even, of a new orientation. Finally there was the skepticism descended from Hume, which led a very faint life indeed, and was generally felt at the time to be quite unendurable.

Dismissing the strategy of outright rejection, we can for each of these deduce first an incorporation of the *Origin* by perversion and second a thoroughgoing disorientation; a reorientation can take any form: Darwinian, Darwinistic, or something quite disconnected from either. The *Origin* implied at least four fundamental orientations: the biological world, and by implication the entire empirical world, is a complexity beyond our comprehension; it is possible to create mental constructs which make sense out of the data; these constructs are most satisfactory if characterized not by straight-line cause-effect thinking but by ecological thinking, that is, by the observation of patterns of relationships within and among fields abstracted from empirical reality; one can hope for increasingly complex and reliable constructs.

Providential thinking incorporated the *Origin* by ignoring most of this and seizing upon the accidental nature of the emergence of new species. It triumphantly insisted that the only possible explanation of such emergence was the operation of the Providential Will. But even that much of the *Origin* was disastrous to a Providential thinking which perceived that the emergence of new species with its waste and suffering could not possibly be reconciled with a beneficent Providence. Hence the bleakness and despair of those whose Providentialism was shattered and who were unequipped to discover a new orientation. This seems to have been what happened to Yeats, and before him to Morris. The Prologue to *The Earthly Paradise* presents a very Darwinian world, beyond comprehension, filled with disconnected gratification and suffering and horror, and populated with a wide variety of false gods.

The effect of the *Origin* upon the orientation of transcendental order was a little more subtle. Whereas not many Providentialists were able to exploit Darwinism, England and the West in general, in the post-*Origin* years, saw an immense revival of Platonism and its related and derivative orientations. It was essentially a defensive reaction, and the dislike of Darwin exhibited by such Platonists as More and Babbitt is an example of how powerfully ideas of transcendental order were challenged. The *Origin* gave science an enormous new vitality and status, and that in turn gave the various antiscientific transcendentalisms immense new energy. But Darwin's uncompromising empiricism meant that if the *Origin* were fully accepted, Platonism and idealism, like Providentialism, crumbled. There is perhaps no logical reason why they should have crumbled, but we are here dealing not with logical relations but with covert culture, which works by half-unconscious and intuitively perceived consistencies. The rigid idealist with profound emotional commitments to his idealism simply erected higher and thicker defenses. The flexible and nondogmatic idealist was disturbed.

As we have seen, the various forms of natural law, the forms of immanent order, including evolutionism, could most easily, of the higher orientations, incorporate Darwinism by misrepresentation and create that odd amalgam, Darwinisticism. It is easy to see today, after the peculiar fate that has overtaken classical physics, that natural law is ultimately antiscientific, although it appears to be scientific on the surface and is, up to a certain point. It is not, therefore, surprising that the effect of Darwinism upon natural law was to popularize it. Similarly, there was a strong reinforcement of cause-effect Determinism. Classical physicists were particularly disagreeable to Darwin, and Huxley himself abandoned his determinism only after some time, perceiving that it was not scientific but Calvinistic. We should remember that the physicists were quite wrong in their insistence, to the great embarrassment of Darwin and to the weakening of his argument, that the earth was not old enough for biological evolution to have taken place. It seems to me unquestionable that the position of Darwin on the nature of science was more advanced than that of the physicists. Yet, because of the superficial content of science in the orientation of natural law and determinism, the disorientation effected by Darwin was to increase that content and to convert its metaphysical content into a heuristic function, even before the heuristic concept of law had been formulated.

It was the "Radical Romantic" who could most readily (with the exception of the Humean skeptic) accept the *Origin*. The Radical Romantic's view of the world as a never-ending series of solutions and dissolutions not only corresponded with Darwin's world, but his concept of moments of vision into the heart of things from which neither moral nor metaphysical nor empirical propositions could be derived was not too far away from Darwin's conception of scientific knowledge as not final. Nevertheless, because of the instability of holding a truth which is expected not to remain a truth or to be eventually revealed as unreliable, Radical Romanticism constantly threatens to turn into a stable metaphysic. But in spite of this weakness, it created the modern environment in which science, the scientific orientation, and skepticism could flourish. Part of the reason for this lay in the fact that it was more interested in patterns than in cause-effect relationships. The Radical Romantic in his moments of vision tended to see truth as a pattern of relationships.

It is thus no accident that Nietzsche, for all his revilings of Darwinisticism, appears in a post-Darwinian world, and that Existentialism, the most recent form of Radical Romanticism, should have followed not long after, built as it is upon Nietzsche and an early Radical Romantic, Kierkegaard. As the case of Browning shows, Radical Romanticism was the least disturbed of all orientations in the post-*Origin* period (except, again, for Humean skepticism, as revived not only by Huxley but far more profoundly by Ernst Mach).

My purpose here has been to create a construct by which the impact of Darwinism might be investigated rather than actually do the investigation itself, and I must leave it to the reader, if he finds the construct useful, to make what use of it he can. However, I should like to examine a couple of literary documents and a pair of writers in order to show how the construct may be used.

I shall begin with some comments on *The Return of the Native*, written within 15 years of the first publication of the *Origin*. If in *Under the Greenwood Tree* we seem to be living in a kind of idyllic Providential world, and in *Far from the Madding Crowd* in a causal world, in the *Native* we have an entirely different picture. It is true that, to begin with, coincidence, or, more accurately, accident, is indeed the means whereby the story is carried on.[5] The vision that we live in a world in which the unexpected, the unanticipated, the totally unpredictable rules our lives can be unbearable, when it is insisted on. However, Hardy holds the story together from the outside. Behind the series of unpredicted events, providing not a causal but a patterned inevitability, lies the cycle of the year. The lovers meet as the sun is turning north, their love grows as the sun moves northward, it is consummated in marriage very nearly at the summer solstice, by September it has begun to go wrong, and the final tragedy occurs in late November, when once again the sun is sinking towards its southernmost point. This pattern is further reinforced by subtle references

[5] Some incidents from my own experience in teaching this novel are particularly pertinent. Some 20 years ago in a Southern college which shall be nameless I had the task of trying to persuade a group of badly educated freshmen to grasp the book. They objected to it violently. They had been taught in high school that a good novel or play does not depend for its plot progressions and resolutions on coincidence. Hardy's novel does depend on coincidence. Therefore it is a bad novel. Again and again I explained that that was Hardy's whole point. They always said that they understood, but at the next meeting of the class the same objection would be brought up again. I fear I failed. Ten years later I was relating my experience to a colleague in a Northern university. He was most condescending, not only to freshmen and Southern freshmen, but especially to me, for my failure in not getting the students to grasp the point. "However," he added, "there's one thing in Hardy I can't swallow. In *Tess* everything hinges on the fact that the letter goes *under* the carpet." Here are two good examples of how profoundly the orientation of causality has penetrated our culture. Reading detective stories is a kind of a metaphysical ritual for reinforcing it. But the *Native* clearly does not belong to that kind of orientation.

to the time of day, particularly in the latter part of the novel, in which the crucial September scenes take place in the afternoon and the final November scenes not long after sunset. But there is a further element of organization: the opening description of Egdon Heath, the careful topography, without which the catastrophe cannot be understood and could not have happened in the way it did, the mixed racial background of Eustacia, Clem's alienation from his native attitudes by his residence in Paris—a thousand big and little elements which show the relation of the characters to their cultural and natural environment and equally their violations of those relations. One great theme of the novel is the ecological relation of personality to, in the anthropological sense, the landscape.

All three of these elements—accident beyond our anticipation or comprehension, control of structure by pattern, ecological thinking—are Darwinian. To be sure, Hardy might have derived the notion of the seasonal cycle from the folklorists, anthropologists, and archaeologists of his day, but they in their turn had been strongly influenced by the *Origin*. And no doubt there is already something of Schopenhauer and von Hartmann in the work. But these last influences on Hardy seem to me to govern more the later novels. The *Native* exhibits, to my mind, a profoundly Darwinian orientation, even to the implication that we can never fully understand the world in which we live, and our relation to it.

My second example comes from something apparently highly remote, though almost contemporaneous, Pater's *Renaissance*, a superbly structured book, from the opening Preface to the famous Conclusion. But its structure—and this is perhaps why it has been taken to be merely a collection of only historically related essays with a conclusion tacked on—is not the structure of logic, which, it is to be remembered, was thought of as descriptive of the cause-effect structure of reality. Rather it is organized, first by the recurrence of themes, and second by Pater's delicate revelation that in each of the individuals or works discussed is to be found a similarity of pattern, the orientational patterns of the modern world, gradually emerging from an early Gothic love story through Leonardo to Winckelman, and crystal clear only in the Conclusion. Here again, I think, is a Darwinian kind of thinking, but much more Darwinian is another ingredient in the basic structure of the Conclusion.

I have pointed out that one of the shocks administered by Darwin to theology was that the one thing which remained un-attacked in the eighteenth-nineteenth-century argument from de-sign, or natural theology, was the perfect adaptation of organism to environment, a subject on which the Bridgewater lectures had been so wearisomely explicit. But Darwin, of course, had revealed that the whole mechanism of natural selection and the origin of species depended upon the imperfect, or less than perfect, adap-tation of organism to environment. Now this, I believe, is the basic assumption for the argument that we should burn with a hard, gemlike flame. In terms of the history of Romanticism, Pater was applying to art, to religion, to metaphysics, to morality, ex-actly the pattern of the momentary spots of time which Words-worth had applied to nature. The problem of the disoriented or Negative Romantic was to re-create the sense of value by estab-lishing an orientation which would relate the self to the universe. Hence Wordsworth makes a romantic and psychological adap-tation of the argument from design, which was already current, when in the passage from the *Recluse* quoted in the Preface to the *Excursion* he speaks of how exquisitely the mind is adapted to the universe. Because of this adaptation we can make the transi-tion from self to nature and perceive it as a symbol of the Divine, or value. But Pater, the post-Darwinian who had lost his Christian faith even before the publication of the *Origin*, can make no such leap. As he sees it, the mind, the emotions, the personality are not adapted to the conditions of human existence. Rather, ideas, whether metaphysical, theological, or moral, are instruments of adaptation by which we adjust ourselves to the world. They are not final truths, nor ever can be. They are, rather, adaptational illusions, but far more satisfactory than any of these is the work of art, since it gives the highest value to the disconnected mo-ments of the personality as they appear and does not pretend to be true. Art, therefore, is the most successful of our adaptational mechanisms. Admittedly, this is in part to translate Pater into Darwinian terms, but it seems irresistible that Pater is saying that the world cannot be known and that our modes of knowing and experiencing are instruments of the observer, not modes of comprehending metaphysical or even scientific truth.

The case of Pater indicates how delicate and subtle is the problem of Darwinian influence. There is always the possibility of cultural convergence. Perhaps he could have come to these conclusions had it not been for Darwinism, but it seems most unlikely. At any rate, that is a question that cannot be answered. We can only say that in the *Origin* is a locus of a novel orientation, and that it seems not to be a misinterpretation of Pater to discover the same orientations in his work. Presumably, the Darwinian orientation entered into Pater's covert culture and left important traces in the Conclusion to the *Renaissance*.

In conclusion, we can examine briefly two figures both currently of great cultural importance, Nietzsche and Freud. In Nietzsche's concept of the will to power (by which he did not mean political tyranny) we have a highly Darwinian notion of the desire to control our environment. This desire has no transcendental source. Rather its roots are physiological within the individual and ultimately biological. The will to power is a way of stating the endless and never-to-be-consummated drive to adapt ourselves to our environment. Hence, for all the suffering in the world, the power of joy is deeper than suffering. The drive towards a sense of value is greater than all its frustrations. The "will to power" thus brings Darwin's ecological vision within the reach of human psychology and human morality.

In the same way Freud, who refused to read Nietzsche because he feared his own originality might be thereby damaged—thus showing that he knew something about him—presents neurosis not only as the repetition of a pattern but something from which everyone suffers and which can never be entirely overcome. Hence analysis is endless. We can never make the perfect adaptation. The only complete adaptation is to adapt our neuroses to those of others in our social environment, to conform; but that is a counsel of despair. It is in the endless effort to solve the unsolvable that Freud finds his peculiar grim optimism closely resembling both Darwin's and Nietzsche's. Yet in Freud we find another example of Darwinisticism, of turning a Darwinian perception into a metaphysic. Implicit and explicit in Freud is an idea which has been so overdeveloped by naïve dogmatic Freudians that it completely dominates their thinking. That notion is that in the psychological world there are no accidents, that all is determined, that cause and effect rule everywhere, and that everything in the individual's psychological past can be understood and accounted for.

It is not surprising that a Freudian metaphysic has become most popular in those areas and levels of Western culture which, to a considerable degree through the impact of Darwinism and Darwinisticism, have been most thoroughly secularized. It has filled the vacuum left by the departure of religion and metaphysics; but the drives of Providentialism are still with us. This new metaphysic, now so popular at middle-class American cultural levels, is only another example of how Darwinisticism has perverted Darwinism, and how the *Origin* has had far less impact than have other orientations, both already existent and more recently emergent, which have misused and misinterpreted that great book for the purposes of their own survival.

11

AESTHETICISM TO MODERNISM:

FULFILLMENT OR REVOLUTION?

[1967*]

A number of years ago I published an article with the title "Modern Art, the Triumph of Romanticism." The only thing about the essay that I can still accept is the title. Today the notion is widespread, though perhaps not yet a platitude, that the breakthrough into the modern styles of the various arts was in the direct line of the kind of artistic and philosophical values that originated in the years on either side of 1800, and that modern art was the first true fulfillment of those ideals. To be sure, among the members of a generation older even than my own, within the circle of the New Critics and their immediate followers, the prevailing idea of the 1920's, 1930's, and 1940's, that modern literature was a revolution against Victorian values, still obtains; but the New Critics are beginning to look old-fashioned, even a little quaint. In the study of music, painting, and architecture, however,

* Reprinted by permission from *Mundus Artium*, I (Winter, 1967), pp. 36–55. Copyright 1967 by Rainer Schulte and Roma A. King, Jr.

the feeling that the modern styles, those that originated toward the end of the first decade of this century, were a realization of the Romantic program seems to be increasingly common. Even in the early 1920's Schönberg changed his mind about the music of Mahler, which, when he was engaged in his own reorganization of musical composition, he found totally unacceptable. Once his new style had been achieved, he was able to see not only the great value and beauty of Mahler's music, but its historical importance, even to himself.

Yet in this conception of stylistic history there lurks a very considerable problem. It comes out in Henry-Russell Hitchcock's judgment that Art Nouveau was the first modern style. For reasons I shall take up later, I believe this decision to be in error. Nevertheless, it has the virtue of suggesting that from Art Nouveau to Modernism there was a continuity, that they were not separated by a revolutionary break; yet it tends to gloss over the strikingly different character of the two styles. To be sure, there was continuity, but the break was so great that like the Mahler-Schönberg break, the new style had the effect of so completely eclipsing its immediate predecessor that the latter was almost forgotten. Of course, the Mahler revival began earlier than the Art Nouveau revival, but I think the reason for that was that nineteenth-century music never suffered the almost complete rejection by advanced taste that the other nineteenth-century arts did. In painting there was a partial exception. French Impressionism and Post-Impressionism were assimilated, by much the same kind of mistaken categorization as Hitchcock's, to the modern styles and their emergence, and as a consequence of that judgment, Impressionism was torn out of its historical context and made to seem a kind of cultural sport, quite unrelated to what was going on in the other arts and in other countries at the same time. Modern painting was made to seem to begin with the Impressionists, just as in the history of English poetry, Hopkins, because he did not become widely known until the 1920's, was called a modern poet. A few scholars, at any rate, are beginning to see how thoroughly Hopkins was of his time, how assimilable his style is to that of Swinburne and Browning, partly because he learned most of his stylistic devices from them, while what he was saying was, actually, considerably less advanced, further from any truly modern or twentieth-century orientation.

So then, both a stylistic continuity and a discontinuity from the late nineteenth-century styles to the modern styles have been discerned, and this antimony demands some kind of explanation and analysis.

My approach to these problems, as I have outlined it in *Man's Rage for Chaos*, leads me to the judgment that art is best understood as the deposit or consequence of a particular kind or category of human behavior. The advantage of this approach is that it makes it possible to assimilate art to other kinds of human behavior and to understand the work of art as the product of decisions made by the artist. These decisions, like any decisions of the past, no matter how recent—a minute ago or thousands of years ago—are inaccessible, for several reasons; for one thing, statements that purportedly refer to decisions are historical statements, and since the past is empirically inaccessible, such statements are constructs; that is, considered as instructions or sets of instructions, they cannot tell us how to locate the phenomenally perceptible, but only how to construct other statements that may, or may not, successfully instruct us how to locate something in the world before us. So a statement that Booth shot Lincoln can, at best, instruct us to look for accounts in newspapers and other documents which, by yet another construct, we postulate as having been contemporary in origin with the actual shooting. Or statements that the eighteenth-century Virginian style in dishes had such-and-such characteristics can instruct us to formulate other statements, based on other constructs, that instruct us to excavate Williamsburg.

For another thing, a decision, even one made, we think, right before our eyes, or made by ourselves, is inaccessible. It occurs in the mind, and "mind" is a semantic bridge by which we cross the abyss of absolute ignorance that lies between stimulus and response. The only empirical phenomenon that "decision" tells us to look for is a certain class of sentences or a class or classes of nonverbal behavior. By metaphor we then apply the word to what in the "mind" we think was, somehow or other, responsible for such verbal or nonverbal behavior. Thus statements that purportedly give accounts of decisions are necessarily historical constructs and metaphorical inferences. This does not mean that they are valid, or particularly invalid. It merely means that they are language, that all statements are necessarily metaphysical, that is, without any necessary or immanent tie or any other kind of relation to the nonsemiotic world. It is always wise, and, in any discourse, sooner or later, necessary to remind ourselves of that fact, and particularly in historical discourse always to keep in the foreground the awareness that we are dealing not with the empirical world but with linguistic constructs. To do this is to be aware that one's construct is inevitably controlled by something inaccessible and discussable only in metaphor, our "decisions," or "intentions," or "purposes," or "interests," or "will," all of which, like "decision" itself, are metaphorical ways of talking about the inaccessible content of the "mind," a dirty word, to be sure, but one we can scarcely get along without.

From this point of view it is easy to understand why in discussing the movement from late nineteenth-century styles to modern styles various critics and historians should have found both continuity and discontinuity. Whichever you find depends upon your interests. That is, there is no reason for quarreling over whether continuity or discontinuity is present, or which is the more important. Obviously, both are present and both are important, and the relative importance of either depends upon one's "point of view"—a very apparent metaphor. Rather, what is needed is a satisfactory explanation of why continuity can be found between such radically different styles, and why at the same time there should be a discontinuity. The question will then arise whether or not both the continuity and the discontinuity can be seen as arising from the pressure of the same cultural values upon the decision-making processes of the individuals responsible for the appearance of the new styles.

Here assimilating artistic behavior to the rest of human behavior becomes particularly advantageous. One of the glossiest words in the vocabulary of the critic and historian of the arts is "creativity." Few words have the power so thoroughly to stun people into the suspension of thought. Indeed, the explanation for this lies, historically, in the emergence in the Enlightenment of the notion of original genius and the transformation by the early Romantics of that word and a group of related terms— "genius," "imagination," "poetry," "art" itself—into a set of terms which ascribed to individuals and works attributes which have paralyzed most thinking on the subject ever since. The whole complex is packaged pretty well in the notion of the Artist as World-Redeemer, an idea most conspicuous in the German Romantic tradition but found equally well in other countries, though rarely in such grandiose terminology. But if we look coolly at "creativity," both the word and the psychic attribute it is alleged to refer to, we can, as our temperatures drop, substitute for it the term "innovation." The initial advantage of this word is that it enables us to look at the products or consequences of human endeavor, rather than to imagine that we are examining the psychic factor responsible for certain features of such products and consequences, something we cannot possibly do. Innovation emerges easily enough when we place a series of similar products or consequences in chronological order. It is then apparent that innovation is the norm of human behavior. One reason is simply behavioral drift, the fact that it is virtually impossible for any human being to learn any behavior pattern with such precision that he can reproduce it exactly, no matter how hard he may try, and we rarely try very hard. Another reason is that any behavior pattern is always inadequate when applied to a particular, or existential, situation, since it is, to use another metaphor, "designed" to meet the demands of a category of situations. In art, furthermore, for reasons which I have discussed in *Man's Rage for Chaos*, but cannot go into here, innovation is peculiarly valued, though that valuation varies with the cultural level: the higher the level, the greater the value ascribed to innovation. For this reason "creativity" has tended to be peculiarly identified with artistic behavior, though once the notion had been firmly established it was extended to other categories of human behavior, principally within this century. Thus "creativity" may be defined as "culturally valued innovation."

In art history an example may be found in Malevich's assertion that Picasso's early Cubism was "academic" painting, a surprising term when one first encounters it. He was referring to the con-

tinuity, to the fact that for all his innovations, Picasso was still
painting human figures and still lifes, like any academic painter.
What Malevich did, in fact, was to abstract from Cubism the innovative characteristics and put them to work in their own right.
But we can also see that the configurations he used and the way he
combined them could themselves be seen as continuous with
what had always been done in art. Indeed, Malevich himself asserted that he had discovered the true universals of art; that claim
is exaggerated, but it is nevertheless true that what he did was
universal in the sense that it is discoverable in all the human art
that we know about. The point is that he could not have been
innovative in his way had Picasso not been innovative within the
academic tradition.

The assimilation of creativity to innovation, therefore, makes it
possible to understand that those who find continuity between
late nineteenth-century styles and modern styles and those who
discern discontinuity are both correct, and that Hitchcock is both
right and wrong in seeing Art Nouveau as the first modern style.
The real problem emerges with the construction of an explanation
for the innovative features of the modern styles. In constructing such an explanation we attempt to examine the forces in the
cultural situation which could conceivably—in our present inadequate comprehension of human behavior and cultural history
—be responsible for that particular kind of innovation and for
its force and degree. On the one hand there are those who would
claim that the innovative characteristics of Modernism can best
be explained by proposing a set of cultural forces radically, rev-
olutionarily different from the forces of Romanticism in its late
nineteenth-century condition. And on the other there are those
who would claim that the forces behind the innovative behavior
were continuous with and a further and unavoidable development of the cultural forces which we call Romantic, or at least
late nineteenth-century.

Certainly at first glance the innovations introduced into the
various arts in the period 1912–1966 are so extraordinary—"creative" to such a high degree—that it seems impossible that their
relation to the immediately preceding stage could be other than
revolutionary. And this certainly seems to be the most common

notion and until recently the dominating one, in spite of certain partial exceptions. It is not difficult to see why; the immediately preceding period was that of the "nineties," of the languorously twining first stage of Art Nouveau and the rich mosaic-like pattern of its angular second stage. It is the period for which the term "decadence" is commonly used. It is the period in which "aestheticism" is felt to have been in its most powerfully debilitating stage. In music, the works of Delius and Mahler have been seen as a prophetic lament for the death of European culture; Debussy and Delius have been judged spineless, "impressionistic," wandering, formless; Mahler has been called neurotic, self-indulgent, marked by the inflation and desperation of declining styles; and similar judgments have been made of Schönberg's "over-ripe" *Gurrelieder.* The fate of Oscar Wilde is felt to be the symbolic essence of a whole period; and the brutal and ugly contemporaneous attacks of Max Nordau, though they have been rejected as a defilement of art and a betrayal of culture, have had, it seems probable, a lasting effect on the usual conception of the period and the most common judgments of the value of its art. The depressing stories of the English poets of the nineties, even the early death of Beardsley, for which he can scarcely be said to have been responsible, are vaguely felt to be the consequence of their miserably mismanaged, self-indulgent, and decadent lives. Perhaps the continuing popularity of *La Bohème* has something to do with its revelation that to live like that naturally results in such an early death as Mimi's—such an unhealthy life!— and after all the artists we see cavorting about the stage are not very talented; the world would be better off, and so would they, if they all became bank clerks. If we move back to the years before the nineties, such dominating figures emerge as Pater, whose Marius is usually considered a pallid English Des Esseintes who, like an Oxford don, could be decadent only about religion and either youths or little girls.

Yeats is, from this point of view, the key and illuminating figure, for he began as they did, but he had the courage—though perhaps he was not very intelligent—to repudiate that whole way of life and art and to see that "there is more enterprise in going naked," though possibly there is no particularly courageous nudity in a belief in the occult. But that, to be sure, was only a hangover from the nineties, an embarrassment that a little ingenuity can explain away.

In short, I believe that I am not setting up a straw man if I assert that the usual picture of the period from, in England, the emergence of Swinburne and, in France, the emergence of Gustave Moreau and Verlaine is one of relaxation of nerve, self-indulgence always hinting in the direction of sexual perversity, and often enough arriving there, remoteness, an unrealistic worship of art for its own sake, of a commitment to Aestheticism as a strategy for escape from a real world which these artists did not have the courage or manliness to face, an escape which often enough involved a return to the more sensate rituals and forms of religion, especially if they were anti-intellectual and mystic in the worst of the many senses of that word. The general conception comes out sharply in the argument as to whether Huysmans's *À Rebours* is to be taken as a serious presentation of Aestheticism in its most extreme form, or as a satire of it. Those who insist on the latter interpretation seem to base their judgment on the conviction that nobody could possibly take such an attitude seriously. Only in Mallarmé's version of Aestheticism, I gather, can modern literary criticism find an exemplar which transcends the limitations of its period; and the other day I came upon the judgment that even he was, at times, sentimental. In the same way the Impressionist and Post-Impressionist painters are felt to have transcended their period, the art of which was headed for a cul-de-sac and a deserved oblivion, because they prepared the way for Modernism, just as, according to Hitchcock and others, we can now see that the same proposition holds for Art Nouveau. This revisionism has been possible, and even required, because all kinds of affinities have now been noticed between Art Nouveau and the Post-Impressionists.

There were, then, a few St. Johns in the wilderness of Aestheticism, a few who saw that late Romantic culture was decadent and doomed, or at least a few who can be seen, with some justification, from that point of view. But I believe with Hegel that nobody is ahead of his time. When we assert this of some figure or some work or group of works, we have merely confessed that such men and works have escaped the categorial net we have woven to catch their period. Nevertheless, even of this kind of useless proposition some sense can be made if we look at behavior instead of works, and if we perceive behavior in its historical-cultural context as problem-solving activity. Then it is by no means pointless to assert that of the various individuals in the same situation some will see the problem before others, some will be aware of the inadequacy of the orientations of their culture before others are. Thus we can give some content to the "individual ahead of his time." He has seen the problem before others and has discovered or made a step toward the solution which later becomes more general, and ultimately widespread. There are, after all, plenty of individuals in our society who have never even discerned any problems that postdate 1600, and are still asserting that the problems of the sixteenth century are not really problems. The question about the relation of late Romantic art to modern art thus can be put more sharply. Was the problem with which the Aesthetics and Decadents were struggling the same problem as that with which the Moderns were engaged, or was their problem and their solution one which the Moderns had transcended? Were the Moderns exposing themselves, perhaps, to a wholly different set of problems? And if so, were they problems which had emerged because their predecessors had found solutions to their own problems which time had shown to be untenable? As I have suggested, I think the most common answer has been that the Moderns were engaged in a new set of problems because the solutions of their predecessors, and indeed their problems, had been revealed to be invalid, even, to use a word fashionable at least until recently, inauthentic.

But this most common answer presents difficulties and problems of its own. Schönberg, Picasso, Matisse, Joyce, Stein, and the other heroes of Modernism were, for the most part and particularly, the very first to make the breakthrough, by no means young revolutionaries. They were stylistically well-established men in their early middle age with an impressive body of achievement behind them in the very style which they transcended or broke away from or revolted against, however one may wish to put it. In the eyes of the knowledgeable, they were already successful artists of great, perhaps the first, importance. After their breakthrough they did not repudiate their early works. In fact, Schönberg completed the scoring of the *Gurrelieder* without rewriting it, and in later years thought well enough of it to rearrange it in a more practicable form. Nor did Joyce repudiate the stories of *Dubliners* after he had written *Ulysses*, or even *Finnegan's Wake*, nor did Stein repudiate her early stories. Joyce, in fact, continued to write poetry in a pre-modern manner, in a very definitely late Romantic or nineties manner. There was nothing, it would seem, of the kind of destruction of his youthful works which Brahms performed when he left Hamburg for Vienna. There seems to have been no such repudiation. Even after Yeats decided there was more enterprise in going naked, he continued to publish collected editions which included his clothed works, and though he revised them, he did not change their style. Those who insist that a revolution was involved, rather than a fulfillment, must find these facts somewhat embarrassing; and if this position is to be taken, an explanation must be offered about the nature of the decisions responsible for the modern styles, and about the cultural forces—the problems, and the available orientations for perceiving them and coming to grips with them— which lay behind the decisions. To put it perhaps too baldly, the thing that needs to be explained is how it was that men who had grown up in, had been trained in, and had been successful in the late Romantic styles and the cultural values that lay behind them could have suddenly and, though unknown to each other, almost simultaneously started responding to an entirely new set of cultural values. Their failure to repudiate their earlier works is not decisive, but is certainly highly suggestive. It is obviously not enough to say that they suddenly evolved or were influenced by modern cultural values, because that is simply to categorize their new styles and to extend tautologically the attributes of their styles to their decisions and their cultural values. It is, in short, to say precisely nothing. The cultural dynamics of the situation need badly to be explained.

So far I have attempted merely to understand the problem more precisely: was the emergence of Modernism a revolt against the Romantic program, which had become moribund, or was it a fulfillment of that program, which was still viable—more viable than ever—and more sharply understood in the period immediately preceding the modern breakthrough? It is apparent from what I have said about the usual conception of Aestheticism and Decadence and Art Nouveau that if the latter answer is to be accepted, then there is something radically wrong with that conception of late Romanticism, and it needs to be thoroughly overhauled.

Of crucial importance at this point is Yeats's famous remark about the fascination of what is difficult. For years I have had this phrase hurled at me by one critic or another, and always with the implication not only that I certainly ought to be very impressed, but also that it was remarkably original of Yeats to have uttered it and that it contains the secret of the Modern and marks him off sharply from his immediate predecessors. Perhaps it does; that is the problem. But it certainly does not mark him off from his ultimate sources in the Romantics of the period from 1795 to 1830. The more I study the early Romantics, the more heroic I find them. I have referred to the Romantic program, and this I think is a better term than the Romantic "attitudes" or "beliefs." A belief is usually seen, it would appear, as an expression of what is in the believer's mind, but such an attitude, of course, is quite untenable. Looked at coolly, a statement of belief is a set of directions designed to control one's activities, and possibly the activities of others. It is a program. The notion of the Romantic attitudes or beliefs arrests them in time, but if we think of the Romantic program a dynamic element is introduced, one which, hopefully, will mesh with the particular cultural dynamics we are seeking.

The Romantic program, then, was nothing if not heroic. Perhaps it was so heroic, so utterly beyond any hope of achievement, that it was comic. But then, the genuine hero is always on the verge of the comic. That is why the atmosphere of tragedy must always be so portentous, why even the humor in tragedy must be extravagant, a little, or entirely, mad. Nevertheless, in the first decade of the nineteenth century Schleiermacher said that any program for man must be impossible of achievement, for only an unachievable goal can bring out man's powers to the full, so that we can know what they are. The program of the Romantic artist was certainly heroic, and certainly impossible of achievement, for the Romantic artist took upon himself the task of the redemption of humanity, that is, of introducing value into human existence. Just as later Feuerbach could insist that every man is and must be his own Christ, so the Romantic artist took upon himself the burden of Christ, the burden of world-redemption. It comes out in Coleridge's conception of the poetic imagination, which, in one form or another, is to be found deeply embedded in the Romantic tradition, right down to the present. The power to make sense out of experience, which is the imagination, is given to every man, but it is given to the poet above all, and to the highest degree, not in spite of the fact that he subjects the world to the demands of the profoundest human needs, but because of it. And this is the introduction of value by the creation of the self. That this Coleridgean conception involved logical and semantic confusions which have invalidated literary criticism ever since is beside the point. The significant factor is that to be fascinated with such a program is to be fascinated with what is difficult.

But this is not all, nor the sole source of the difficulty in the Romantic program. The case of Blake is to the point. Let me be frank; Blake as man, thinker, poet, artist, and engraver I detest. Whatever I say about him is biased, but I am no more biased, I think, than those who admire his performance of these various roles. He did not, to my mind, become more than a failed Romantic. That is, he saw the problem; the Enlightenment dissolved beneath him, but he retreated in fear to an early sixteenth-century position. If the Romantic program was deeply committed to the fascination of what is difficult, the Enlightenment program was deeply committed to the fascination of what is easy, a program which led to an ideal even more hopelessly unattainable than that of the Romantics. Blake certainly saw this, and reacted against it in an initially Romantic direction. But, as he said, he had to have a system, and a system is what he soon had, a closed system. The Enlightenment, as Blake clearly saw, had as its aim to dissolve the subject into the object. Blake's system was merely a return to a late medieval and early Renaissance determination, as Northrop Frye tells us, "to destroy the antithesis of subject and object." As a contrast, consider a genuine Romantic, Hegel, commonly, and perhaps vulgarly, identified as the most devoted of system-builders. Yet even if he was—and this is doubtful—what a difference between his system and Blake's! His aim was not to build a system but to discover the true method of philosophy, the one philosophy. And he was convinced that once it had been discovered, its practice would reveal that it was continuously self-transforming, and self-transcending. He did not claim that philosophy ended with him. He merely claimed that his position presented the most advanced form of this endlessly self-transforming and self-transcending philosophizing available within the historical limitations of his own time. That is, far from collapsing subject into object, as the Enlightenment wished, or object into subject, as the regressive Blake wished, he proposed that the only way out was to maintain an eternal and irresolvable tension between subject and object. Far from being undercut by his own principles, he used his own principles to undercut himself. That Blakeian itch for finality the Romantic Freud has taught at least some of us—not that others had not tried before—is the mark of childishness.

Here then is the heart of the Romantic fascination for what is difficult. It was not merely the introduction of value into the world; it was the determination to introduce it in such a way that the self would never be threatened by the fusion of subject and object in either direction. That in turn meant that any final statement of value in the form of a belief must be undercut and transcended (*aufgehoben*, as Hegel put it) as soon as it was arrived at. Thus the ultimate difficulty which fascinated the Romantic was to maintain the tension between subject and object. Psychologically, it meant that the individual must always keep himself under extreme pressure, and that as an artist he must work under the guidance of the most cruel and demanding rules he could devise (the notion that Romantic art is formless is one of the silliest ever to have been introduced into the immense body of critical platitudes.) The history of the culturally emergent styles of the nineteenth century is one of steadily mounting pressure. It led in the 1880's to Browning's *Parleyings*, that ambiguous, equivocating, and Wittgensteinian study of the word "truth." Within the next twenty years it had produced the symphonies of Mahler. Each of these vast works stretches out and coils and returns upon itself and shudders and writhes like a huge snake struggling to cast its dead skin. To call them neurotic touches just enough of their character to miss the point. To call them shapeless betrays an inability to grasp a large-scale plan.

From this point of view it is possible to understand Yeats a little better, whose transformation occurred in the decade of the last Mahler symphonies. It was perhaps unfortunate that so tender and weak a mind as his ever encountered so brutal, so powerful, so egocentric, and so half-educated a mind as Blake's. Apparently what appealed to him most was the concealed and veiled presentation of Blake's doctrine, not the doctrine itself, which he probably never understood. The appeal was the same that led him to Theosophy and the comic fantasy of the dictation of *A Vision*. That late nineteenth-century interest in the occult, in Rosicrucianism, in alchemy, in Satanism, in all forms of bad and non-European mysticism is embarrassing. Such a betrayal of European culture seems hard to comprehend, and harder to forgive. The basic character of Romanticism is an uncompromising tough-mindedness, and all this seems like a collapse of the Romantic program, unless we take as our clue the necessity for the Romantic to devise strategies for putting himself under pressure and for steadily increasing that pressure. It is not entirely a safe thing to do. A little bad luck, a few bad choices, with drugs, or alcohol, or mysticism, or religion, and the individual can be destroyed, either literally or psychically, by being squeezed by a greater pressure than he can endure out of the Romantic program into some intellectual backwater, as Blake was. It was a risk Yeats ran often enough, yet never quite fatally. For always before him, as Frank Kermode has shown, was the image of the dance, the dance that is the dancer, a nearly perfect emblem of the kind of self-imposed pressure and discipline the Romantic tradition is always seeking strategies to achieve. One has the impression that the European artists of the late nineteenth century who became involved with experiments in everything from the occult to traditional Catholicism were never quite serious, were always toying with these matters, never quite committing themselves. The reason for this ultimate failure of commitment seems to be that they were not really seeking for finality, in spite of what they occasionally may have said, but were actually interested in exploring these esoteric areas of human experience as possible sources for strategies of self-imposed pressure. Their immediate aim, as Professor John Lester has shown, was ecstasy, a key word in the period before the breakthrough into Modernity.

Strategies for maintaining pressure, lest the self's endless task of introducing value into the world be extinguished by the finality of collapse of subject into object, or object into subject—this perhaps is the key to Aestheticism. Several years ago (in *Beyond the Tragic Vision*) I proposed that for that term be substituted "Stylism." A justification for this proposal will, I think, help illuminate the problem at hand. By the end of the 1850's a number of the most advanced individuals had come to the realization that the superficial aspect of the Romantic program—the redemption of the world and the redemption of the personality—could not possibly be achieved. The difficult thing now became keeping up the pressure without the aid of either of these goals, even as heuristic and unrealizable aims. They came to be seen not as the heart of the Romantic problem, but only temporarily valuable devices; but once a faith is perceived as a strategy, though it is possible to maintain it in that status, it is difficult; and sooner or later the question arises as to whether or not it might be better to do without it. If that next step is taken, what was once a faith becomes an illusion. This process was implicit in the dynamics of the Romantic program, as we have seen; sooner or later it was bound to move to the foreground, as it had, for the advanced Romantic, by the end of the 1850's.

A new problem now arose. With the abandonment of the superficial aspect of the Romantic program, there was also lost a moral imperative, which, by the logic of the cultural situation, was now perceived as easy, rather than difficult. Moreover, such a loss left the self and its creation of value absolutely exposed, with neither transcendental justification nor protection against the non-Romantic society and the culture, from which the Romantic was alienated because it was engaged in the quest for finality by the destruction of antithesis between subject and object. A functional substitute for faith was obviously needed, a substitute which would be metaphysically neutral; it would not commit the individual to any illusory goal, nor would it leave him defenseless. The answer lay in the commitment to style in its own right.

The psychological process can be understood if we conceive it in the terms of neurosis and psychosis, or, to use a more recent term, the progression of dysfunctional behavior. It seems reasonably obvious that one of the symptoms of breakdown of ordinary functions, one of the ways, perhaps the most important way or even the only way, we can tell that a personality is disintegrating is that its behavior becomes increasingly stylized, that is, more limited and less flexible in its responses and more repetitive. It becomes formalized. The behavioral pattern is applied almost indifferently to an increasing variety of situations without correction or adaptation. On the other hand, these dysfunctional symptoms can be seen just as well as functional strategies to prevent further disintegration, and for the majority of those people classified as neurotic, such strategies are successful. Dr. Johnson's compulsion to touch everything was a strategy for holding himself together. Indeed, in this sense, we are all neurotic, for the personality is always threatened with disintegration, precisely because none of our behavior patterns are perfectly prepared to meet any actual situation with total adequacy. Further, from the inside of the neurotic or psychotic looking out, one of the indications to himself that something is wrong is that he becomes aware of differences between his faiths, his programs, and those of the bulk of the individuals in the society around him. His strategy for holding himself together in the face of this discrepancy, which is so disturbing, is either to adopt the position that their faiths are valid and his are not, or vice versa.

I do not wish to suggest for a moment that the Romantic was neurotic, or, in the sense suggested, any more neurotic than is the norm. On the contrary, from his point of view, from the modern point of view, he was less neurotic. What the Romantic did from the beginning of his history was to engage deliberately and rationally in a process which the severe neurotic and psychotic adopts because he has no choice. The Romantic responded to a cultural crisis and a cultural problem, but in doing so he necessarily entered upon and exposed himself to the psychological process characteristic of disintegrating personalities. This is why his behavior so frequently has a superficial resemblance to the behavior of the mildly disturbed and even the insane. A striking instance of this appears in the art of the Aesthetic movement, or as I prefer to call it, Stylism. An examination of the art of the disturbed and the insane shows clearly that as functional breakdown proceeds and one strategy after another is discovered to be inviable, their art becomes increasingly stylized, that is, both formally and semantically overdetermined, or less flexible. That is particularly evident in the case of schizophrenics who have had artistic training. As each strategy is abandoned, the next, and more regressive, strategy becomes more desperate, both more limited and more violent. More energy flows into a narrower range of behavior. And precisely that formal and semantic overdetermination is the characteristic of the art of Stylism. Swinburne's poetic style is an easily comprehensible example, but the style of the mature Monet, of Cézanne, of Debussy, is just as much to the point. The most striking instance of all is the style of late Stylism, Art Nouveau.

However, the strategies of the Romantic Stylist differed in both their origin and their function from the superficially similar styles of progressively dysfunctional personalities. Unlike these individuals, the Stylist saw the faiths both of his non-Romantic cultural and social environment and of his own Romantic tradition as invalid. He was not faced with an either/or choice, as is the dysfunctional personality, but with a both/and rejection. Furthermore, the strategies of the dysfunctional are designed to relieve the pressures from what he perceives either as a disintegrating personality or as a disintegrating sociocultural environment. But the Stylist strategy was, of course, designed to increase pressure. The one is interested in a body of rules that will protect him, that will enable him to maintain what functional processes he still has control of; but the other was interested in a body of rules that would force him into an entirely new position. Robert Schmutzler has pointed out that the practice of Art Nouveau was accompanied in its practitioners by a desire to discover a wholly new form of life. The artistic activities of the Stylists were designed as defenses within which they could work out, obscurely and with great difficulty, a new Romantic program, nothing less than self-transformation by self-transcendence. Nietzsche, the greatest Stylist of them all, summed it up in his famous "transvaluation of all values." Thus, paralleling the explorations into the possibilities of religious occultism was a similar interest in other culturally transcended possibilities, particularly a superficial interest in Naturism (to distinguish it from Naturalism, which is pre-Stylist) of an Enlightenment character. That is, some of the propositions of religion and of the Enlightenment were adopted for strategic purposes; the same things were said, but for a different reason. This Stylistic Naturism was, as is to be expected, particularly an English mode of Stylism, found in Meredith, whose verbal style was almost as difficult as Browning's, and whose Naturism, as in "The Woods of Westermain," had the Romantic attribute of difficulty rather than the Enlightenment attribute of ease and the psychologically comfortable: "Enter these enchanted woods, ye who dare." This Naturistic mode of Stylism continued into the novels of E. M. Forster and of D. H. Lawrence, and the poetry of John Masefield; but it was also found in Germany, as in certain youth movements of the time, and the German form of Art Nouveau is commonly known as *Jugendstil.* Browning himself, whose later poetry is notoriously difficult, even impenetrable, and has been most unjustly neglected as a consequence, when asked why he wrote in so difficult a style, replied that it was to warn people off his property who did not belong there. The defensive aspect of Stylism comes out better in this remark than in any other I know of.

An examination of Pre-Raphaelitism will serve to make my position clearer. The Pre-Raphaelitism of the 1850's was of course of quite a different character from the work of the period after 1860, which, confusingly, goes under the same name, that of the later Rossetti, Morris, Burne-Jones, and so on. The earlier belonged to the pre-Stylist and post-Transcendental stage of Romanticism, which I have called Objectism, to indicate the naked exposure of the self to the non-Romantic world without any defenses at all. The dangerous and self-destructive aspect of Objectism comes out in that original Pre-Raphaelite program, which required such exact transliteration of phenomenal appearance that, to be blunt, no painter could possibly make a living at it; and that the early Pre-Raphaelites rapidly acquired a market is now well known. Further, current studies of Victorian painting show that they were by no means alone in undertaking this program; other English painters with no connection with them were pursuing the same goals. The corresponding French style, the naturalism of Courbet and the Impressionism of Manet, was economically much more efficient. Some of the Pre-Raphaelites continued to paint as they had begun, notably William Holman Hunt, but the other leaders, for the most part, entered upon a Stylist program. The poetry of Rossetti, rather than his painting, shows most clearly the character of this cultural transformation, particularly *The House of Life*. It is not surprising that this should be so. The weakness of the first stage of Pre-Raphaelite painting, and even, though to a lesser degree, the second, was that, unlike Courbet and Manet, the English painters continued, in spite of their protestations, to organize their paintings according to the academic tradition established by Raphael himself and the other painters of the High Renaissance. Semantically, their art was genuinely innovative, but formally it was not. This is probably why their painting has lost its popularity, while the various corresponding stages of Impressionism (for there was an Objectist and a Stylist Impressionism, as well) have not.

The House of Life, however, is considerably more innovative. For one thing, it is characterized by an extraordinary concentration. The first necessity for good poetry, Rossetti said, is fundamental brain-work. Consequently it is marked by a difficulty, that is, a semantic overdetermination, which was paralleled in English poetry only by Browning's *Sordello* and by the work he was beginning to do while *The House of Life*, for the most part, was being written, the 1860's and the 1870's. It is, however, the general plan which is most illuminating for an understanding of Stylism. It is divided into two parts, "Youth and Change" and "Change and Fate," but the overriding subject of the first is love, and of the second, art. The first is, in itself, a fascinating exploration of eroticism, but an eroticism presented not for erotic purposes. We live in an interpreted world, and part of that world, perhaps to all of us the most significant part, is to be found inside our own skins. The internal environment of forces which can never be completely mastered or understood, any more than the external environment, includes the sexual drive. Eroticism is the interpretation of that drive, which has to be interpreted as every other force and phenomenon has to be. What is the significance of that interpretation to the self, with its task of creating value? What unique set of value-laden interests is manifest in these erotic interpretations of sexuality?

The second part uses art as the first uses eroticism. In the Romantic tradition, as we have seen, the imagination is the instrument that makes sense out of experience, or, more melodramatically, creates the world; and that art is the prime instrument and manifestation of the imagination is a virtually unquestioned doctrine not only of the Romantic artist but also of the Romantic critic and often enough of the Romantic philosopher. (It is the most common conception of art to be found today, though, to my mind, pretty nonsensical.) Love, then, is the instrument of the self, or the imagination, that introduces values into the internal world, and art is its complement for the external world. Thus, late in the century, in a somewhat vulgar and, except for the music, non-Stylistic setting, Tosca lives for art and lives for love. But Rossetti presents both love and art as failing in their prescribed tasks, only death offering blessedly a flower in a fountain, finality. That is to say, there is no finality in life, nor is there any resolution of the necessarily conflicting claims of art and love. Both are means for placing the individual under the extremest pressure, and the pressure is redoubled by the power of each to reveal the inadequacy of the other. Thus each pulls the self, the imagination, in opposite directions and threatens it constantly with disintegration. Over and over again, during this period, one finds style used, not as the neurotic does, to decrease the threat of disintegration, but, on the contrary, to increase it. It is for reasons such as these that I find it meaningful to say that Stylism (or Aestheticism) does not abandon the heroic tradition of Romanticism for escapism or self-indulgence. On the contrary, it seems to me more heroic than its predecessors, because it does not parade its heroism, but disguises it behind an elaborate defense of the sumptuously beautiful, or sometimes the perversely repellent. Rossetti's work brings to the foreground a theme which had been introduced but not fully developed earlier in the century, the theme of the *Doppelgänger*. Rossetti, however, does not treat it emblematically, but psychologically, thus developing it into one of the most remarkable themes of Stylism, a self-imposed and controlled schizophrenia. Dorian Gray and Jekyll-Hyde are subsequent instances, and some have professed, I think correctly, to perceive the same kind of thing going on in the symphonies of Mahler.

The perverse itself was an equally important theme during the period, and in English literature also dates from the 1860's, Swinburne's *Atalanta in Calydon* and, above all others, his *Poems and Ballads*. At times one thinks that the latter work must have been written after Krafft-Ebing, Swinburne presents so many forms of erotic perversity and in "The Triumph of Time" analyzes their psychological origins with such care and penetration. The theme of the book is really Baudelaire's *"Hypocrite lecteur,—mon semblable,—mon frère!"* It is the open admission, and even assertion, of the polyperverse character of the erotic manifestation of the imagination. This is, no doubt, why it is continuously downgraded as poetry and denied all intellectual content, why it has been treated as an expression of Swinburne's perverse erotic personality, rather than as what it really was, an exploration of what is found in all humans and what, hitherto, had been carefully concealed both from ourselves and from others. I know of no one who has been willing to admit that Swinburne let the cat out of the bag so early in the game. Indeed, deeper than this bringing into light the perverse and hidden was Swinburne's profounder aim, the exploration of the nature of the psychological bondage that makes a genuine transformation and transvaluation of the self impossible. After these poems he went on to explore those forces in the religious and social and political worlds responsible for a similar failure in public life. Like Rossetti, he puts himself under the most extreme possible pressure in both the internal and external environments. (Our dishonesty about pornography and politics makes his work still more than pertinent.) Looked at this way, Swinburne's use of the sexually perverse, a strategy in which innumerable authors and painters were to follow him, can be seen as a manifestation of the program responsible for the exploration of the religious occult and Naturism.

This brings us back once again to Art Nouveau. Whatever one thinks of its charms or failures as a style, its significance in cultural history can scarcely be exaggerated. It was the culmination and the ineluctable consequence of the Stylist program. What it set out to do was to create a style that would be viable in all areas of artistic behavior, that would be a fusion of all styles in European culture (it is historically self-conscious in the Hegelian manner to an almost super-Hegelian degree), and that at the same time would transform and transvaluate those styles into something absolutely novel. The example of Beardsley makes the psychological process involved understandable. He stripped away nearly everything from drawing except the line, itself controlled by a highly restricted range of possibilities, and the patch of black or white. Again, not the result is to be considered, but the character of the decision of which the result was the consequence. And that decision was an heroic self-limitation combined with the fantastic productivity so characteristic of the Romantic artist, and the sheer hard, continuous work and application responsible for it. Historically, the most important matter was the stripping away. It must be conceived behaviorally; that is, the artist deliberately altered and transcended the behavioral patterns in which he had been so highly trained. That deliberate stripping away made Beardsley the most significant Art Nouveau artist, as many people recognized at the time, for what was to follow as a prelude to the breakthrough to Modernism was precisely that stripping away, that unlearning of carefully learned behavioral processes and patterns. It is an astonishing—and heroic—going against the grain. It can be seen in the behavior of the Fauvists, for example, but it can be seen just as well in philosophy, as in G. E. Moore's "The Refutation of Idealism" (1903). The artist's aim was the transformation of the European stylistic tradition, that is, the transformation of the artist's behavior, of his decision-making processes, and the philosopher's aim was not very different.

This is the great achievement of Art Nouveau; it makes it not a minor episode in the history of art but a major and necessary step in the cultural dynamics of the Romantic tradition. I have said that the obscure and difficult and half-realized program of the Stylists was self-transformation by self-transcendence. What does this mean when we ask what such a proposition tells us to look for? If not the process itself of decision-making, certainly the decisions themselves of individuals can be examined. Decision-making is one of the many areas of human behavior which we are just beginning to explore, but it may be that here is exactly what the Romantics were talking about when they spoke of the self, and of the introduction of value into the world, or of the imagination as the instrument of the will. In any event, we can say with some certainty that there are styles of decision-making, visiting one's astrologer or psychoanalyst, praying, summoning every nerve to make decisions quickly, or summoning every nerve to postpone them. If that is the case, then the Romantic intuition that in art lay the redemptive key may have not been so far off, in a way, for, since artistic style shows a higher rate of change than any other mode of human behavior, decision-making is most easily observable in art; and further, since art is irresponsible, since neither artistic production nor artistic perception demands manipulation of the environment to one's own benefit, or requires adaptation to the nonartistic environment, it is the perfect instrument for the exploration of the character and strategies of decision-making. Hence it is also the perfect medium for experimentation in decision-making, since, as the Stylists themselves were the first to realize, the specific intellectual and moral content of art ("Art for art's sake," that is, art can do something nothing else can do) is a matter of indifference, at least if one is alienated and seeking strategies for self-transformation and self-transcendence. Hence, also, it is an area of behavior in which it is least dangerous to apply the maximum pressure upon oneself. Even philosophy does not offer the opportunities for irresponsibility that art does. (Or one can say just as well, for responsibility; for the Romantic nothing is so irresponsible as conventional moral responsibility of a non-Romantic kind.)

Thus the appearance of Art Nouveau upon the scene was a sign that the pressure which the Stylist was seeking strategies to achieve had very nearly reached the necessary degree. One can feel in the art that immediately followed, in the music of Scriabin and Mahler, for example, almost tangibly the struggle to break through into a new mode of being. When the pressure was enough, the lid blew off, and the modern styles emerged, not in an embryonic form, or only briefly, but almost at once in maturity. Modern art does not develop as previous styles have. In the sense in which Art Nouveau is still a style, modern art has no style at all; it is a bewildering and marvelous succession and simultaneity of styles, a happy chaos of modes of decision-making. For something genuinely new had emerged. Up to this time the Romantic had explored decision-making, the self, the introduction of value into the world, from within. With the coming of modern art he transcended it. The parallel with what Hegel hoped to do for philosophy is striking and exact; not philosophy within the bounds of philosophy, but meta-philosophy, philosophy from above. Thus for Modernism the aim is not the mere continuation of artistic behavior in the European tradition, but controlling artistic behavior, that is controlling decision-making from above and outside of it. The hierarchy of understanding and reason which Kant set up is achieved by the behavior of the modern artist. This is why no culture has ever shown a stylistic discontinuity so abrupt and so historically divisive as that achieved by the first generation of Moderns. It is why modern art, in an odd way, is about itself, has as its subject the decision-making process of making a painting. It is for this reason that I think Hitchcock and others are in error when they call Art Nouveau the first modern architectural style, or Impressionism the beginning of modern painting, or Hopkins the first modern English poet. They all live on the other side of the breakthrough in the years immediately preceding the first World War. But given the program of the original Romantics, and the revised Romantic program of the Stylists, who invented a new mode of Romantic heroicism, they were "logically necessary" strategies for encompassing that breakthrough into the comprehension of the very principle of self-transformation, which is Modernism.

12

WHAT DID

LADY WINDERMERE LEARN?

[1956*]

Although on first reading, the plot of *Lady Windermere's Fan* seems to consist entirely of the melodramatic clichés of the well-made play, in *Understanding Drama* Professors Brooks and Heilman have given Wilde's comedy a close and sympathetic analysis. To them it is a play about Lady Windermere's education: "And what has she learned? Not merely that Mrs. Erlynne is a good woman. But the more general truth that good and evil are not easily determined by simple rules, that they do not often exist in pure form, so to speak; hence one must measure the evidence carefully and must avoid hasty conclusions."

Yet it is odd that Wilde thought so highly of his plays if this is all *Lady Windermere's Fan* amounts to—a few witty epigrams, a trite plot, and a dull moral. True, Wilde was capable of self-deception, but perhaps his talent was more subtle than these

* Reprinted by permission from *College English*, XVIII (October, 1956), pp. 11–14. Copyright 1956 by the National Council of Teachers of English.

days we are inclined to believe. And so I am going to assume that his first comedy is worth looking at again.

The plot consists of three simple situations, all so worn out that it is hard to believe that anyone, let alone Wilde, would use them. The primary situation, the Long-Lost-Child pattern, is one of the oldest in the world. But Wilde does several curious things with it. First, it is the parent who is lost, not the child. This in itself would not be very significant were it not for something else. The usual emotional release of this plot is the recognition scene, or else the acquisition of a substitute parent or child. But Wilde neither permits a recognition nor supplies a parent.

It is not enough to say that a recognition scene would be incurably melodramatic. So common is the plot that any audience must anticipate the recognition, and when it does not occur must wonder why not. The whole fourth act builds toward it, but it does not happen. Mrs. Erlynne is on the verge of telling the truth, but she keeps her secret. Furthermore she is rewarded for her silence; she gets Lord Augustus. Why is she rewarded? Mere Wildean cynicism? I think that the crux of the matter lies in finding out why Mrs. Erlynne is silent.

The second simple plot pattern is the Meeting of the Rival Women. Exhausted as this device is, in a serious situation it can be effective if carefully handled, whether the rivalry is social or sexual, or both. The last part of Act I and the first third of Act II build toward the encounter of Lady Windermere and Mrs. Erlynne. When they meet, what happens? Lady Windermere "bows coldly to Mrs. Erlynne, who bows to her sweetly in turn, and sails into the room." Again we have the nonfulfillment of a traditional plot device. The audience anticipates what is going to happen, but it is disappointed. There is, however, a meeting in Act III. I have pointed out that the encounter theme can depend on either a social rivalry or a sexual rivalry. Wilde completely disposes of the social rivalry, while by dramatic irony—by the end of Act II the audience knows that Mrs. Erlynne is Lady Windermere's mother—he completely disappoints the audience's anticipation of an encounter based on sexual rivalry.

The third antiquated trick is the Discovery Scene. Like Sheridan, Wilde conceals two people, but he lets the important one escape; Lady Windermere would lose more by discovery than Mrs. Erlynne. The latter might lose Lord Augustus, but she at least can take care of herself. Her daughter cannot. So the scene really revolves around whether Lady Windermere is to be caught, as the discovery of the fan makes very clear. Lord Windermere is heading straight toward his wife's place of concealment when Mrs. Erlynne appears, gets everyone's attention, and lets her daughter escape. And again we have the nonfulfillment of a traditional stage device.

The play, then, is built upon the frustration or nonfulfillment of three of the most ancient and common theatrical plot devices imaginable. Wilde has put it together by *not* completing traditional patterns. The disappointment of the encounter between the social rivals leads to Lady Windermere's flight. Her arrival at Lord Darlington's room leads to a false encounter between sexual rivals. And that in turn leads to the disappointment of the discovery pattern, which, by changing Lady Windermere's attitude towards Mrs. Erlynne, in Act IV leads us to the major theme of the play, the disappointment of the lost-child pattern in the nonfulfillment of the expected dénouement of recognition between child and parent. If we look at the play from his point of view, we are led straight to the question I have already asked. Put in another way, it is, "Why is Lady Windermere not allowed to learn the truth?" It appears to me that Wilde has unmistakably and most ingeniously forced our attention to that point. And if this is so, it is a mistake to say that there is really nothing left to happen in Act IV, as do Brooks and Heilman. Everything happens in Act IV.

Now it would appear that if Lady Windermere has really learned her lesson, she may be considered able to learn the truth. She says she has learned her lesson, and Professors Brooks and Heilman believe her. She has been through terrible experiences: convinced her husband is false to her; forced to receive a scarlet woman in the last pure home in London; driven to flight, abandoning her child; humbled before a detested woman, whom she has been forced to learn to respect. She has been forced to learn that she is capable of wrong judgments and that people are a mixture of good and bad. But she has not questioned the *standards* by which she judges. She discovers that she is capable of evil; but she knows that she is good. She has discovered that Mrs. Erlynne is capable of good; and she concludes that Mrs. Erlynne is not bad. She has understood nothing about Mrs. Erlynne. On hearsay she decided that Mrs. Erlynne is bad; on gossip she refused to trust her husband, whom she professes to love; because of a social embarrassment she abandoned home, husband, and child—for a lover. She thought Mrs. Erlynne a devil; she concludes that she is an angel. She learns to question her conclusions, not her categories.

Her final scene with Mrs. Erlynne is the crucial scene of the play.

Mrs. E. You are devoted to your mother's memory, Lady Windermere, your husband tells me.
Lady W. We all have ideals in life. At least we all should have. Mine is my mother.
Mrs. E. Ideals are dangerous things. Realities are better. They wound, but they are better.
Lady W. If I lost my ideals, I should lose everything.
Mrs. E. Everything?
Lady W. Yes.

And that is the end of the matter. Lady Windermere is not permitted to learn the truth because she hasn't earned the right to the truth. Her ideals are still the same. She is condemned to live in a world of illusions. She has learned nothing. Freedom is not for her. She has neither the brains nor the courage. And so Mrs. Erlynne forbears. Who is the good woman of the subtitle? If it is Lady Windermere, she is good only because she is stupid and shallow. The truly good woman is Mrs. Erlynne, but not because she rescues her daughter. Any mother would do that under the circumstances. She is good because she has brains enough to realize that some people must be forever separated from realities. She is good not because she saves her daughter from making her own mistakes but rather because she spares her daughter from facing the realities which would destroy her. The final exchange between Lady Windermere and her husband shows how very little she has learned.

Lady W. There is the same world for all of us, and good and evil, sin and innocence, go through it hand in hand. To shut one's eyes to half of life that one may live securely is as though one blinded oneself that one might walk with more safety in a land of pit and precipice.
Lord W. Darling, why do you say that?
Lady W. Because I who had shut my eyes to life, came to the brink. And one who had separated us—
Lord W. We were never separated.
Lady W. We never must be again. Oh, Arthur, don't love me less, and I will trust you more. I will trust you absolutely. Let us go to Selby. In the Rose Garden at Selby, the roses are white and red.

The irony of Lady Windermere's final sentence is one of the best things in the play. In the world of innocence, things are clear and simple. If the innocent discover evil in what they thought was good, they can remain innocent, nevertheless. But only by questioning and revising their categories can they become experienced. And to revise one's categories takes intelligence and courage.

Lady Windermere, then, is not allowed to learn the truth because she is one of those who cannot tell the difference between ideals and illusions, not an uncommon type, and she is therefore incapable of true moral growth. Through his ironic and subtle analysis of a particular kind of personality Wilde attacks the inadequacy of the traditional categories of good and evil. Lady Windermere began as an absolutist and remains an absolutist. Wilde's attack is directed against absolute morality, not against the absolutist's inadequate realization of his own moral absolutes. Arnold has identified the source of this rigidity, the Evangelical conscience, in which Lady Windermere was trained, and had demanded that the middle class transform itself. Wilde showed how improbable it was that Arnold's desires should be fulfilled. For in fostering absolute morality, the Philistine trained his children in rigid moral ideals, and so condemned them to a life of illusions, a life forever separated from reality. "Realities are better," says Mrs. Erlynne. "They wound, but they are better." "In the Rose Garden at Selby," her daughter replies, "the roses are white and red."

13

THE CURRENT CRISIS

IN THE ARTS: POP, OP, AND MINI

[1967*]

In the entire history of art nothing so strange has ever happened as the astonishing developments of the 1960's. The shift into Modernism at the end of the first decade of this century was extraordinary enough; no culture had ever experienced so radical a redirection in its artistic styles. But that change can, after all, be seen in terms of the great tradition of Western painting. Malevich, indeed, called Cubism academic art, a strange term with a recognizable justice to it. Abstract Expressionism itself is clearly in the tradition of modern art; it belongs to the same impulse that early in the movement led to Kandinsky's Improvisations. The emergence of Pop Art, however, which appeared simultaneously in the work of a number of artists independent of one another, which was not, in the traditional sense, a movement, with a manifesto, which seems not even to have been a typical avant-garde

* Delivered at Conference on the Arts, McMasters University, November, 1967. Reprinted by permission from *Studies in the Twentieth Century*, No. 1 (Spring, 1968), pp. 21–38. Copyright 1968 by Stephen H. Goode.

development, was a strikingly different matter. When it was shortly followed by Op Art and then by Mini Art, it was evident, although each had quasi-precursors within the modern movement, that at work behind these new styles was a wholly new attitude toward art.

Nor have the new developments been confined to painting alone, although most easily accessible there. Similar changes were taking place in music, and attempts, at least, have been made to do the same thing in poetry and fiction; Andy Warhol, perhaps the most interesting artist in the world, as a phenomenon, if not for his products, has extended his revolution to film. One kind of response to these new works is instructive. It is that of art-lovers, connoisseurs, and critics who have devoted their lives to art, or one of the arts, and who have been proud of their ability to master each new style of the twentieth century as it has come along. One such friend of mine, an eminent music critic, is appalled. He sees the destruction of everything he has ever valued and has devoted his life to. Such men are convinced that the new artists are savagely aiming at the denigration of art, the trivialization of art, the destruction of the whole magnificent tradition of Western painting, music, poetry, the novel, the dance—everything. Another response is even more instructive. It is that of the critics in such magazines as *Art News, Art Magazine, Art Forum, Art in America*, and who knows how many others on the West Coast. The history of art criticism, like that of literary criticism, is, on the whole, something to make a sensible man blush for his species, but the essays on the new artist in these journals are quite beyond belief. Either excruciatingly funny, or excruciatingly tragic, depending on one's point of view, they are attempts to make meaningful or profound, something which is not meaningful or profound, something which is deliberately trivial, something which, as many of the artists themselves say, is out to denigrate art and to render it absurd, not Absurd, but merely absurd. A third clue to what is going on is the inconceivable commercial success of the new art. The art-buying public is buying it up as fast as it possibly can; it is difficult today, once one has breached the first publicity barrier, not to be successful.

What is going on? A glance or two at each of the three major movements so far may help a little. Pop Art is, of course, perfectly named. It is the repetition on a different scale, or sometimes merely the display, of typical products of commercial art, such as Campbell's soup cans and boxes, or of the art of the lower cultural levels, as in Liechtenstein's enormous versions of comic-book panels. Now it is worth observing that Liechtenstein did not use as his source the comic strips of the newspapers, and for good reason. As recent research has shown, if you see a man on a bus reading the newspaper comics, the chances are high that he is a college graduate, and they are low that he never went beyond primary education. The comic books, however, are a different matter. Their audience is composed of children, not very intelligent adolescents, and rather stupid adults. They are clearly the art of almost the lowest cultural level, at least the lowest cultural level with a significant commercial life. Similar are Warhol's endless pictures of Marilyn Monroe, the same photograph, sometimes colored variously, sometimes in a single color, sometimes just black and white, in what appears to be a random order. Even more instructive is Liechtenstein's recent work, sculptures inspired by the architecture and decoration of the 1930's, a style regarded today as one of very low status.

Still more illuminating is Warhol's movie *My Hustler*. The most extended sequence simply points the camera at two men in a bathroom, grooming themselves endlessly, and discussing whether or not the blonde should take the advice of the brunette and become a professional hustler, a homosexual prostitute. Fairly sensational material, one would think, but not when Warhol gets through with it. The effect moves from the shocking to the funny to the banal to nothing at all. It is, I believe, supposed to move that way. It is a superb and virtuosic demonstration that Warhol can trivialize anything, can remove the emotional power from any subject whatever. As he says, he likes to make things boring; he likes boring movies. Well, they are not really boring; comfortable, perhaps, would be the better word, or cozy. His factory, judging by the pictures, his comments, and the recording in the recent *Andy Warhol's Index (Book)*, has all the relaxed *Gemütlichkeit* of the old-fashioned extended family, with neither the snobbishness nor the moral and artistic seriousness of Jane

Austen's world, though in other ways it does remind one more than a little of the Victorian country-house gathering, as we know it from Victorian novels. And "factory" is his new word for the traditional "studio," so charged with an aura of magic creativity, the highest realm of civilization. But Warhol is at his most enchanting when he submits to an interview. For the most part he simply says nothing, though at times he says a little more than that. On the whole, however, he simply refuses to play the journalist's game, or to perform the role of the avant-garde artist. Does he take himself seriously? Does he take his art seriously? When Warhol is through with a reviewer, the questions have become irrelevant, indeed, quite meaningless.

From this it is reasonably evident what the Pop Artist has done. In one way or another he has refused to say anything at all. In these comic-book frames, Rinso boxes, and 1930's bric-a-brac, and so on, there is no irony, no implied social criticism, no nostalgia, nothing. The artist has simply presented something and divorced himself from it by trivializing it, if it is something once important, or blowing it up to a heroic scale, if it were originally trivial. The result is the same. There is nothing of "I shall show you fear in a handful of dust," nothing portentous, nothing in the slightest degree significant. These works are not parodies; they are not affectionate imitations. As Warhol says, they are simply something to do. He has, in short, abdicated one of the basic demands of the artist's role as we have known it and as all cultures have known it, that he say something important. Even the oral artist who is the master of telling dirty jokes says something important. He makes sex and defecation funny, or outrageous; he adds something to his material. He comments. The Abstract Expressionist, the practitioner of the last modern style, presented, he insisted, his emotions, or more precisely, his feeling states, and made possible for the observer what he considered to be significant feeling states, just as the composer does. Since the coming of Romanticism, the artist has also been supposed to say something original as well as important, and before that the society saw to it that he said something the society considered important. When the importance of the subject was abandoned in painting and the motif took its place, then the artist's comments were considered to be of sole importance, until the Abstract Expressionists discovered that a motif was not necessary for an important comment. The comment could exist free of all phenomenal situations. But the study of the iconography of motif paintings shows that even in such paintings the motif had a significance; it was, after all, this and not that.

The next step after Pop, Op Art, offered the spectacle of a further abdication. Although there are a few practitioners left, it was obviously not a very fruitful line. All it set out to do was to give a visual shock. To be sure, all innovative artists give a visual shock, but only because their style has radically changed from its predecessor. Abraham Rattner, for example, gave a certain shock years ago because of the intensity and purity of his colors. Others have shocked by their novel modes of distorting recognizable configurations. But Op did nothing of all this. Taking its cue from the designs in psychology textbooks to illustrate problems in understanding the nature of perception, and from certain textiles, the Op artist reduced his work simply to presenting a perceptual ambiguity or something so dazzling it was hard to look at. In traditional art, the closest precursor is to be found in Christmas tree ornaments, and some of the Op works were simply such ornaments, foil icicles, for example, blown up to an enormous scale, larger than the viewer. The Pop artist abdicated all comment on his subject; the Op artist abdicated both comment and subject, nor, unlike the Abstract Expressionist, were his works to be construed, except in the most primitive and unavoidable way, as signs of feeling states, or emotions. Actually, the Op artist presents, for the most part, two similar visual regularities out of phase. Once the perceiver has figured it out, there is nothing else to be responded to, except some bright and pretty colors. But at least the Op artist preserved what I have called perceptual discontinuity, the one attribute that distinguishes art from non-art. (See my *Man's Rage for Chaos: Biology, Behavior, and the Arts*).

The Mini Artist has now abandoned even that. All over the world children go through the same procedure in their early experiments with two-dimensional signs, making the cross, the X, the square, the circle, the triangle. There is good reason to think that in mud-pie making they do much the same thing with three-dimensional signs. Such signs are of the highest importance to art, for they form the configurations which the configurations in art imply, and occasionally present. The higher the cultural level, the more remote the implication. What the Mini Artist does is simply to present these signs, frequently on an enormous scale, and the scale seems to get bigger as each art season arrives. In New York City this past fall there were on display a number of enormous Mini sculptures, and for a recent exhibition the Corcoran Art Gallery in Washington commissioned several so large they had to be built inside the museum. Two-dimensional Mini Art, of which Frank Stella may have been the first practitioner, simply presents such signs. Occasionally there are variations. Kenneth Noland has created a massive reputation by painting stripes. The result looks like a rather elaborate wallpaper or canvas awning. This is no denigration, at least on my part. I believe they are supposed to look like that. The sculptors present huge cubes and rectangles, or great X's, forty feet high. These are simply children's blocks on an enormous scale, and some sculptors are particularly pleased when children play on them. They are properly called Mini Art (minimal, not miniature) because they have no visual ambiguity or discontinuity at all. They can be perceptually grasped at once, with no loss of effort. They exactly match the cognitive-perceptual models for children's two- and three-dimensional signs, which everyone has at his disposal in the perceptual transaction. Mini Art has abdicated everything in art except scale. But the scale makes them easier to grasp. The Mini artist creates what a child would create if the child had the materials, the tools, and the craftsmanship, which is that of a good carpenter or draftsman.

Since 1960, then, the American artist, who is the leader in the world of international art, has abdicated every essential attribute of the artist's role as his society, and any society, has traditionally conceived of it. Everything, that is, except making things, and that is why Warhol, with his extraordinary penetration (Is it intelligence? It is impossible to tell.) calls his studio the factory. And he makes things only to deny the validity of the artist's role and the validity of his culture's demand that he play it. He has deliberately stripped that role of all of its glamor, all of its importance, all of its quasi-religious significance. He has, in short, completely overturned the Romantic conception of the artist, as the alienated, cursed, tortured redeemer of the world. He offers comfortable art, art that imposes no challenges, demands no intellectual or even perceptual effort, refuses all questions, turns serious critical effort into a mockery of itself. It leaves nothing for the spectator to do, and nothing for the critic to do, and nothing for the public to do, except to buy it, if they are silly enough to do so, as they most assuredly are. Why this revolution?

To understand it we must go back to the beginnings of Romanticism itself. The real question is whether these artists have denied the validity of the Romantic conception of the artist, have denigrated and trivialized it and turned their back on it, or whether in some odd and unforeseen way they are in fact carrying it another step, a step dictated by the logic of the situation.

The Romantic artist took upon himself an extraordinary task, the introduction of value into the world. Art accrued to itself what had been for the sophisticated the task of philosophy and for the unsophisticated and the historically remote sophisticated the task of religion. A few philosophers, such as Hegel, felt that the highest activities of man were philosophy, religion, and art, in that order, while artists, such as Wordsworth or Caspar David Friedrich, claimed that philosophy was properly conceived as the offspring or consequence of art, and this view became the predominating one in the Romantic culture of Europe and America in the nineteenth and twentieth centuries. The demonstration of this position usually hinged upon the notion of the imagination—more completely, the creative imagination. Few phrases have, even today, or especially today, such power. Merely to say "the creative imagination" is a means of ascribing to oneself great value; to understand the importance of these words one has only to think of the self-intoxicated look of the typical English teacher when he utters them—or for that matter, of the teacher of anything, particularly kindergarten, or of the scientist, or even, since "style" was added to the vocabulary of government by the late Kennedy administration, of high Federal officials. "Creative imagination" has come to excuse all sins of intellect and art; it is the universal solvent of established positions about anything. To understand what the new artists are up to it is useful to examine this phrase with some care.

"Creative" identified the artist with God or with a surrogate of God. The idea that the artist is divinely inspired was, of course, an old one, but the Romantic conception was, though dependent upon it, something novel. It metamorphosed the artist from instrument into agent, from sacred vessel into sacred rod, or magic wand. Consequently it is not surprising that a good many artists, critics, and philosophers of art identified the artist with Christ, either as a surrogate of God or as an avatar of God, who takes upon himself the enormous task of redeeming the world, that is, of introducing value into experience. But let us look at this term a little more coolly. Since it is laden with such intense value, it is useful to substitute for it a much more colorless word, a quieter word, innovation. Now innovation is the norm of human behavior, for several reasons. If we employ the cognitive-model theory of perception and knowledge, it is apparent that human beings pick up from each situation certain clues which bring into play certain pre-tuned psychic sets, or cognitive models, which make sense out of the situation by selection, reduction, structuring, and simplifying. It is evident, then, that there is always a disparity between the total phenomenal data of a situation and the cognitive model used to comprehend it. There must, therefore, be an adaptation of the model to the situation, though the most characteristic human behavior is to avoid as much adaptation as possible. Every perceptual-cognitive activity, therefore, introduces innovation into human behavior. The consequence is behavioral drift.

A second source of innovation emerges from the fact that our various semiotic systems, verbal and nonverbal, with which we interpret the situation and communicate our interpretations, are both categorial and conventional. The consequence of the first is that we understand any configuration only in categorial terms; we cannot know what it really is, only how it may be categorized. This is the distinction, to use Coleridge's terms, between the actual—the phenomenon—and the real—the interpretation of the phenomenon, an activity of the mind—to use a dirty four-letter word—never derived from the data immediately before it. Hence there is no empirical test for the adequacy of the semiotic categories. Since our whole tendency is to believe that the categories are derived from the data, are immanent within the data, from which we draw them, it follows that on the whole we have very little control over categorial application. Consequently every situation for which there is a semiotic response (that is, all situations) introduces innovation in the attributes of the category, the range of phenomena which the categories cover, and the ways the categories are bundled or logically structured together.

The conventionality of categories, both verbal and nonverbal, brings in a further source of innovation. The categories have to be learned, and since that is the case, humans learn categories as behavioral patterns. Now since, in any learning process, the unique experiences and interest of each individual govern his cognitive activities, no pattern of behavior is ever learned precisely. And to this it is necessary to add that each individual therefore has not only psychological limitations to what he *can* learn but also physiological limitations, which, apparently, involve not merely muscular movements but also the highest centers of the nervous system, the brain itself. Learning, therefore, invariably introduces innovation.

Every culture, consequently, is faced with the problem of selecting from the endless torrent of innovation those innovative patterns which, for whatever reason, frequently bad or inadequate, it considers valuable. Creativity is culturally selected and validated innovation. The Romantic notion of creativity and the creative artist means, as an irresistible consequence, that whatever innovation an artist produces is automatically valuable, ought to be culturally validated, and is, potentially, at least, redemptive of that culture. But since this is a claim quite beyond rational acceptance, Romantic criticism and aesthetics has centered upon the question of what is truly creative. The answers, of course, are infinite; since the question is a pseudo-question, there is no possible way of limiting the available answers.

"Imagination" is a term with equally built-in confusions, as it has been transmitted by Romantic culture and absorbed into the society. Before Romanticism it meant, roughly, the power to make up that which is not the case. Diseased, it is the source of madness. In sexual behavior, it is the source of love. In art, it was the root of the artist's power to invent a better or at least more interesting world than the one we live in. Hence, as Shakespeare said, the lunatic, the lover, and the poet belong to the same species. In the course of the later eighteenth century, however, it was decided that such inventions reveal the structure of thinking more clearly and more purely than any other behavior. Since the artist had been culturally designated to present signs of the values most highly regarded in the culture, it was almost automatic that he was the one chosen—though the lover and the lunatic were not without interest—as the highest revealer of the mind. Consequently, with the coming of Romanticism, the imagination came to mean not merely the power of invention but, much more significantly, the power to make sense out of experience, a sense which is not immanent in the world but which the human mind brings to it. This is the proper distinction between Coleridge's actual and real. The artist, then, reveals the real.

In the English tradition, Coleridge is more responsible than anyone else for the resultant confusion. In his exaltation of the imagination he made both a semantic and a logical error. In his famous distinction between the fancy and the imagination, he attempted to distinguish between the power to invent and the power to make significantly real. However, as his examples, which nobody has ever been able to understand, make abundantly clear, the distinction is not between two kinds of behavior but is a value distinction. The power to make up may very well reveal the structure of the mind, but that is simply because the results are not empirically tested; the cognitive model thus emergent is not corrected, as it is when our cognitive models are actually engaged with the world and used to control it and change it. Thus, as it turned out, it is impossible on these grounds to distinguish between the scientific and the poetic imagination. Coleridge's attempt to define the imagination resulted in the mere assertion that the cognitive models made by artists are superior to those made by anyone else.

His logical error entailed a similar confusion. If the imagination means the power to make sense out of experience, then it is obvious that everybody has it; without it no one could cross a crack in a sidewalk, let alone get to the other side of the street. To say that it is the peculiar gift of the artist is exactly similar to Orwell's justly famous, "All animals are equal, but some animals are more equal than others." Whether the sense one makes out of the world is better than the sense another makes is a matter for investigation, and that investigation, in its sophisticated form, we now call science. But Coleridge, and the other Romantics, claimed that, because artists are particularly good at making things up, the sense they make out of the world is superior to everyone else's. After a lifetime spent in the study of the arts, I can only say that I see no reason to believe this notion. It is true that some artists make better sense out of experience than other artists and even than a great many non-artists, but that is because they are intelligent, not because they are artists. On the whole they tend to make a much richer sense, but that is a different matter, for elegance and economy are the characteristics of the more adequate scientific constructs.

To innovate a sense-out-of-the-world which is subsequently culturally validated—that is all "creative imagination" amounts to. It is something that everybody does because he can't help himself, and something that the culture does because it can't help itself, and by "culture" here is meant merely "other people." The condition of man, then, can be seen as an endless and desperate attempt to hold his ground in the face of a continuous avalanche of human innovation, and at the same time to select those bits of innovation of some merit, such as a novel twist to the technique of laying bricks. But we can say more than this to the detriment of the imagination. The cursed human paradox is that the imagination, the power to make sense out of the world, is man's deadliest enemy. The exercise of the imagination is something we cannot avoid, but, since it makes sense out of the world, our primary interest is to maintain the sense we currently have. Hence the paradox that although the flow of innovation is constant, a stated program for achieving innovation is usually resisted. Even for a psychotic the sense he makes out of the world is what keeps him going. To abandon an imaginative model means, to use the terms of Coleridge, the collapse of the real and the helpless exposure to the actual. Thus imaginative models are psychological defenses. Since that is the case the psychological processes involved in constructing a truly radical vision of the world, or any aspect of it, are by no means smooth. On the contrary, before such a breakthrough occurs, the individual is so disoriented that his overt behavior often enough cannot be discriminated from certain kinds of psychotic behavior; and a similar breakdown of normal functioning usually follows the breakthrough. A cognitive model, or imaginative construct, does not give easy birth to a new and more adequate one; on the contrary, when it collapses under the pressure of empirical testing, the consequence is the confusion of the exposure to the actual; it occurs when data cannot be categorized by the existent cognitive model. That is why it takes courage both to create a new scientific theory and to have a thoroughgoing nervous breakdown. The task of the psychiatrist is to exploit the opportunity given by the collapse of the current self-conception either by preventing the construction of new defenses against the unassimilable material or by frustrating a desperate return to the previous self-conception. The task of the scientific partner is precisely the same. Indeed, all large-scale innovation is always the result of some kind of dialectical personal interaction. On the one hand, then, we gain new and more adequate notions of the world by exercising the imagination; but on the other hand we are the victims of the imagination. We can't live with the imagination, or live without it.

The glamorization of the creative imagination meant that the Romantic artist was supposed to make a supremely important new kind of sense out of material of the highest possible cultural status; the Pop artist presents material of low cultural status and makes no comment. The Romantic artist was supposed to create extremely complex and richly organized formal structures; the Op artist offers simple visual puzzles. The Romantic artist was supposed to present the most sophisticated, cultivated, and complex products of human endeavor; the Mini artist offers us the spoils of the kindergarten, and of the pre-kindergarten. It is evident that the new artists have seen through the pretentions of the "creative imagination." The sacred enclosure, the divine dancing ground at which the humanly ennobling imaginative creativity bursts into flame—the artist's studio—has become Andy Warhol's factory. It is not surprising, then, that art-lovers who have conceived themselves as worshipers of the Romantic creative imagination, whose very self-valuation is founded upon this particular way of making sense out of the world, should be horrified, enraged, and filled with despair when they observe what is going on. Pop, Op, and Mini have swept away the foundations of their being. And this explains the excruciating absurdities of current art criticism. The critics are making a desperate, a courageous, a heroic, even a noble attempt to assimilate the new art into the Romantic conception of art. But their efforts are vain. Pop, Op, and Mini are unassimilable.

Apparently, then, these new arts do not belong to the Romantic tradition, and it would seem that their emergence marks the end of Romanticism. But that does not necessarily follow. Romanticism is an exceedingly rich and various way of thinking, the virtues of which, to my mind, are still being explored. The possibility that the new artists are still Romantics comes out when what they have done is expressed as an alienation from the cultural tradition which formed them, that is, the Romantic tradition through Abstract Expressionism; the dynamic power of Romanticism is precisely alienation from one's culture and one's society. However, it does not follow that the new alienation is necessarily Romantic alienation. Some further common attribute must be discovered before such an assertion can be made.

Pure, unadulterated alienation is an extremely difficult position, indeed, one almost impossible to maintain for very long. Some psychological strategy is necessary to overcome the inability to act which is the manifestation of alienation, or perhaps is alienation. The Romantic solution has always been cultural transcendence, the construction of a metaphysics or a way of making sense out of the world and the derivation of set of values which have an antithetical and dialectical relation to the metaphysics and values of the existent culture. Cultural transcendence is in particular something to be achieved by denying the validity of the form of human behavior which currently has the highest status and is believed to be the area in which the most important problems are to be found and the most important solutions are to be achieved, the area of human activity which is the ultimate source of human value. From this point of view Hegel's philosophy can be seen as a magnificent exploration of the possibilities, strategies, and techniques of cultural transcendence. He did not say, after all, that he had arrived at the ultimate philosophy; he merely said that his philosophy was the most advanced possible at his time, and he saw the history of philosophy, a subject which he introduced into professional philosophical studies, as a history of successive achievements of cultural transcendence over positions which human experience had invalidated. Thus, in common with all the great Romantics, he saw his position as open-ended, that is, a position which could and must be itself transcended. The history of man is the history of the self-transcending *Geist*.

Now at the end of the eighteenth century there were two areas of human activity considered to be the ultimate sources for human value; their historical emergence was successive. Both are still with us. The earlier one was, of course, religion; and the one which transcended it, beginning to emerge in the fifteenth century, was politics. To the Romantic both had failed; instead, the most common Romantic solution was, as we have seen, art. It is within what we may, perhaps carelessly, call the logic of the Romantic situation that sooner or later art itself must be transcended; the only question was, when and under what circumstances. Much has been said about the cultural revolution that has occurred in the United States since World War II. It has been roundly affirmed, and as roundly denied or at least minimized. That it has happened, however, is I think undeniable. All over the country art centers are being built, at enormous cost, and at considerable sacrifice, both to the wealthy in the form of gifts, and to the less prosperous and to the poor in the form of taxes. It is the recognition of the Romantic assertion that the success and value of a culture is to be measured by its productivity in the arts and its respect for them, both in cherishing them and teaching them. Thus the Washington Center for the Performing Arts was having great difficulty in getting together funds until the assassination of President Kennedy. Congress then voted funds for its completion as a memorial to the late President. It was an astonishing decision. But that is not all. Of late, $2,000,000 has been spent for a second-rate Rembrandt, and nearly $1,500,000 for at best a second-rate

Monet, and all this by a museum already filled with second-rate paintings, not to speak of, as it admits from time to time, forgeries. Nor is this all. The art market in New York City, and elsewhere as well, has become so active that art dealers and even artists are becoming wealthy. The day of the reproduced masterpiece is over, or at least has receded to the lower middle-class level. To be chic, one must now have an original. Yet enormously expensive books of art reproductions sell fantastically. Its publishers expected 2,000 subscriptions for the new *Encyclopaedia of Art*; they received, initially, eight years ago, 10,000, at a price of over $500 for a set of fifteen volumes. It is well worth the price—but 10,000 copies! What has happened is that the upper cultural half of the society has accepted the Romantic conception of art as the redemptive area of human activity. Furthermore, it is instructive that this acceptance began to appear on a massive scale concurrently with the undertaking of the new art centers, shortly before the appearance of Pop and its two successors. An explanation is possible.

The psychological dynamism for cultural transcendence comes from alienation. So long as the culture refused to accept art as primary in human affairs, the Romantic alienated artist could continue to find in art the ultimate source of human value. Art could be his religion, his redemption, and the world's. However, that is no longer true. Politics has bowed to art, and so has religion. All over the country ecclesiastical architecture of the most elaborate and innovative sort is receiving the support and the money of the wealthier suburbs, and the nighttime illumination of churches can now be found in the remotest hamlet. Night illumination was developed in Europe in the 1930's as a way of attracting tourists by making great works of architecture available by night as well as by day. Does the rage for building splendid and splendidly modern churches come from the desire to validate art by religion, or religion by art? The circumstance is equivocal, but the cultural situation seems to indicate that the latter is what is really going on. At any rate, art is now a commercial success as it never has been; it has become a major area for capital investment. It is impossible to assert that the Romantic artist is alienated, not when business corporations build the most dazzling modern buildings and fill them with the most fashionable works of art. This triumph of the Romantic status of art, therefore, has compromised the Romantic artist; it has destroyed the very source of his psychic and cultural dynamism, his alienation. The only possible immediate solution is the cultural transcendence of the Romantic concept of art.

This is the cultural situation which is responsible, I believe, for the deliberate denigration and trivialization of art and of the artist's role, for the current crisis in the arts, for Pop, Op, and Mini. The Romantic artist's cultural logic now requires that he alienate himself from his own tradition. Romanticism separated the self from the role, and developed the role of the Romantic artist as an anti-role, a role that could maintain his alienation and from which he could achieve cultural transcendence, for it made possible the symbolization of the self as antithetical to the socially validated role and hence to the culture. But that anti-role is no longer what it was; it is now merely another culturally validated role. The artist must now, therefore, give away the secret, reveal his anti-role as only another role and attack it. The new art is out to prove that the Emperor of Art is wearing no clothes, or, more accurately, is only clothes, as Carlyle would have put it.

Looked at this way, I believe, Pop, Op, and Mini are developments logical, rational, and necessary. Nevertheless, with their emergence the culture is exposed to a grave danger. It has often been said that Romanticism and the Romantic tradition place their primary emphasis and indeed find their primary source of value in the irrational, and as a corollary to this it is still too often asserted that the Romantic writers and artists were antiscientific. Though there is a certain validity in these statements, they distort the situation badly. Consequently, to give but one instance, the New Criticism, which is a pallid form of the Transcendentalism of the 1830's and the 1840's, has, for example, misunderstood Coleridge's concept of the imagination and has, as with Tate and Brooks, set up a sharp antithesis between poetry and science, an antithesis which none of the major Romantics would have accepted. For example, to Carlyle the factuality of fact was as important as the mind's transcendence of fact; Carlyle's epistemology was at heart a kind of operationalism, or philosophical pragmatism, in which the imagination cannot operate without the fact. To give a couple of other examples, Constable studied and reorganized his rendering of clouds and sky on the basis of the newly founded science of meteorology, while Turner controlled many of his choices of color by the principles of Goethe's *Farbenlehre*, which then, at least, was still considered by many a scientific treatise. Wordsworth's presentation in a poem of the exact dimensions of a pond shows the same interest.

The Romantics, then, were interested not in the irrational for its own sake or even directly, but rather were concerned with the borderline between the rational and the irrational; their primary interest was in the limits of the rational, with, as a twentieth-century philosopher has put it, the limits of scientific thought.

But the very term "irrational" is filled with semantic perils; it appears to have two principal semantic functions. If the rational is thought of as the human capacity to make sense out of the world, to create, for instance, scientifically useful linguistic constructs, then the rational can be seen to be frustrated, to find its limits, in two directions, to use a common spatial metaphor. Between the stimulus and response lies an abyss; the ongoing activities of these depths are unknown to us, and always will be. Whatever goes on, it is responsible for the varying interpretations of the world which different people offer of precisely the same situation. Thus, instead of the traditional S→R formulation, we should use something like S→I→R. Consequently, when we examine the mental activities of ourselves or others, we discover inevitable limits to the rational comprehension of the uniquely personal and the universally human interests that govern our interpretation of a stimulus and hence our response to it. Now the rational may be considered those "mental" constructs, or cognitive models, which we use to control our behavior, to predict the world, and to find our way about in it and control it. Claude Lévi-Strauss's *The Savage Mind* is a fascinating study of this organizing power, the theory of which he calls "structuralism" and which is nothing more nor less than an anthropological reassertion of Romantic epistemology. (This should not be surprising; he depends on Freud and Marx, and they in turn emerge from Hegel. However, his admiration for Rousseau confuses his interpretation of what he has found.) Even his proposal, which makes me want to stand up and cheer, that the study of logic is properly the domain not of the philosopher but of the psychologist and the ethnographer is directly in the Romantic tradition. Thus the roots of the rational are deeply embedded in the irrational.

In the other direction lies the phenomenal world. Here the rational, or structuring, imaginative power finds its limits in the failure of its structure and its categories to exhaust the phenomenal attributes of any situation. No matter how rich and complex the mental structure, or, to be a little more careful, the verbal or nonverbal semiotic construct put to use in any situation, there are always sensory data left over. In this direction, also, then, the mind encounters the irrational.

However, at this point a second semantic function for "irrational" emerges. Not to recognize the limits of the rational in either direction is to be irrational. To put one's entire faith in the rational is to forget its limits and is to be irrational. Thus "irrational" can direct our attention to those interests, or emotions, as some people, rather more loosely, would say, which may be properly thought of as controlling the rational and providing its roots and nourishment; it can direct our attention to that emotional turbulence—to use Lévi-Strauss's term—which interrupts rational processes only because such processes are ultimately inadequate; or "irrational" can direct our attention to the way we use our constructing powers as a defense against the irrational in the mind and the irrational in the world. Such is, for example, the interest of many psychotics, both schizoids and manic-depressives, in building unbelievably elaborate constructs which are absolutely resistant to the recognition either of their irrational sources or their empirical limits.

The Romantic tradition, then, is interested in both the rational and both senses of irrational. To distinguish these two senses, I shall use "extra-rational" to indicate what lies beyond the borders of the rational, and "irrational" to point to the blind confidence in the constructing powers of the mind, the exclusion of the awareness that those powers must always be corrected by the world and compromised by their irrational roots. The Romantic, from this point of view, is consequently primarily interested in the frontiers of the rational, in the tension between the rational and the extra-rational and the tension between the rational and the irrational. To ignore that tension, to imagine that the categories of the reason exhaust the attributes of either subject or object—to use now old-fashioned Romantic terms—is to be irrational, as it is to ignore the fact that the grounds for any decision are extra-rational. Hence the Romantic's interest in science, which is the organized and sophisticated technique of revealing the limits of the rational and thus extending its powers farther into the realm of the extra-rational.

The real importance of all this lies in the Romantic's placing the ultimate source of human value in art. If value comes from our power to make sense out of the world, then the emotional temptation to surrender to that power without correcting it and compromising it is enormous. It makes, therefore, an enormous difference in human affairs in what area of human behavior the individual and his culture are exposed to the maximum temptation to surrender to the irrational. By defining art as that area, the Romantic protected his mind and his culture against that temptation, for what happens in art is of no importance. Art is blessedly irresponsible, even more irresponsible than philosophy, and that is saying a good deal. Obviously, by "responsible" I mean the refusal to surrender to the power to make sense out of the world. Now art does not really make sense out of the world, but only out of signs of the contents of the world, interpreted as signs and not as the world itself. Thus artistic activity is at best a rehearsal for the encounter with the world, not that encounter itself. Moreover, it is not a rehearsal for the encounter with those phenomenal configurations for which the signs are categorial signs, but only of a desirable attitude toward the world when it is responsibly encountered; specifically, it is a rehearsal for the endurance of cognitive tension, of the awareness of the frontier quality of the mind, of the sense we make of the world and of the necessarily compromising roots of that sense, what Polanyi calls personal knowledge. Thus by ritualistically relegating the temptation of the irrational to the area of artistic behavior, the Romantic opened the way to science, the correction and extension of our constructive powers by a responsible encounter with the world. What I am proposing, then, is that the extraordinary development of science in the nineteenth and twentieth centuries is something that occurred neither in spite of Romanticism, nor independently of it, but was in fact made possible by Romanticism. The fact is that many of the greatest scientists of the nineteenth century were deeply interested in Romantic culture, particularly in Romantic philosophy, and in any case insofar as they were interested in art, as many of them were, they were exposed to the Romantic tradition. To give one instance, Freud, who certainly attempted to construct a scientific psychology, emerged from Romantic philosophy and art, as his early letters and his lifelong interests—his admiration for Dostoevsky, for example—plainly indicate. It is my own experience—and I say this with a certain regret—that sophisticated scientists whom I have met tend to be not only more knowledgeable about the various arts than most humanists, but also more penetrating, more subtle, and more responsible. On the other hand, the early Romantic philosophers were keenly interested in the empirical world, as their speculations on *Naturphilosophie*, picked up by Coleridge, show.

If then, one can accept the hypothesis that the Romantic tradition and the astounding forward leaps of science since the late eighteenth century are indeed complementary, then it is obvious that the denigration and trivialization of art by Pop, Op, and Mini—necessary though this development may be according to the logic of Romanticism—does indeed expose the culture to a grave danger. By denying that art is the ultimate source of human value, the new art threatens us with the evaporation of the defense against the irrational that at least high-level European culture has profited from. For the most part, the lower cultural levels still place their primary source of value in either politics or religion, and thus are relatively helpless against the temptations of the irrational, the blind confidence in the constructing power of the mind, its power to make sense out of the world, against, therefore, the imagination. Already threatening signs are appearing. If indeed hippiedom is not a temporary aberration but the archaic effort to forge a new life style, then its emphasis upon love indicates that for such individuals the mind is no longer protected against the irrational. Likewise, the interest in psychedelic drugs both in hippiedom and outside of it is a similar danger sign, for the sole effect of such substances is to expose the individual helplessly to the onslaughts of the imagination and to give him the most sublime confidence in the adequacy of his mental constructs. The fervor with which both drugs and hippiedom are preached by their adherents is also disturbing, for "religion" is used to indicate not only formal religion but any field of human behavior in which ultimate value is alleged to have its source. Similarly, sophisticated scientists are themselves exhibiting a new awareness of epistemological problems and a new and intense interest in the philosophy of science, a sign that their security is threatened by cultural forces of which they are only obscurely aware. And all these developments have been historically concurrent, a fact which suggests that what is involved here is the phenomenon of cultural convergence. The only protection against the collapse of art's defenses against the irrational is highly sophisticated philosophy; but this is not much of a consolation, for even at the highest cultural levels philosophy is available to only a few. If this cultural analysis, then, of the emergence of Pop, Op, and Mini has any validity, it would seem reasonable to predict that our culture, after a brief respite of less than two centuries— a respite which admittedly only a minority within the culture was able to profit from—is once again to be victimized by the imagination.

III CONSEQUENCES

14

ART

AND DISORDER

[1966*]

I

It is an honor and a privilege to have the opportunity to address
the members of this division of the American Psychological
Association and to submit my notions about art to their judgment. I daresay I am not far wrong if I think that, in spite of
divergences of opinion, we are all in agreement that traditional
philosophical aesthetics is hopelessly bankrupt. I feel quite sure
that a good many of us have felt the frustration and bafflement
of attempting to derive operational propositions from that aesthetics and to set up experiments based upon such propositions.
Indeed, aesthetics seems to provide no directions even for the
simple observation of human behavior when it can be categorized
as artistic behavior. Nor, to make matters worse, can it provide

* Delivered at the annual meeting of the American Psychological As-
sociation, September, 1966. Reprinted by permission from *Literature and
Psychology*, XVI (Spring, 1966), pp. 62–80. Copyright © 1966 by Leonard
F. Manheim and Morton Kaplan.

any rules for determining when a human being is, or is not, engaged in artistic activity.

Happily, we are not alone. In recent years a number of philosophers have subjected traditional aesthetics to the most penetrating analysis and have arrived at uniformly negative results. Briefly, the denial of any validity to traditional aesthetics reduces itself to the denial of the basic assumption of all aesthetics: all works of art have something in common. Or, more precisely, the word "art" refers to a category all members of which have in common at least one attribute. If this is not the case, then it follows that traditional aesthetics collapses. And not only aesthetics. The theoretical and practical criticism of any of the arts of which I have any knowledge is full of sentences of the form: "Poetry is x"; "Music is y"; "Painting is z"; and so on. The fact that thousands of such sentences have been uttered by critics, that any number of times critics of poetry have said, "At last we know what poetry really is," seems to discourage no one. They go right on making such statements, and the fact that no such statements have ever been widely or more than temporarily accepted never seems to suggest to them that there might be something radically wrong.

Nevertheless, in spite of the happy clearing of the air which is the result of the revelation of the logically unsound assumptions of aesthetics and criticism, a new and severe difficulty now appears. If "art" is not a valid category, then, strictly speaking, there is nothing to talk about. The category "art" collapses into the category "artifact." Or, if we shift ground to artistic behavior, whether of artist or perceiver, it collapses into all behavior. To talk about art at all involves the assumption that art can be distinguished from whatever is not art; but if all works of art have nothing in common, then it is impossible to make that distinction. To be sure, for psychologists, or even for critics and aestheticians, what the highest cultural level currently calls art is good enough. The psychologist has merely to say that he is investigating what his culture calls art. For him the term need not convey anything more. He still has a field of investigation. But when he wants to move outside of that particular culture, into, let us say, the cultural level in which comics and jokes and blue movies may or may not be art, he is in trouble. And he is in worse trouble when he wishes to move into societies other than his own, societies in which the term "art" does not exist. After all, in the current sense, it has existed in our culture for only a few hundred years. Paleolithic man had paintings, but are they art? Or rather, they are certainly art to us, if we want to call them art, but were they art to a people of whom we can reasonably be sure that they had no category "art"?

Nor is it satisfactory to talk about "artistic behavior." In some ways it helps a great deal to do so. It helps so much that I should like to assert at once than I myself am not interested in art but in artistic behavior. To me a work of art is the deposit or consequence of artistic behavior. But even this shift of reference leaves us worse off than before. The artifactual definition of art, even though only a matter of cultural convention, permits us to investigate whatever surviving from the past is currently called art, but we can scarcely investigate the artistic behavior of the Middle Ages, or even of yesterday. Clearly, if the term "art" is going to be of any use at all, we must find some way of distinguishing works of art from other surviving artifacts.

II

I cannot here give my argument in full, which is developed in my recently published book *Man's Rage for Chaos: Biology, Behavior, and the Arts*. I can only offer my solution to this difficulty and explain what I mean by it. To begin with, not only do I assert that the only proper object of investigation is artistic behavior, but also that such behavior is most usefully considered as a social role, patterned, learned, culturally transmitted, governed by rules, and elicited by the semiotic stimuli of a particular class of situation. A work of art, then, is any artifact in the presence of which an individual plays a particular social role. Furthermore, a work of art is what the perceiver observes in what has been culturally established as an artistic perceiver's space. Thus Andy Warhol's piles of Brillo boxes are works of art because they are exhibited in an art gallery; the situation defines them as works of art, by eliciting in the observer the art perceiver's role. An assertion that such works are not works of art by an observer actually in such a culturally defined artistic space is itself an admission that they are art. That is, it has occurred to such a perceiver that they are. That he should deny what the situation tells him is so is of no importance. The denial of the high-status term "art" to a work we dislike is too common to be taken seriously. The point is that the question should arise. And that it should arise is itself an answer to the question.

Extending the role metaphor for human behavior, I go on to assert that a work of art may be defined as an occasion for a human being to perform the art-perceiving role in the artistic situation, that is, on the artistic stage. An artist is merely one whose social role it is to produce such occasions. As the recent rash of happenings has vividly demonstrated, the artist can produce anything so long as he can persuade his audience to play their art-perceiving roles. It is also obvious that some members of the audience will and some will not. As to why this should be so, I will return. In any case, with this definition of the artist we can dismiss him from further consideration. Clearly, he has to learn the perceiver's role before he can play the artist's role. But what kind of occasion he produces, his famed creativity, is no different from any other kind of cultural innovation. Artistic creativity presents no special problem, other than the problem as to why some people want to be artists. But that problem does not differ from the problem of why some people want to be policemen, or psychologists, or English teachers. All the tremendous amount of verbiage about the special problem of artistic creativity is, from this point of view, barking into an empty cave. It tells us something about the high status of the artist in our culture, but that is about all.

But we may go further than this, and proceed to what I call my final definition of a work of art. It is any perceptual field which an individual uses as an occasion for performing the role of art perceiver. A piece of driftwood placed upon a mantel becomes a work of art, because in our culture the mantelpiece has been conventionalized as an artistic space. But to the man who placed it there, it was a work of art as soon as, having found it on the beach, he perceived it as a work of art. Thus the Chinese placed interesting rocks in their gardens not in order to make them works of art but because they were works of art as soon as they decided that they were. The advantage of this position lies, for example, in its explanation of the confusion in traditional aesthetics between art and nature. A landscape is a work of art as soon as the individual decides to perform the art perceiver's role when he is looking at it. If he does not so decide, then it is not a work of art. And this accounts for the constant arguments in criticism as to whether a particular work should be accepted into the canon. For some people there may be something about it which makes it impossible for them to play the art perceiver's role.

On the basis of these definitions, it is possible, I think, to solve the conundrum of how we are to know whether or not a particular work was produced to be the occasion for the art perceiver's role, whether or not it functioned as a work of art in its particular culture. Any object, then, or perceptual field, from any culture, may be properly categorized as having been the occasion for artistic perception if a chronologically arranged sequence of such objects shows both functional identity and nonfunctional stylistic dynamism. I do not think I shall here arouse much antagonism if I assert that all behavior is styled, though in some critical and aesthetic circles such a statement would probably arouse intense disagreement. By style I mean this: all behavior is patterned, and patterns are stabilized and culturally transmitted because they are biological adaptations, or functional. But a behavioral pattern is, after all, a construct based upon innumerable unique percepts. It is apparent, then, that a functional pattern continues to be functional even though each individual exhibits unique variations of that pattern. That is, every pattern is styled. But even style is a construct, because in fact every recurrence of the individual's uniquely stylized performance of the pattern exhibits a novel configuration. Further, all behavioral patterning drifts. Not only is there the physiological limitation of the individual, but patterns must be transmitted by a semiotic or communication process, and any such transmission invariably involves loss both of content and of structure. Normally, an individual develops his unique style of performing a pattern and adheres pretty closely to it, although the limitations of memory and the exigencies of particular situations are responsible for a certain drift. After all, one of our tests for determining that an individual is disturbed is that his style, his way of performing cultural patterns, begins to disintegrate.

However, when we examine the behavior of artists, the producers of occasions for artistic perception, we find a striking difference. We find something more than drift; we find a dynamism. Let me give a couple of examples. The American axe handle is famous for the elegance and beauty of its curves as well as for its superior efficiency. The European axe handle is still a straight shaft. The reason is easy to find. Europe had few trees and a lot of people; America had a lot of trees and very few people. It was, therefore, adaptational to increase the man-hour productivity of the American tree-cutter by designing a more efficient axe handle. But the point is that once the new axe handle had been established, it remained unchanged. Its stylistic dynamism was functional.

The teakettle has had a different history. It took a long time to develop, but apparently by the end of the nineteenth century it had achieved functional perfection. The last change of importance was to make it of aluminum. Yet I daresay that among my readers there are a number of people young enough never to have seen the old-fashioned gooseneck teakettle. For along in the late 1930's the manufacturers of teakettles began to subject the teakettle to "design." The result is that it is now impossible to buy in any department store and almost any neighborhood store anything but a teakettle which is a handsome enough piece of sculpture but is also a functional disaster. You burn your fingers on the handle, and when you pour, the steam scalds your hand. The teakettle, like almost everything else in the modern kitchen, has become a work of art. Its sad fate is a salutary reminder that art can be terrible nuisance. The teakettle, then, has exhibited in the past thirty years nonfunctional stylistic dynamism. As a tool it has become dysfunctional, though this is not to deny that artistic behavior has an adaptational function, but merely to assert that the tool function of an object, whether a teakettle or a religious painting, and its artistic function can be, and probably always are, incompatible. Lest my point should have been lost, let me repeat that any object, or perceptual field, from any culture may, then, be properly categorized as having been the occasion for artistic perception if a chronologically arranged sequence of such objects shows both functional identity and nonfunctional stylistic dynamism.

But it is possible to go further than this. It appears that we may categorize as a work of art any artifact or any perceptual field, if it can be placed in a sequence of similar objects or fields which shows a greater rate of dynamism than other such sequences from the same culture. If, moreover, we find a series of sequences ranging from a low rate of dynamism to a high rate, we may say that in that culture the last sequence was the occasion from the most intense and devoted artistic perception. The higher the rate of stylistic dynamism and the more frequent the stylistic revolutions, the higher the cultural level for which the art is being produced. Properly applied, this principle is a way of determining the cultural level for which a particular sequence was made; further, as an artistic style descends from the higher cultural level to the lower, its rate of stylistic dynamism slows down, and vice versa.

It appears, then, that art is, after all, a valid category, and that for the category art there is a defining attribute. But that attribute can never be located in a unique work of art, or a unique instance of artistic behavior, whether artist's or perceiver's, but only in a sequence of functionally identical artifacts or behavioral patterns. The commercial amphora of the ancient Mediterranean world remained virtually unchanged for centuries, but the amphorae used for banquets and other ceremonial occasions show all kinds of changes in both profile and decoration. The defining attribute of art, then, can only be located in functionally identical sequences of artifacts or behavioral patterns, and it is nonfunctional stylistic dynamism.

III

I think it may be said that the central interest of all human beings is to create a predictable world. This may be an explanation of why it is that behavioral patterns are transmitted with as much exactness as possible and why it is that unpredicted behavior in ourselves or others should be taken as a sign of behavioral crisis and should often bring about crisis in the observers of such behavior. It would certainly seem to be an explanation of why innovation is usually resisted. Or perhaps it is not an explanation but merely a tautological restatement. Certainly, it may be said with some confidence that the unpredictable person is precisely the socially useless person, and that the goal of social training is to produce predictability. Of an individual whose behavior is unpredictable we say that he is disoriented. From this point of view the behavior of artist and perceiver is extremely atypical. The artist's role requires him to create occasions in which the perceiver's predictions will be frustrated, and the perceiver's role requires him to look for them. Hence the erection of artistic innovation into a special problem is no more than a response to this extremely peculiar condition. On the other hand, it is of course not true at all that innovation is to be found only in artistic behavior, nor do I wish to imply that it is or that it is not uniquely found there, only that artistic innovation in the perspective of tool function is nonfunctional or even dysfunctional. Nevertheless, an investigation of the innovating situation, when it conforms to the demands of social roles, shows a striking parallelism with the artistic situation. When we examine the circumstances in which such innovation takes place, such as the situation of the scientist, the scholar, or the great corporation president, it is obvious that it is characterized by psychic insulation. The laboratory, the study, the presidential office, even the design of university campuses, localities in which innovation is at least *supposed* to take place, are all marked by insulation from sensory stimulation which is not immediately pertinent to the problem at hand. Now it is obvious that the artistic perceiver is also psychically insulated; and the more the work of art to be perceived is characterized by nonfunctional stylistic dynamism the greater the insulation. Popular music can be successfully experienced in situations in which considerable extraneous stimulation is present. Yet when jazz moved to a higher cultural level in the 1940's and was characterized by a higher rate of such dynamism, people stopped dancing and started listening. The nightclub devoted to progressive jazz suddenly became a concert hall.

Innovation involves, of course, problem-searching, problem exposure, and problem-solving. I do not suggest that artistic perception is a matter of problem-solving, though artistic creation is. Rather, what problem-solving and the behavior of the art perceiver have in common is psychic insulation that permits disorientation, a discontinuity of perceptual experience. Henceforth, instead of nonfunctional stylistic dynamism I shall use the term "discontinuity," and the theory I am about to propose I call a general theory of the discontinuity of artistic perception.

It is obvious, therefore, that what is needed here is a theory of perception; and the theory I have adopted is the one frequently referred to, at least a few years ago, as the New Look in perception theory. It goes by various names, and has been arrived at by various schools of psychologists on quite different routes. Directive state theory, expectancy or expectation theory, transactionalism, TOTE theory, and perceptual model theory are the terms most frequently encountered. The essence of this position has been well stated by George Miller: "The organism struggles to reduce the mismatch between its own criteria and perceived reality." In this proposition the two elements I would emphasize are "criteria" and "perceived reality." The heart of the matter is that in any perceptual situation the criteria are not derived from perceived reality. Or, to use the terminology I prefer, the orientation which the organism applies to a given situation exists *a priori* to the perceptual phenomena of that situation. Now that orientation is best considered, I believe, as a system of categorization which the individual applies because he has responded to conventionalized clues in the situation. That is, an orientation does not prepare an individual to deal with a particular situation but only with a category of situations. The orientation may also be identified as an expectational set. For "mismatch" I substitute the term "cognitive disparity." The extraordinary thing about perception, therefore, is that cognitive disparity may be reduced by, to use a currently popular term, feedback. The orientation, or set, is capable of being corrected. However, two other qualifications need to be introduced at this point.

First is that before cognitive disparity can emerge and feedback take place, the individual must sense that something is wrong, that somehow or other his orientation is not successfully organizing the perceptual data. This experience I call cognitive tension.

Thus in the perceptual situation we have the following sequence: orientation, or expectancy, cognitive tension, cognitive disparity, problem location, problem-solving, feedback, corrected orientation. But all kinds of things can go wrong. The problem may be wrongly located; the solution may be incorrect; the feedback may be incomplete; and the orientation may be even less well adapted to that category of situation than it was at the beginning.

But something even more important may happen. The statement from Miller comes from a passage in his *Psychology: The Science of Mental Life*, which certainly leaves the reader with the impression that return to homeostasis is achieved by carrying through the entire procedure from application of criteria to reduction of mismatch and, presumably, correction of criteria. But to my mind he has left out an element of great importance. In this sequence it seems to me obvious that the critical stage is the stage of cognitive tension. The organism must endure cognitive tension until it has recognized that something is wrong, and it must endure that tension until it has located a problem, and it must endure the tension of problem exposure until it has solved the problem. But the critical stage is the first stage: enduring cognitive tension.

Now although Miller is, of course, perfectly correct when he says that the organism struggles to reduce the mismatch, it must also be added that it doesn't struggle very hard. Miller gives us too much credit. Homeostasis is not achieved by going through the whole cycle. It is ordinarily achieved by resolving the tension before disparity and problem location have emerged. The great human motto is, "Millions for the orientation but not one cent for the reality." The defense of the orientation and not the tribute to reality is what we prize above all else. As I have suggested above, only in conditions of psychic insulation is there a tendency for the entire cycle to be carried out, and certainly the history of culture, and even the history of scientific investigation, indicates that cognitive short-circuiting can and usually does occur at any stage in the cycle. Thomas S. Kuhn, in his study of the history of scientific research, has shown how even the scientist, whose role requires him to seek out problems and whose situation provides him with a high degree of psychic insulation, nevertheless commonly ignores perceptual data which his orientation—Kuhn uses the word paradigm—cannot organize. In short, the organism prefers homeostasis to any awareness of mismatch, or cognitive tension. There are two ways which it can use to dissolve that tension without going on to problem exposure. One is simply to suppress the awareness of data which violate expectancy; the other is to find new grounds for justifying the orientation. One might even say, sanctifying the orientation.

Perception, then, selects, simplifies, reduces, and organizes. That such behavior is adaptational, or biologically functional, is obvious. But on the other hand, the very character of perception, which enables us successfully to find our way about in the world, is the element in our behavior which disqualifies us for successful adaptation. The reason is that the perceptual model must eliminate data which are essential to successful situational adaptation. The hunter concentrating on spearing a charging lion ignores the tickling of the poisonous spider; the man with a fear of all authority figures misses the data which if properly observed would have shown him how to defeat the authority, when it was to his interest to do so. The very aspect of our behavior which qualifies us to deal with the environment disqualifies us. Functional perception is dysfunctional as well. I was interested to read in the conclusion to Berelson and Steiner's *Human Behavior* a statement of precisely this point. But these authors, quite understandably, considering the limitations of their fascinating task, do not go on to draw what seems to me an inevitable conclusion. Given this condition, there must be some form of human activity which is devoted to the practice or rehearsal of the endurance of cognitive tension; and this rehearsal must occur in situations in which nothing is at stake, in which the appearance or nonappearance of a genuine problem is a matter of indifference. That activity is, I believe, artistic behavior, and works of art are produced to provide occasions for the rehearsal for the endurance of cognitive tension; they train us to stand our ground when we encounter disorienting situations.

If such a position can be sustained, we will have an adaptational or biologically functional explanation for art; and we will be able to understand the expenditure of enormous, inconceivable resources of energy, intelligence, innovation, and economic wealth upon creating, exhibiting, and contemplating works of art. For my part, I think it astounding that a couple of thousand human beings should sit in silence and darkness while a hundred more make peculiar noises on odd instruments. The explanation I have suggested is the only way I can understand such strange behavior, and I should add that the only way I can ultimately think about human behavior is in terms of biological adaptation of the organism to the environment. It is, if you wish, my metaphysic.

IV

My next task is to offer grounds for the acceptance of this proposition by analyzing a few works of art and explaining the terminology and justification of my mode of analysis, but before I can do that, a couple of digressions or qualifications are desirable.

The obviously weak point in my argument is this. Only too easily can it be asked, "Are not such terms as orientation, expectancy, set, directive state, perceptual criteria, perceptual model, and so on—are these words not hypostatizations? Are not you and the psychologists you depend on victims of the fallacy of misplaced concreteness? Has anyone ever seen an orientation? If not, what evidence is there that there are such things? Furthermore, are not these merely substitutes, intervening variables, for mentalism? Are they not merely means of smuggling into a behavioristic framework substitutes for the naughty and forbidden word 'mind'?" The only answer to such questions is, "Well, unfortunately, yes." It helps, of course, to say that there is no claim that these terms refer to phenomenally existent entities, but that rather they are constructs. The question still remains, "On what empirical grounds are such constructs erected?"

Now the perceptual theorists I have depended on insist almost to a man that such explanations of perception invalidate behaviorism, or at least neobehaviorist S→R theory. To be sure, of late neobehaviorism has been getting some terribly hard knocks. Attack has particularly come from something called phenomenology, and it is of interest to note that phenomenology, as found in Heidegger and, particularly, in Sartre is a remarkable parallel to those theories I shall lump under the general name of expectancy theory, just as that theory shows remarkable similarities to recent philosophy of science and also of certain new developments in philosophical ethics, or value theory. But profound as the phenomenological philosophers may be, nobody would call them elegant, or even very clear. My reading in current attacks on behaviorism, in spite of my original feeling that expectancy theory irreparably damaged it, has led me to reconsider the matter, to attempt to meet these embarrassing questions; and here, unqualified as I am to deal with such matters, I am very much on my own. I have encountered no efforts to meet these questions, and only one to reconcile expectancy theory and behaviorism. In short, current attacks on behaviorism, though consonant with my own directive state, have made me much more sympathetic with behaviorism, though aware of its limitations. It is wise to remember George Miller's caution: "No one can now foresee what benefits or dangers may some day come from these fumbling efforts with caged animals and nonsense syllables—but we had better be prepared for success."

The irresistible advantage and appeal of all forms of behaviorism is that the behaviorist insists that all conclusions be based on, and only on, phenomenally observable behavior. "What is the organism doing?" the behaviorist asks, and that is the rock on which he builds his house. It is a very firm rock, though we have yet to see very much in the way of a house. By eliminating the word "mind" from his vocabulary, the behaviorist hoped to get away from talking about the unobservable, but in doing so he denied himself the opportunity to talk about a whole class of observables. Consequently, nearly 20 years ago it was felt necessary to introduce our old and now somewhat limp and bloodless friend, the intervening variable. But this self-denial was, I believe, quite unnecessary, and was based upon a logical error, which in turn was based upon a misconception of language and all signs. We are instructed from childhood that a noun is a name for a thing. Even the great Wittgenstein, to whom I must refer as a matter of ritual, asserted that "Objects can only be named. Signs are their representatives." A sign, then, names an object.

If no object can be located, then the sign or name is invalid. If mind cannot be located, then we should stop using the term "mind."

But, for reasons I cannot go into here, I believe that the notion that a word, or any sign, verbal or nonverbal, refers to an object is entirely in error. A sign refers not to an object but to a category of perceptual or phenomenal configurations. Such a category has a range of configurations and a set of attributes, that is, denotation and connotation. But a word does not denote an object; it denotes a range or community of configurations. And I would go even further and assert that categorial stability is almost impossible, that in any situation in which a word is used the range and attributes of its category differ from its use in all other situations, even though very slightly.

The proper question to ask, then, is what is the range and what are the attributes of this word in this situation. In the very loose situation of psychological investigation "mind" has a perfectly valid function; it refers to interpretational variability, the observable phenomenon that individuals act differently in the same situation and that the same individual acts differently in various instances of the same category of situation. That is, the way an individual interprets a situation varies independently from the variability of the situation itself. In turn, my use of the term "interpretation" depends upon a general theory of semiosis, according to which all configurations are, to the perceiving organism, signs. Such sign functions are conventionally established, even if the convention is held by only one individual. Numerous experiments have shown that if a configuration is encountered which is not conventionally interpretable, which has no semantic function, which cannot be categorized by some existent categorial system, the perceiver cannot tolerate such a degree of cognitive tension and forthwith makes sense out of it, makes it meaningful, by assigning it to the range of an existent category, even when such assignment is wildly inappropriate. It seems to me that Professor Ralph Stogdill's proposal that expectation theory and behaviorism can be reconciled is well founded. There is no such thing as "mind," just as there is no such thing as "tree," and no such entity as Morse Peckham. But when we use the word "mind" we are, after all, talking about observable phenomena, phenomena which the behaviorist can theoretically handle and, I should say, is already beginning to handle with some success.

Perhaps this digression was unnecessary and irrelevant, but I always like to display my assumptions quite openly. At least it permits me to say, I believe, this. When an individual uses the term "orientation" or "directive state," and so on, he is in fact predicting that the particular organism he is examining will behave in a particular way whenever it finds itself in a particular situation. Thus, even when the psychoanalyst talks about an unconscious fear of the father in language which I find hopelessly unacceptable, he is nevertheless predicting that his patient will tend to categorize authority figures in any situation in such a way that they have to him the same attributes of the feared and hated father, and that he will behave accordingly. The psychoanalyst may fancy he is talking about the unconscious mind; he is really making predictions, and many that he makes are highly reliable.

My second digression is less of one. It is the question of the semantic function of works of art, or content, as it is traditionally referred to. In recent decades a considerable fuss has been made about the abandonment of the distinction between form and content, or the demonstration that they are both one. So far as I am concerned the result merely serves to deprive both terms of what little referential value they formerly had. I propose frankly to reinstate the distinction, with a difference, analyzing the problem from the point of view of a roughhewn but I believe adequate general theory of signs. In my book I go into this problem at some length. Here I can but give briefly my conclusions.

Since I believe all experienced perceptual configurations are signs, it is no great trick for me to assert that works of art also are sign structures, if they consist of words, or sign packages, if they do not. The function of signs, including verbal signs, I believe to be, in the last analysis, behavioral control. Two classes of signs may be distinguished, natural and artificial. Artificial signs may further be broken down into arbitrary signs, of which words are the most prominent instance; configurational signs, of which traditional European painting is an example; and what, for want of better words, I call nonsituational or primary signs.

These are the signs of music; of color, depth, verticality, horizontality, and so on in painting; in architecture, verticality, horizontality, shadow, plasticity, screen opening, and so forth; and in poetry the various kinds of phonic overdetermination. Merely to give an instance of what I am talking about, but not to suggest that anyone at this point accept my position uncritically, I find the sense of demand signified in poetry by alliteration and assonance, in music by upward pitch motion, in painting by verticality, and in architecture by verticality and solidity. The only point I wish to make here is that I can discover no kind of semantic function in art which is not to be found also outside of art, and, for primary signs, also in the natural world.

Thus, departing sharply from the most common kind of contemporary poetic theory, I believe that nothing can be said in a work of art that cannot be said outside of art. There is nothing that a poet or any artist says by virtue of the fact that he is an artist. What he says is in response to extra-artistic cultural demands. The culture may demand that the poet devote himself to a particular kind of statement, or that the artist devote himself to a particular kind of subject matter, but his role as artist in itself, as distinguished from other socially established roles, provides no unique rules or directions in this matter; nor does his medium make it possible for him to say something which non-artists cannot say. The semantic or conventional aspect of art may be conveniently regarded in terms of the tool metaphor, in the sense that a Madonna is a religious tool, or an abstract painting is a tool for separating from situations signs of the sense of demand and acceptance, adequacy and inadequacy, fixity and flexibility, expression and inhibition, and so on. What stylistic dynamism the semantic aspect of art exhibits, therefore, is a matter of functional dynamism, not of nonfunctional dynamism or discontinuity.

V

One of the most common criteria for excellence in art is that it serves as a stimulus for intense emotion. Now there are only two ways emotion can be elicited; by presenting a sign configuration to which the perceiver is conditioned to respond emotionally, or by disorienting him, by violating his expectations, by offering the occasion for a discontinuity of perceptual experience. A work of art may or may not offer the first kind of emotional elicitation, just as any sign structure or package may or may not. Art's distinguishing attribute is that it always offers the second kind, but only for the observer who has been properly trained by his culture to bring the appropriate expectational set to that particular work. There are two sources of this training, normal experience and special experience. Of the second kind music is the most obvious example. One must be trained to expect certain musical processes before one can experience their violation. Nevertheless, the individual, because of the tendency to simplify and organize perception, can, if sufficiently sensitive and intelligent, build up a weighted average of exposure to a particular musical or other artistic style without special training. But the ordinary mode in our culture is special training for the high arts. As for normal experience, let me give two examples.

I shall begin with fiction, because it was a long time before I could understand how to apply my theory to this kind of art. A fiction begins by presenting a problem, usually in the form of something that doesn't make sense, or something that is not readily comprehensible. For most of us here the purest kind of fiction available is the detective story. Now in normal behavior, when a problem is encountered, the individual either suppresses awareness of it or devotes his energy to solving it. But fiction makes both impossible. On the contrary, it postpones the solution of the problem and prevents its suppression. And what we call well-made fiction introduces a number of problems related to the major problems. Fiction is endurable only because nothing is at stake, because it is made up, invented, because it is a lie. Consider the mild and amused contempt we have for the reader whose tolerance of cognitive tension is so low that he must peek at the back of the book to find out how the story comes out, how the problem is solved.

Another example of the violation of normal expectations is to be found in the language of poetry in English, and in a good many other languages as well. English poetry is characterized by badly made sentences; the poet is constantly messing up the syntax. In teaching poetry even at the college level it is necessary constantly to require the students to straighten it out. Their tendency is to do what is normal in any disorienting situation, to seize upon the recognizable feature and ignore the rest of the syntactical and semantic information. But this is true at much higher levels. I have seen graduate students helpless before Browning's *Sordello*, which, to be sure, is the most syntactically disordered poem in English before the twentieth century. Professional students of poetry have been arguing for decades over the syntax of Hopkins' "The Windhover."

But poetry also requires special training, or lengthy experience, so that the correct set of rhythmic and junctural expectations be acquired. Current theory, though it has been questioned, asserts that there are four levels of stress in English. Poetic convention recognizes two kinds of syllables, accented and unaccented, or, more properly, stressed and nonstressed, or, sometimes, weak and strong. Now rhythm, if it means anything, refers to the regular recurrence in time or space of identical or interchangeable perceptual configurations. Rhythm, by this definition, is the one thing that English poetry does not have. Or rather, it has it in patches, and the higher the cultural level for which the poem was written, the less frequent the patches of regularity. But when we see a poem our expectation is for rhythm, that is, for the recurrence every second syllable or every third syllable of a stress. These are the only two possible rhythms in English poetry. In recent years the metaphor "counterpoint" has been used to describe this phenomenon, but it is a very bad metaphor. In music counterpoint refers to the simultaneous presentation of two or more melodic configurations; but in poetry we expect a regular or rhythmic stress configuration and we are offered a violation of that expectation. Hence we experience a constant disorientation, the poet offering only enough patches of rhythmic regularity to reinforce our expectation.

This principle also explains the line, which is a typographical device to indicate the recurrence of juncture, or pause, or hiatus in the phonic stream. In English blank verse, a fairly long juncture is required at the end of every tenth syllable. The violation of that expectation, when it has been reinforced for a number of lines, is one of the most powerful effects in poetry; it is usually called the run-on line. The poet also has another means of discontinuity, though less powerful, in the internal juncture, or caesura, which is prescribed to occur after the fifth syllable, but which he can move back or forth, multiply, or eliminate. When Shakespeare's plays are examined in the more or less reliable chronological order objectively established, a striking phenomenon leaps to the attention. The order of the plays corresponds to the increasing frequency of violated line and junctural expectations. All kinds of explanations have been offered for this, but on the theory presented here, it is obvious that a highly gifted poet writing for twenty years in the same verse form unavoidably increases the frequency of this kind of discontinuity. This Shakespearean phenomenon is an instance of what I call external discontinuity, and it is to be found in the work of every artist of the higher cultural levels I have examined.

Whenever I encounter in aesthetics or criticism the word "form," my mind goes blank. But from the point of view presented here, it is possible to locate a semantic function for this almost meaningless term. In artistic perception form refers to the expectancy; form is not a character of the work, which is irregular and indeed in any normal use of the term, formless, but of the perceptual *a priori*. Form, then, is a mode of perception; and art violates form. Hence I call this aspect of the work of art the formal aspect, as opposed to the conventional or semantic aspect. External discontinuity, as we have seen, refers to the violation of the expectations a particular series of works has built up. But the individual work also exhibits, as I have pointed out, discontinuity which can be experienced independently from the series. The kind I have examined is implicit discontinuity. It is the violation of any perceptual form implied by the perceiver's recognition of a perceptual field which, in his culture, is an art situation, or by his application of those rules to any perceptual field not hitherto, in his culture, so conventionalized. This is why the Chinese connoisseur can see a naturally formed rock as a work of art, and also why a contemporary sculptor can so perceive a mashed automobile.

A second kind is internal discontinuity, which is the violation of a perceptual form established in that particular work of art.

It, too, can be experienced in the perception of fields not hitherto defined as works of art. Let me give a few examples. In poetry, the seventeenth-century Pindaric ode proceeds by presenting a rhyme scheme often enough to build up expectation for its continuation, and then violates it. Another device is to present a pattern of lines of varying length, to repeat the first couple of lines of that pattern, and then to violate. Ordinarily, internal discontinuity depends upon the establishment of a pattern within a work, but in the Pindaric ode the poet can depend upon the practiced reader to expect a familiar stanzaic line pattern upon the presentation of only the first part of it. What we have here is an instance of implied discontinuity which is then used for internal discontinuity before the implication is made explicit.

The final kind of discontinuity I identify is modal discontinuity. It is the violation of those perceptual forms which are the sources of implicit and internal discontinuity in a given work of art. It is also the violation of an expectancy that a particular mode of sign structure or package already established in a work should be continued in that work. That is, it is the violation in the latter case of a functional style for nonfunctional purposes. The shift from a comic mode to a serious or tragic mode in the Shakespearean tragedy is an obvious instance. Another is the introduction of songs into a spoken play. The first kind of modal discontinuity is less common in nondramatic poetry. An instance may be found in Spenser's "Epithalamion," in which 23 long stanzas of either 18 or 19 lines are followed by a stanza of only seven. This also shows the second kind of modal discontinuity, a shift in verbal functional style. But the most common kind of modal discontinuity is syntactical discontinuity, from patches of rhythmic regularity to patches of rhythmic violation, and from junctural explicitness to junctural violation.

To clarify what I am talking about I shall turn to music, compared with which poetry is comparatively poverty-stricken. Or rather, since poetry can depend upon the violation of syntactical expectancies, which are reinforced millions of times in the experiences of any individual, poets have not found it necessary to develop other possibilities. Music, however, is the art which requires the greatest amount of special training for both the artist and the perceiver. Consequently, of all the arts it is perhaps richest in discontinuity. There is still another reason why this should be so. The problem of the poet, the painter, and the architect is to adjust the degree of formal discontinuity he wishes to the semantic aspect. This is by no means easy. From this point of view a study of European images of the Madonna is extraordinarily instructive. The iconographic, or semantic, regulations were fairly stringent, and the ingenuity displayed by painters in creating continuous external discontinuity and interesting internal, implicit, and modal discontinuities is very great. Music, on the other hand, for the most part has only to present primary signs. Up to the nineteenth century, these were under considerable situational control, but even so the possibilities for musical discontinuity are so great that the composer can say the same thing over and over without boring us. Indeed, compared with poetry and painting and even architecture, music cannot say very much. Its semantic aspect is limited, but its formal aspect is extraordinarily rich, at least in our culture.

The simplest kind of musical internal discontinuity is the theme and variations. Imitation, it has been said, is the breath of life in music; but of course, as might be expected, it is not imitation at all, but the violation of a unique pattern or melody. The principle of musical development, then, is internal discontinuity. Melody itself depends upon implicit discontinuity. That is, diatonic music, the kind which is most familiar to all of us, still, creates melody by violating scale and triad expectations. For instance, the concerti grossi of Vivaldi almost invariably in the fast first and third movements present melodies which violate triadic expectations, while the slow second movements violate scale expectations. If C is given and followed by D, the expectancy for E is very great. If E is followed by F, the expectation for G is even greater; but if instead of G the melodic line offers A-sharp, which is not even in the scale of C major, the violation comes as a real shock. All melodies are created in this manner. Or rather melodies are melodies because they imply a scale or a triad but do not make the scale or triad explicit. The typical sequence of movements in the Vivaldi concerto grosso is an example of both kinds of modal discontinuity; the first accounts for the shift from triadic implication to scale implication and back again; the second for the shift from fast tempo to slow tempo and back again, for to my mind the continuum from slow to fast tempo is a sign of the sense of the continuum from energy conservation to high energy release.

At this point I should like to offer an instance of what I believe to be the explanatory powers of my proposal. One of the most common phenomena in the history of music is the assertion that a new musical style has no melodies. A nineteenth-century example is *Tristan and Isolde*, of which numerous original perceivers asserted that it was utterly unmelodic. To us that is an almost inconceivable statement. Another instance is Schönberg's *Pierrot Lunaire*, which for years to me was just one damned note after another. But suddenly one day I heard the most delicious melodies. What accounts for this? *Tristan* offers a degree of chromaticism hitherto unparalleled in Western music, as well as a frequency of large and unusual melodic leaps. In other words, the triadic and scale expectations are so frequently and intensively violated that the expectancies themselves disappear. *Pierrot Lunaire* is quite a different case. *Tristan* should be listened to with diatonic expectancies, but Schönberg, beginning with *Pierrot*, is properly listened to with the expectancies of the chromatic, not the diatonic, scale. Melody requires the perceiver to make a new form as he listens. But if the requirements are too great, many a perceiver cannot do so, let alone experience its subsequent violations. My own experience with Schönberg's twelve-tone music moved from total disorientation, to the perception of individual notes, to the perception of melody and the acceptance of the harmonies, to the realization, which came after the event, that the appropriate perceptual form was the chromatic scale. My judgment moved correspondingly from irritation to boredom to toleration to emotion to, now, the experience of finding this twelve-tone music ravishingly beautiful and as easy to listen to as Vivaldi— and a lot more interesting. Clearly, acceptance of a really striking external discontinuity depends upon the personality, both experience in the appropriate artistic series and toleration of cognitive tension. It is only too evident that most people can tolerate so little cognitive tension that they can never accept a radically new artistic style. But at the highest cultural levels there is considerable support, for there innovation in all areas of human behavior is highly valued.

I shall now turn briefly to painting. To begin with, painting is like fiction and the syntactical aspect of poetry: the formal expectations are developed in normal experience, rather than by special training. In recent years, it has been discovered that all over the world children start making the same visual signs more or less in the same order; the smear, the line, the cross, the x, the square, the circle, the triangle, and finally the free or biomorphic closed form. The development of iconicity follows, the ability to create complex signs with an increasing configurational isomorphism to perceptual configurations. These packages of signs have been called children's art, and to a sophisticated observer they are, of course, art if he wishes to categorize them as art. But they do not function as art for the children. Rather, the emergence of these signs in children's behavior is the emergence of configurational sign behavior, and is parallel to the emergence of verbal, or arbitrary, sign behavior. These signs, up to the biomorphic free shape, are the implicit forms of perception before paintings. Children also make three-dimensional signs out of mud, sticks, stones, and, in our culture, blocks, and these are the implicit forms for sculpture and architecture.

VI

There remain two further problems and my theory is complete, though most sketchily presented. Here again, I can scarcely defend in detail my solutions to either of them, but I do wish to present them to you as indications that I have tried to create a complete theory.

First I should like to offer a more thorough and formal definition of external discontinuity. The term refers to the discontinuous relation between a work of art and its predecessors in the same category. An example would be Tchaikovsky's Sixth Symphony with the slow movement at the end. The explanation for external discontinuity lies in the fact that when particular devices for achieving implicit, internal, and modal discontinuity have been used for any period of time the perceiver comes to anticipate them, or predict them; the artist's role, therefore, requires him to innovate new devices. This predictability explains why it is that art has a stylistic history, and why, at least for individual observers, works of art wear out.

What predictability does *not* explain is why the historical dimension of art is also characterized by stylistic continuity, why we can recognize, say, Baroque, or Rococo, or modern styles, and why the boundaries of these stylistic fields can be approximately determined, or why stylistic historians working in entirely different kinds of art so often tend to agree that the stylistic boundaries of different arts occur at about the same time. For example, in music, architecture, painting, poetry, and the novel, universally recognized modern styles all appeared between 1905 and 1912, although the artists responsible were quite unknown to each other. It is an extraordinary instance of cultural convergence. Such convergences are the only empirical evidence that the formal aspects of the arts are somehow related to each other. Certainly there is no other evidence, for the various discontinuities in each are entirely dependent upon rules manipulating quite disparate media and work by violating quite different perceptual forms.

The answer I propose comes from examining not works of art, but rather the behavior of artists. I cannot present my evidence here, but only my conclusion. When an artist makes a decision which results in external discontinuity, what controls that decision? To what values is he responding? It cannot be the formal medium, which he can manipulate any way he pleases, nor can it be the values of the semantic aspect, which vary quite independently. The artist's decisions, then, are not controlled by anything uniquely characteristic of art. The values which determine what he does must, then, be extra-artistic. They must come from somewhere else in the culture, and they must have continuous control over several generations of artists.

From about 1720 or 1730 to about 1800 external discontinuity in all the high arts moved steadily toward a reduction of implicit, external, and modal discontinuity. What could have caused this? This was the period of the Enlightenment, and the Enlightenment ideal was the perfect adaptation of organism to environment. Everything, whether in thought or politics or economics, was aimed toward problem-solving and tension reduction. Consequently, for reasons I have already presented, the preference for problem-solving over problem exposure and for tension reduction over endurance of cognitive tension meant that a great many problems were too hastily resolved, to put it very mildly. It was the great era of facile pseudo-solutions. It was also the era in which sentimentality, that great technique of tension reduction, was identified and made into a cult.

With such values regnant at the higher cultural levels, it is apparent that the decisions of artists influenced by such values must lead to a steady reduction of internal, modal, and implicit discontinuity. On the basis of my examination of this period, of the seventeenth-century or Baroque styles, and of the nineteenth- and twentieth-century Romantic styles, including the modern styles, I conclude, therefore, that stylistic continuity is the consequence of the fact that the decisions of artists about discontinuity are responses to the regnant values of their cultural milieu.

This proposition also accounts for the common chronological boundaries of the historical styles. When there is a major shift in regnant cultural values, there will be corresponding redirection of the formal aspect of the arts. And this also is how the arts are related. Attempts in the manner of Spengler or Wylie Sypher to relate them on the assumption that a style is a symbol of a set of values or a metaphysic are bound to fail, and in fact have never been widely accepted. The reason is that a discontinuity is not a configuration but the violation of an expected configuration and therefore cannot be a conventionalized sign. Discontinuities have no semantic function, except to the stylistic historian. The arts are related because the accumulation of external discontinuity in each art moves in the same direction as in all the other arts.

To conclude, the role of the artist demands that he offer violations of formal expectancies, that he offer occasions for the rehearsal of the endurance of cognitive tension. And the role of the perceiver demands that he search for such occasions and that he respond to them to the best of his ability. Artistic behavior, then, is not a pretty ornament to life but a terrible necessity which keeps man alive, aware, capable of perceiving that he is neither adequate nor inadequate to the demands of his environment but a perilous mixture of the two, capable of evading the sentimentalities of comedy and of tragedy. Art is the ingredient in human behavior which enables man to innovate, because it trains him to endure the cognitive tension which is the necessary preliminary to problem perception and genuine and meaningful innovation. To me, only such a psychological and biological explanation of artistic behavior can serve to make comprehensible the outpouring of energy, devotion, treasure, and creativity at the feet of the terrible idol of art. Of all man's burdens, art is one of the most unendurable, and one of the most necessary. Deprived of it, he could not continue to be man.

15

ART AND CREATIVITY:

PROPOSAL FOR RESEARCH

[1966*]

When I wrote *Man's Rage for Chaos: Biology, Behavior, and the Arts*, one of my goals was to construct a theory of art useful to the psychologist—the typical behavioristically oriented psychologist of the current academic establishment, whose point of view, in part, I attempted to share and use. This ambition arose from the same source as the theory in general, i.e., my dissatisfaction with traditional philosophical aesthetics. One way of looking at the history of philosophy is to recognize the fact that the sciences have all spun off from philosophy and to conclude that the explanation, from the linguistic point of view, is that the task of philosophy has been to get a specialized area of the natural language ready for scientific, empirical use. In the past 60 years, for example, analytic or linguistic philosophy, of various schools, has progressed to the point at which the philosophical investigation of language is proving to be less and less rewarding, while

* Reprinted by permission from *Art Education*, XX (April, 1967), pp. 5–8.

certain linguists are boldly taking upon themselves the task of creating an empirical "philosophy of language," as in the recent book of that title by Jerrold J. Katz. Consequently, philosophy is beginning to return to its traditional task, metaphysics, the generation of novel explanatory statements and the refinement of vocabulary. Such an event is, I believe, typical of the relation of philosophy to science.

After 200 years of philosophical aesthetics, however, no psychology of art worthy of the name "science" has developed. What has been accomplished—and it is by no means negligible—has been done by psychologists who have improvised research problems from a general theory of human behavior, in itself by no means satisfactory. Because, for example, of the extremely unsatisfactory concept of "art," they have been pretty well forced to operate within their own culture, that is, to accept what their peers among art historians and art critics call "art." It is with a justified sense of considerable daring and of working in the dark that they have investigated all the arts of lower cultural levels. The explanation is that aesthetics emerged at a high cultural level in the eighteenth century, and the term "art" was used to refer to the range of works of art accepted, valued, and canonized at that level. With great difficulty, aesthetics has adjusted itself to emergent artistic styles at the highest cultural level, but it has remained extraordinarily ethnocentric within canonized limits. It may seem hard to believe, but I have encountered any number of sophisticated individuals, including aestheticians and even philosophers in fields other than aesthetics, who have been shocked and even horrified at my suggestion that artistic perception is a social role which functions by developing a particular mode of normal perceptual breakdown, or discontinuity. It seems to them strange, outlandish, and wrong-headed to consider poetry, for example, as a particular mode of verbal behavior. For this reluctance to see art as the deposit or consequence of a particular kind of behavior, I feel that the only explanation is a Neoplatonic background, which considers the artist as having access to a unique kind of transcendental truth. Psychoanalytic explanations of artistic behavior are formally another instance of the same kind of thinking, while the most popular current notion of poetry is that it has unique semantic functions and reveals a unique kind of non-scientific truth, more valuable than the scientific sort.

With such considerations in mind, I hoped to construct a theory of artistic behavior which might be usable for psychologists properly trained in setting up problems in empirical research, which I am not. Nevertheless, I should like to make a suggestion for a research project which, if the results are positive, should be of great practical usefulness in college education.

My position, in very brief form, is this: Artistic behavior is most usefully understood as a social role. By that I mean that it is an activity which is organized, codified, and taught. Thus my preliminary definition of a work of art is "an occasion for a human being to perform the art-perceiving role in the artistic situation, that is, on the artistic stage," while my final definition is that "a work of art is any perceptual field which an individual uses as an occasion for performing the role of art perceiver." (This definitional extension is necessary to account for the functioning of found objects as works of art.) The artist's role is quite simply to be defined as making perceptual configurations to be used for the performance of the art perceiver's role. The basic human activity which art perception as an organized and socially sanctioned role exploits and develops is the perception of disorder, that is, the violation of expectations, or, more generally, the awareness of a disparity between the perceptual model we use to organize every category of situation and the actual data a unique situation offers. The normal and necessary human tendency is to suppress the awareness of such disparities, but that means that every time a perceptual-cognitive model is successfully used, it is reinforced, with the consequence that the chances of suppressing the disparity are increased at each subsequent use. Perceptual models, from this point of view, both enhance the adaptation of the organism to the environment and weaken it.

It is obvious that the principal departure of this position from traditional aesthetics is its emphasis upon art as characterized by disorder rather than order; it is my conviction that in characterizing art as showing an unusual degree of order, aesthetics has prevented itself from forming a theory capable of empirical exploitation. The sources of this notion are multiple, but a few are worth a word or two. The primary source is perhaps the unquestioning positive value given to the word "order," which has interfered with the observation that insofar as such a sanctified word has reference at all, in actual use, to the empirical world of art, it explains second-order rather than first-order statements. Another important source is the confusion between the work itself and the situation in which the art perceiver plays his role; that situation tends to be characterized by psychic insulation (as the darkened concert hall) and the higher the cultural level, the greater the insulation. A third stems from the assumption that art has unique semantic functions. Such a position is, I believe, untenable. All works of art have a semiotic aspect (a front door is designed to indicate "enter here"), and all semiotic structures have, of course, structure, even if it is only conventional and not logical. From this point of view, the notion that art has order is a mere tautology. The assertion that art has as its defining attribute the presentation of perceptual disorder—or "discontinuity," to use the general term offered in my book—refers to its formal aspect, as with the violation of the prosodic pattern in poetry or the violation of scale expectations which is the source of melody. The simplest example of the point I would make is the theme and variations plan in music, in which the perceiver is constantly misled by the variation's approach to and departure from the theme.

I have already touched on the aspect of my theory which I think offers a useful basis for investigating artistic behavior and for applying the results of that investigation to education. In my book I discussed it briefly, but it is a consequence of my position. The general principle is that the lower the cultural level, the less discontinuity the work of art offers, and, contrarily, the higher the cultural level, the more it offers. From this point of view, the process of formal education can be seen as training the student in the socially sanctified modes of behavior and role performance at as high a cultural level as his genetic endowments and personality limitations permit. For example, in verbal behavior, the lower the cultural level, the more verbal discourse involves a semantic continuum of exemplary or particularized discourse as well as the continuous and highly redundant assertion of value propositions. What formal education entails is training the individual to engage in longer and longer periods of explanatory (or theoretical) discourse together with a steady reduction of value propositions, particularly of an unanalyzed sort. In the same way education involves training the student in problem exposure. For ranking students, examinations are of questionable value, but it is probable that their real function is training in problem exposure. It is believed that formal education is finished with the production of a dissertation. That is, ideally, the student has located a problem in the field of his interest and has offered an acceptable solution which he is able to defend against the attacks of his cultural superiors in that field. From this point of view, the final oral examination, or defense of thesis, is particularly designed to be an emotional test. Can the student stand the emotional as well as the intellectual strain of the solemn and minatory atmosphere of the doctor's orals?

Now a necessary preliminary to the perception of any problem is the awareness that the cognitive-perceptual-interpretive model used in a particular situation is inadequate to the unique sensory data and demands of that situation. That is, awareness of a disparity, an obscure feeling that something is wrong somewhere, is the clue to the individual that the proper mode of behavior is to look for an explanation of that awareness or feeling by locating something in the perceptual field or some failure in the model. When that has been done, a problem may be formulated. When the individual is convinced that the problem has been successfully solved, it is possible to correct the original model by feedback, a currently fashionable but quite useful term. The adaptational function of art behavior is, I believe, training in the endurance of the cognitive tension which occurs when the feeling that something is wrong is accepted, though the most frequent, or normal, tendency is to reject or suppress that feeling. That tension is also relieved when a problem has been formulated. (A new kind of tension, of course, now appears, but that is a different matter. That is where science, in the widest sense, comes in.) The universality of art is a consequence of the fact that something is always wrong, that the model is always inadequate to the demands of the environmental situation. Hence human beings spend an enormous amount of time asserting that semiotically formulated models are indeed adequate. Such are the functions of religion, socially sanctioned constitutive metaphysics, and the astounding redundancy of unexamined value statements at the lower cultural levels. On the other hand, they also spend a great deal of time in training themselves to endure cognitive tension by exposing themselves to discontinuity in playing the role of art perceiver.

It is, I think, meaningful to say that there are higher cultural levels in the various areas of human activity only because some people need them, that is, are more capable of enduring cognitive tension than others and in some areas of their behavior find gratification by explaining that tension in problem formulation rather than in suppressing that awareness. At the highest cultural level, the recognition of that awareness that something is wrong, i.e., the experience of cognitive tension, becomes a gratification and a reinforcing reward in itself. This would seem to be a useful way of accounting for creativity, which I would define as innovation to which the culture ascribes positive value. To put it another way, an individual is judged to be performing his social role adequately at a high cultural level to the degree to which he is creative. Artistic behavior, then, can be theoretically described as training in the necessary psychological preliminary to creativity. If that is the case, the importance of artistic behavior to the training of all individuals to operate successfully at the highest cultural levels in the various activities and roles established at that level is firmly grounded.

There is some empirical evidence that this position is well taken. Professor D. E. Berlyne of the University of Toronto has given us reason to accept the notion that exposure to perceptually problematic configurations improves learning ability (*Scientific American*, August 1966). Indeed he uses some of the terminology I use in *Man's Rage for Chaos*. To be sure, he does not mention that his experimentation took place in situations of a high degree of psychic insulation, but it is significant that the higher the cultural level, the greater the discontinuity in the work of art, and the greater the psychic insulation of the artistic situation.

The work of Professor Irvin L. Child at Yale University also provides support for my position. Though he has not expressed it precisely this way, he has accumulated evidence that indicates

that there is some positive correlation between the I.Q. and apti-
tude scores of college students and the extent to which they agree
with the judgments of pairs of works of art made by "experts,"
that is, individuals familiar with the proper performance of the
art perceiver's role at the highest levels in our culture. Indeed, I
would almost rest my case on the remark of a boy, one of Professor Child's subjects in another series of experiments, who,
informed after each pair which the experts judged the better, said,
"Oh, I get it! The best one is always the crummy one." Professor
Child has also said, "As children grow older, some of them begin
to tolerate complexity and even to seek it out. They will look for
more challenging emotional experience in art and will tolerate incompleteness and lack of abundance."

The research I would like to see done is focused squarely on
that phrase, "some of them." In its practical aspects it has to do
with the problem which has been located independently in both
Britain and the United States, i.e., why college students with a
humanistic training show greater creativity than those with a
scientific training. It is a question which has the scientific establishment in both countries seriously worried. Now it has been my
general observation in years of talking with academic scientists
that those who have reputations of being unusually creative, or
who deserve such reputations but have not, principally because of
youth, achieved them, are ordinarily interested in one or more of
the arts; frequently they are themselves practitioners of the arts,
especially music. It is to be observed how heavily manufacturers
of high-fidelity playback equipment advertise in the very expensive pages of the *Scientific American*. It has also been my observation that such scientists are more frequently responsive to
highly innovative artistic styles than humanists, even professional students of the various arts. They seem, on the whole, to be
more tolerant of the cognitive tension caused by exposure to
thoroughly radical works of art.

The question is: Can the production of creative individuals be
improved at the college and graduate-school level, whatever the
subject they are specializing in? The first project I would propose
would be to find out if there is a positive correlation between the
records of students and the frequency, depth, and range of their

experience with the art of the highest levels in our culture. If it turns out that there should be such a correlation—and there certainly ought to be—the next, and more difficult, problem is the question of why the correlation is not greater. I mean by this that we may assume that there are individuals who are, perhaps genetically, equipped to develop their tolerance for cognitive tension. Now, in theory, training in high-culture art should improve that tolerance, and there is some evidence that it does so. But it is also evident that various personality factors can inhibit the development of that tolerance. If there is, as I think to be the case, a transference of the capacity to endure such tension from artistic perception to other areas of behavior (in my book I cover this by considering "rehearsal" as an aspect of role-playing), then it ought to be possible to isolate such personality factors. It is doubtful if psychiatric records currently include material about the patient's experience with high art, but college and university psychiatrists could be requested to gather such information. Unfortunately, Freudian psychiatry puts all the emphasis upon the semantic aspect of art, insofar as it considers it at all, but psychiatrists, as I know from my own discussions with them, are quite prepared to consider seriously my position. But there are of course other techniques for gathering such information available to the psychologist, although I am not competent to recommend any. The question then would be: Can artistic experience be used therapeutically to break down those inhibiting factors and to enhance the individual's capacity for exploiting his capacity for enduring cognitive tension and, ultimately, his creativity?

If solid results are obtained from these investigations, then it would be possible to consider the best way to implement the conclusions in structuring college and graduate education. If there is indeed a central importance in art to developing flexible and creative personalities, then training in artistic perception could acquire a solid and assured place in education. At the present time, the study of the arts is tolerated, more or less, as the desirable but decorative equipment of a gentleman; but the gentleman has all but disappeared from our culture. On the other hand, a good many scientific educators for the past generation have been convinced that artistic experience is essential to the making of a first-class scientist, and they have implemented this belief; but they are quite frank in admitting that they have precious little theoretical support for their convictions. Furthermore, such training just teaches students to look for and respond to the perceptual discontinuities that art offers. Here I can only offer the testimony of my students, many of whom have asserted that other courses in the arts teach them adjectives, but the way of perceiving presented in my course on the relation of the arts teaches them how to go about perceiving and responding to painting, poetry, architecture, and music.

To summarize, I think it is true that the highest cultural level of all modes of behavior is characterized by an active interest in problem exposure, and that the arts at that level are characterized by the greatest amount of perceptual discontinuity. What we need is a thoroughgoing verification of the theory that there is a relation between these two phenomena, and if that is forthcoming, a means of exploiting that relationship in college and graduate-school education for the sake of increasing the amount of creativity available to the society. It is, I admit, a grandiose proposal, but I have the utmost confidence that our psychologists, if they think the necessary research is worth doing, will find a way to do it.

16

ORDER AND

DISORDER IN FICTION

[1966*]

Why do people tell stories? Webster informs us that a fiction is "the act of creating something imaginary: a fabrication of the mind," and that the word is derived from the past participle of *fingo*, to make, to shape, or to form. And indeed, I suppose most people would say that a story is the result of the exercise of the imagination or is the expression of the imagination. And from there we can wander in all sorts of explanatory directions, with the psychoanalyst in the direction of unconscious fantasy or with those who would point to the instinct to play. All such theories depend upon the notion of the imagination, but that notion is really most unsatisfactory.

The evidence that the imagination has operated is something, verbal or otherwise, innovated, originated, or created—to use a word which is so splendid in its aura and so uninformative if one

* Delivered at the University of Wyoming, L. L. Smith Lecture Series, November, 1966. Reprinted by permission from *Sage*, Spring, 1967, pp. 225–43.

stops to think a moment—something which has never existed before. How does such a something come into existence? Well, the answer we usually get when we ask that is that such some-things are produced by the imagination. We appear to be involved in a tautology. Even when, taking a hint from Webster, we add something new by asserting that the imagination is a faculty or function of the mind, and substitute "mind" for "imagination," we are faced with the same difficulty. The mind produces a fiction by means of the imagination; the evidence for mind and imagina-tion is that a fiction has been produced. It would appear, then, that if we wish to say that a humanly produced something is characterized by novelty, originality, or creativity, we say that it is the consequence of an imaginative act, or the expression of the imagination, or the product of that faculty or function of the mind which we call "imagination"; for the mental mode imagination produces something which is novel, original, or creative. The word "imagination," then, seems to be no more than a means for characterizing certain humanly produced somethings and differ-entiating them from other humanly produced somethings. Such somethings are placed in the same category only because we thus characterize them. It follows that a verbal something so character-ized and a nonverbal something do not necessarily have any other character in common. A fresh ice-skating figure and a freshly in-ventive story do not necessarily have a common origin, or motive, or function in the human economy. If it is argued that after all both are fresh, are creative, are novel, it is not difficult to demon-strate that all human behavior is innovative, but that some behav-ior is singled out as uniquely innovative because of our interests and our values, while the innovative character of other behavior is ignored. But I shall not attempt to argue this here, having gone into it elsewhere, in my recent book *Man's Rage for Chaos*. Rather, here, it is an assumption on which I shall proceed.

Since, then, it is, I believe, improper to differentiate human behavior on the grounds of innovation, we cannot account for a special class of behavioral somethings by tracing them to an innovating instinct, or motive, or drive, or personality causation, that is, to the imagination, or even to the mind. Such a position frees us, and indeed forces us, to explain the telling of stories by looking elsewhere. What I wish to propose is that instead of trying to locate a cause or origin for story-telling in something outside of language we should properly account for it by looking at language itself. Telling stories is, after all, a mode of verbal behavior. In the character of verbal behavior itself, therefore, may be found an explanation for story-telling.

A word of caution and explanation may make what I have to say a little more palatable—or possibly less. The language I shall be using will sound at times like philosophical language, and at times like psychological language of a behaviorist variety, or at least as behavioristic as I can make it. Philosophers, I suspect, will consider it improper philosophical language, and psychologists might well be disturbed by the appearance of terminology they would rather not hear, at least in such a context. The first possibility should not be an occasion for too great concern, on either my part or anybody else's. A philosopher always considers any language improperly philosophical except his own, and he is quite right to do so. We should respect his attitude, but not be excessively concerned with trying to submit to it. After all, philosophers have developed propositions usable outside of philosophy, though not as often, perhaps, as we would all like to think. Insofar as a philosopher is a philosopher of language, he tries, it would seem, to discuss language from within language and to stay within the bounds of language. The classic modern instance of such philosophizing is Wittgenstein's *Tractatus*. But in his later years he repudiated that work and turned to the problem of how language is related to the world. As soon as a modern philosopher does that he finds himself making empirical statements about how people use language; willy-nilly, he becomes an odd kind of psychologist. Part of the fun of modern philosophy is watching philosophers tumble out of language into psychology.

I am not, then, trying to do philosophy, though I shall use certain notions developed by modern philosophy. My effort will be in the direction of psychology, towards verbal behavior; I am concerned with how language functions in human activity. Psychologists may well consider some of my language and propositions too philosophical, but it should always be remembered that psychology, like all the sciences, issued from philosophy and needs now and then a pull at the nourishing maternal breast. Philosophy may not be the queen of the sciences, but it surely is at least the illegitimate mother.

I shall begin with certain assumptions which I consider basic simply because I cannot get beyond them. Hence I shall not attempt to justify them but rather to explain them and their consequences. The first is that all referential words are categorial, including proper names. We are all taught as children that a noun is a name of a thing, and hence we grow up thinking that a word refers to an entity. That, for example, is why we think that there is such a thing as "imagination." We think that since there is a word there must be an entity to correspond to it. But "imagination" only categorizes certain humanly produced somethings and ascribes to them a valued novelty. And our arguments over whether, for example, a literary work is truly imaginative or not, or whether or not an author displays evidence of a first-rate imagination indicates how slippery the term is and how little agreement its use gives occasion for. A word, then, does not refer to an entity. Rather, it ascribes certain attributes to a certain range of perceptual configurations. All words are potentially, and most actually, as slippery as "imagination." As for proper names, every person here has had a different set of experiences with the bearer of the name L. B. Johnson. That name does not refer to the bearer of that name. Rather for each of us it ascribes different sets of attributes to different sets of ranges of perceptual configurations, or, more simply, experiences. If the name were "Clifford Trevelyan," and if everything else, bearer and sets of attributes and sets of ranges of configurations, were the same, the word would have the same semantic function, or, in this sense of the word, "meaning."

From this innocent-looking proposition that words are categorial emerge some surprising and disturbing notions. It means that at no point is language tied to the world. We tend to think, since we believe nouns to be the names of things, that all words have referential power of themselves, that reference binds language to the world, and that we determine meaning by discovering existent links between language and the world, or by being informed of such links. But it appears that such is not the case.

Language is by no means tied to the world. Rather it hovers above it, or it slips and slides and slithers on top of it; all language is as slippery and unstable as the word "imagination." To put it another way, all language is equally metaphysical. Or, the relation of language to the world is anamorphic, not isomorphic. The structure of language is different from the structure of the world. Having, therefore, nothing in common with the world, it cannot be related to the world either by something in itself or by something in the world, but can only be related to it by something else.

This brings us to my next assumption. That "something else" that relates language to the world is human behavior. Language is not directly related to the world, but only indirectly, by human behavior. The word "imagination" does not refer to anything in the world; it is I who decide to use it to categorize certain humanly produced somethings. And this is true also for such a word as "tree." Until I make that decision, the word is quite functionless; and indeed I encounter too often words which do not make it possible for me to make any decisions. I do not understand them; I do not know their meaning. That is, I do not know what range of configurations I am supposed to catch by what categorial net. Therefore, if I do know, it is only because I have been properly instructed. That is, all language is conventional. If I know those conventions I know how to link the discourse I have heard to the world. If the utterer of the discourse assumes that I know those conventions, and if I employ them as he would, then he has controlled my behavior. Language functions, then, by controlling behavior, or more precisely it functions because someone, including ourselves, is attempting to control our behavior. But since it functions only when the one attempting to control actually succeeds, even though the subsequent behavior may not be what he has predicted it would be, we may say that language functions by controlling behavior. Even when the utterer fails completely to control to a predicted result the behavior of the hearer (let us call him the interpreter), he has, insofar as the interpreter does nothing at all and thus does not do something else, controlled him. From this emerges another rather distressing conclusion. As far as the interpreter is concerned, the world always happens *after* language. (The utterer may, of course, also be the interpreter.

Language is one of the ways we control our own behavior.) Since the notion of controlling behavior includes not only overt behavior, but also covert behavior, that is, attitudinal or orientative behavior, the consequence of interpreting an utterance is that the interpreter now faces a different world. It is not merely that language slips and slithers over the surface of the world, but, from this point of view, the world slips and slithers underneath it. The reason is not merely that the act of interpreting language creates an unstable world, but also, and even more important, it is that the act of interpretation is itself unstable. That interpretive instability or variability, which, incidentally, we are talking about when we use the categorial term "mind," emerges from a state of affairs such that interpretive conventions are learned, that learning processes involve loss of both structure and content, and that all behavior, including interpretive behavior, is necessarily innovative. We have then, three instabilities—the language, the interpretation, and the world. It is not surprising that we spend our lives lost in a linguistic bog. This is what I mean, then, when I say that language happens after the world. From that point of view, the sole function of language is predictive. I know of no more scandalous a proposition; at this point I expect all philosophers to leave in disgust, but perhaps on the way out they will remember that I am trying to talk about behavior, not doing philosophy.

By the notion that all sentences are predictive I mean that all language is equally metaphysical, that language cannot be descriptive, since for the interpreter the world happens after language, not simultaneously with it, that language is not isomorphic with the world, and that language does not communicate or convey information, except in a very loose sense. An utterance amounts to a speaker's prediction that if the interpreter categorizes the world as the utterer recommends, the interpreter will encounter such-and-such a world; or the interpreter predicts that if he interprets the utterance as the conventions, as he uses them, recommends, he will encounter such-and-such a world. To put it another way, I cannot tell you what the world is, or what anything in the world is, but only how to find it. I cannot tell you what the taste of a mango is, but I can give you sufficient instructions to enable you to select a mango from among ten unfamiliar fruits by tasting each one of them. Returning to our original point, I do so by offering you through language an interlocking set of categories. If the conventions are sufficiently stable, I can tell you how to locate a perceptual configuration to the exclusion of all other possible configurations. I can tell you not only how to find a tree but also how to find a particular tree in Yellowstone National Park. Precisely in this power of language to particularize through interlocking categories is our only linguistic salvation, but that power is also responsible for the illusion that nouns are names of things, rather than, as is really the case, of categories.

From this point of view an empirically true statement is one that so controls the behavior of an individual that his consequent behavior leads to a predicted result. In this the variable of the interpreter must not be neglected. Much of the confusion in speculation about the nature of science has arisen from the failure to observe that the conventions of the interpretation of propositions involve not merely a knowledge of the categorial conventions of semantic function but also a knowledge of an extremely complex behavioral paradigm, which is adapted and modified for the unique particularities of a unique situation. The statement that the combination of hydrogen and oxygen under proper circumstances produces water is true only because someone knows how to perform the operations and to select the conditions which the statement itself does not specify; frequently, in science they are never specified. This is the important point of Thomas S. Kuhn's fascinating work, *The Structure of Scientific Revolutions*.

Such a question may seem irrelevant to the problem of why people tell stories, but is exceedingly pertinent. It has often been maintained, indeed is usually maintained, that there is a radical difference between statements found in a work of fiction and statements found in a work of science, when both are equally particular. But whether I find in a guidebook or a novel a statement about the location of the city hall makes no difference. If I know how to interpret such a statement and how to behave in order to achieve a predicted result, namely, finding that building, it makes no difference where I find the statement. The difference between fiction and nonfiction lies not in the character of the statement, but rather in the character of the subsequent behavior. The appropriate behavior when I read a guidebook is to follow its directions if I feel like it. But whatever I do when I read a novel, the socially established role of novel-reading involves quite different behavior from that of the role of reading a guidebook. Since all statements are metaphysical, in an odd way all discourse is equally fictitious. The question is whether we wish to control our behavior to a predicted result when we read them, that is, whether, in the scientific manner, we wish to verify them. Those scientists who claim that their work is as imaginatively creative as that of any novelist are quite correct, but I am not sure if it is of much point to boast about something one can scarcely avoid.

Linguistic behavior, then, involves continuous exposure to three instabilities, that of language, that of interpretation, and that of the world. At the heart of this whole mess is the factor of polysemy. Webster defines it as multiplicity of meaning and quotes from Stephen Ullman, "English is less exposed to polysemy than French." If Ullman really believes so, it is only because his native tongue is English. All languages are equally polysemous. That is, all terms have multiple and ever-shifting semantic functions, or "meanings." We have seen the reason. Terms being categorial, they can only tell you, no matter how particular they are, how to behave in a category of situations. The interpretative act requires the adjustment of the linguistic control to a unique situation. But there *is* a feedback. As far as the interpreter is concerned, every successful use of discourse in a unique situation changes both the range and the attributes of the categorial network in which he catches a bit of the world. If this recategorization is conventionalized to other human beings besides himself—and it would seem that that happens at least most of the time—the conventional categorial structure of that speech-community changes.

It is not that English or any other language is exposed to polysemy. It is that interpreters and speakers are continuously exposed to polysemy. This is the basic reason why language slips and slithers and slides over the surface of the world. The only way, as we have seen, to be sure a discourse is true is to put it to the operational test, by means of behavior. That is why science claims to be the only source of true statements. It is an assertion that is not true at all, but it is the case that scientists are equipped by conventionalized training to demonstrate and test the truth of a small class of statements. And it is true that, not their propositions, but their behavior is paradigmatic, i.e., the best model for generating and testing particular statements. In the vast majority of human behavior such stringent requirements are simply impossible. It is necessary to proceed, unsatisfactory though it may be, by interpreting statements through verbal behavior, that is, other statements. Most of our verbal behavior links statements not to the world but to other statements.

In such situations, which are most situations, that link between statements is also behavioral. That is, we must know the proper behavioral paradigm to link two statements together. The beginning student of literature does not know the conventions for linking statements about Fielding's novels to statements about Richardson's novels. Nor does he even know that he is supposed to. Further, he must not only be taught the behavioral paradigm for moving from the Fielding class of statement to the Richardson class, but he also must be able to justify it. The relation is of course analogical; and that is why, of course, again, it is possible to make the link without being able to make the justification, for analogies can be grasped although the interpreter is unable to offer a justification for what he has done. If he can offer a justification, it is because he has learned an explanatory statement; if he is sufficiently advanced, he will be able to offer a novel justification for the link. On the basis of what he has learned about the behavioral paradigm of the student of literature and his kind of language, he generates an innovative explanation. From that moment he is marked for graduate school. The Richardson class and the Fielding class of statements are particular statements, the kind of statements which the student of literature would treat as a physicist treats his statements, if he could. But all the student of literature can do is to control his behavior so that the interpretation of Richardson's or Fielding's work will be as he predicts, and he does this by linking the statements with explanatory statements. This is why, though the study of literature properly belongs to the group of studies known as the behavioral sciences, it runs no danger of being absorbed by any one of them.

An explanatory statement, then, does not explain the world; it only explains other statements. What shall we call these statements, which so far I have been calling "particular" statements? By examining some of the uses of the highly polysemous word "meaning" it is possible to make a useful proposal. When we ask for the meaning of a particular statement, we are offered an explanatory statement which links it to what is claimed to be other particular statements. For example, if I do not understand discourse that asserts that the American government is engaged in military activity in Viet Nam, a statement that, for all I know, may very well be true, I do not mean that I do not gather from such discourse that the American government is militarily active in Viet Nam. I understand that as well as if I had encountered it in a novel, and exactly the same way. What I mean is that I am asking for an explanation of that particularity. *Why* is the government active there? Here are three possible explanatory statements, each of which, formally, serves equally well as an explanation. "The American government is interested in the economic development of underdeveloped countries." "The American government is interested in holding back aggressive Communism." "The American government is an imperialist neocolonialist power." If I ask for proof of any of these statements, I may be offered as proof of the explanation the government's support of the defeat of the Greek Communists, or the government's aid to India, or the government's behavior toward Cuba. Or the government's behavior toward South American countries can be offered as proof, or supporting evidence, for each of these explanations. But these statements are proof, or more weakly, evidence, or most weakly, examples, only if I accept them. The reason is that they are none of these three. Proof, evidence, examples are some things that happen in the world, but I have been offered only language. If I assert that the American government is an imperialist neocolonialist power, and I am challenged, I will, if I am scrupulous, say, "I can't offer you proof, but I can offer you language that asserts that certain examples of American relations with other countries demonstrate, if properly interpreted, the truth of my explanation." And if I am very scrupulous I will put "properly" and "explanation" and "truth" in quotes. Or again, "I can't offer you examples, but I can offer you sentences that purport to refer to examples." That is, "I can offer you exemplary propositions; they will not be examples of the world but exemplifications of my original explanatory statement about America as a neocolonialist imperialist power." For "particular" statements, then, I pose the term "exemplary" statements.

I suggest that as behavior language has two polarities, the exemplary and the explanatory. That is, these are not two kinds of statements but two opposite directions in which discourse moves. A statement is exemplary if it is explained by another statement; it is explanatory if it explains another statement. The limit of exemplification is reached if a statement controls behavior to a predicted result, but two things must always be remembered. Even at that limit an interpreter and his behavior are required for a statement to have any semantic function at all; and it is always possible that a more exemplary statement may be generated through further discoveries in the world. That is, indeed, how science progresses. But it also progresses by making explanatory statements to which previous explanatory statements serve as exemplary statements. Linguistically, that is what makes possible the linkage of two once disparate fields such as biology and physics into biophysics. That is, both polarities point in the direction of infinite regressions, a process which is halted in either direction by satisfaction on the part of the interpreter.

Let me now offer some exemplary statements of this general or explanatory proposition about the exemplary-explanatory polarity of language. We say that a man really knows his field when for every explanatory statement he can give numerous exemplary statements. And we say that he really understands what he is talking about when he is familiar with the accepted ways of covering and linking his exemplary statements by explanatory statements. Or we say that he is truly creative if he can offer novel explanatory statements to link exemplary statements, or if by introducing new exemplary statements under the cover of an existing explanatory statement he can extend the range of such an explanatory statement. Or again, when we ask for the meaning of an explanatory statement we are offered exemplary statements, and vice versa. Further, we consider a teacher excellent in his profession if he can develop an explanatory argument by continual recourse to exemplification. Moreover, if we examine the matter of the learning process from this point of view, it is apparent that education consists of training students to sustain increasing spans of nonexemplary or explanatory discourse. But again, we never trust the most brilliant student, unless for a novel explanatory position he is able to give numerous exemplary statements. But in this matter there is a clear difference between cultural levels. It was pointed out more than 150 years ago by Jean-Paul Friedrich Richter. The lower the cultural level, the more the verbal behavior is confined to exemplary statements, but intelligent conversation at a high cultural level occurs between and among people able to engage in explanatory dialectic, though ready at any moment, when there is any failure of lucidity, to demand and provide exemplification.

From this it is clear that to maintain understanding of sustained explanatory discourse requires both high intelligence and elaborate training. This is the reason for philosophy, which attempts to control polysemy in explanatory discourse. Hence philosophy is highly disorienting when it is first encountered. The student is quite unable to provide exemplification for even the simplest philosophical statement that lies in the direction of the explanatory pole. The terms have so many possible references that they have none. In other words, the more explanatory the statement the more exposed is its interpreter to polysemy. The ultimate philosophical statement is one which covers all possible exemplary statements, such as God made the world. Not a few philosophers, and theologians, have made them. The general principle, therefore, is, the farther from the exemplary pole the greater the exposure to polysemy. But even at lower cultural levels there is a constant exposure to polysemy. Consider an automobile mechanic instructed to repair a carburetor on a foreign car which he has never seen before. He is an expert on American carburetors, but this particular carburetor is put together in what to him is a wholly novel way. The category carburetor no longer means to him (has the same range and attributes) what it did before. It has attributes for the moment bewildering. By extrapolation he is able to repair it successfully, but henceforth for him the word "carburetor" has a different semantic function. And such situations are increasingly encountered today, because of social mobility and worldwide trading.

Consider now a lower middle-class or workingman's bar. There is little in life so instructive as eavesdropping. In such a bar you overhear almost exclusively exemplary statements: jokes, stories clean and dirty, incidents at work or at home. And so on. But in a group of academics relaxing at the bar at a professional conference, such as the Modern Language Association, you hear exactly the same sort of thing: academic or professional gossip, as exemplary a verbal dialectic as they can make it. It seems to me to be clear what the connection is between relaxation and sustained exemplary dialectic and discourse. It is relaxation and escape from the exposure to polysemy, for which, be it remembered, there are two sources. One is explanatory discourse and dialectic; the other comes from the fact that even the most particular exemplary statement, when it is used to control interaction with the world, rather than the other language, is prepared to control behavior only in categories of situations, not in unique situations. Adjustment, interpretation, polysemous exposure are always necessary.

When the cook's recipe calls for two eggs and a cup of flour, she must consider whether or not the eggs are larger than average, and, if so, "a cup of flour" means a certain amount more than a cup of flour. Exposure to polysemy means confusion, uncertainty, hesitation in interpretation. It means perceptual, cognitive, interpretive disorientation. And the experience of disorientation is precisely what I mean by perceptual and cognitive disorder. For to my mind, the word disorder does not refer to the character of the world. It cannot; no word can. Rather "disorder" categorizes those encounters with the world in which perceptual disorientation entails cognitive tension, the experience of a disparity between the cognitive model and the sensory data which are being scanned. Relief from the cognitive tension that results from exposure to polysemy accounts for sustained exemplary dialectic and discourse. And of the various devices to obtain that relief, sustained fiction is one of the best. What fiction does is to repeat frequently a limited number of words, of which the proper names are the most obvious instances. It creates an increasingly fine-

meshed, limited, and interlocking set of categories. Because it is
highly exemplary it seems, for reasons I have already discussed,
to be closely and directly linked to the world, even though we
know perfectly well it is not. But our role as readers of fiction
enables us to suspend criticism, or testing, and we assume, usually
correctly, that anything not immediately comprehensible will
eventually be made so by analogical exemplification or by explanatory statements. Thus, *a* world, not *the* world (but the relief and
irresponsibility of our role enables us to ignore the distinction),
emerges. As the fiction proceeds, the possibilities of polysemy
decrease, because of what we may call thematic repetition, of
characters, places, categories of events, and so on. Since exposure
to polysemous disorientation is the experience of disorder, the
relief from such real-life disorientation is the experience of order.
We tell stories, then, to experience a particular kind of order,
relief from exposure to polysemy.

That is why we tell stories, but that is not why stories enter the
realm of art. As I get older, I prefer, for relaxation, history to
fiction. It is, I believe, a not uncommon experience. For one thing,
psychologists tell us that abstract thinking, what I would call
exemplary verbal behavior, is the enemy of memory, that is, of
particularity or exemplification. History is a continuum of exemplary statements. This may be the reason why as I become
more able, successfully or unsuccessfully, to operate in comfort
toward the explanatory pole of verbal behavior, I find it harder
to remember that my students need constant exemplification, and
harder to think of exemplary statements, though 15 years ago
they rolled off my tongue. But mainly, I think, I prefer history to
fiction, though I faithfully go to the movies at least once a week,
possessing no television, because fiction at the cultural level at
which I am accustomed to operate offers, since it is art, more
disorder than I want or, I like to think, need to expose myself to.

A year ago I published a book with the title, *Man's Rage for
Chaos: Biology, Behavior, and the Arts.* The three main conclusions of that book are: (1) Art offers an occasion for playing the
art perceiver's role, and therefore one may turn anything into a
work of art by playing the art perceiver's role before it. (2) The
defining attribute of the art perceiver's role is exposure to per-

ceptual discontinuity, or, as I have defined it above, disorder. Whether the world is disorderly or ordered, we can never know, but we can experience it either way. (3) The function of art as biological adaptation is that it enables us in protected situations in which nothing is at stake, in which we are not required to interfere with the world, to rehearse the endurance of cognitive tension, the result of being aware of the disparity between the perceptual-cognitive model and the actual sensory data fed into it, so that in real situations we may be better able to endure cognitive tension until we have located a genuine problem and dealt with it as adequately as we can. My principal exemplification would be that at the highest cultural level one finds the greatest interest in problems, the greatest capacity to endure cognitive tension, sometimes, as with a great scientist or philosopher, for decades over one problem, and art that offers the richest occasions for experiencing perceptual disorder.

I should now like to apply this to fiction, by which I mean all kinds of story-telling—romances, tales, novels, plays, movies, comic strips, jokes, and so on. As Aristotle said, the heart of fictional narrative is the plot; at least he said it of tragedy, comedy, and epic. But what is a plot? In perceptual-cognitive-interpretive activity (for these words are different ways of categorizing the same experience) a problem emerges, as I have suggested, when there is a disparity between the perceptual, or cognitive, or interpretive model and the actual sensory data, as with the cook, whose egg situation requires her to interpret a cup as somewhat more than a cup. The unusually large eggs make a problem. The careless cook will ignore the size of the eggs, and her soufflé will collapse. That is, when we become aware of a disparity between model and data we have two choices. Either we can suppress that awareness and apply the model without correction—sometimes with no noticeable results and sometimes with self-destruction as the consequence—or we can devote our interpretive energies to locating the problem, solving it, and correcting the model. Life requires action; that is why an activity, such as art, or science, or scholarship, devoted to problem awareness is ordinarily granted a high degree of psychic insulation. Now, as our discussion of polysemy brought out, the ordinary way of behavior is to repress the awareness and avoid problem exposure. Either that, or we expose ourselves to the problem and arrive at a reasonably acceptable solution as fast as we can.

What happens in a fiction? Such narratives always begin with a problem, or sometimes a hopeless anomaly, such as the murder in a room locked from the inside. But the opposite from real situations takes place. The reader is exposed to the problem and the solution is postponed. The devices by which these two goals are accomplished is what we are talking about when we use the word "plot." It is often said that a plot should be so constructed that the problem is fully worked out and the solution explains all the twists and turns of the plot. That is what Aristotle thought, but Aristotle was a philosopher, and philosophers like things to be reduced to an overriding explanation. They tend to be terribly monistic. It is usually the judgment of most people at the highest cultural level. But it is simply a cultural prejudice. It has nothing to do with the character of plot, which consists of problem exposure and solution postponement. Indeed, we have a certain contempt for people whose capacity to endure cognitive tension is so feeble that they have to peek at the end of the book to see if the butler really did his master in. And even people at the highest cultural level not only gossip, they go to the movies or, like Paul Elmer More, read a new detective story every night. As for the logical working out of the plot, that again I fear is an illusion. It is by no means accidental that Shakespeare's tragedies are all about the same length, that detective novels are usually between 70 and 80 thousand words long, that all Greek tragedies last about the same amount of time, and that most Victorian novels were three-deckers. The author can postpone his solution for as short or long a time as he pleases. Frequently he knows the length of the book before he has even decided on what problem to use to get the plot started. Nor has this anything to do with the intellectual or moral seriousness of the writer, nor does that have anything to do with the triviality or seriousness of the problem. A very serious book can have a trivial problem, and a trivial book, as a detective story, can have a serious problem, murder.

Consider the most famous work by the greatest problem-setter and plot-starter in the business—*Hamlet*. Why is Barnardo so nervous? Why is Francisco sick at heart? What thing has appeared? Why is there an apparition? Why is it the ghost of the king that's dead? Why does it refuse to answer Horatio and stalk away? Why does Horatio think the ghost bodes some strange eruption to our state? (There are, after all, other possible explanations.) And Marcellus has a whole series of questions: Why the strict and observant watch? Why the daily cast of brazen cannon? Why are implements of war being bought? Why are the shipwrights working round the clock? Is Fortinbras really planning an attack on Denmark, and will he succeed? Why are the current rulers of Denmark—and as yet we know nothing about them—so fearful? Why does the ghost reappear but give no message? Who is young Hamlet? Should he not be the king? But the next scene reveals that he is not. Why not? Why has the king married his sister, as he calls her? Why is Laertes shown such favor? Why do the clouds still hang on young Hamlet, "my cousin and my son"? Why does his father's death seem so particular with him? Why is young Hamlet not permitted to return to Wittenberg, if Laertes is permitted to return to Paris? Why does Hamlet long for death? Why must he hold his tongue? And then, on a larger scale, is the king guilty? He is. What shall Hamlet do about it? Kill him? And then we have a couple of the most shameless solution postponements in the history of fiction. (But shamelessness is the mark of the really great artist.) Hamlet finds the king, but he will not kill him while he is praying. Then he does find him, and does kill him, but it turns out to be only Polonius.

The real motive for these events was Shakespeare's: to keep the plot going, i.e., to maintain problem exposure and postpone solution. If we are to find an explanation in the play, Shakespeare did such a bad job offering it that there has been very little agreement on the matter. But whether it was a bad job or not depends not upon the laws of plot-making, but simply on one's taste. I am perfectly willing to believe Hamlet when he refuses to kill a praying king. But then I am willing to believe anything an author tells me, unless he gives me some good hints that I shouldn't. Why not believe it? It is merely fiction. Both of these failed attempts at revenge are what I call discontinuities. Expectation is built up for revenge, and then it doesn't happen. The solution is not offered; the audience continues to be exposed to the problem.

I call them instances of implicit discontinuity. That is, in normal experience, characterized by as much continuity as we can possibly manage, so that we perceptually discard occasions for discontinuity, it is implicit that we will repress awareness or devote ourselves to problem solution. Plot offers us the opportunity to experience such occasions, not discard them, or repress them, or ignore them. It violates, then, the implicit pattern of behavior. One source of emotional effect in fiction is certainly the semantic content. As Aristotle said, the most horrible deed, killing a close kinsman, makes the best tragedy. But the other source is precisely the element of discontinuity. For all his philosophical monism, Aristotle himself was aware of the fictional value of surprise. But that in itself marks fiction off from life, for the values of life are all reducible to the effort to make experience predictable. The socially useless person is precisely the unpredictable person. As all business executives know, and as all academics know, if you want to say or do something genuinely novel, something really surprising, you had better be in a very secure social and economic position, or you will be ignored and perhaps discouraged. In great corporations, idea men are specifically designated. Their job is to offer surprise. From them surprise is predictable; the role makes the character of the surprise endurable and makes it possible to consider it seriously. The best place to study how a narrative presents anomalies and problems, and maintains them, and introduces both related and unrelated problems, and postpones solutions, so that the audience is simultaneously exposed to a number of problems, is in the major plays of Shakespeare. Directors and producers and actors are always very ill advised to cut the initial lines of a Shakespearean work. The Olivier movie of *Othello* lost much of its potential power by cutting the opening scenes savagely. Perhaps these egocentric maniacs will one day realize that Shakespeare was a very intelligent man.

To all this it may be objected that in good fiction surprise is always "logical," to use a word which in this kind of situation seems to be very quaint. What the word appears to direct our attention to is that as one looks back over the course of the story it is possible to generate an explanatory statement, or at least possible to see that the surprises are analogically related, or form a certain pattern. This objection is telling, provided we forget certain factors. The first person we know of to make that assertion was, as we have seen, Aristotle, but even he was talking about a good plot, that is, what he, as a man of the highest cultural level, recognized as a good plot. That is, to underline a point which is frequently forgotten, Aristotle was, in his *Poetics*, writing a recipe for a plot that would be morally functional at the highest cultural level in the Greek city-state. He was not making a taxonomical study of plots, or even of plots that might have some other than a moral function, which, as we know from his *Politics*, was the only way tragedy could be justified. Like Aristotle, at the highest cultural level we demand that there be a point to the plot, that its interrelation of characters, events, and places force a meaning to emerge. That is, what the highest cultural level requires is that a fiction give hints, or clues, or sometimes statements to which the appropriate verbal response is the utterance, covert or overt, of an explanatory proposition. So reliable is this convention that certain modern writers can offer quite pointless fictions with the reasonably sure knowledge that the more intelligent readers will regard that very pointlessness as in itself implying an explanatory or "philosophical" statement. But this is only a manner of speaking. A fiction implies nothing; it is only interpreters who decide that it implies a nonexemplary or explanatory proposition.

Now the basic reason for this behavior at the higher cultural levels we have already seen. The higher the cultural level, the more adept the individual is at generating explanatory statements and at sustaining explanatory, nonexemplary discourse. Further, he is intensely interested in problems and puzzles. People whose jobs operate at that level are, in fact, required by their roles to devote themselves to looking for problems and solving them. The efficiency experts called in to evaluate a corporation office or factory are asked, in effect, "What is wrong here? What problems, what anomalies, what events requiring explanation can you find?"

But also, it is to be observed, such people, once they have found problems, are expected to solve them as soon as possible. All this gives us a clue to another important source for implicit discontinuity. At the lowest cultural levels it is barely existent, if at all, just as at the lower levels long works tend to proceed episodically, in short spans of problem exposure and solution postponement. In Proust, the problem solution is postponed for thousands of pages.

Aristotle, then, was pointing to something important when he said that the surprises of the plot must be capable of explanation. But that is only part of the matter. St. Augustine came closer, for he believed that in true poetry the poet presents figurative language, that is, exemplary statements, in such a way that they can be penetrated by the properly trained mind to reveal the invisible truths of God. And he also thought, apparently, that the pleasure to be found in reading poetry was the satisfaction gained from overcoming the enigmatical difficulties of the figurative language. That is, he proposed that literary satisfaction comes from using hints and clues and analogies as the occasion for uttering explanations.

Students, first encountering difficult works, are often exasperated by this character of high literature. "If that's what he meant, why didn't he say so? Why do these authors you tell us are so good have to hide their meanings?" Indeed, if the purpose of fiction is to offer an explanatory statement or series of explanatory statements, these querulous cries are quite justified. Why go to so much trouble to conceal what, as often as not, is a mere platitude? But then, man does not live by bread alone but principally by platitudes, so that objection scarcely counts. Yet it is an objection that, like Augustine's position, points in an interesting direction.

It is claimed by certain medievalists that a unique character of medieval literature is that it is allegorical, or, to be more technically precise, consists of tropes. It seems hard to believe that such a notion could be seriously entertained, and yet Professor D. W. Robertson certainly seemed to entertain it when he wrote his famous *A Preface to Chaucer*. Perhaps the technical terms of medieval exegesis and rhetoric misled him. Certainly nothing in medieval literature offers more of a puzzle than, let us say, *Who's*

Afraid of Virginia Woolf?, not to speak of *Tiny Alice*. Further-more, in those works, the method is fully one of *alieniloquium*, language foreign to the discourse. That is, when the events of a work do not make much sense in themselves, are bizarre and in-explicable, we take it, if it is operating on a sufficiently high cul-tural level, that what we are supposed to do is to provide an explanation. Furthermore, the data, or exemplary materials, which serve as hints and clues, are thoroughly mixed in with super-ficially similar materials which do not and cannot so serve. In a movie, the hero's exit from a room may be such a hint, but how he grasps the doorknob, and whether the door opens in or out may very well not be relevant. In the simplest sense, we encounter disorder, uncertainty of categorization. No, the difference between medieval literature and the literature of today is that in the Middle Ages you always ended up, apparently, with the same explanation, the same invisible truths of God, whereas today you end with multifarious *invisibilia saeculi*, invisible interpretations of the world. It may be, as Professor Robertson maintains, that the *Canterbury Tales* are properly interpreted on the system of medieval exegesis, but it is also undeniable that Chaucer, far more than his predecessors, included material that did not serve as clues and hints.

At the higher cultural levels it is implicit in behavior, as we have seen, that when the individual faces an anomalous or con-fusing situation, the appropriate response is to make sense out of it. When I was in the army, I was always offering explanations for what didn't make sense, and in the army, to the casual ob-server, that is almost everything. Alas for my pains. I bored and often infuriated my fellow soldiers who lived at a lower cultural level—except for a few, and to them my pedantry was manna from heaven. They hungered for it, they had been hungering all their lives, and they were delighted to get it. Their timidity and their eagerness were most endearing, because, after all, they encouraged me to do what I loved to do—offer explanatory statements.

Fiction, then, as it moves towards the higher cultural levels, increasingly offers hints and opportunities for an explanatory response. This is the source of the interpretational problem in literature, and one of the reasons, though it is not the only one, why great works inspire varying interpretations, many of which would quite astonish the author. Enough of the anomalous, or *alieniloquium*, is given to indicate that the appropriate response is interpretation, the generation of explanatory statements. But as with plot, the arrival at a satisfactory explanation is continually postponed by introducing new anomalies as well as large quantities of data which serve no exemplary purpose. Thus the author of fiction has at his disposal two ways of arousing cognitive tension, the plot problem and the interpretive problem, and he handles them both the same way, by postponing the presentation of data sufficient either to solve the problem of the plot or to facilitate the construction of an adequate interpretation.

A second way of categorizing discontinuities in art and in fiction is what I call internal discontinuity. The easiest example of this is the theme and variations plan in music. The important thing about a variation is not its resemblance to the theme, but its difference, and its fascination and emotional power comes from the fact that it is impossible to predict when the variation is going to adhere closely to the theme and when it is going to wander far away. In fiction, the prime source for internal, or thematic, discontinuity is character.

As I suggested above, it is one of the most common of human illusions to imagine that a proper name refers to an entity. It is hard for us to think ourselves out of the fancy that we exist, and for practical purposes, of course, it is necessary to imagine that we really do. What applies in all other perceptual and cognitive behavior applies also in this area of experience. Nowadays, the notion of image, and of self-image, in particular, is distressingly common. It has become so vulgarized that one hesitates to use it. To avoid it, and to keep coherence with my terminology elsewhere in these remarks, I shall use instead the term "self-model." We have a cognitive model of ourselves, and like all cognitive models we maintain its stability by repressing our awareness of behavior that is inconsistent with that self-model, and by controlling our behavior so that we behave the way we think such a self ought to behave. Thus we attain stability and maturity, and, I fear, a certain dullness. Perhaps that is why, as Einstein said, when we are young to be lonely is terrible, but when we are old, to be alone is delicious. Then we do not have to be exposed to other people's dreary consistencies, and, isolated and protected, we can at last expose ourselves to our own delicious inconsistencies. At last we can afford to surprise ourselves. Be that as it may, to be surprised by the behavior of a fictional character, especially if it is one which we can categorize together with ourselves, is one of the major delights, and discontinuities, of fiction.

One of the reasons other people become such a bore as life goes on is that we tend to see most of them, sometimes even members of our families, in a very small category of situations. When we are young and college students, we often have the experience of coming to know well, we think, and to like and respect a friend for his, as we call it, maturity and adult independence. Then we go to his home, and we see him, before our very eyes, regress to an immature dependence on and domination by his parents. We scarcely recognize him. And no wonder. The facial and gestural and costume signs and clues by which we had so successfully come to predict his behavior are, in this situation, of no predictable value whatsoever. But this experience, so disagreeable in life, unless we are enormously flexible, which we are not likely to be when we are young, is precisely what happens in fiction, and is one of its greatest sources of emotional power. Consider the discontinuity in the personality of Baron Charlus. When we first see him, he is young, haughty, aristocratic, proud, superbly self-controlled and self-disciplined. At the end we see him tied to a bed in a homosexual brothel, begging to be beaten harder, and harder yet. Who among our friends can offer us so interesting and so instructive a range of behavior? Or consider the superb Othello, who has married, blackamoor that he is, a fair Venetian, and see him plunge through jealousy, convulsion, and murder to suicide.

Now this is why the fictional characters which exhibit the greatest discontinuity of behavior are infinitely more vivid to our memories than all but a few people we ever know, and to some people more vivid than anybody they ever know, including themselves. The reason is that we see a central fictional character in a great variety of situations, to which he responds in ways ranging from the predictable to the completely unpredictable. How many people see even themselves in so varied a series of situations with so varied a series of responses? To be sure, one of the pleasures as well as one of the tribulations of travel is that we thrust ourselves into novel situations and respond in novel ways. But even as travelers we are tourists, that is, detached from the society around us, observers, insulated from most requirements for action, and by our very garb and behavior protected from the animosity of the natives toward our unpredictable behavior. To be sure, they frequently laugh. And so do we when we are reading or seeing fiction. For in fiction the formal source of tears and laughter is one. It is the semantic aspect that tells us that we should laugh or cry, but it is the discontinuity that provides a powerful emotional stimulus, and the role that permits overt emotional expression.

To be sure, as with plot, we frequently demand that some single explanatory overriding statement be available or at least derivable from the material before us. But again as with plot, that is always a matter of current cultural values, and simultaneously a measure of the perceiver's tolerance for discontinuity, which varies enormously from individual to individual, and from time to time for one individual. A report that a character is inconsistent is very frequently a report that the perceiver's toleration for inconsistency in personality is always or momentarily low. Further, as in plot, an explanatory statement, like all explanatory statements, can be generated only by omitting a great deal of the data presented. When we assert that we have an explanation for a plot or a character, we can be sure that we have neglected many of the problems presented or many of the responses and much in the situations. A fiction is unified according to the stringency of our requirements for unity. If our requirements are extremely stringent, no fiction is unified; if they have little stringency, it all is.

Another aspect of character or internal discontinuity is worth pointing out. Characters are discontinuous according to their distance from the central character. Spear-bearers are always the same. Anyone off the streets can successfully carry a spear and wear a costume, with minimal instruction. A curious instance of this appeared in Maurice Evans' film of *Macbeth*. An entirely new non-Shakespearean character was created by simply giving three different characters the same actor and costume. It is only the proper name that unifies a character and makes the discontinuity possible. In revising *The Human Comedy*, Balzac took three separate stories about three different women, gave all three the same name, made a few other necessary adjustments in lesser characters and in setting, and had a novel about three stages in the same woman's life. A splendid example of how the interpreter imposes a unity upon character and plot through the repetition of proper names is to be found in Marc Saporta's *Composition No. 1*, which consists of several hundred episodes printed on separate sheets. To get a new novel you merely shuffle the sheets. I have done it several times, and the device works very well. One gets a limitless number of novels for the price of one. The reviewers were surprised, but to my mind it was the most natural thing in the world.

The general law of fiction, therefore, is that the less important the character the less discontinuity in his personality, the more predictable his responses, and the smaller variety of situations he appears in, down to the character who appears in only one situation and does almost nothing in that. But this can be put more accurately. The importance of a character is defined by the amount of discontinuity he displays. That is, we know that a character is unimportant precisely because he has a narrower range of responses than other characters and appears in a smaller variety of situations. He is minor because he is, unhappily, just like us, while the major characters are deeply attractive, or repulsive, because they exhibit a range and discontinuity of behavior which, in our daring moments, but rarely in public, we would like for ourselves.

There are other sources for internal discontinuity, such as landscapes, houses, interiors. One mark of the fiction-writer at the highest cultural level is his power of giving such nonhuman elements life by ascribing to them a certain emotional tonality which turns them into characters, and then by varying them by discontinuity just as he varies human characters. Dickens is a particular master of this device; an example would be what he does to Pip's stuffy chambers at the end of *Great Expectations*. The cumbersome, heavily upholstered furniture is gone, as are the heavy drapes. It was a room seen only at night. Now there are white curtains on the bed and at the windows, and the windows are open and the sun is streaming in. The effect is far more powerful than if Pip had awakened from his fever in a different room.

The final category of discontinuity I have called modal, by metaphorical extension from musical modality. This is above all a matter of, in written fiction, rhetoric. A very obvious instance is the shift from prose to verse and back again in Shakespeare. But discontinuities from narrative to dialogue in fiction serve just as well to show what I mean, or from description to narrative, as in the often berated and praised opening of Balzac's *Père Goriot*. Or it can be a matter of shift in emotional tone. Ivy Compton-Burnett is extraordinary in that she depends almost entirely upon rhetorical discontinuity to create modal discontinuity. Sudden bathos is another device. Generally speaking, modal discontinuity is a matter of emotional tone. It can be done by such a simple thing as having a cloud come over the sun during a picnic. It is by missing such discontinuities that some people judge Jane Austen to be placid and monotonous. She works within a narrow range of discontinuities, but that narrowness makes the oscillation the more powerful. An adequate response to Jane Austen is a pretty dizzying experience. To miss it is to miss utterly, for example, *Emma*.

Again, modern critics of the novel have decried the omniscient and intrusive author, but it is precisely that device that adds enormously to the possibilities for modal discontinuity. A sharp and abusive comment by the author on the behavior of one of his characters brings about a sudden, unexpected, surprising discontinuity in the point of view. The prejudice against the intrusive, omniscient author is merely a modern cultural prejudice, which will prove to be quite temporary, and critically is about on the level with those seventeenth-century theorists of the drama who insisted on the unity of place because the audience cannot believe that people are suddenly transported from Athens to Rome. Who ever has really believed that they were in Athens? Actors are on a stage and everybody knows it, and knows it all the time, though every member of the audience may be crying like pigs.

These are but instances of the vast repertoire of discontinuities available to the creator of fiction. That, of course, does not mean that everybody responds equally well to them. In spite of critical yammering about authorial control, the author has, in fact, very little control; in the thousand members of the audience at a play there is a great variety of behavioral response. Some may be completely under the author's spell; some may be bored to distraction. The reason is that to experience a novel, like every form of art perception, involves learning a response, specifically, learning a socially conventionalized role. We laugh or cry because we have learned that it is proper to laugh or cry. That does not prevent some people from being rebellious. There are always those, fortunately, who refuse to play the social role they know perfectly well they are supposed to play. And like everything else that is learned, and that is everything human beings do, the role of fiction perceiver can be learned badly. Teachers of that role are parents, companions, friends, artists, critics, and, of course, professional teachers of literature. But it is to be observed that such teachers do not teach literature. There is nothing, literally, to teach. For language too, though we may separate it for certain purposes from the world, is experientially part of the world. Whether spoken or written, language consists, to the interpreter, of phenomenal configurations which he must learn to interpret. And we do not teach the world; neither do we learn it. What we teach, and what we learn, is behavior. So the teacher of literature teaches the proper behavior for playing the role of reader of literature. And that is what the interpreter learns. That does not mean that he does not innovate. One of my assumptions, it may be remembered, is that we cannot help innovating, and there is nothing to prevent us from exploiting what we must necessarily do. And so the critic, likewise, does not criticize literature. He criticizes the behavior of the author, behavior of which the work itself is the mere consequence or deposit or trace. Applying his cultural values, he praises or blames him for not playing the writer's role properly, for being too innovative or not innovative enough, for offering too little discontinuity or not enough.

I come, therefore, to my final paradox that the telling of stories, and the listening to stories, is motivated both by the desire for order, for cognitive and perceptual and interpretive continuity, and by the desire for disorder, for cognitive and perceptual and interpretive discontinuity. I hope I have made myself clear enough so that it will be seen that this is not a paradox at all. The ultimate motive for story-telling is, I believe, the desire for relief from exposure to the continuous disorienting effect of polysemy in the ordinary and extraordinary affairs of life. Its consequence is a set of richly interlocking exemplary statements which seems to create a world of solidity and of "meaning," in still another sense, the sense that polysemy is controlled and even eliminated. A constructed world of intense particularity is the result. In such a world, protected from the vagueness of language in the real world, one can afford to enter upon artistic experience, one can afford to expose oneself to a different kind of disorientation, a nonsemantic discontinuity, even though it is presented, like everything in the real world, in a semantic costume, or, as Carlyle would almost put it, in semantic clothes. But semantic function is a matter of convention, and, to make momentarily a dangerous distinction, whether a discontinuity is cognitive or perceptual, it is a discontinuity precisely because a configuration is offered which is not conventionalized, for which there is no conventional interpretation. Fiction, then, satisfies our desire for a semantic order we cannot experience in our everyday and endless and hopeless task of trying to link language surely and permanently to the world, and this satisfaction permits us to encounter a nonsemantic disorder which trains us to endure the slippery instability of the real world, and of interpretation, and of language itself. Our reward is that if the instability of language is our cross, it is also our opportunity and our salvation, for only because language is unstable can we say something new.

17

DISCONTINUITY IN

FICTION: PERSONA, NARRATOR, SCRIBE

[1967*]

When I published *Man's Rage for Chaos: Biology and Behavior in the Arts*, I did not discuss the problems of fiction. It is evident that if such a novel, odd, and, to some, even outrageous theory of art cannot say something about fiction without seriously distorting itself, it is not worth very much. I have already published one essay on the subject ("Order and Disorder in Fiction," *Sage*, Spring, 1967; see pp. 290–317 in this book), in which I attempted to show not only how the theory can be thus applied without suffering any damage, but also why people tell stories at all. In the present essay I should like to extend my speculations, with particular attention to the persona, or narrator, or, in another terminology, official scribe.

For those unfamiliar with my position, I had better present at least the heart of the matter, but I shall do so in a way I have not

* Delivered as the Invited Address at the Annual Meeting of the South Central Modern Language Association, November, 1967. Copyright © 1970 by the University of South Carolina Press.

hitherto used, for the sake of those who have come across it. My assumption is that we confuse statements about playing the role of artistic perceiver with the experience itself. When we disregard overt and covert verbal behavior that purportedly gives information about that experience, thus jettisoning metaphysical explanations and justifications, and examine instead the configurations of works of art themselves, it is apparent that individual works present not continuity of configurations but discontinuity, and when we examine the perceptual transaction, it becomes evident that our perceptual expectations and cognitive patterns are by no means fulfilled but on the contrary disappointed, frustrated, violated. A ready example comes from prosody: meter is the pattern of expectancy violated by the actual configurations of stress the poem offers.

An analysis of the language of discourse about order in art will perhaps serve to make my position clearer. Statements about the order and organic unity and so on of art are second-order statements; that is, they organize statements about the phenomenal configurations in the work. Regarded as sets of instructions, they instruct us in what kind of statements to generate about the work, rather than what to look for. Thus an individual who makes such a second-order statement will respond, when challenged, with such a statement as, "The painting is dominated by a set of triangles, some contiguous, some separated, some overlapping others." This first-order statement gives instructions about what configurations may be discerned in the painting. Now there is nothing wrong in all this, but two things are to be noticed. First, this first-order statement does not give instructions about what other configurations are to be discerned, nor, more importantly, does it give instructions about perceiving that the triangles are not all of the same size, that in each the angles are of different degrees, that some may be seen readily, that others can be discerned only with difficulty, that others are only implied, or suggested, and that others are ambiguous, that is, a line may be interpreted as a side of any of three or four triangles. Second, where in my exemplary sentence I have used "dominated by," it is common to use such phrases as "planned around," "is organized by," or "is given order by." Any one of these phrases, including "dominated by," has traditionally been considered as a justification for such a third-order sentence as, "Art is characterized by order." Such statements are explanatory statements, but they do not explain the phenomenal world; they merely explain other statements, themselves explanatory of exemplary statements (or concrete or empirical statements, to use terms which I myself cannot accept), and these statements give only partial information, selected by instructions deduced from second- and third-order statements.

My theory of artistic behavior, therefore, amounts to the assertion that second-order statements about art function by giving instructions for generating first-order statements. That is, they generate verbal behavior, not perceptual behavior. But further, when they are used to generate perceptual behavior, the results are deplorable. The history of criticism, as well as professional teaching and writing, and so on, shows that what we foolishly call "evidence" for order in a work is a matter on which there is continuous disagreement. The reason for this is that the attributes of the word "order" and similar expressions are highly unstable. Within our culture are to be found innumerable metaphysical or explanatory systems (though Stephen Pepper says there are only seven basic types), each of which prescribes differing sets of attributes for such terms. Ernst Cassirer says, for example, that "in every artistic creation we find a definite teleological structure, . . . Each individual utterance is part of a coherent structural whole. . . . Not even a lyric poem is wholly devoid of this general tendency of art. . . . In every great lyrical poem we find this concrete and indivisible unity" (Essay on Man [New York, 1953], 182–83.). This is all very well if you are a neo-Hegelian, but if you are not, your notions of the attributes of order may not be teleological at all. Actually Cassirer says, "In every act of speech and in every artistic creation." That first phrase makes it very hard for me to understand the statement that "not even a lyric poem is wholly devoid of this general tendency of art." If a poem is an act of speech, I do not understand how it can be even slightly devoid of that teleological structure which is responsible for "the coherent structural whole." This is but one of endless instances of what happens when metaphysical justifications for the attributes of the term "order" are used constitutively instead of instrumentally. That is, when we are given instructions, no matter what their metaphysical explanation and justification, to look for a set of configurations, we use them constitutively when we observe and report on only what we have been told to look for, but instrumentally when we also observe what we have not been told to look for and use those observations to correct both the first-order instructions and their second-and third-order explanations and metaphysical justifications. There is, moreover, a further difficulty about metaphysical explanations and justifications when such words as "order" are used in general statements about art or more restricted statements about individual works. When I ask, "How shall I know whether the work is ordered or unified or not?" an appropriate and certainly very common type of reply is to give a list of criteria. Now in fact there is no field of perception which cannot be judged to be disorderly if the criteria are sufficiently stringent, and none that cannot be judged to be ordered if the criteria are sufficiently loose. In short, it is my conviction that statements about order are misunderstood in their function, are intellectually damaging, and at best are useless. But this is to be expected. "Millions for the statement," is the great human motto, "and not one cent for the phenomenon."

The quotation from Cassirer can serve as introduction to the kind of discontinuity in fiction I want to discuss. I was led to it by a recent article by Professor Bernard J. Paris on *Vanity Fair*. ("The Psychic Structure of *Vanity Fair*," *Victorian Studies*, X [June, 1967], 389–410). In this interesting essay Professor Paris is concerned with the distinction Wayne Booth makes in *The Rhetoric of Fiction* between "the author as historical persona and the author as the writing self, the official scribe." Booth's book, of course, is principally focused on the scribe, and one has the impression that for some time it has been, or recently was, the central question in any theory of fiction. It is the great merit of the book that it shows how many different ways this writing self can appear in a novel, and to how wide a range of degrees. It seems to me apparent from what Booth has done that the degree to which the official scribe appears can best be thought of as a continuum from the virtually inobtrusive to the virtually omnipresent, while the ways for introducing him are best thought of as indefinably large in number.

But this, of course, is not the conclusion to which Booth comes. On the contrary, he objects, on what he calls aesthetic grounds, to any ambiguity or inconsistency or lack of clarity in the presentation of the scribe. Paris quotes from Booth: "Our sense of the implied author includes the intuitive apprehension of a completed artistic whole; the chief value to which *this* author is committed, regardless of what party his creator belongs to in real life, is that which is expressed by the total form." Booth's regret for "the absence of moral norms in modern fiction"—the consequence of scribes whose attitudes toward their stories and their characters puzzle the reader—betrays clearly that he is not making an "aesthetic" judgment at all, but a moral judgment. Like so many critics, he wishes to be a moral re-educator; possibly he should have been a psychiatrist, the moral policeman of middle-class culture. Or if he wants fiction to be a guide to life, he has but to devote himself to *The Ladies' Home Journal*.

Now Paris will have none of this. He demonstrates, I think to anybody's satisfaction, that the scribe of *Vanity Fair* is at least of two minds about his material. These Paris explains by using terms from Karen Horney. This scribe is superficially compliant towards the society he is presenting, but unconsciously aggressive toward it. Thus he is inconsistent. According to Booth such moral inconsistency would damage the aesthetic merit of the book. But Paris disagrees; for him the author's task is to grasp human behavior "in its concreteness and inner reality." And he concludes that Victorian fiction is not the poorer because the author "does not know what he is talking about."

To dispose first of a couple of minor issues, had Paris remembered that the publication of *The Snobs of England, by One of Themselves* overlapped that of *Vanity Fair*, he would have realized that Thackeray knew perfectly well that he was both "compliant" and "aggressive" toward his society. He wanted to be a snob, and was, but he also held a set of values that made that snobbishness contemptible. This conflict of values, also to be found in the values of *Vanity Fair's* scribe, was anything but

unconscious, as Paris is convinced it was. Further, the disagreement between the two critics about the basis for valuation—the
one moral, the other epistemological—indicates that it may be
impossible—to my mind it is certainly impossible—that any
aesthetic judgment can be made on aesthetic grounds. Judgments
about the merit of a work of art are invariably made on extra-
artistic grounds, and any grounds can be chosen, according to the
interests of the critic. An artistic judgment may be a social act;
it is, I am convinced, never an artistic act.

Nevertheless, both Paris and Booth share a common assumption—that the healthy personality suffers no inconsistencies.
Booth's position is that, whatever the author may be, the scribe
should be healthy, not neurotic. Paris' is that if the scribe is
neurotic—and that is what he calls the scribe in *Vanity Fair*—it
is because the author and his society are neurotic, and he supports
his position by referring to Karen Horney's notion that the test
of neurosis is inconsistency, though a trained psychiatrist can
see a consistency in the neurotic's patterns of inconsistency. Thus
all three entertain the assumption that the personality is structured, and that even when superficial inconsistencies are evident,
a unifying explanation is available which demonstrates that the
neurotic's inconsistencies have a structural relationship to each
other. Encountering such words as "structure" and "inconsistency," we should be immediately suspicious. Is such a statement
a first-order statement or one of the second order? I think the
answer must be that it is a second-order statement, designed to
generate first-order statements. Further, as I have already pointed
out, it is difficult if not impossible for second-order statements
so generated to be unsuccessful. But supposing we begin with
the statement that the personality is not a structure but a package,
a position justified by the notion that behavioral patterns are
learned from the culture, and that each of the total patterns available within a culture has historically originated in the culture's
struggle to master infinitely varied and unrelated situations. From
this position it becomes immediately obvious that the test for
neurosis is not inconsistency but inappropriateness, and that
what the trained psychiatrist—or anybody else—observes is that
when the neurotic is judged to behave inappropriately in a variety

of situations his patterns of inappropriateness show a high degree of coherence, or that when his behaviors are inappropriate according to the cultural protocol for a situation they tend to be inappropriate in the same way. Consequently inappropriate consistency is the test for neurosis, a very different matter from simple inconsistency. Further, as the neurotic continues to regress, his behavior becomes inappropriate to an increasing range of situations, until he may decide to curl up naked in a corner. Here, at last, is structured and consistent behavior.

It seems reasonable to ask, then, what is the source for this consistency and structure? Certainly, the neurotic feels that the continuity of his ego is threatened with disintegration. His increasing consistency of behavior is, therefore, a strategy of defense against a feeling of disintegration. It follows that the healthy personality is one that experiences no such feeling, or that, when he does, he is able to endure it without adopting defensive strategies, and that, even more to the point, he is not troubled by inconsistency of his own behavior in different categories of situation, or, if he is, is able to endure it without resorting to defenses. From this point of view, though we may admire Paris for seeing the inconsistencies in Thackeray and his scribe, we need not conclude, as he does, that both are neurotic. Quite the contrary. Furthermore, we need not justify that inconsistency by an appeal to "concreteness and inner reality." Thus why the inconsistency is there is left an open question, concealed neither by Booth's and Horney's sentimental moralizing, nor by Paris' desperate effort to justify it by an appeal to a fuzzy notion that art is predictively reliable.

The problem is best attacked first by exploring the problem of why all three make the assumption that the personality is structured. That almost everybody assumes that the personality is an entity and is therefore structured, or internally coherent, is no help. The weakness of that assumption comes out in Paris' conviction that the relation of the scribe to the author's "historical self" is a highly complicated matter. If both are entities, it is certainly a complicated matter, but if neither is, the problem virtually vanishes. The notion of a relation between the two involves the conviction that statements derived from scribal information can be converted into statements about the author and thus can become highly predictive of informational statements about the author, and vice versa. Put in this way it becomes evident at once that the degree of predictive reliability in either direction can be arranged along a continuum from completely reliable to utterly unreliable. If that is the case, no general rules are going to emerge, except for the possibility that the degree of reliability may be culturally linked. I suspect that a thorough study of the matter would show this to be so, but until such a study is undertaken, we had all better keep quiet. Paris' puzzlement about this scribe-author is, of course, a very common puzzlement, virtually universal in the current critical situation. But, as I have tried to show, the puzzlement arises not from the relation itself but rather from the verbal form in which it is put. That is, both Booth and Paris, and Horney too, and almost everybody else, have assumed that a proper name and the word "I" refer to entities; they have hypostatized or reified these terms.

Consider what actually happens. When we first encounter a person we learn (a) his physical appearance, (b) his name, and (c) certain attributes. His appearance and his name are now signs for his attributes, and the succession of encounters we have with him becomes the range of both appearance and name. That is to say, physical configuration and name have become categorial signs, like all signs, of which the encounters are the range—the extension—and the phenomenal observables of his physical configuration, including costume and his behaviors, are the attributes —the intension. Because language gives us directions on how to find a unique phenomenal configuration, the universal tendency is to assume that the sign or name for the category of which the configuration is a member is in fact the name for the configuration. In the behavior of locating phenomenal configurations, we use all terms as proper names. This is responsible for the illusion that a name refers to a configuration, and that notion of reference is hypostatization, or reification, if no configuration can be located. Psychologically, what we do is to build up expectancies or cognitive models for the configuration. When it comes to persons, our hypostatization is not challenged so long as the physical configuration of the individual and his behavior, that is, the attributes for the steadily increasing range of encounters, vary only within the culturally accepted protocol for appearance and behavior in the situations in which we encounter him. This comes out in our judgment that his behavior is consistent. But it is not his behavior that is consistent; it is rather that his attributes have not fallen outside of the attributional limits permitted by the expectational set and the tolerance of the cultural protocol for that category of expectations, or, to put it in semiotic terms, of that categorial sign. Hence, when the attributes do fall outside of the tolerated limits, we call the individual inconsistent or neurotic, and if the categorial term is "I," the individual who so designates himself is threatened with a sense of ego-disintegration, to which he may respond either by generating defensive consistencies or by standing his ground and eventually incorporating the emergent attributes within his self-tolerated categorial limits. An individual, therefore, is interested in maintaining his behavior within the limits of his self-expectancies, and likewise anyone is interested in having his expectancies confirmed, for any reorganization of a set of expectancies involves disorientation, contamination of other expectancy sets, and the energy expenditure of readaptation to a category. What we call neurotic defenses against inconsistency in one's own behavior and the moral rejection of others on the grounds of their inconsistencies of behavior are therefore different instances of the identical psychological strategy.

Yet this strategy is necessary for survival and personal interaction. It is only the predictability of experience that we really care about and cherish, for the most part, particularly when it comes to other people. Only love and friendship make such violations acceptable, and thus love and friendship may be seen as strategies for tolerating unpredicted behavior. Be that as it may, it is evident that such toleration varies enormously. In fiction, at any rate, Booth cannot tolerate scribal inconsistency, but Paris has greater resources of toleration, though even he must say that inconsistency is neurotic, must justify it epistemologically, and must assert that Thackeray didn't know what he was talking about, although it is quite obvious that he did.

At this point, however, a difficulty arises. Is there not a difference between real persons and fictional persons? Is it not true that one is real, and the other is not, is, rather, imagined? The conviction that there is a radical difference has generated a problem which seems incapable of solution. It is, of course, often stated that Coleridge solved the problem with his "willing suspension of disbelief," but for the life of me I have never been able to understand that he did more than restate it. Now certainly never are hypostatization and reification so obvious as in critical discourse about characters in fiction, including that character who has recently received so much critical attention, the fictional scribe or, in poetic criticism, the persona. The irresistible psychological tendency to interpret a word as a real person makes both critics and their readers forget that they are talking about a term, and frequently, so far as the scribe or persona is concerned, an implied term. But that, let us firmly remember, is the phenomenal object of our discourse, an "I," a "he," or a "Joe." Thus discourse that uses such expressions as, "The author gets into the mind of his narrator," such as is so common in discussions of *The Confessions of Nat Turner*, is utterly superficial and entirely misleading. Yet it depends, for all that, on something that is entirely the case. There is no difference between a real and a fictional person. What an author does is to present a proper name and then verbally ascribe a series of attributes to that name while presenting it in an increasing range of verbally signified situations. The reader, therefore, is required to adjust his expectations for that name, initially barely existent, to a constantly growing set of attributes. That is, there is no difference between an experience of a real person and an experience of an imagined person. As I have pointed out, for real persons both the configuration and the proper name of a real person are categorial signs, with range and attributes.

The real difficulty in such expressions as "getting into the mind of a fictional character" is that it at once leaves us defenseless before the degree of our tolerance of violations of our expectancies. From this emerges the endless and wearisome discourse about the "believability" of a fictional character. The readiness with which professors of literature enter into such discussions argues an extraordinary naïveté in their intellectual tradition. But listening attentively to such discourse, and that of nonprofessionals, as in theater intermissions, is very instructive, as all eavesdropping is, if conducted in the right spirit. We categorize not only individuals; we also categorize groups of individuals into types, or, pejoratively, stereotypes. Some people reject the believability of a character because his attributes violate their expectations for the behavior of that particular type, but sometimes, and this is most instructive, because the character does *not* violate the expectations for what a more tolerant individual tends to call a stereotype. This requires that we add to the notion of toleration of attributional violation the notion of demand for such violation. Generally speaking, the toleration for the violation of any set of expectancies, in or out of art, is a function of cultural level; the higher the level, the greater the toleration. It is also a function of psychic insulation, as with the scholar, the scientist, the corporation executive, and above all the perceiver of art. In discussions of fiction, two generalities are highly reliable. First, the lower the cultural level, the lower the toleration for violations of attributional expectations. This was pointed out long ago by Hegel in his brilliant essay, "Who Thinks Abstractly?" It is the untrained mind that thinks abstractly; it is the untrained mind that is victimized by its own categories. Second, the lower the cultural level, the less the fictional character violates the attributes set up at the beginning of the presentation of the range of the successive appearances of that character. L'il Abner has changed very little since the 1930's. On the other hand, I have heard Nat Turner criticized as a fictional creation because he is too consistent. That is, Styron seems to imply and sometimes presents explanations for Nat's attributes which can be subsumed under a limited and interconnected set of explanatory statements. Such complaints were uttered by individuals at a very high cultural level, particularly of sensitivity to fiction. One, in fact, was himself a young Negro who has recently published a first novel of extraordinary promise. That is, from fiction at the highest cultural level the reader at the same cultural level tends to demand, at least from the principal characters, a violation of both typical and individual categorial expectancies. To use the term I used earlier, he demands discontinuity in his experience of the novel, and as a descriptional term of my theory of art, I use the expression, "general theory of discontinuity."

With all this in mind, it will, I think, be fruitful to turn once again to the disagreement between Booth and Paris. In the first place, Booth has come to a conclusion about what a scribe ought to be which to my mind is quite worthless. What he has done is to set up for the scribe a set of attributes the violation of which justifies a judgment that the work is an artistic failure. He had made the scribe into a characterological type, and would like to convert him into a stereotype. He has denied the validity of scribal discontinuity. Yet in the second place he has performed two great services. First is his demonstration of the continuum of the degree to which the scribe is given categorial emergence. At one end is the scribe whose only attribute is to present information about the behavior of the characters and their situations, that is, the attributes and the range of a set of proper and generic names. At the other end is the scribe who is given such a high degree of categorial emergence, such a rich set of attributes, that all information about the attributes and range of other proper names must be interpreted as controlled and perhaps distorted by the scribe's attributes. Booth of course wants these attributes to be a set of moral values which will be for the reader a moral model. Yet in spite of this, such is his sensitivity and intelligence that he also presents a wonderful array of scribes whose attributes are highly discontinuous. What these scribes do is respond to the various situations as if they were characters in the novel, characters above all at a high cultural level of fiction. Such scribes are puzzling; that is, as their range is extended, their emergent attributes are unexpected. In the full-blown Jamesian novel they are, often enough, full-blown characters, in the sense that they participate in the interpersonal actions of the situations and respond in unexpected ways. The scribe can thus be seen to vary along these two continua from a nearly empty category to an extraordinarily rich one. And this, I would say, is the value of *The Rhetoric of Fiction* that will give it considerable critical longevity.

The case of Paris is somewhat simpler. After quoting Booth

on "our sense of the implied author" as including the "intuitive apprehension of a completed artistic whole," he interprets Booth in the following statements: "In a novel which is organically unified the impulses toward representation, interpretation, and aesthetic patterning are harmonized; and the implied author emerges as a deeply integrated and coherent being. But there are many novels, including some great ones, which fail to achieve such organic unity." How does one demonstrate such matters as a completed artistic whole or organic unity, phrases which, I must admit, enrage me? A novel is made up, after all, of words, of statements. As we have seen, the generation of first-order statements from these second-order statements instructs us how to select from the novel statements and combine statements in such a way as to confirm these first-order statements. I suspect it is impossible to generate first-order statements from second-order statements about organic unity and coherence and all the rest which cannot be confirmed. But let us assume what is probably impossible, that for a particular novel one can account for all statements in the novel and all possible statements which can be derived by selection from the novel with a hierarchy of subsuming statements of such a character that ultimately one statement can be said to subsume all the statements in the novel and all statements between the ultimate statement and the statements in the novel. Such a novel would, I should think, be organically unified. The sheer impossibility of such a verbal construction is recognized by Booth's expression, "intuitive apprehension of a completed artistic whole." But if it were possible, what would we have? A proof that the novel is indeed organically unified? Not at all. If the history of philosophy shows anything it shows that a metaphysical system—for such an explanation would be a metaphysical system—is capable of including all possible statements. But no metaphysical system has been constructed the subsumptional character of which has not been successfully criticized by someone else. Indeed, the assertion of organic unity as implying the possibility of a consistent and successfully reductive explanatory system implies both that induction and deduction are understood and that the rules for valid induction and deduction have been codified. But neither of these propositions is true. In short, what I am simply pointing out is that the construction of what one man and many of his colleagues may accept as a satisfactory system of explanatory statements about a novel is not the same thing as asserting that the statements which make up the novel itself are coherent and consistent. In short, making statements about the novel is not to be confused with experiencing the statements of the novel in the order of their appearance.

An obscure recognition of this may lie behind Paris' assertion that the "great illuminative value of most fiction" is "that it helps us to grasp in their concreteness and inner reality phenomena that philosophy and social science treat objectively and categorially." First of all, a novel consists of language, and thus it can do no more and no less than language can do. Lurking behind Paris' statement is the assumption that literature has unique semantic functions, a widely held position that does endless amounts of damage and for which there is no basis at all. One way of showing its inadequacy must suffice here. If this semantic uniqueness is true of novels, then novels present unique interpretational problems. But since there is current no general theory of interpretation and scarcely the beginnings of trying to construct one, there is currently no way of knowing whether or not a novel presents unique interpretational problems, and hence no way of knowing whether or not it has unique semantic functions. Next, it is hard to understand how a discourse can be concrete which is generally accepted to be a construction of the imagination; that is, as a set of instructions, whatever it may do the novel certainly does not instruct us to locate phenomenal configurations. Further, if all terms are categorial, then the terms of novels are as categorial as those of philosophy and social science. Moreover, what is one supposed to do with a term like "inner reality"? I believe that all this means is that the novelist gives examples of the explanatory statements of philosophers and social scientists, and that he frequently gives examples for which neither he nor philosophers and social scientists can offer explanatory statements. Since most of human behavior remains unexplained, and since there are rival explanatory systems for explaining what can be explained, this is not at all surprising. Indeed, Paris goes on to say that the novelist is better off if he cannot interpret "what he grasps intuitively." If I understand him correctly, his final claim is that the greatness of Victorian fiction lies in the fact that "the author as interpreter usually does not know what he is talking about."

Paris' case, then, is really quite simple. Like Booth, he has responded to the discontinuities of the scribal category, but instead of being able simply to accept them, he has felt it necessary to provide a philosophical explanation of an extremely feeble character. But then, just before the end, he tosses in a statement for which there has been no preparation in the paper at all. The trouble with *Vanity Fair*, he says, is "that the narrator's attitudes are not, as in *Henry Esmond*, made part of the drama." He wants, in short, a Jamesian narrator. Oddly enough, in his prologue, "The Author: Before the Curtain," Thackeray has established the "I" category, and has ascribed to it a complex set of categories, among which is the warning that "I" 's responses to the range and attributes of his proper names—his dolls—is going to be varied and unpredictable; that he keeps this promise Paris shows us very well. I suggested above that the degree of predictive reliability back and forth from scribe to author is culturally linked, and I would now suggest that the continuum of what I have called scribal categorial emergence is also culturally linked. That is to say, Paris, who obviously plays the role of fiction reader at a high cultural level, though not at the current stage of that level, is convinced that the scribe should be a Jamesian narrator, and the explanation for this is not to be found in anything characteristic of fictional scribes but is to be found in Paris' cultural situation.

What he has done, then, in uttering this rule is what most critics have always done: they universalize and make into an aesthetic imperative a literary trait dominant in the literature of their own period. This is usually an emergent trait. Living on the high cultural level, they are quick to recognize and approve what I call external discontinuity, the historical emergence of violations of artistic expectancy. I sometimes wish our critics would read Hegel and learn something about how one transcends the limitations of one's own cultural situation. At any rate, attuned to a demand for discontinuity by the high cultural level to which they have ascended, both Paris and Booth report extremely well on what they experience when they read fiction written to be consumed at that level. However, the tradition of explanatory discourse in which they have been trained makes it impossible for them to do anything but betray their experiences when they attempt to explain the statements which report their experiences. I cannot forbear pointing out that my general theory of discontinuity provides an explanatory discourse which preserves the integrity of the experience from experience to first-order statement to second-order statement. If I did not know better, I would call it inductive, and perhaps it is.

At this point let me clarify a matter which has caused readers of my book considerable confusion and which has led many to accuse me of inconsistency myself. This is the assertion that my theory is a concealed value theory, and that I claim that the greater the discontinuity, the better the work of art. This is to misunderstand me. Rather I assert that the individuals trained in the mode of playing the role of art perceiver currently considered appropriate at the higher cultural levels will tend overwhelmingly to ascribe positive value to works which offer a great many powerful discontinuities. Being such an individual myself, I tend to prefer such works. However, it is my misfortune that, victimized by my culture and my society, I have been trapped into a gross overvaluation of art. Consequently, when I seek a little therapy for the purpose of tension relaxation I turn to art. That is, I read the comics and I go to the movies, and the older I get, the more I prefer movies which do not violate my expectancies of what a movie at a middle-cultural level may offer in the way of discontinuities. Some people for this purpose prefer westerns; I have a shameful liking for Walt Disney family-type movies, especially if they give me a chance to cry a little. In short, I have attempted to construct a theory which will account both for what is to be found in the formal aspect of art and for the behavior of perceivers of art, and to do this by scrupulously avoiding any recommendations about what artists ought to put into works of art or what perceivers ought to get out of them.

To introduce my final problem, the relation of the fictional persona to the persona of lyric poetry, I must present briefly the other kinds of discontinuity which fiction offers.

I have discussed scribal discontinuity and have mentioned discontinuity of characters, that is, categories the sign of which is personal proper names. A proper name, according to the view of language I am using, is a substitution for a lengthier discourse which offers a set of interlocking categories which gives instructions for locating a unique phenomenal configuration. The function of this substitution, then, is to stabilize that set of instructions, since, as situations vary, the same set of categories can be appropriately and successfully used for locating quite a different configuration. The language of fiction, which, of course, one does not respond to by behavior which attempts to locate a unique configuration which has been assigned a proper name, does not differ in any respect from language in response to which locating behavior is appropriate. It does not, in this sense, link language to the nonverbal and phenomenal world. It does not differ from nonfictional discourse by constructing verbally an imaginary world; all language constructs an imaginary world. As a consequence, the novelist has an unusual freedom in creating proper-name categorial expectancies and in violating them. But he also has an equal freedom in constructing those sets of interlocking categories for which proper names are substitutes. Consequently he does not have to provide a proper name for a person or a place or a house or anything else for which proper names are culturally conventional. On the contrary, because his instructions are never used for locating a configuration, are never tested, he can use a term for an attribute of a category instead of inventing a proper name for that category. This is what happens, for instance, in not naming the scribe. But this in turn makes it possible for him to use on the next appearance of that category still another attributional term. Thus the novelist has at his disposal a technique for creating discontinuity by withholding information. That is, he can make it uncertain precisely which of his categories is being presented. He can tease and puzzle the reader. It is a device which when used on the scribe profoundly shocks the morally upright Wayne Booth, but which Paris, perhaps, rather likes.

Proper-name and equivalent unnamed categorial discontinuities depend, of course, upon the fact that the novelist's imaginary world, forever untested, can include as much categorial repetition as he likes. And this circumstance gives him further enormous resources for discontinuity. But the principle of withholding information, of teasing and puzzling, can be extended.

The kind of discontinuity I have so far discussed is what I call internal discontinuity. That is, the categorial term is presented within the novel and then subjected to various devices of attributional violation. Plot, however, is a different matter. Consider the opening of *Vanity Fair*. After a couple of pages a problem emerges, a mystery is posed: Why is Becky Sharp *not* to be given a copy of Johnson's *Dictionary*? At this point the plot begins. For a twentieth-century novel it is a late beginning; for a Victorian novel it is early. Now the rest of the novel can be seen as an explanation of why poor Becky is thus deprived. But this leads to still another problem. Why, when she has been given a dictionary surreptitiously, does she throw it out of the carriage window? And this leads to still further problems. That is, it is incorrect to say that the rest of the novel is devoted to explaining why she is not to be given a dictionary. The correct statement is that the rest of the novel is devoted to postponing that explanation. That is, the immediate explanation we are given turns out to be a pseudo-explanation, one that is a problem in itself. I call this an implicit discontinuity because in nonfictional discourse, or normal expository or controversial discourse, as well as in nonverbal behavior, problem exposure implies that the appropriate response is to devote all one's energies either to solving the problem or to suppressing one's awareness of it, avoiding it, going around it, ignoring it. Plot, therefore, is a technique for postponing problem solution while maintaining problem exposure. In other problematic situations problem exposure is maintained in order to arrive at a solution, or problem solution is avoided in order to avoid problem exposure. The solution of the problem of *Vanity Fair* is ultimately that Becky and everybody else are products of their culture, dolls, puppets, with only rare experiences of cultural transcendence. Perhaps Dobbin is the only one who manages it, except for the scribe, who sometimes is victimized by his culture and sometimes rises above it. But this dual aspect is carefully signaled in the prologue. Furthermore, the length of the novel, that is, the degree of postponement of problem solution the author wants, is also, like all other discontinuities, entirely at the author's disposal, within the limitations imposed by his publisher. But even in accepting that decision he makes it his own. Again, the kind of problem he chooses, the technique of solution postponement he invents, the subordination of all problems in the novel to one or the coordination of various problems—all this is the consequence of decisions derived not from the character of fiction, but, on the contrary, from the author's response to his cultural circumstances, and this again is a matter for which there are no rules.

Finally, there is what I call modal discontinuity. In nonimaginative discourse rhetoric is controlled by cultural protocol. There are conventions for the rhetoric appropriate to the various categories of situation, as the culture has discriminated them. The novelist, however, is an artist. His product is the occasion for playing a role which has no immediate consequences for the reader, and it is consumed in a culturally isolated and psychically insulated situation. Above all, therefore, there is no need for the rhetorical conventions which obtain in all interpersonal behavior. Consequently, he can shift as he pleases from one rhetorical mode to another, and as frequently as he wishes. Such a position depends upon a definition of rhetoric as overdetermined language. That is, from the phonetic, syntactic, and semantic resources of language a rhetoric makes a selection for the purpose of facilitating interpersonal relations, including, for example, what we all learn in graduate school, the various rhetorics considered appropriate for the various kinds of scholarly and critical articles we are so careless as to compose and publish. The novelist can choose as he wishes the rhetorics available within the fictional tradition of his culture, the rhetorics available outside that culture, and such rhetorics as he chooses to invent himself. The greatest master of this, of course, was Joyce.

However, the novelist, like any artist, has one further burden and opportunity for discontinuity. As techniques of discontinuity are innovated within the fictional tradition of a culture, they are imitated and established. Thus the novelist, and the reader, builds up sets of expectancies for discontinuities, and the discontinuities begin to lose their effectiveness in violating expectation. It is consequently necessary for the novelist to innovate new kinds of discontinuities, of what I call the interior discontinuities, internal, implicit, and modal. This is responsible for the historical dimension of fiction; and it is this aspect of the novel that has scarcely been explored. Such an analysis, which, as I have said, maintains the integrity of the experience into the second-order statements about that experience, will make it possible to write a history of fiction. All we have now, at best, is a history of the values which are exemplified in fiction; but, as we have seen, that takes care of only some of the statements of a novel.

With this preparation I can now turn to the very puzzling problem of the relation of prose fiction to lyric poetry. We have all wrestled with this, and we have all read mountains of material in which others have wrestled with it. Not much has been gained. What we have attempted to do is first of all to make a semantic discrimination between verbal discourse which is art and that which is not. I hope it is evident from what I have said so far that no such discrimination can be made. No semantic function has yet been found which obtains in verbal art but does not obtain in verbal non-art. Indeed, the very notion of fiction is unacceptable, since all language is equally fictional; the difference between verbal art and verbal non-art lies in the response, not in the semantic character of the discourse. A similar failure marks the efforts to make semantic distinctions among lyric poetry, narrative poetry, and narrative prose. We cannot even say that the fictional scribe and the poetic persona mark a boundary between verbal art and verbal non-art, for the fact is that we make a cognitive model or set of expectations for every bit of verbal discourse we encounter. Thus all statements imply a scribe or persona. The difference between verbal art and other discourse is formal, that is, it is characterized by a maximization, depending upon cultural level, of the various kinds of discontinuity I have discussed. Furthermore, the difference between prose fiction and poetry is that poetry adds the various kinds of discontinuity made possible by prosody. Non-narrative poetry merely dispenses with the kind of discontinuity offered by plot.

A glance at the informal essay, such as that of Lamb, will help at this point. Plot is not the only way of presenting a problem and postponing a solution. Plot depends upon interpersonal behavior: the novel offers a series of proper-name categories and adds attributes by a verbal dialectic of agreement and contradiction among the categories, that is, by the verbal presentation of personal interaction. The informal essay, however, presents the internal, or attributional, dialectic of but one proper-name category. The problem is, so to speak, examined in terms of these attributes, and the discontinuity is accomplished by manipulating the category of scribe or persona, that is, by withholding attributional information, by adding unexpected attributes, and by emphasizing dialectical disagreements among the attributes considered as categories. Lyric poetry adds the prosodic discontinuities to non-poetic verbal art, and like the informal essay eschews plot. In both informal essay and lyric poem, then, the proper-name categorial focus is upon the persona, or spokesman, or scribe. Short lyrics rarely have the space to do more than present a problem and leave it unresolved. Hence their peculiar emotional power. But scribal discontinuity can be accomplished with greater rapidity. The turn in the traditional sonnet is an example. At the same time, although, that lyric poetry may present a problem and may offer scribal discontinuity, it need not do so, because it has the resources for discontinuity made possible by prosody and, especially, syntactical distortion, rarely, until the twentieth century, used in prose narrative or even in the informal essay, though Lamb plays a little with it. But here again a general law is observable; the lower the cultural level, the less the scribal discontinuity, as well as the less the prosodical and syntactical discontinuity.

To conclude, art is a category not definable by its semantic attributes, but only by formal attributes. Prose narrative or plot-centered fiction, as a subcategory of art, is, therefore, also definable not by semantic attributes but only by formal attributes. If we wish to understand fiction as art, it is these attributes we must study. They are the various kinds of discontinuity as I have outlined them. It may well have occurred to the reader that there is a deep inconsistency in my position. It certainly can be asked of me: Are not your proper-name and problem and rhetorical discontinuities presented in language, and are they not therefore semantic categories, and does it not follow that verbal art may be distinguished from verbal non-art by semantic discriminations? After all, did you not yourself specifically include semantic overdetermination in your definition of rhetoric? True, but the distinction is, nevertheless, tenable. I believe that "meaning" is best understood as the behavior, verbal or nonverbal, which is appropriately generated by a bit of discourse of any length, and which can be regarded as an acceptable substitute for the original discourse. The key word here is "appropriate." The link between the utterances of successive speakers is the cultural convention of what is appropriate, and this is also true of the link between individual statements in the discourse of a single individual, as in fiction. Indeed, it looks very much as if the philosophical effort, which has been going on for several thousand years, to establish logic as a set of rules governing discourse which transcends the conventions of language behavior is about to be given up as vain; in that event logic itself would have to be subsumed under the general category of appropriateness. Logic would then emerge as a special kind of rhetoric. (Work of great importance on the problem of links between utterances is being done by Professor Richard Gunter, of the University of South Carolina. He has defined the problem as "context grammar" or the "grammar of relevance.") It is this possibility for the semantically inappropriate—the appropriate being defined psychologically as an expectancy, set, or cognitive model—that the artist of fiction exploits.

I do not deny, of course, that prose fiction has a semantic aspect. All art does. In offering an interpretation of that semantic aspect, that is, in generating in response to it verbal behavior which they regard as, for some purposes, acceptable substitutes for it and thus appropriate verbal behavior, Booth and Paris have responded to that semantic aspect. The formal aspect is the experience of discontinuity, and is not to be confused with the attempt to reconcile, for example, a new attribute of a proper-name category with the attributes already presented. As Paris has acutely seen, though he has misunderstood it, a great deal happens in a novel which cannot be explained, for which generating verbal explanatory responses is inappropriate and even impossible; and some fiction is entirely constructed in this way—detective stories, for example, for which only sociologists or sociologically minded critics would bother to attempt to draw a moral. To put it very inexactly, the experience of not understanding a discourse is common; the responder is unable to generate appropriate verbal responses. The art of literature exploits the possibilities of this experience. The semantic aspect is understanding the discourse; the formal aspect depends on not understanding it. It is the failure to realize and comprehend and provide an adequate theory for this psychological distinction which has made it so difficult to assimilate literature to the arts, and to include it in the general category of art. What I have tried to demonstrate is that very pure semantic material, without the admixture of nonverbal configurations, can offer an opportunity for the psychological discontinuity which is the defining character of playing the artistic role, of the artistic experience, if you wish. And on this I rest my case for including fiction among the arts.

18

LITERARY INTERPRETATION AS

CONVENTIONALIZED VERBAL BEHAVIOR

[1967*]

I

The question of how a work of literature ought to be interpreted is the most perplexing question in the study of literature, so difficult and confusing that many a critic—by which I
mean anyone who purports to generate valid statements about
literature—obscurely feels that the very enterprise of studying
and teaching literature, as it is now practiced, and perhaps as
it has always been practiced, is somehow fundamentally fraudulent. The problem emerges sharply in the embattled garden of
the classroom whenever a student asserts that he disagrees with
his teacher's interpretation, that he prefers his own opinion, and
that in such matters his opinion is as good as anyone's, including
the author's. The poor teacher can do little more than gnash his
teeth, or, with luck, intimidate the student by a show of authority.

* Delivered at Pennsylvania State University, January, 1967. Reprinted
by permission from *Penn State Papers in Art Education*, No. 2, 1967.

Yet if he feels that the position of the student is wrong, his trouble is that he has no way of falsifying the student's position. Or he may agree with him, as a colleague of mine asserted, when I pointed out the syntactical and grammatical confusions in one of Blake's poems, that these confusions made a richer variety of interpretations possible and proved, therefore, that it was a good poem.

The attitudes of the student and my colleague are both the consequence of what still is called the "New Criticism" and will perhaps eventually be known as "contextualism." It rests on the proposition that poetry (and by implication all literature and art) has unique semantic functions, meanings not to be found elsewhere in verbal structures, or, more properly, closed verbal sequences. It is by no means a novel position, though it has had an extraordinary recrudescence in this century. I shall call it, for reasons to emerge later, the Augustinian position, though it is older than St. Augustine. It is, I believe, a position totally in error. Yet its constant recurrence in the Western literary tradition, beginning with the Alexandrians and, apparently, even before them, indicates that its very existence involves serious issues, and that to defeat it requires not merely a formal demonstration of its inadequacy but also an explanation of why it should exist and of its function in the uses we make of literature. It has been successfully argued against, but it never dies.

The best attack on the Augustinian position that I know of is in Isabel Hungerland's *Poetic Discourse* (Berkeley and Los Angeles, 1958), a work which has been, so far as I can discern, pretty much neglected in literary circles. "In brief," she says, "there is no such thing as a poetic language, either as a diction or as a mode of sentential meanings. The nearest approach to this occurs when a tradition in poetry has so cut itself off from the ordinary spoken language as to have a diction and grammar confined almost exclusively to itself." Yet, though I certainly agree with her, and though in her second sentence she has pointed in a very important direction, her arguments, I think, are not powerful enough to settle the matter. Indeed, as I shall try to demonstrate, those determined to accept the Augustinian position cannot be defeated. Yet it may be possible to show them what they are doing.

To begin with, it appears to me that if poetry (a word I shall henceforth use as an abbreviation for "work of literature") has unique semantic functions, there would be no way of finding out what they might be. It amounts to an assertion that there is a radical discontinuity between the semantic functions of poetry and those of ordinary language, that there is a chasm between the two and no way to bridge it. The recognition of this consequence of the Augustinian position emerges with the contextualistic assertion that paraphrase is heresy, that poems cannot be translated. Now, in one perfectly valid sense, no expression can be translated or paraphrased. It has its unique semantic function in a never-to-be-repeated situation. Unique semantic function is a property of poetry, only because it is a property of all verbal expression. And immediately the terrifying question arises, "What do we mean by any assertion of meaning?" At any rate, either unique semantic function is not a property of poetry or it is a property of all language.

Nevertheless, it is well known and has been pointed out a thousand times that the contextualists themselves are constantly telling us what a poem means, though to be sure they also assert that the meaning of the paraphrase or interpretation is not to be confused with the total meaning of the poem. But since the total meaning is by definition inaccessible, there is no way of knowing whether or not the meaning of the interpretation is or is not identical with that total meaning. And we are back where we started. If poetry has unique semantic functions, there is no way of knowing what those functions are or, indeed, of knowing that they exist. In truth, this form of the position seems to be little more than the truism that the subjective experience of the reader of a poem cannot be stimulated by any other proposition or set of propositions. That is perfectly true, but it is equally true that such a point is just as true of any proposition. Also, there seems to be no way of denying that any proposition or set of propositions always stimulates any reader or listener to a different subjective experience every time he encounters it. And finally, the subjective experience is inaccessible anyway, and consequently all of these propositions about subjective experience are quite useless, at least for the purpose of validating the Augustinian position, as well as for invalidating it.

Nevertheless, the "heresy of paraphrase" notion and the opinionated student's position point to the most striking characteristic of literary Augustinianism. An Augustinian interpretation cannot be falsified. To be sure, it is easy enough to account for the cultural possibility of such a position. Though it is not true that poetry has a unique semantic function, it is obvious that in a given culture a poet is supposed to write about some things rather than others. The culture has, so to speak, assigned him a subject matter as well as an attitude toward that subject matter, and these are called poetic insight, or some such name, and true poetry. The fact that these assignments are, historically, constantly being changed is usually recognized by the Augustinians with the assertion that assignments other than those they approve of are not truly poetic and do not result in true poetry. Rather, it is that fact of their recalcitrance that needs to be accounted for. The "unique poetic truth" theory rejects, bafflingly enough, attempts at falsification. But it is equally true that it rejects attempts to validate any interpretation. This is the consequence that my colleague revealed in his assertion that the more mutually exclusive meanings a poem has, the better it is. In actual practice, there are innumerable Augustinian modes of interpretation, of modes of asserting what a poem really means. Granted the Augustinian position to be absurd, as I would readily grant and assert, it is in spite of that quite true that it raises serious questions about meaning, questions crucial to the study and teaching of literature and all art.

II

The crux of the matter lies in the word "has" in the phrase, "the more meanings a poem has," and in the words "really means" in the phrase, "asserting what a poem really means." Well, a poem doesn't have any meanings; it doesn't *really mean* anything. The reason is that no sentence, no word, has meaning. Meaning is not immanent in language. When I say, "X means so-and-so," I am in actuality asserting that, "under the circumstances, the appropriate way to interpret X is so-and so." Meaning is not a property of language; it is something that human beings do. Meaning is not a property of language; meaning is a property of behavior. Further, the word "meaning," like all words, is characterized by polysemy; it has a good many semantic functions, none of which can ever be finally fixed. Again, like all words, it is categorial; it categorizes a great many aspects of behavior, and there is no particular reason to think that such semantic functions are necessarily continuous or overlapping. When I use the word I may be directing attention to an individual's overt behavior, that is, his performance, which I judge to be a consequence of his ascribing meaning to a particular sentence, as in, "Close the door." Or to what happens between the stimulus and the overt response, an abyss which we conceal from ourselves by one of the semantic functions of "mind." Or to his verbal response. Or to the speaker's "intention," whatever semantic function may be ascribed to that word. Or to a paraphrase, or to an example, or to an explanation. I must confess that in all the reading I have done about "meaning" I cannot remember anyone's recognizing this multiple semantic function of the word; instead, whoever I am reading offers *his* monolithic explanation of the essence of "meaning." And again I must confess that I have read so many of these that I have become a little weary of all of them, not, I daresay, an uncommon phenomenon. At any rate, rightly or wrongly, I have concluded that the enormous efforts to locate the essential meaning of "meaning" have failed because they cannot succeed; the wrong question has been asked.

I should like to approach the problem from a slightly different direction. My colleague who asserted that the more meanings a poem has the better is really asserting that poetic meanings cannot be falsified, indeed, that it is impossible to falsify any proposition, if we accept the notion that poetry and ordinary language are continuous. Indeed, can any proposition be falsified? Can any be verified? Now it is apparent that the Augustinian interpretation of poetry, and any theory of interpretation that has appeared so far, assumes meaning to be immanent in a poem, and that one's task is to discover it and utter it. But it also seems to me, I must admit, that the notion that any proposition can be falsified or verified rests upon the same assumption. I would suggest, first, that that is why theories of verification have been so unsatisfactory, and second that it is why, in spite of all efforts to dispose of it, the term "proposition" continues to be necessary, in the sense that it involves the notion that the meaning of a sentence is not identifiable with the sentence, or that two sentences, such as "It is raining" and "*Es regnet*," express the same proposition. A proposition, then, is a very mysterious affair, but I am convinced that the mystery vanishes if we observe that both the German and the Englishman, under similar circumstances and with similar interests in keeping dry, will get an umbrella, if they happen to believe the statement.

Briefly, I am convinced that language is linked to the world by behavior, that language functions by controlling behavior, and that the control is effective only because the interpreter of the sentence can respond to it by an already learned and pre-established conventionalized behavioral paradigm.

Consider the notion of falsification. How can we falsify a simple proposition like, "It is raining"? We can, in Wittgenstein's famous phrase, look and see. But we can do this successfully only because we know what to look *for*. That is, the sentence elicits in us an interpretive condition. We must be pretuned, or set, if we are to make sense out of the sentence. We must have a perceptual, interpretive, cognitive model. Or consider one of the small class of sentences which we take as models of true sentences—scientifically verified sentences. What, in fact, does a scientist do? Take such a proposition that hydrogen and oxygen combined in the proper proportion and under the proper circumstances will manifest themselves as what he calls water. Here, "under the proper circumstances" is the clue to what happens. That is, he knows how to interpret that sentence and how to behave appropriately, given the fact that he is currently performing the role of chemist. That is why one can read all the chemistry textbooks in the world and still not be much of a chemist unless one has been trained in a laboratory by a chemist, and it is why great scientists are produced only by some form of the apprentice system. The chemist must learn the appropriate behavioral paradigms; and if he is to be a creative chemist, he must learn them so well that he can control and exploit the innovation which necessarily results from the fact that no behavioral paradigm can be reproduced exactly. A sentence is true, in this sense, then, if it controls behavior to a predicted result, but that formulation conceals the fact that the person being controlled has learned how to link the sentence to the predicted result by appropriate behavior. In short, I suspect that the term "proposition," in at least one of its semantic functions, categorizes the behavior consequent upon the response to the stimulus of the sentence. Considering the conventional nature of semantic functions, and the impossibility of learning perfectly any behavioral paradigm, particularly that of interpreting language, it is by no means surprising that the same sentence should elicit different overtly observable behaviors, and that different sentences should elicit the same behavior.

But when we apply this conception of the link between language and the world, or that which is extra-linguistic, to the study of literature we immediately find ourselves in appalling difficulties. For the sad fact is that literary interpretation links language not to the world but to other language. That is, what the student of literature learns is behavioral paradigms of language. He learns, therefore, what kinds of propositions his culture considers appropriate when he ascribes semantic function to poems. At first glance, therefore, the scientific model of verifying propositions seems to be wholly inapplicable. Basically, and in verbal shorthand, the scientific model is a "look and see" model. The scientist manipulates a nonverbal world. Seemingly, at any rate, the literary interpreter does nothing of the sort. If he looks, there is nothing for him to see. To be sure, he thinks there is, because the scientific model is but a refinement of any behavior linking language and the world, and he thinks that is what he is doing; but he is not, for he manipulates nothing nonverbal. But his task is not to see, because meaning is not immanent in the poem. His task is to ascribe meaning, that is, to look at the poem and decide what verbal paradigm is appropriate.

Further, in that word "refinement" lurks another perilous difference between the scientist and the student of interpretation. The refinement has come about through the development of scientific theory. But the interpreter has no corresponding theory of interpretation. To be sure, there are innumerable theories of interpretation. But these are merely generalized forms of kinds of verbal paradigms. They are not theories of what the interpreter does. They are not, in the scientific sense, theories, but merely generalized instructions for modes of interpretational behavior, directions about what he ought to do. And it is precisely here that one finds the source of that distressing feeling of fraudulence in the study of literature. What we need is an understanding of what we do, not of what we ought to do. In that direction we have an embarrassment of riches, if one can call them that. If we have an understanding of what we are in fact engaged in doing, we can perhaps decide what we ought not to do, or possibly learn how to do better what we appear to be doing well, or at least what appears to be on the right track. We can hope to jettison a great many modes of interpretation and innovate more adequate ones. We can perhaps hope to accumulate something reliable instead of seeing every generation or so the dissipation of what we have accumulated.

Theoretically, there is nothing insuperable in our way. If we assume that poetic language is continuous with ordinary language, then it is perfectly obvious that there is such a thing as a correct interpretation of a sentence, in the sense that the uttered sentence is responded to in a way which the original utterer would consider appropriate. But, of course, in dealing with literature the original utterer is inaccessible. The complexities of interpretation are compounded by the unresolved complexities of the truth-status of historical statements. And further, no theory of what we do in interpretation can be regarded as complete or adequate unless what I have called Augustinian interpretation is accounted for and either utterly rejected or admitted to a comprehensible place in the activity of literary interpretation.

III

It is obvious that the principal embarrassment is the lack of a general theory of the interpretation of language, a general hermeneutics. Until a general theory is forthcoming, the question of whether or not poetry presents special problems must remain open. But further, even a general theory of language interpretation must be adequate until we have a general theory of signs and sign interpretation, since language signs form only one class of a very large class which also includes nonverbal signs. We live in an interpreted world; any configuration for which a semantic function is conventionally established or for which we innovate such a function is a sign and is interpreted. Moreover, I believe that every sign is a sign of a category, not of an entity. In that sense I can tell you nothing about the world, but only how to find something and what it will be like when you do. Or rather, you can find it only because I can predict by offering signs of interlocking categories what it will be like. Thus you can find it. If that is the case, then there will always be a gap between the perceptual-interpretive-cognitive model I use to locate something and the particular something I locate. Consequently, the categorial sign always has a unique function in a particular never-to-be-repeated situation. Hence, every time a sign is used there is a possibility, perhaps a certainty, that the range and attributes, or denotation and connotation, of any particular category are shifted, even if ever so slightly. This is particularly true of verbal signs, which are arbitrary. That is, there is no phenomenal analogy between the word "tree" and a tree, while there can be various degrees of analogy between a picture of a tree and a tree. The instability of semantic function characteristic of all signs is even more of a threat, then, to verbal signs than it is to configurational signs. That instability results in multiple semantic functions, the phenomenon of polysemy, and it is polysemy, therefore, with which any consideration of verbal hermeneutics must begin. Polysemy is the very heart of the puzzle of language, or, more precisely, meaning. Nor is there any point in concealing the fact that the very instrument with which we examine polysemy is itself language, and therefore subject to precisely the same difficulties and limitations as the phenomenon we wish to examine. Any attempt to deal with the problem, therefore, must ultimately be unsatisfactory, but that after all is the task of philosophy, to demonstrate the unsatisfactoriness of philosophical propositions. At least that seems to be what philosophers principally do.

We may begin by observing a more limited semantic function of the word "meaning." One way of locating that function is to observe what kinds of answers people give in ordinary language when they are asked to explain the meaning of a statement. Such a question arises when the respondent is so exposed to a possibility of multiple interpretations that he has no notion of what an appropriate response would be, that is, so exposed to single or multiple polysemy. Two kinds of answers are possible. One is to give an example or examples; the other is to give a more general explanation, one that covers a wider range of examples. Thus, if the proposition to be explained is that poetry does not have unique semantic functions, the speaker can give examples of identical propositions in both poetry and non-poetry, or he can offer the proposition that poetry belongs to the category of language, and that language can function only if the semantic functions of specialized language are continuous with those of ordinary language.

I submit, then, that language can be usefully conceived of as having two poles, exemplification and explanation. Explanatory sentences cannot explain the world, they can only explain exemplary sentences, and they do this by categorial substitution and logical manipulation. At the same time exemplary sentences cannot *prove* explanatory sentences. True examples, evidence, and proof, whatever that may be, are to be found only in the nonverbal world, and can be linked to language, as we have seen, only by behaving according to nonverbal paradigms and manipulating the nonverbal world. Exemplary sentences can only illustrate explanatory sentences. They can only indicate what the speaker, in this sense, "means" by his explanatory sentences. Nor are these, unfortunately, two clear-cut kinds of sentences. A sentence is explanatory, no matter how exemplary—or concrete, or particular—it may be, if a more exemplary sentence can be provided to illustrate it. From this point of view all language is equally metaphysical, in the sense of being discontinuous from whatever is extra-verbal, linked to the world only because someone decides that it should be for whatever purpose he may have.

It is an often asserted value that poetry, to be good, must be concrete. This is nonsense, but it does recognize the fact that poetry tends to be more exemplary than explanatory. Indeed, I have suggested in "Order and Disorder in Fiction" (*Sage*, Spring, 1967, reprinted pp. 290–317 of this book) that our interest in gossiping and telling stories takes its origin from our desire to be relieved from exposure to polysemy, which the use of language in the real world continuously subjects us to. However, an enormous amount of poetry contains not merely exemplary sentences but also explanatory sentences. Shakespeare, for example, liked to conclude a quite exemplary sonnet with a stately explanatory couplet. Similar are Aesopian fables, which present exemplary material and then instruct us in what general moral truth that material exemplifies.

Sir Philip Sidney, in his *Apology for Poetry*, develops very interestingly the idea that poetry is superior to both philosophy and history. History, he says, gives us only events, while philosophy gives only truths. Poetry is superior to either, for it illustrates the truths of philosophy with the materials of history. In terms of the discussion offered here, he is asserting that the task of poetry is to exemplify philosophical truths. The origins of such a notion extend all the way back to Aristotle, but the tradition Sidney was working in was St. Augustine's.

It was Augustine's position that poetry is veiled or hidden discourse, and that the delightful task of the reader is to penetrate that veil and discover the invisible truths of God. Augustine is here making two assertions which must be carefully distinguished. One, which he makes more clearly and usefully than any critic I have come across, is to recognize that the appropriate response to the exemplary material of poetry is to generate an explanatory proposition, but the reader is frequently at a loss to know which particular bits of the exemplary material are to be explained. For reasons to be forthcoming I do not believe this proposition to be universally valid, but it tends to be true of much literature, particularly at the higher cultural levels. On the other hand, if to generate an explanatory proposition or propositions is the appropriate verbal response, then it is overwhelmingly true that the reader tends to be uncertain about which exemplary bits he should use, about which ones, as it were, need explanation. I shall return to this interesting phenomenon of uncertainty in literary interpretation.

As for the assertion that the task is to penetrate the veil and discover the invisible truths of God, there is much to be said.

To begin with, we do not penetrate any veils. We respond by generating explanatory sentences. Such an approach clears up, I think, the vexing metaphor of literary levels. Consider the fully developed medieval system of exegesis. This postulated that a poem does, or could, have four levels of interpretation: the literal or historical, the allegorical, the moral, and the anagogical. The first was what I have called here the exemplary polarity; the second had to do with the church, as in the allegorical interpretation of *The Songs of Songs*; the third had to do with subjective religious states; and the fourth, the anagogical, had to do with the future life. The significance of these is more readily understood if we extend them to a non-Christian range of meanings. Thus, the allegorical, or church, can be extended to the social meanings of the work, the moral to the psychological, and the anagogical—to what? In a narrative fiction, for example, the anagogical had to do with whether the protagonists were rewarded with hell, heaven, or purgatory. Such a judgment indicated whether their behavior was to be approved or disapproved. It was a way of indicating the moral validity of their lives. Thus the anagogical can be extended to the more general notion of validation of particular attitudes or actions, i.e., whether or not the reader is supposed to approve.

Now these four kinds of meanings are almost invariably referred to as levels of meaning, just as today a poem is said to have levels of meaning. But if we look at them in terms of verbal behavior, it is evident, first of all, that they cannot be levels of meaning, for the notion of immanent meaning is unacceptable. Rather, instead of being levels of meaning, they are modes of interpretation, paradigmatically learned and transmitted, and, it is thought, theoretically justified. But, if what I have suggested above is at all adequate, such justifications are not properly theories of interpretation. They are, rather, generalized instructions for responding to a poem by generating explanations in particular modes. The four medieval modes were developed in the same way as I have extended their range. The medieval modes are explanatory propositions for exemplary material, but I have considered them as exemplifications of more inclusive explanatory modes, the social, the psychological, and the validational. But this hierarchical explanation of explanation brings out another instructive character of Augustine's *invisibilia Dei*. Augustine, apparently for nostalgic reasons, was interested in preserving the culture that he loved and, as a Christian, had had to abandon. Thus, learning the general model from the Alexandrian allegorical explanations of Homer, he subjected classical myths to a Christian interpretation and established the Christian explanatory modes.

Yet he has not explained those myths at all. What he has actually done is to exemplify Christian truths by drawing his illustrative material from non-Christian mythology. No matter what Augustine and his followers interpreted, he invariably generated the same Christian truths. It is as if I were to use the word "rectangle," and my hearer asked what I meant, and I pointed out to him the rectangular frames of doors, windows, pictures, and so on. I have not in any sense interpreted or explained the functions of those doors and windows in the room and related them to an explanation of the function of the room in human affairs. For purposes of exemplification, I have simply ignored that function. In the same way Augustine, for the purposes of his exemplification, ignored the semantic function of the myths in the culture in which they originated. It is not satisfactory to say that it would be possible to generate explanatory sentences for which the explanations offered by Augustine and by an ancient Greek would be exemplifications. If I were to say to Augustine that his allegorical, moral, and anagogical modes were really exemplifications of my social, psychological, and validational modes, he could and no doubt would reply that on the contrary my modes exemplified his more inclusive terms. That is, it is a question of what, for the individual, is his ultimate explanatory mode.

We can get out of this impasse only if we cling to the notion that in ordinary language there is a correct way of responding verbally to a sentence. I suggested earlier that in ordinary language the judge of whether or not the response is correct is the utterer of the sentence the response to which is in question. It is obvious that the peculiar characteristic of Augustinian exemplification is that it cannot be falsified, or verified. It is evident, then, that what is desired is a way of explaining the exemplary material of a poem which can be falsified or, in some way or other, verified or somehow validated.

IV

Let us return to Augustine's other, and very valuable, notion, that it is a characteristic of poems that the reader is uncertain as to what literal or historical details, as he would have said, or exemplary material, in the terminology proposed here, requires interpretation. Consider a play and a movie which most of my readers will have seen, or read, in one form or another, *Who's Afraid of Virginia Woolf*? It seems to be the judgment of most competent people, critics and others, that this work demands interpretation. The particular material which more than anything else seems to indicate that we are supposed to offer an explanation is the extreme symmetry between the older couple and the young couple, which is specifically directed to our attention when the young man cries out that at last he understands what has been going on. Most people seem to think that the mode of explanation would be some kind of general proposition about marriage, and the names of the two principals, George and Martha, seems to suggest that the proposition should be about American marriage, while the setting of the play suggests that the proposition should be further qualified by the word "today" or "now" or something of the sort. The principal hint apparently is that rarely in literature, let alone in life, do we encounter so rigid a symmetry between couples. Were we to encounter it in life, it would seem so disparate from our general cognitive model of the relations between married couples that, I believe, almost anyone who noticed it would cast about for an explanation. Explanations, then, are generated, among other reasons, when something does not make sense, that is, does not correspond to our expectations in the situation in which we find them.

Consider, for example, the details of the setting. According to the conventions in which the movie was made, the setting had to be "realistic," crammed with details which are not to be interpreted in the sense that the rigid symmetry of the couples is to be interpreted. For instance, on the hero's shelves in the movie are not one but two sets of the Heritage Press edition of Gibbon's *Decline and Fall of the Roman Empire*. What are we supposed to do with this? Is it something that is supposed to generate an explanation? Since he has two sets, our professor is, I suppose, rather careless, and since I could not see anywhere the J. B. Bury edition of Gibbon, I daresay the two sets of the Heritage Press edition explain why he is not a full professor. But why would anyone trouble to keep two sets of the Heritage Press Gibbon, even if they were presents? It certainly seems to make more sense to explain that not the professor but the set-dresser was careless. If he himself noticed what he had done, I doubt if he expected anyone else to notice. This, then, is but an instance of something of which we have little understanding, that is, how do we go about eliminating material from the category of material that needs explanation?

But before such a question can even be considered—and I shall have a few things to say about it, though not as much as I would like—it is necessary to understand why there are these two categories of material, why poetry has its own uncertainty principle. In my recent book *Man's Rage for Chaos: Biology, Behavior, and the Arts*, I have proposed that art is characterized not by order but by disorder. That is, art exposes us to the disparity between the perceptual model and the sensory data; it is a violation of expectancy. The simplest example is the theme and variation plan in music, in which the source of the effect which is the defining attribute of artistic behavior is the violation of the perceptual model set up by the theme. Another readily apprehended instance is the formal aspect of English verse, in which the effect is the consequence of the disparity between the expected rhythmic regularity of stress and the actually perceived irregularity. Art depends for its effect on, and finds its function in the exposure to, perceptual discontinuity, and I call my theory of art the general theory of discontinuity. In the book itself I did not extend this theory to fiction, but in "Order and Disorder in Fiction," I have now done so. One of the applications I have made is in fact derived from Augustine's uncertainty principle in poetry, and my application explains why I admire that principle so highly. What Augustine has pointed out is that in poetry the literal or historical mode of interpretation is continuous, but that at unpredictable moments something happens which implies that more than an exemplary mode of interpretation is required, that, in fact, the appropriate response is in terms of an explanatory mode, and that the explanation is generated according to an already existent verbal paradigm. When one is actually experiencing *Virginia Woolf*, the rigid parallelism of the two couples gradually emerges and becomes something of a puzzle, something which requires explanation. But the evidence for that parallelism is discontinuous, while the literal aspect and the literal-historical interpretation of the material are each continuous. To be sure, literal continuity is not always present in a poem, as I pointed out above, but that is not a point that cannot be accounted for. Hugo von Hofmannsthal's libretto for Strauss' *Ariadne auf Naxos* is a case in point. Two different plays, one an *opera seria* and the other a *commedia dell'arte*, are presented alternately, and at the end are seen to have a relation; that is, one sees that an explanation for this oddity is possible and appropriate, and in the final song a clue about the nature of that explanation is provided.

Such a theory would also provide an explanation as to why novel metaphor is so common in poetry. What metaphor does is to import a term into a semantic context in which it does not belong. We know that it is a metaphor and requires interpretation simply because, initially, it makes no sense. That is, it requires explanation. Metaphor is itself a normal and necessary feature of ordinary language. It is virtually the only way we have of establishing new categories. It works by applying some of the attributes of the imported term to the local situation, thus selecting some of the attributes of the local category or categories. The problem in metaphor is always to determine which categories are appropriate. That is, the first test of whether or not an exemplary item needs explaining is whether or not it makes sense in the context. By contrast, Augustinian exemplification completely ignores that question, for, as we have seen, it is not interested in the local context, but only in how it can use selected exemplary material to exemplify its explanatory propositions. Further, this kind of discontinuity is not a semantic discontinuity, though it depends upon that feature of language which I have called polysemy. The question is now how it should be interpreted. The disorientation comes not from the uncertainty of how it should be interpreted, but from the uncertainty of whether it should be interpreted or not. Frequently, as in *Virginia Woolf*, it is only the accumulation of identical kinds of such uncertainty that finally convinces us that we ought to start interpreting. In my own case, it did not happen until I had seen both the play and the movie. I had an obscure feeling that it ought to be interpreted, that explanatory propositions were expected of me, but it was only when I thought over the exemplary material and became aware of the rigid symmetry of the two couples that I felt that I had a clue as to how to proceed.

Now it is evident that in fact we have to be trained by our culture to recognize the failure of some item to make sense in the context, to decide that we are supposed to generate explanations. But this fact is true of discontinuity in all of the arts. The basic psychological equipment, so to speak, is there and, for some, would be brought into service by repeated exposure, but the fact is that in our culture, for the arts at the higher culture levels, we are trained to become aware of formal discontinuities, of violations of expectations. To be sure, we do not know that that is how we are being trained, nor do our teachers, unless, of course, they have read my book, and that does not include very many people, and never will. In the same way the teaching of literature involves, paradigmatically and through generalized instructions, teaching students to pick up these various hints and clues. Although their variety is infinite, they are basically of two types: hints, interpretational discontinuities, items that do not make sense; and clues as to what should be the modality of the required interpretational response.

Of the hints of uncertainty, or interpretational discontinuities, I have, I think, said enough to make my point. But of clues as to the interpretational modality, something further needs to be said. One of the great puzzles in the interpretation of literature is this: Once it has been decided that an interpretational response is appropriate, what is the character of the clue? That is, is it a symbol, is it allegory, is it an emblem, is it a metaphor, or what? When a great many intelligent people have continued to be puzzled by something for century after century, there is a strong possibility that the wrong question has been asked, or that the wrong assumptions are at work. Having wrestled with this problem for nearly 35 years and having, like so many others, thought I had found a solution, only to be disappointed, I approach the question with considerable wariness. Nevertheless, I think that from the point of view I am presenting here a solution is possible. It is clear that in virtually all discussions of the matter it is assumed that the difference between sign and symbol, or symbol and allegory, and so on, is a difference in the character of the term or terms. That is, the symbolical or allegorical nature of the semantic function involved is believed to be inherent or immanent in the language itself. The initial difficulty, then, is precisely the same as that we have already encountered in the literary interpretation, the assumption that semantic functions are immanent. Or, that allegory and symbol are different kinds of meaning. The first step is to recognize that whether a term is symbol or allegory is a question not of its meaning or of its character but of the appropriate mode of interpretation and of the character of the information which we decide is offered by the work or which we import into the interpretative act from outside the work which instructs us as to what the appropriate mode is. But even when this decision has been made, the assumption that different modes of interpretation can be categorized as allegorical or symbolical, or emblematic, or metaphorical, and so on, remains to plague us. But it may be that such terms are historical flotsam and jetsam. The frequent redefinitions of symbol, for example, suggest that the words are redefined whenever a new mode of interpretation emerges: that is, when an author or authors begin providing new kinds of interpretational uncertainties and new kinds of hints about the appropriate character of the explanatory modes to be employed in response. In *Man's Rage for Chaos*, for example, I proposed that symbolic interpretation emerged from the Romantic cultural situation, and was radically different from the former meaning of "symbol," which was not to be differentiated from allegory. I feel now that I was in at least partial error in asserting that symbolic interpretation moves backwards from the sign to an orientation while sign interpretation moves forwards from the sign to the world. What really happened is that with a new meta-physical explanatory system there emerged poetry for which the appropriate explanatory propositions derived from that meta-physic. In other words, formally there was no difference. The difference lay neither in the character of the sign nor in the character of the category of interpretation, but rather in the modality of the appropriate explanatory propositions.

I believe it to be correct, therefore, to say that attempts to differentiate between symbol and allegory and so on are responses to pseudo-problems and that all these different kinds of literary signs can be resolved into the single notion of clues controlling our behavior toward modes of explanatory propositions, as *Virginia Woolf* directs us, I believe, to make a general proposition about the current state of American marriage. It is hopeless to try to decide whether it is symbolic or allegorical. If a term is needed, we might as well adopt the one most commonly used today, "symbol," and let it go at that. What we call it doesn't make much difference, so long as we know what we are doing.

In short, we say that a poem or an exemplary item in a poem is symbolic when we realize that the appropriate behavior is to generate an explanatory proposition. This definition covers all cases that I have been able to think of, and if it proves acceptable will be one of those radical simplifications which puts a study on a sounder base.

I have not, it seems to me, departed from my original model in ordinary language behavior. I do not see that I have crossed any line that separates my position from the notion that the judge of whether a verbal response to an utterance is correct or not is the individual who generated that utterance. Years ago when I tried my best to be a New Critic—and clearly failed—I believed that the poet was in no special or privileged position when it came to the interpretation of his poems. It is a common position in modern criticism. Obviously, I now think it in error. Rather, I now think it is evident that the poet can verify or falsify an interpretation. That is, theoretically, an interpretation can be falsified or verified or at least validated. I shall call this way of responding to discontinuous hints and to clues in poems "interpretation," and I oppose it to Augustinian exemplification. The movement in each is different. Exemplification moves from the explanatory pole of language to the exemplary, while interpretation moves from the exemplary to the explanatory. But it is further to be observed that the two ways of explaining poems are not antithetical. If they were, if one were false, the other would be true, and attempts to distinguish between the two have usually been efforts by the protagonist of one to dispose finally of the position of the protagonist of the other. On the contrary, they are not antithetical but contrastive. The reason, of course, is that falsification and validation are not questions in Augustinian exemplification, but they are in literary interpretation.

I said earlier that a place in human affairs must be found for Augustinian exemplification. To give some modern examples, Freudian and Jungian explanations of literature are, insofar as they claim to be interpretations, not interpretations but exemplifications. The system which Northrop Frye presents in his *Anatomy of Criticism* is Augustinian exemplification. And the notion of my colleague that a poem is better if it can be subjected to a greater variety of unconnected interpretations and the notion of the stubborn student that his opinion is as good as the teacher's are Augustinian. A production of *King Lear* that shows that that work is "really" Existentialist and that Shakespeare held the Existentialist position is Augustinian exemplification; it is not interpretation. None of these positions can be falsified. What, then, is their function? It is clear that, at least in the Western tradition, Augustinian interpretation is one of the things that people do with literature. They have always done it. Even if we desired to stop it, there would be no way to do so. The insidious danger today, though, is manifest in the helplessness of the teacher to oppose the stubborn and opinionated student. He has no theoretical basis on which to do it. There is no doubt that the New Criticism has been responsible for an enormous proliferation of Augustinian exemplification into innumerable modes. The reason, as we have seen, is the revival of the Augustinian notion that poetry has unique poetic functions, which took its local form in the assertion that it always revealed the same invisible truths of God. On the basis of an unjustified notion that poetic language is discontinuous from the rest of language, Augustinian exemplification has re-established itself in a position which appears to be impregnable. Yet if we are engaged in teaching the interpretation of literature we need desperately to know whether we are doing that or whether we are teaching exemplification. For instance, a younger colleague of mine has asserted with great pride that he has a wonderful lecture demonstrating that Cleopatra in Shakespeare's play is an artist figure, is an example of the explanatory category "artist." This is astonishing. Though I have not heard the lecture, I find it impossible to believe that such an explanation can in any way be called interpretation, is anything other than exemplification. I do not blame him. The present critical scene makes it virtually impossible to distinguish between the two, even though many of us are convinced that there is a distinction, and a valid one.

Nevertheless, I hold no brief against the literary exemplification of explanatory propositions. It is clearly one of the things that human beings do with their literature, and I see no reason that they should not. After all, it is their literature. It is important to exemplify important explanations. One way is to write a new work, but another is to use an old one as a vehicle for the new purpose. It is only desirable to recognize what is going on, and to be able to distinguish between the two. Actually, if the position offered here proves tenable and acceptable, it is clear that an important new area of literary study is before us; an immense vista of how literature is used opens up, and a marvelous source of insight into the values of different cultural epochs becomes available to us.

Yet certain questions remain, of which the most important is, how do you tell one kind of literary explanation from the other? A clue to a partial answer is to be found in the fact that Augustine and his followers always found the same *invisibilia Dei*. That is, Augustinian exemplification is characterized by a striking stability of its explanatory modes. To give a modern instance, the practicing psychoanalyst does not have a body of knowledge which he applies to the patient. He too is engaged in the interpretation of the patient's behavior, and his body of explanatory propositions consists of verbal tools. The history of psychoanalysis is characterized by considerable instability. School after school has come and gone. Far from being, as many people think, a sign of weakness, this is one of the few things about psychoanalysis that suggests that we ought to give it some confidence. After all, it merely asserts, in its modern form, that the individual organizes current experiences on the basis of cognitive models or patterns he has derived from previous experiences, all the way back, without break, to infancy. Psychoanalysis is not necessary, really, to tell us that; we have other and more reliable reasons for believing it. What a psychoanalyst is specifically concerned with is explaining why in some individuals some models are incapable of correction by feedback from current experiences, why the individual is unable to observe and exploit the disparity between the model and the experience. The instability of psychoanalytic theory is the consequence of predictively applying the psychoanalyst's model to the behavior of his patient, to his observation of the disparity between the model and the patient, and the consequent feedback into and correction of his theory. It is true that there is not nearly enough feedback, but that is true of all science and all behavior.

Literary Freudianism, however, is a different matter. An interesting recent example is Steven Marcus' *The Other Victorians,* a book about Victorian pornography. Marcus, I fear, merely uses his material to exemplify a weary, dreary, motheaten, literary, out-of-date, orthodox Freudianism. There is no feedback from such stuff to Freudian theory, and there never will be; for there is no prediction about the nonverbal behavior of the author. And this, I think, is the general situation in both Freudian and Jungian literary interpretation of works not written to be exemplifications of psychoanalytic explanations. Psychoanalytic theory has been unaffected by such exercises. Professor Norman Holland, however, who is one of the very few literary Freudians who really comprehends Freudian theory and is *au courant* with it, has made it clear that he is not engaged in the interpretation of literature, nor in using literature to exemplify Freudian propositions. Rather, if I understand him correctly, he is engaged in explaining the emotional response of individuals to poems on the basis of Freudian theory as a general theory of behavior. If he can progress to the point where his efforts result in changing psychoanalytic theory, it will be indubitable that he will have succeeded in making an important contribution. That will prove that he has been engaged in an explanatory enterprise that involves verification and falsification. But perhaps his contribution will not be to the study of literature, but rather to the instrumental repertoire of the practicing analyst. If poems can be made into the functional equivalents of Rorschach and TAT tests, I see no reason why they should not be.

Instability of explanation, then, is a mark of scientific enterprise. The enormous scientific advance of this century has been the result of the fact that scientists have accepted theoretical instability as a necessary condition of their enterprise. As Darwin said about 100 years ago, a natural law is a mental convenience. It follows that, if literary interpretation is characterized by falsification and validation, it is possible to create a theory of interpretation. For many years I have been engaged in an effort to introduce into the study of literature the instability of scientific theory. As I might have expected, the answer was right in front of me.

V

In considering interpretation two problems are before us. The first is one of the intention, in this form. Suppose I say to Edward Albee that I think his *Virginia Woolf* is an exemplification of the general explanatory proposition that modern American marriage is characterized by a crusting over and sealing off of emotional vitality, and that married couples renew a flow of genuine and original feeling by improvising rituals of renewal characterized by tearing at each other savagely until once again the emotion is flowing and real. And suppose he says, "That's correct. That's what I meant." Splendid. The original utterer has now verified my interpretation. But suppose he says, "I had no such intention. I had no intention at all. I wasn't exemplifying anything; I was just writing a play and it took the shape it did because that's the way I felt it and that's the way it came out." Apparently my interpretation has now been falsified, and it is true that, Augustine to the contrary, there are a great many poems which present only exemplary material and exist only to provide the occasion for experiencing the other kinds of discontinuity which literature offers. Detective novels are an easy example. But is it necessarily true that I am wrong in interpreting *Virginia Woolf* and wrong in my interpretation? I think not.

I hate to use the word, but one of the ways we think, one of the ways we solve problems, is by generating exemplary sentences without being able to generate explanatory sentences to cover them, to explain them. An illuminating instance is Röckl's puzzlement about why Erda in *Das Rheingold* tells Wotan that if he does not give up the Ring the Gods will be destroyed, but that they will also be destroyed if he does. Röckl's puzzlement is understandable. Ernest Newman merely thought it was a flaw, a mistake. But Wagner wrote to Röckl that though he could not explain it in so many words, Erda's conundrum concealed the whole point of the *Ring*, and indeed that the rest of the tetralogy existed only in order to explain it. Shaw once said that a great artist writes one early work in which he says everything he has to say, and then spends the rest of his life figuring out what he has said, that is, providing explanations for his exemplary material, or such of it as it is appropriate to explain. I think this has been the experience of anyone who has attempted to think about some matter difficult to him. A book I published several years ago is, I think, very well organized, but it was not until two years after publication that I was able to explain that organization. At the time, it merely felt right.

In the case of Albee's play and his second answer, it would be perfectly possible for him to write a work which presented hints and clues without knowing he had done so, that is, without being able to tell us what they were and what the appropriate interpretation would be. Since we have no controlled knowledge, as interpreters, of these hints and clues but have merely learned paradigmatically to respond to them, it is not at all surprising, it is to be expected, that the author himself, trained in the same culture, should be equally uninformed. He has learned them as we have, and he puts them in just as we exploit them, because it feels right.

But suppose on my way to New York to interview Mr. Albee and to ask him my question, I read in the paper that he had died.

Albee has now, alas, entered history. Interpretation becomes an historical problem. Are falsification and validation still possible?

Now whether Albee is alive or dead, I have proceeded in the same way. Assuming that I was right in interpreting the play and that my interpretation was correct, how was it possible? In ordinary verbal behavior a correct answer is possible because, putting it very roughly, both speaker and responder belong to the same culture, and both recognize and interpret in the same way the same features in a particular situation. Indeed, one of the most instructive kinds of information we could possibly have—and some day it will have to be provided—is a thoroughgoing study of what is involved when, in ordinary conversation, people make the wrong response, misinterpret each other. In this situation, both Albee and I are not only products of the same culture but we are also equally aware that for years, but particularly since World War II, the nature of modern marriage, particularly the changing of the social roles of husband and wife, has been discussed endlessly in every medium of communication, from the most trivial magazine to the most strictly controlled sociological and psychological monograph. More trivially, both of us are aware that to use the names George and Martha, particularly for a childless couple, is for an American to provide a powerful hint and clue for proceeding to interpretation. Whenever the utterer of a sentence is not present, or at least frequently, we control our response to the sentence by first making a verbal construct of the speaker's situation and his intention, that is, the problem or feature in the situation to which he was responding. And in interpreting the play that is precisely what I did.

From this it is but a step to building a model for the interpretation of literature which was written in previous periods of our own culture or in alien cultures. That is, in historical interpretation, what we do is create a theoretical construct of the cultural situation in which the poem was written. We then use that construct to guide and control our decisions about the kind of interpretational modality we should use in responding to the hints and clues offered by the author in his poem. For instance, a knowledge of Augustinian interpretation in the Middle Ages suggests the possibility that some individuals wrote poems in order to exemplify the Christian *invisibilia Dei*. Indeed we know this to be so. And one current school of literary interpretation, headed by the formidable Professor D. W. Robertson, Jr., of Princeton, has applied this theoretical construct in a more thoroughgoing fashion than any of his predecessors in medieval studies. It is interesting, however, that his principal inspiration seems to have come from students of the iconography of medieval art. That is, many of the semantic functions he purports to identify had already been identified by art historians. This troubles some people, but there is no reason that it should. Without a given culture, particular semantic functions can find their vehicle in any number of semiotic systems. Professor Panofsky, for example, has suggested quite convincingly that the organization of Gothic cathedral architecture intentionally exemplifies Augustine's theory of music. On the other hand, Professor Robertson's application, though few competent students deny his theory, is highly contentious. It is thought to be extreme. My own feeling is that he has taken into insufficient account Augustine's proposition that not all but only some exemplary material in poetry needs to be interpreted. This brings out another aspect of the position I am proposing. It makes it apparent that one of the most important things to be done in the study of literature is the investigation of the interpretational hints and clues, and historical investigation into the changing styles of hints and clues. Just as in our theoretical construct our propositions assert what is probably appropriate in the way of interpretational modes, so we need a comprehension of what, in a given culture, is probably a hint or clue, what hint or clue the author *could* give, given the limitations and possibilities of his cultural situation. I think it is obvious that such an investigation would be one of the most delicate and difficult—and important—literary inquiries possible.

Nevertheless, the position I have proposed, that formally the interpretation of the sentence of an absent though living speaker and the interpretation of a poem of a dead writer are identical, presents various difficulties and problems. The first is this: Are these two positions identical, or at least continuous, with the interpretation of a sentence when the speaker is both living and present before the responder? It is evident that throughout this paper I have been using the perceptual model theory of perception, variously called directive state theory, psychological set theory, transactionalism, and so on. In the late 1950's it was called the New Look in perception theory. What happens when we hear an utterance or encounter any situation is, very roughly, that we take clues from the situation in order to arrive at a perceptual model which is also, looking at it from other points of view, an interpretational and a cognitive model. A sentence elicits in us an interpretative condition or orientation which controls what we see, how we interpret it, and how we know it and judge it, for it may also be called a conative model, or an intentional model. Loosely speaking, when the gap between that model and the utterance is so great that we cannot make sense of it, we experience cognitive tension, which we resolve either by suppressing our awareness of the disparity or by exploiting the cognitive tension to discover a problem, that is, some kind of explanation for our failure to understand, which, by feedback, can readjust our model so that we do understand. ("Model" is here, of course, used metaphorically, and so long as we remember that it is a metaphor we will not encounter any severe difficulty.) All this can happen without overt verbal behavior, and it can happen without covert verbal behavior, one of the categories of behavior to which the word "thought" directs our attention. But the process of problem location, problem solving, feedback, and correction can also be accomplished by means of both covert and overt verbal behavior. Thus writing tends to be better controlled than speaking continuously, for writing permits pauses of any length and thus permits more thorough feedback and correction while the problem is being investigated and the discourse is being constructed. If this is the case, it then follows that though interpretation of the sentences of a living speaker before us is not always identical with interpretation of an absent individual or a dead author, the two processes are continuous and sometimes identical.

The second problem is the status of historical explanations. I can scarcely go into this vexing problem here, but I wish only to suggest at least a partial solution to it which indicates that the behavior of the historian is sufficiently analogous to that of the scientist to permit at least a useful assimilation of the two. Briefly, there is a regularity in history, but it is not in the sequence of historical events. For one thing, any sequence of known historical events is so highly and accidentally selective, depending upon the small amount of material the historian is able to recover, that it is pretty obvious that such regularity comes from the structure of the explanation, not from the structure of the exemplary material the historian is explaining. He is, it must be remembered, engaged not in explaining events, but in explaining sentences that purport to give information about events. Rather, the regularity of history lies in the fact that the distribution of historical documents and artifacts over and within the surface of the earth is not random. That is, the historian can predict successfully where he is going to find what, what its character will be, and, frequently the kind of statement to be found in the document and the kind of character of information the document presents. He can predict, therefore, what some dead individual has said, and there is no formal difference here between such prediction and predictions of what some living individual is going to say, a matter in which we have all been very successful, especially wives and husbands. And again, as with the scientist, his language is linked to the world by behavior; that is, he has learned research techniques.

This leads to the third problem. On the grounds just offered I think that it can be said that the behavior of the scientist and the historian, including the literary historian, can be successfully assimilated. They are sufficiently analogous for useful purposes. But, as we have seen, the theoretical constructs of the scientist are characterized by instability, by accumulation of information, and by increasing reliability. Is this true of the historian, particularly the literary historian, or the interpreter of poems written by men now dead in previous stages of our own culture and in alien cultures? I believe the answer to be yes. First, a bit of terminology. I call the interpretation of poems from alien cultures "cultural interpretation," and of poems from previous stages of our own culture "philological-historical interpretation." Now the first thing to be observed about the latter is that its rise is coeval with the rise of modern science, beginning in the fifteenth century, and perhaps earlier. The cultural redirection amounted to the realization that it was possible to arrive at Christian truths by methods other than those validated by Christian institutions, the most important methods being mathematics and humanistic scholarship. At any rate, just as the seventeenth century was the great period in which science finally freed itself, with the aid of mathematics, from dependence upon a Christian mode of ultimate explanation, so literary scholarship in the century, and inspired, at least to some extent, by the same leaders of thought, Bacon and Hobbes among others, freed itself from Augustinianism, which predominated in the Renaissance, though it was not exactly what it had been in the Middle Ages. Likewise in the same century, literary scholarship and philological-historical interpretation took a tremendous step forward. However, most students of the modern literatures know very little about this, for it took place almost entirely in the study of classical poems. It was not until well into the eighteenth century that the techniques of philological-historical interpretation began to be applied to the modern, vernacular literatures. This coeval development, then, of science and philological-historical interpretation seems to me to indicate that they have a common cultural source and suggests that on these grounds also a certain assimilation between the two is possible.

Furthermore, the history of such interpretation has been characterized by exactly the same kind of instability and exactly the same kind of accumulation and increasing reliability of theoretical construct which has characterized science for the last five centuries. The history of the explanatory term "Renaissance" is a case in point. Adumbrated in the earlier nineteenth century, it became firmly established in the later part of that century, and for a time all students of literature knew exactly what the Renaissance was and what happened in it. There followed a period of increasing accumulation of information and weakening of the "Renaissance" as a theoretical construct which controlled interpretational modes. By the end of the 1940's it was in ruins. Since World War II, however, it has been revived; it is now in better shape than it ever was, and more reliable, in the sense that it is less damaged by the accumulation of information. But most scholars of the period now, I believe, are willing to grant its status as a construct and not as a set of statements which purport to describe what actually happened. At least I hope so; perhaps I am too sanguine. But it is certainly my impression from recent reading in the subject that Renaissance scholars are now prepared for instability and much more willing to exploit it. So long as that instability is maintained, the study of the Renaissance will continue to be in a healthy state. As soon, however, as with all such constructs, it becomes stable, then it will threaten to drift into Augustinian exemplification. That is, the best way to tell the difference between exemplification and interpretation is to determine, on the basis of historical investigation, whether or not the theoretical constructs which control exemplification or interpretation, as the case may be, are characterized by instability.

VI

I began with a confession of the widespread feeling of the possible fraudulence in the enterprise of studying and teaching literature, of which the very heart is interpretation. I have attempted to show why that feeling is entirely justified, in the confusion between the formal differences between Augustinian exemplification on the one hand and philological-historical and cultural interpretation on the other. Yet I feel that a more hopeful picture has emerged. The two have been distinguished, I hope successfully, and a place in the human use of literature has been found for Augustinianism, a respectable and important place. At the same time I think—though there are many more problems which I am aware of but have not explored here—that the enterprise of the interpretation of historical material is sufficiently analogous to scientific research to be assimilated to it well enough to relieve our anxieties. Whether we like it or not, in our culture, today, the scientific enterprise is the recognized model for meaningful and valid interpretations of the world in which we find ourselves. I have hoped, therefore, to open up a way for what we must do before we can proceed with confidence; we must understand what, in fact, we are doing when we interpret literature. Ultimately, as students of literature and as practitioners of humanistic disciplines, that is all we care about.

19

THEORY

OF CRITICISM

[1967*]

We have been asked to consider the question, "Is there a purely literary study?" Or, "How far can the writing of literature or the reading, teaching, and criticizing of it be considered 'pure' or distinct from its possible bearings on history, philosophy or other disciplines?" Two kinds of solutions may be offered. One would be some recommendation that among existing modes of criticism one should be preferred, perhaps to the exclusion of all others, or that some novel mode should be preferred to all known modes. I have no interest in making such a recommendation. The history of criticism has seen the emergence of innumerable modes of criticism, though they can perhaps be reduced to a limited number of types. This century has seen such a proliferation of them that the paradigm of developing new modes

* Delivered at Geneseo State University College, SUNY, Conference on Literary Criticism, April, 1967. Copyright © 1970 by the University of South Carolina Press.

has been well established. Any well-educated critic possessing a certain ingenuity can develop new ones, or at least modes that look new. An examination of the history of such modes shows that it is easy enough to trace them to the extra-literary problems, issues, values, and metaphysical modes of the cultural situation in which they emerge. Predominant critical modes seem most generally to appear as means of explaining and justifying new modes of composing works. It is my own conviction that such emergent literary modes are themselves a response to cultural redirections, but it is not necessary to accept this in order to see what novel critical modes are up to. There would be nothing wrong in this were it not for the fact that the new critical modes are invariably presented in the form of universals. The New Criticism of this century, for example, as a set of statements about what works really are and what they ought to be, is for me a thin and torn tissue of absurdities. But as a set of instructions for reading the stylistically novel works of the twentieth century, and of one or two previous periods, it is not bad, and occasionally quite helpful.

The second kind of solution to our problem would be, to use a currently fashionable prefix, a kind of meta-criticism. It would be an inquiry into what we are in fact doing when we engage in criticism and it would result in a taxonomy of criticism. To such an enterprise, however, there are grave difficulties. For example, most critical modes, though certainly not all, can scarcely proceed without some decisions about the "meaning" of a work, or at least a decision that the work "has" a meaning. It is hardly necessary to emphasize the perplexities involved in understanding the word "meaning." The two disciplines from which we might hope to gain some genuine aid are of very little help. Philosophy has a good deal, of course, to say about meaning, but aside from the fact that not much has emerged on which there is agreement, it can offer little in the way of models; philosophers pretty much concern themselves with the semantic analysis of very simple statements. Even with these they often confess themselves more or less helpless; consequently they offer no patterns to follow in dealing with statements of the enormous complexity literary critics try to handle. The other discipline, linguistics, has been of considerable help in the phonic and syntactic aspect of literature, but it is only beginning to dip one little toe into the bitter cold water of semantic function.

In such a situation a critic can scarcely be blamed for attempting to run up a theory of meaning which might be at least heuristically valid for his purposes. The wonder is that there are so few efforts to do so. In this century the only important one seems to be the New Critical notion that the semantic functions of poems are unique either to poetry in general or to particular poems. Though this position is frequently asserted, I have yet to see any attempt to justify it from the position of a general theory of meaning. Since I have discussed it elsewhere,[1] I shall here simply assert that pragmatically I have never been able to find any semantic function in literary works which I cannot find in extra-literary language, and also that on theoretical grounds I believe it is impossible to do so. Further I have never found any philosophical or linguistic theory of meaning which would offer the slightest grounds for such a position, which, in any case, is a very ancient one. I shall have more to say about it later.

But the New Critics certainly arrived at one exceedingly important conclusion. Edmund Wilson once jeered at them because they had discovered that poems are made out of words. Those who can remember back to the 1930's know how exciting a discovery that was; but its development was immediately terminated by the cultural ethnocentricity of the practitioners. The result was the emergence of the question about what is inside a poem and what is not. It is this, I believe, which is responsible for the question of whether there can be a "purely literary study." Such a study would be confined to what is inside the work. Statements that informed us about that, and only such statements, would be relevant. However, the problem of what is and is not inside a poem is entirely a pseudo-problem. There is nothing inside a work. Everything we say about it we import, we bring to it, we ascribe to it. We derive nothing from it. Some will find such a position obvious; others will judge it to be absurd to the highest degree. In any case, I shall now try to sustain it.

[1] "Literary Interpretation as Conventionalized Verbal Behavior," pp. 341–370 of this book.

1

In what follows I shall use a theory of language which I have worked out in rough detail elsewhere.[2] It will be necessary to begin, therefore, by giving a rapid rundown of the principal propositions about language which are my assumptions in constructing a meta-criticism.

First, I believe language is best understood if it is conceived as linked to the world by behavior, not by reference. To say that language controls behavior is to state only half of what is necessary. The other half is that behavioral response to an utterance is possible only if the responder has at his disposal one or more behavioral paradigms which he uses in order to manipulate the extra-linguistic world. From the point of view of the responder, the world happens after language; the ultimate function of language is predictive.

Second, the notion of semantic function as referring, then, is inexact, blurring over what actually happens, which is substitution of a word for a set of phenomenal configurations. Conceived, however, as reference, all terms other than structural terms are categorial. That is, the responder, if he knows the appropriate behavior, is equipped to look for a class of phenomenal configurations. Location of an individual configuration is made possible by the relationship of terms in propositions. Even so, the utterance conceived as a set of directions for which the responder knows the appropriate behavior requires the adjustment of the behavior to the demands of a unique situation. That is, he must determine the intention of the utterer; and the sole judge as to whether he has responded correctly to the utterance is the original speaker of the utterance. The process by which appropriate behavioral paradigms are learned can be, and has been, observed in the training of children in culturally correct behavioral responses to utterances. It is obvious that in this formulation the word "intention" is exceedingly unsatisfactory, but I shall return to it.

Third, I believe a semantic universal of language, and indeed of nonverbal signs as well, to be polysemy, or multiple semantic function, or multiple meanings. The responder to an utterance,

---

[2] "Order and Disorder in Fiction," see pp. 290–317 of this book.

then, must first resolve the various semantic functions of all the terms in the utterance into an appropriate interlocking set of categories, then select from his repertoire of behavioral paradigms the appropriate one, and finally adjust that paradigm to the unique requirements of the situation. How all this immensely complex process happens we have but little idea, if any. That it does happen can be observed in our own behavior when we respond to all four kinds of uncertainty by overtly or covertly uttering or by visualizing or otherwise planning alternative possibilities. Thus we may speak metaphorically of resolving semantic multiplicity, categorial incoherence, alternatives of behavior paradigms, and behavioral adjustments as decisions.

Fourth, it is obvious that action cannot proceed unless alternative possibilities for decisions of these kinds are resolved. Another way of putting this is to say that such alternatives disorient the responder, that disorientation is accompanied by tension, and that the discomfort of tension can be resolved only by action, and one mode of action is verbal behavior. Thus, a common way of resolving a polysemy and/or categorial incoherence is to submit to the original speaker an alternative or substitutional statement. It is evident, then, that an element in human behavior the importance of which cannot be exaggerated consists of strategies for the resolution of polysemy.

Fifth, one of the most frequent ways of responding to an utterance is by verbal behavior. One way of responding to an utterance is to link it to the world by nonverbal behavior which manipulates the extra-linguistic world. To do this is to test the validity of one's decisions. The significance and process of such testing is blurred when we call it a test of meaning. The mastery of strategies for such decision-testing is what we call science. However, it is evident that when we respond to an utterance by generating another utterance, when our responsive behavior is verbal behavior, the possibility of that kind of testing is eliminated. What, within verbal behavior, is a substitute? I believe the question can best be answered by postulating for language a metaphoric polarity. At one pole is explanation; at the other is exemplification. Thus, when we are asked for the meaning of an utterance, we often reply by subsuming it under an explanatory statement, or, on the other hand, by giving an example. Sir Philip Sidney, interestingly enough, asserted that history offers events, while philosophy offers truths; but poetry exemplifies the truths of philosophy with the events of history. It is an inadequate definition of poetry, but it is a penetrating observation, for which, to be sure, there is a long philosophical history, although I have never seen it so neatly put. The more exemplary a sentence is, the less polysemantic uncertainty it offers. Hence the illusion that such sentences are concrete, or empirically true, or referential; or synthetic, in the sense of "having the truth determined by observation or the facts of experience," a definition which merely blurs the observation of what is going on. On the other hand, an explanatory sentence also resolves polysemantic uncertainty by subsuming a hierarchy of less explanatory sentences which shade into exemplary sentences. This is why Sidney, and others, have called explanatory sentences philosophic truths, for philosophy has historically been engaged in constructing explanatory sentences under which all possible exemplary sentences can be logically subsumed. Such verbal behavior is called the construction of abstract truths, or analytic sentences, or general truths, or universals, or metaphysics. From the position presented here, all sentences, exemplary as well as explanatory, are equally metaphysical. The distinction between the two poles is that exemplary sentences can be more easily tested by nonverbal behavior because they can be tested in a more limited category of unique situations.

Finally, I believe it to be true that literature exploits polysemy in a special way. It exposes us to uncertainty as to whether or not several semantic functions are to be regarded as simultaneously operative at some point or points in the work. Currently, the usage seems to be that when there is little or no question we use the terms "emblem" or "allegory." On the other hand, when we recognize that there is some uncertainty and we decide that several semantic functions are to be considered as operative, we are likely, at the present, to use the term "symbol."

I would define criticism, then, as verbal behavior in response to a work of literature. The most obvious characteristic of a critic's behavior is that he responds to a set of sentences which he has characterized as literature by generating other sentences.

He judges that he is faced with a set of exemplary sentences, even though many sentences in the work may be explanatory in relation to other sentences in the work, and that his task is to subsume these sentences under a set of explanatory sentences. Further, just as nonverbal behavior in response to utterances is performed by a selection from the responder's repertoire of behavioral paradigms, so any verbal response to an utterance is performed in the same way. That proposition holds, of course, for criticism as well; hence the modes of criticism. These are the 'verbal-behavioral paradigms which we have learned from our culture. The critic employs these paradigms by making decisions in the form of either covert or overt verbal behavior, though his social role as critic requires him to make them, sooner or later, overtly. That is, he makes decisions which resolve polysemy, including the special polysemantic problem that literature offers, decisions which resolve categorial functions into an interlocking categorial set, decisions about what explanatory paradigms he shall use, and how, or whether or not, these paradigms should be organized into paradigmatic or innovative modes.

A glance at how verbal-behavioral paradigms are learned will perhaps make this definition a little clearer. From the widest point of view, learning behavioral paradigms is the socialization process. It is apparent from the above theory of language behavior that any learning process involving language is bound to be imprecise, and I believe this to be true of any communication process, which appears always to involve loss of both structure and content. This is what makes it necessary to use such terms as "paradigm," "model," "pattern," or "archetype." The consequence of this imperfect socialization is that each individual performs the paradigms and links paradigms together, that is, performs paradigms of paradigms, in a unique manner. This is his style. Parents, or parent-substitutes, initially teach children, almost from the moment of birth, paradigms and paradigms of paradigms. More precisely they teach what the appropriate paradigm is for given situations; and in the course of time they teach not only what behavioral paradigms are appropriate for various classes of statements, but also what paradigms of verbal behavior are appropriate as responses to various classes of statements.

Teachers of literature engage in the same kind of activity. They do not teach literature; they teach appropriate verbal responses to literature. Again, like parents with children, they subject students to various tests to discover how well they have mastered these verbal paradigms. And, as in all teaching, a certain latitude of range of response is permitted. This is in tacit recognition of the imperfection of the socialization process, but it is also designed to encourage the student to innovate within a certain range.

A reasonably valid generalization is that all behavior involves both testing and innovation. Innovation is unavoidable, and the child takes over from the parent the testing process. A test determines whether the various decisions made in verbal or nonverbal response to an utterance have resulted in appropriate behavior. The parent grants or withholds approval according to the success with which the test is passed. This may very well be the origin of the universal demand for reassurance, whether one demands it from another or provides it oneself. The one is generally judged immature behavior, the other mature or independent. Scientific experimentation can be understood as strategies to acquire reassurance, as can the vain efforts of philosophers to establish an unfailing test for verification. Hence the emotional satisfaction of a successful conclusion to an experiment which scientists so often talk about. The original judge of whether or not the response to an utterance is appropriate is the parent, that is, the speaker of the utterance. Since the process of response to an utterance is not complete until a test has been performed and reassurance is experienced, that reassurance can be forthcoming only from the speaker or from a functional substitute for the speaker, which may be, as we have seen, provided by the responder. That functional substitute, constructed by the responder, is a statement, overt or covert, of the speaker's intention.

This notion of intention as a substitute for the speaker who furnishes reassurance that the responsive behavior is appropriate can be understood a little better if we examine a case in which it seems in error: a scientific statement which experimentation shows to be false. If the above analysis, however, is at all correct, the statement has not been falsified, for what is really tested is the appropriateness of the four stages of decision which I have discriminated above. When we assert that a statement is false, we are actually asserting that the resultant behavior would be considered inappropriate by the speaker, or that, if the speaker were to go through the same decisional-behavioral process as the responder, he would judge the behavior as appropriate and rescind his statement. Assuming, as is necessary in science and similar activities, that the speaker was attempting to utter a statement which would lead to a response he would judge to be appropriate, the responder concludes that the "meaning" of the statement and the "intention" of the speaker can be discriminated as not being coherent. He gains the necessary reassurance by substituting for the original utterance one that he considers to be "true," that is, under the cultural rules obtaining, one that will lead to a series of decisions resulting in appropriate behavior. The substitute utterance may, of course, be a single sentence or it may be an entire scientific theory. The substituted utterance the responder now asserts to be coherent with the original speaker's intention, even though it may be a complete surprise to him. But also it may not.

A recent instance may shed a little light on this formulation. Not long ago I was talking to a young linguist about a recent book by an older linguist with whom she had studied. She asserted that the author was a very careless writer, that he said in the book many things which were in error, that certain other linguists were indignant and contemptuous, but that she knew how his mind worked and what he intended to say, and that indeed she had spoken to him about these errors and he had asserted that of course what he said was not what he meant. He meant what she said he meant.

Here, of course, we have an instance of verbal, not non-verbal, response, but it is also an instance of utterance being incoherent with intention. How had the young woman come to her conclusion? I think it can be described as follows: She is familiar with the situation, advanced contemporary linguistics. She is familiar with the problems in the field, particularly the problems with which the older linguist is engaged. She is familiar with the paradigms of decision-making, as I have outlined them, which the older linguist customarily employs. She concludes, therefore, that certain of his utterances are incoherent with his intention, the first step of her conclusion being the realization that the statements in the book were not coherent with and not redundant with his other statements of the same semantic family. Perhaps the most important element in her conclusions was his carelessness. The situation is precisely the same as the one in which the mother tells the child to go buy a loaf of bread and the child replies, "You mean a pound of butter, don't you?" The child, of course, knew that there was plenty of bread in the bread box but no butter in the icebox, that his mother was planning to cook something that needed no bread but lots of butter, and that she frequently made slips of the tongue of this sort.

In short, I propose thus to account for situations in which the speaker, upon questioning, asserts that he had no formulated intention but insists that there was a purpose or meaning in his utterance. It is necessary to do this because the critic generally deals with situations in which the speaker of the utterance he is attempting to explain is inaccessible.

When the critic assumes that a question about the intention of a speaker can be answered, what he does is (1) construct a theory of the situation which the author was confronting at the time he made his statement, (2) construct a theory of the problem or kind of problem he was capable of perceiving in that situation, and (3) construct a theory of the decisional process which resulted in the utterance the critic is attempting to explain. In short, the critic does what everyone else does in responding to an utterance. In all cases the aim is to test the appropriateness of the response and to gain reassurance. In the critic's case he needs to test the appropriateness of his verbal response, that is, his explanation. And that test consists of the coherence between the literary utterance and the author's intention, as I have defined it.

This formulation makes it possible to distinguish between conscious and unconscious intention. Actually the word "intention" has differing semantic functions in the two phrases. "Conscious intention" merely draws our attention to a particular class of authorial statement. In "unconscious intention" the semantic function of the word is a metaphorical extension. A critic's statement of "unconscious intention," like a psychoanalyst's or anybody else's, is a verbal construct of the sort I have outlined. It is one mode of the critic's verbal response, designed to test the appropriateness of his explanatory mode. I shall call these two kinds limited and extended intention.

I shall now attempt to apply this schema to criticism itself.

II

To begin with, I shall not be dealing with critical responses to what I have called elsewhere the "formal aspect" of art.[3] I mean such matters as prosody, syntactical deformation, plot, personality inconsistency in characters, shifts in rhetorical modalities, and so on. I shall be exclusively concerned with the critic's verbal responses to the semantic aspects. I should like to repeat here, though it is probably unnecessary, my assertion that a statement of the meaning of a work is the consequence of a series of decisions by a particular critic. What the critic is attempting to do is construct a hierarchy of explanatory statements between an ultimate explanatory proposition or propositions and the work regarded as a set of exemplary statements. It is a matter of taste, temperament, style, and cultural conditions whether he attempts to resolve that hierarchy in a single explanation, or whether he is content with a group of unrelated ultimate explanations, that is, whether he is a monist or a pluralist. But even if he is a pluralist, his pluralism is supported by the reassurance of the statement that no monistic mode of explanation is either possible or desirable. Even a pluralist, at least emotionally, is a kind of monist.

To show how this position is applied in practice I shall begin with a mode of criticism which, to me, is only of mild theoretical interest, evaluative criticism. For many critics evaluation is the defining attribute of the critic's role; and for them, of course, it is. But for me it is not. It is only one mode of criticism, and the least interesting mode at that. Thus my recent book on art[4] can be seen as a strategy for postponing as long as possible the utterance of a critical judgment, for as soon as a judgment of value is uttered, the critic is engaged in justifying that judgment. That is, he is no longer responding to the work but to his own utterance.

[3] *Man's Rage for Chaos*, Philadelphia, 1965.
[4] Ibid.

He proceeds in two directions. In the explanatory direction he applies to the work a criterion or set of criteria. He tests it. Sets of criteria which can be applied to any work are indefinably great in number. If I wish, I can say that to be good a work must use the word "God" or some substitute, and that any work that does not is bad. Generally speaking, sets of criteria, in the form of statements, actually employed by an individual playing the critic's role tend to be somewhat more elaborate than this, though a good many are only a little less simple-minded. The next step is to justify these criteria further by subsuming them under more general propositions. Thus the critic moves toward the explanatory pole of language behavior. He decides that he has justified his criteria and therefore his judgment when he has arrived at an ultimate explanatory proposition.

The other direction in which he moves is extended intention. He regards the author as having been in a particular situation and having responded to that situation by making a series of decisions the result of the last stage of which is uttering a series of sentences, or their functional equivalent, according to a culturally established or innovated verbal paradigm or paradigm of paradigms or even paradigms of paradigms. These paradigms have been traditionally called genres, though the theory of genre is in a most unsatisfactory state and always has been. The critic, therefore, is judging the author's performance of such paradigms, measured against the requirements of the situation and the paradigms available to the author. A judgment that the author has not fulfilled his intention is a statement that the utterance is not coherent with the requirements and possibilities of the situation and responsive paradigms. Critics, of course, vary enormously in the degree to which they accept innovation or flexibility within the established paradigmatic range.

Now in both directions the critic is playing the role of judging parent in the parent-child situation of learning culturally acceptable paradigms. As the parent perceives the situation, the child is required to behave in a particular way. Applying what he believes to be appropriate criteria, he then offers or withholds reassurance. He says that the child's performance is good or bad, or somewhere in between. And like the critic the parent is always capable of offering explanations for his criteria, if only, "That's the way everybody does it." I must confess that the principal reason evaluative criticism is so uninteresting to me is that so much of it employs so simple a form of the parent-child learning model. It never seems to occur to such critics that the author was sensitive, learned, and intelligent, and that he had a better perception of the situation as it was than the critic has of the situation as he constructed it. The tone of the overwhelming proportion of such criticism is that of a stern parent to a naughty and rather stupid child. The more adequate parent is one who is always prepared to entertain the possibility that the child has responded to important ingredients in the situation to which the parent has not. That is, the inadequate evaluative critic forgets that he has constructed the intention in order to test the appropriateness of his own utterances, in this case his basic exemplary utterance of ascribing goodness or badness to the work. Only too frequently evaluative critics neglect constructing an extended intention, and even constructing an explanation. They merely make the judgment and then apply their criteria, and let it go at that.

Evaluative criticism, taking into account its complete form, I would call "justification," but, as we have seen, in actual verbal behavior justification is a mode of explanation. The next critical mode is of quite a different sort. I shall deal with it very briefly, because I have discussed it at some length elsewhere.[5] I call it Augustinian exemplification. In this critical mode intention is entirely ignored. Augustine exemplified Christian doctrine by using materials from classic myths. In response to classic myths he uttered statements which exemplified Christian explanatory statements. A modern instance of Augustinianism is the New Critical theory that literature has unique semantic functions and therefore that the series of decisions which lead to statements about a work's meaning is entirely free from the cultural rules that govern decisions in ordinary behavior. This theory is the background for the theory of the intentional fallacy. Or rather, that theory was designed to protect Augustinianism and provide the reassurance which disappears when the construction of intention is omitted. For Augustine the reassurance was provided

[5] "Literary Interpretation as Conventionalized Verbal Behavior."

by Christian doctrine, but for most critics of the twentieth century this is not so. It might seem that my position would require me to judge Augustinianism not to be criticism at all, but I have defined criticism as "verbal behavior in response to a work of literature." It is incomplete criticism, but it satisfies all the other criteria. That is, the situation and consequent problem of the Augustinian critic is such that he wants to locate occasions for generating utterances that will exemplify some explanatory mode. In responding to Augustinian criticism, the intention of the critic is all that is pertinent. I hold no brief against Augustinian criticism. I merely wish it to be recognized for what it is and to account for the ease with which it is confused with criticism which is concerned with intention. That confusion arises from the fact that in both Augustinian and intentional criticism the utterance of the critic is the consequence of a series of decisions which resolve polysemy, categorial incoherence, alternativity of behavioral paradigm, and the possibilities for innovative adjustment to the unique situation. The divergence between the two begins at the first stage, resolution of polysemy. The intentional critic attempts to resolve this by employing his construct of the author's intention, in the extended sense. The Augustinian controls his resolution by his own explanatory mode, by his own intention, or the intention of someone other than the author. In the case of narrow Augustinianism the polysemantic and susequent resolutions are controlled by the intention of God in creating the world and in controlling the utterance of divinely inspired texts. Thus, if you begin at the explanatory pole, you will seek reassurance at the exemplary pole. If any utterance can be responded to with an exemplification of your explanatory statements, it serves its purpose.

The next critical modality I would discriminate is very similar in form, although it involves consideration of the author's intention. It is what I shall call Aesopian interpretation. The appropriate response to an Aesopian fable or a New Testament parable is to utter either covertly or overtly a general truth, that is, an explanatory statement. Here the author proceeds exactly as the Augustinian critic does. He exemplifies an explanatory proposition in a work. That is, one of the appropriate responses, but by no means the only appropriate response, is to utter that explanatory proposition or its approximate equivalent. I call such criticism Aesopian because it is from Aesop's fables, or their equivalent, like *The Little Engine That Could*, that as children we learn that the utterance of a moral or similar explanatory proposition is the appropriate verbal response to some works, and there also we learn the verbal paradigms in which our culture considers it appropriate to cast them. Such works exploit polysemy and are to be found within a very wide range. At one end is the obviously didactic; the work includes both the exemplification and the explanation. At the other is the work which contains only hints that some of the sentences are polysemantic and very little in the way of clues as to what explanatory mode the explanation should be cast in. It is, in this kind of work, the author's intention, in either sense, that the reader should become a critic and utter an explanatory proposition. It is worth noting that at this end of the range there is frequently considerable uncertainty as to whether or not Aesopian interpretation is appropriate. The reason for this is that, first, a great many of the sentences, perhaps most, are to be ignored in constructing the appropriate verbal response and, second, that we respond to what I have called hints and clues paradigmatically. That is, the critic frequently cannot point out exactly what element in the work was responsible for his series of decisions leading to an Aesopian interpretation. And this is also often true of the author. It is my own conviction that a great deal of research needs to be done in codifying those hints and clues which authors present and Aesopians respond to.

A couple of examples may make this clearer. Suppose that I were to respond to the first book of *The Faerie Queene* by asserting that there are hints that I should resolve the polysemantic problem by using the paradigm of allegory, but that then I responded by asserting that the work is an allegory of the game of Monopoly, that it includes terms and statements which are exemplifications of the rules of Monopoly, in the narrow sense of intention. I could point out the remarkable similarities between the two. In both the player moves toward a goal of success, and in both there are both frustrations and sudden forward leaps, hindrances and helps, Orgoglios and Prince Arthurs. Furthermore, both are made up of a series of separate stages or spaces, each of which has its peculiar character of advance or retreat from the goal. Again, in each, from the point of view of any single player there are other players, Archimagos and Duessas, who can win only if he loses, and vice versa. In short, I am asserting that my test for appropriateness of responsive verbal behavior is a structural coherence between Monopoly and Book I of *The Faerie Queene*. Why should this seeming interpretation not be accepted and included in the canonical criticism of that work? As we all know, modern criticism is full of explanations of this sort, usually presented under the categorial term "myth."

Here it is sufficient to invalidate the appropriateness of the response by asserting that Monopoly was not invented until the 1930's and that Spenser wrote in the 1590's. This amounts to an assertion that the cultural situation in which Spenser found himself did not make it possible for him to respond by uttering sentences appropriate for playing the game of Monopoly. The question for Aesopian interpretation, then, is whether the author, given his cultural circumstances, could or could not have exemplified a particular explanatory proposition in his work. The mother who told her child to go buy a loaf of bread could conceivably have meant a pound of butter. It is improbable that she intended the child to go to the corner grocery to buy an astrolabe. Thus the Aesopian interpreter constructs a set of probabilities which limits the possible range of explanatory propositions the author could conceivably exemplify in the work.

A second example is a much more difficult case, but illustrates the same processes. One of the works I lecture on with some frequency is Swinburne's *Atalanta in Calydon*; to exemplify my position on Aesopian interpretation I shall discuss a set of my utterances in response to that work. In my lectures I assert that Swinburne has put into conflict two opposing views of the proper attitude toward life: Meleager's, that we should trust the world and our spontaneous responses, and that of Althea, his mother, that we should trust neither. What I have done is to consider a number of sentences spoken by Meleager and Althea as exemplifications, to which I have responded by uttering explanatory propositions. At this point it seems to me that some students, perhaps most, have never formulated their relation and response to the world in either of these ways. I therefore explain what I mean, that is, my own semantic intention, by drawing upon philosophy, psychiatry, and other literature for explanatory statements and exemplifications, taking care to distinguish this pair from apparently similar pairs, such as timidity and aggressiveness. In this I am pursuing a course parallel to that of the evaluative and Augustinian critics. I am explaining my own utterances by offering explanatory statements and exemplifications other than those to be found in the work. Speaking very roughly, I am asserting that it is reasonable to utter such statements and to put them in a contrastive relationship so that as statements they make sense.

I then continue by explaining the chorus "Before the beginning of years" by the utterance, "Every human gratification is matched and accompanied by an equally compelling frustration." Or, in more general form, "Every human pleasure is inseparable from an equally powerful human pain." And then for the chorus, "Who hath given man speech?" I offer the explanatory statements, "Language is responsible for our awareness of value conflicts and of the inseparability of pleasure and pain, gratification and frustration. Language, therefore, is responsible for our longing for death, since it makes us aware of the fact that these conflicts are irreconcilable." Before proceeding further, I offer explanations for these statements, including non-Swinburnian exemplifications. It is not necessary to give further examples. It is enough to conclude that on the basis of the coherence and redundancy of my explanatory statements, I explain them by the more general explanatory statement that the effort to resolve the contraries of human life brings about disaster, but that the failure to make that effort eventuates in the desire for death. This is my Aesopian interpretation.

The problem is now to test it by constructing an intention. To condense the process, in *Songs before Sunrise*, published six years after *Atalanta*, I find not only a series of poems which present explanatory statements about the irresolvable conflicts of human interests, but also in one poem the phrase, "the divine contraries of life." In *Atalanta* divinity is presented as something evil, since it is responsible for these irresolvable conflicts, but here the term "divine" ascribes to them positive value. On the basis of statements made by Swinburne about himself I assert that Swinburne's peculiar erotic temperament made him extraordinarily sensitive to the inseparability of pleasure and pain, gratification and frustration. At this point I introduce the propositions that Swinburne was writing in the Romantic tradition and that the primary problem for Romanticism was perceiving and accepting the irresolvable tension between subject and object, to use an old-fashioned terminology. I conclude that this element in Swinburne's cultural situation and personal mode of perception made it possible for him to perceive in his situation the problem of contraries and subsequently to *Atalanta* to ascribe positive value to their existence. For me, though perhaps not for many other critics of Victorian literature, a construction of extended intention has been successfully substituted for the speaker; the result is the experience I have called reassurance. What has happened is that in the absence of the speaker I have uttered statements about his intention which are coherent with my explanations of some of his utterances in the work. On these grounds I assert that response by Aesopian interpretation is appropriate.

The ultimate model or paradigm for this kind of response to a work is to be found in my earlier remark that one way of resolving polysemy (and categorial incoherence as well) is to propose to the speaker an alternative statement. If the speaker judges this to be appropriate, it is then admitted as an acceptable substitute for the original statement. However, Aesopian interpretation could perhaps better be named subsumptional interpretation. The justification for such a terminology is the fact that explanatory hierarchies are constructed by subsuming under explanatory statements sets of exemplary statements.

There is a fourth kind of criticism which is appropriate for non-Aesopian works, that is, works for which to offer an explanatory statement would be inappropriate behavior. Such works are not "about" anything. It is inappropriate to judge such a work to be a set of exemplary statements the appropriate verbal response to which is the utterance of an explanatory statement which subsumes them. The appropriate behavior is to substitute for each statement in the work an alternative statement which is coherent with the extended intention. The most common term for such verbal response is "paraphrase." It is, as a technique, frequently the first and appropriate step in constructing an Aesopian or subsumptional statement, but the process ceases before such construction is begun. Such substitutional criticism, as I shall call it, is most commonly found in responding to poetry, but in the criticism of extended fictional prose paraphrase or substitutional criticism takes the form of statements of such weak explanatory power that they are properly, perhaps, called summaries, as the statement, "The hero takes a walk in the country," may substitutionally summarize a number of pages. Paraphrase, of course, has been said to be a heresy, but as I have indicated above it is a norm of ordinary verbal behavior and one of the most common means of gaining reassurance. The notion that paraphrase is a "heresy" derives, not surprisingly, from an Augustinian theory of criticism. Both Aesopian and substitutional criticism may be properly called "interpretation."

This brings me to the particular problem to which we have been asked to address ourselves. What is the bearing, if any, of history, philosophy, and other disciplines on literary criticism? The first problem to get out of the way is the term "discipline." In the sense in which I think most people would take the word, there are no disciplines. In fact each of them is bothered with the same question that bothers the critic and that we have been asked to examine. In every discipline one finds the same question under discussion: What is history? What is psychology? What is philosophy? What is sociology? Is there such a subject and discipline as molecular biology? Biologists and biochemists tend to deny it, and molecular biologists disagree with each other. From the point of view of this paper each of the so-called disciplines consists of a loosely organized, discontinuous, and unstable set of explanatory hierarchies. It will be easier to understand what is going on in criticism if for "discipline" we substitute "culturally available explanatory modes."

In Aesopian and substitutional interpretation these modes are brought in for two purposes. One is to provide an explanation and justification for the substitutional statements of the critic. One aim of the critic is to explain his explanatory substitutions by constructing an explanatory hierarchy which permits his statement to be a reasonable and acceptable statement in its own right, that is, without reference to the work. There is nothing purely literary about such statements, about the moral to an Aesopian fable, or about my interpretation of *Atalanta*. Something here may be learned from the Augustinian exemplifier, who uses literature to exemplify any explanatory mode he pleases. In the interpretation of *The Faerie Queene*, for example, the aim of the critic is, in this sense, to justify his interpretation as a comprehensible proposition. To do this he must either explain in terms of the explanatory modes of his own culture or construct an explanatory chain between such a mode and a mode the language of which belongs to a mode comprehensible to Spenser's contemporaries but not to the critic's. In order to explain his statements, any individual uses the explanatory modes available to him, either paradigmatically or innovatively. Much of what we call the interpretation of literature is actually the explanation of a critic's explanatory statements, not an explanation of the work, in the sense of being a substitution for a set of the author's statements by explanatory subsumption.

The other way in which various explanatory modes from various "disciplines" enter into criticism is, of course, in the construction of extended intention. This is undoubtedly the most difficult verbal behavior the critic engages in, the one which necessarily involves the greatest uncertainty. Yet if we keep in mind as example the child who knows his mother wants butter and not bread, or the young linguist who knew, correctly, what the older linguist intended, even though he had said something quite different, we can see that theoretically nothing lies in our way.

What the critic does is to construct verbally the cultural situation the author found himself in and the modes of perceiving that situation concurrently available. He attempts to state what the problems of the culture were, and how the author responded to those problems. He attempts, therefore, to construct a theory of the decisional process which led to the statements of the work. His evidence for all this consists of other literary and nonliterary

documents and of artifacts presenting other than linguistic semiotic systems to be found in the author's situation. At the present
time he finds available within our culture numerous explanatory
systems for which this material offers the occasion for exemplary
statements. Any explanatory mode, no matter what discipline it
is found in, which organizes exemplary material within the situation of the author is usable by the critic. It is at this point that
something properly called literary study emerges. In selecting
material and explanatory systems for constructing his theory of
extended intention the critic needs as a selective instrument a
hypothesis of what his kind of author would be likely to perceive
in his situation as appropriate for literature. If the work is not
anonymous, and if other materials, both literary and nonliterary,
exist and are available, the critic has a more selective instrument
for the kind of situational aspect the author was likely to respond
to, how he was likely to perceive, and what series of decisions
he was likely to make in arriving at the literary utterance. To be
succinct, the study of literature boils down to the study of the
behavior of authors in their cultural situation, just as children
study the behavior of mothers in their situation. The aim of the
critic is to make an appropriate verbal response to an author's
utterance, and this is precisely the same as anybody's effort to
make an appropriate response to any other person's utterance.
To do this one must examine the behavior of the speaker in his
situation, whether directly perceived or constructed. Sooner or
later it will be recognized that the study of literature belongs to
the behavioral sciences.

A final type of verbal response or criticism remains; I call it
"accounting for." The child who decides that his mother meant
butter and not bread may also explain why she made the mistake,
or an individual, say a psychoanalyst, to whom is available a
richer variety of explanatory modes, may offer such an explanation. In either case, the slip of the tongue is accounted for. Such
criticism may be the verbal consequence of constructing an intention for either Aesopian or substitutional criticism, or it may
be used when the critic feels that the author's statement is so self-
evident that not even substitutional criticism is necessary. For

example, in *Atalanta* there is a catalogue of heroes which has nothing to do with Aesopian interpretation. For reasons I have gone into elsewhere[6] a work of literature offers material for which interpretation is inappropriate, and a work can consist entirely of such material. Nevertheless, the critic generally feels that he is not playing his role completely if he fails to respond verbally to such sentences. What Swinburne did was to import into the paradigm of Greek tragedy a verbal paradigm from Greek epic. In responding to such material the critic does not interpret it; he accounts for it. Here the famous critical aberrations of Thomas Rymer are most instructive. His judgment was that *Othello* was a poor work because it contained no moral. And in his explanation I believe he was right. *Othello* does indeed contain no moral. That is, like all of Shakespeare's tragedies, there are no hints that an appropriate response would be to utter an explanatory proposition. It is not, I believe, an Aesopian work. It is not, by limited or extended intention, an exemplification of an explanatory proposition. What the critic does is to account for the presence of the sentential and other material, such as stage directions, in the work. That is, he constructs a theory of intention and then accounts for the decisions which resulted in Shakespeare's presenting such material in *Othello*.

Another example will perhaps help to clarify this. Using once again the *Faerie Queene*-Monopoly instance, suppose I responded by asserting that within Spenser's situation was the universal of human behavior that goal-directed activity encounters unanticipated helps and hindrances, and that this way of patterning behavior was accessible to him from other works and from Christian psychology. It is to be found in his own work, then, because it was available to him through numerous paradigms. This is accounting for. I then respond to my accounting-for statement by uttering my sentences about Monopoly, my purpose being to exemplify both the pattern and my use of the term "universal of human behavior." This, as I have suggested, appears to be what happens in much so-called mythic or mythopoetic interpretation.

[6] "Literary Interpretation as Conventionalized Verbal Behavior."

It is not interpretation but an exemplification of an explanatory "accounting-for" statement.

III

Justification of evaluation, Augustinian exemplification, Aesopian and substitutional interpretation, construction of intention, and accounting for—these I believe to be primary modes of criticism. I would add only one final point. It has been said that the role of critic is not an autonomous role, or that it is parasitical upon literature. I believe such a position to be in error. The role of critic needs no defense. Any literary work, like any sentence, exposes us to polysemy and categorial incoherence; the consequence is disorientation and tensions. Any behavioral strategy designed to alleviate that tension is justified simply by the fact that the development of such strategies is unavoidable. All the anthropology that I have read indicates that primitive people who have literature also have criticism. Asking if criticism is justified is like asking if eating is justified. If you decide that being alive is not justified—and great numbers of people daily decide that it is not—then neither eating nor criticism is justified. Otherwise, both are. The only way to avoid the verbal response to literature we call criticism is to avoid works of literature, but that is so difficult that virtually the only way to do so is to sunder all relations with all other human beings. And that too is a kind of suicide. Criticism is a self-justifying activity, dependent only upon the willingness to live.

20

IS POETRY

SELF-EXPRESSION?

[1953*]

Traditionally, the problem of whether or not poetry is self-expression has been attacked by an analysis of "expression"; that is, behind such analyses lies the assumption that the "self" is an entity, and in this sense such theories about poetry have the characteristics of metaphysical thinking. In the nineteenth century, men like Newman and Ruskin expressed in various parts of their writings the typical idea of that century—the idea which still dominates most thinking on the problem. In these terms, the poem is thought of as a kind of window between the inner and the outer world. And in Tennyson's "Lady of Shalott," the picture of the lady weaving her designs from what she has seen in the mirror, which reflects reality, is an allegorical visual image of the nineteenth century's idea of the relationship of the poet to reality: The poet is conceived of as living within the inner world

* Reprinted by permission from *Four Quarters*, II (May, 1953), pp. 1–5.

of the "self"; and when the poet leaves that inner world and moves into the outer world, he is, as a poet, destroyed.

This window into the soul (or the "self") has, of course, also the dimension of time, and, consequently, the poem is thought of as a record of experience. This being so, the relationship of the reader to the poet is that of someone who relives or recreates the experience, which was originally lived by the poet and which is recorded in the poem. It may be said that this has led, possibly, to a misunderstanding of nineteenth-century poetry, the dramatic fiction of which is that it is a spontaneous overflow of powerful emotions, a record of experience; but this, it may be, is only dramatic fiction and really has no relevance to what actually happens in both the reading and the writing of the poem.

As we have seen, this kind of thinking posits the "self" as an entity. What I would like to do is to take three propositions which are accepted by some people at the present time and apply them to this problem of poetry as self-expression. Primarily, my attack will not be upon "expression" but upon "self." These propositions, as variously expressed, can be presented in the following way: First, metaphysical language is without "meaning"; that is, metaphysical linguistic structure is not the same kind of linguistic structure as scientific linguistic structure. It is not cognitive language. Second, the "self" is not an entity and the word does not refer to an entity the existence of which can be empirically verified. This, however, does not mean (as I shall shortly try to explain) that when we use the word "self" we are not talking about anything at all. The third proposition has been, perhaps, most strikingly set forth by Beardsley and Wimsatt in their famous "The Intentional Fallacy." This proposition is that in reading the poem we must assume that the spokesman of the poem is not to be identified with the author and that we go from spokesman to author by an act of biographical inference. If my analysis is correct in stating that to posit the "self" is to use metaphysical language and not, loosely, scientific or cognitive language, we can dispose of the proposition that a poem is self-expression in the sense that something inside the "self" goes out into or is projected upon, or is reflected in, something outside the "self," namely, the poem. Because if this is metaphysical language it is meaningless language. But can we say that we are not talking about anything at all when we speak of poetry as self-expression? I think if properly understood the term does yield something. Psychology has taught us that the root of emotional life lies in the sense of identity, which apparently begins to emerge about the age of two. It is possible, for example, that the fear of heights or the fear of death is not a real fear in the sense that it is a recognition of a real threat to existence but is, rather, a fear not of death or of heights but of loss of identity, which is so hardly won and which is maintained with such difficulty.

Now if we examine the actual behavior of people, we find that it is an inconsistent and discontinuous mixture of conscious and unconscious reactions to a storm of ever-differing, constantly changing phenomena. Further, analysis shows us that each person has a self-portrait which is a construct (or a selection on the basis of models learned from the society) from all of the individual's bits and pieces of behavior, one which does not correspond to the full range of behavior. This self-portrait is, in itself, inconsistent, but it does have a certain kind of structure, that is, each person lives according to a predominating role. It is only a madman, though, such as the man who imagines himself to be Napoleon, who maintains an absolutely consistent and fixed self-portrait and acts according to it. The healthy person is constantly changing his self-portrait and actually has at his control a wide range of roles and differing self-portraits, which he can adopt as the situation demands. It is, perhaps, something of this sort that was in Yeats's mind when he developed his doctrine of masks.

Now if, from the behavior of the individual, we isolate his linguistic behavior, we will observe that it has all the characteristics of the self-portrait; that is, it lacks logical structure and is adapted to a wide range of varying roles. In this sense, we might almost say that every sentence an individual utters in normal life in social relationships reflects a slightly different role, and, sometimes, a profoundly different role. It is immediately apparent that there are certain kinds of linguistic behavior which have, for instance, the characteristic of logical structure. There is, of course, at the present time, a profound disagreement on what logic is and its relationship to reality (or what lies outside of the structure which includes signs which point or refer to something outside the structure) and even on the origin of logic. But this disagreement need not affect the argument. All that is necessary is to accept the proposition that a series of sentences organized according to logical structure is a unique and special kind of linguistic organization, of which we cannot say much except that it has that strange quality known as structure and that it is a linguistic activity profoundly different from ordinary linguistic behavior.

Poetry also has structure—in rhythm, in rhyme, in stanzaic organization, and, for some poetry, in symbolic organization, as well as in the organization of images. The various kinds of poetic structure have not, so far as I know, been carefully distinguished or even recognized. One of the reasons for this critical lack lies in the very assumption that the whole poem is thought of as a sign with reference to the "self." But if, as we have seen, the "self" is not an entity, we can scarcely have a sign which points to it. Furthermore, this structure of poetry is like logical structure, a most untypical or anormal kind of linguistic behavior.

Certain words which are used by both reader and writer give us a hint of what is going on in the poetic activity of either. The poet speaks of inspiration from a source outside of his "self." He often speaks the way the reader speaks; that is, he will say he loses himself in the activity of poetic creation. For many people with a somewhat naïve tendency, this is, in fact, their single aesthetic test—they lose themselves in reading the poem or in looking at the play or the movie, or in reading the novel. This is the equivalent of what the poet calls "inspiration."

What could they possibly be talking about? I think it is something like this: Like the man who thinks himself to be Napoleon, they experience, for the time being, a consistent role. Their linguistic behavior is organized according to the structure of a role and does not, as it does in ordinary life, skip rapidly from one role to another. The teacher, for instance, experiences something like acting: During the time of his teaching performance, he acts according to a certain pre-existent model or pattern of "the teacher."

Perhaps, to digress a moment, the more conscious he is of the difference between this role and his ordinary self-portrait, the better the teacher he is; just as we, I think rightly, make a distinction between the acting of Tallulah Bankhead, who seems to confuse art and life, and that of a disciplined artist, such as Helen Hayes. When we say, then, that a poem is self-expression, do we not mean, rather, that through its linguistic structure it is the creation of a temporarily consistent "self"? The implications of this are really very great. For it means that a poet can achieve an understanding and an acceptance or rejection of a particular emotional attitude which he cannot practice in life. In Swinburne's "Anactoria," we have a complete description by Sappho of masochistic love, which arouses her to a fury of aggressive verbalization. And an analysis of the poem shows us, in the flight of Venus from the Isle of Lesbos, that Swinburne is saying that this kind of love is a wrong kind of love; yet in his own life he was never able to solve that problem, and he could get along only by submitting himself to the control of the ineffable Watts-Dunton. In the traditional kind of biographical criticism, the poem would be taken as proof that Swinburne had solved this problem; or else, working from Swinburne to the poem, it would be taken as an expression of Swinburne's emotional life, and it would be said that the poem does not imply that this kind of love is a failure. And, indeed, this has been done by several English critics in recent years, one of whom has rejected Swinburne wholesale on the grounds that his poetry is the expression of a neurotic "self." If my analysis of the situation is correct, however, it will be seen that Swinburne was capable of understanding, describing, and rejecting an emotion which dominated his whole life. Obviously, to move from a poem directly to the emotional life of the author is an act of biographical inference which cannot be justified.

Psychologically, then, we can say that the function of the creation or reading of a poem is to give us relief from our continuous struggle to maintain the sense of identity. It is the kind of relief which children have on Hallowe'en. By dressing up they create an image of themselves which is the basis for a self-portrait according to which they can act with emotional consistency for a few hours. It is for this reason that poetry can be so profoundly moving, and it is for this reason that we can give content to the proposition made by I. A. Richards (among others) that a poem is the organization of emotional attitudes or of the emotional life. To relate images which have emotional significance or color or suffusion is to organize and relate the emotions themselves; the varying effects of one emotional attitude upon another are thus, for the time being, made consistent and structured and, consequently, have "meaning." The true psychological function, then, of poetry is to give us the experience of maintaining identity. The more profoundly, the more richly we have this experience, the more successful we will be in creating this sense of identity. Poetry, then, is one of the healthiest of human activities, and it is not surprising that its particular appeal should be strongest to those people who, for whatever reasons, are especially aware, perhaps unconsciously, of the difficulties that lie in the way of the struggle for identity.

Finally, then, we can say that the task of criticism is not, as it has usually been in the past, to find out something in the poet's life to which the signs within the poem point, but rather to discover whether or not the poem has a consistent structure. To find out whether it has or has not a consistent structure will require the development of techniques which are yet scarcely in existence or even thought of, except by a very few critics, who are studying structure because they have arrived by intuition at the realization that the study of the linguistic structure of the poem is the important task of criticism. Perhaps a development of a true criticism will involve the development of a meta-language, that is, a special limited language whose signs will refer to the structure of poetry and not to anything that lies outside of that structure. Furthermore, the acceptance of this proposition must involve a reconsideration of the portraits of the "selves" of poets which biographers have created over the past several hundred years. At the same time, this kind of thinking sheds considerable light on the problem of why individual biographers extract from a consideration of poems and of nonliterary biographical data such differing and inconsistent pictures, such as, on the one hand, Shelley as a completely aimless and irresponsible neurotic, and on the other hand, as a human being with aim and direction and a steadily growing sense of identity and a steadily growing responsibility toward himself, his family and friends, and society as a whole.

To conclude, the poem is not self-expression. It is the creation of a "self" or a role which temporarily gives the writer and the reader a continuous sense of identity, a sense traditionally called inspiration. The term self-expression, therefore, should be dropped from the critical vocabulary as essentially meaningless and metaphysical, and in its place we should try to create a meta-language which will explore and describe the various kinds of poetic structure.

21

METAPHOR: A LITTLE

PLAIN SPEAKING ON A WEARY SUBJECT

[1962*]

So long as metaphor was regarded as a mere figure of speech, as a literary ornament, it did not cause too much trouble. Nevertheless, the possibility for trouble was present, for Aristotle had stated that the power to create new metaphors was a mark of genius. When the philology of the late eighteenth and early nineteenth centuries moved toward the notion that metaphor is the source of the development of language and the cause of semantic change and refinement, the Romantic poets and critics hurried to adopt a notion filled with potential for exalting the status of poetry. The notion had already emerged that poetry is not a way of using language but a way of thinking, and that it is ultimately the only way of thinking which brings into consciousness something deserving to be called "truth." Poets, linguistically and semantically inventive, could be identified by their power to

* Reprinted by permission from *Connotation*, I (Winter, 1962), pp. 29–46. Copyright 1962 by *Connotation*.

create novel metaphors. By Aristotle's assertion, that made them geniuses, and by the discoveries of the new philology, they were revealed as the originators of thinking and therefore of "truth." Poetry, truth, and metaphor were virtually identified, and though this equation was half forgotten for a time, it was revived by the pallid transcendentalism of this century's New Critics. The most common position today, the position that carries with it the richest critical and academic status and self-approval, is that poetry is a means of discovering a "truth" which is accessible to no other way of thinking, and that the technique of such thinking is metaphor. Ultimately, it follows, and at the profoundest level, poetry is metaphor. Myth and symbol, which are special forms of poetry, are also metaphor, and Stanley Edgar Hyman, armed with this vision, has asserted in his recent *The Tangled Bank* that science is likewise ultimately metaphor and a mode of poetic thinking; and he has, explicitly and implicitly, extended this notion to something he calls the "moral imagination," by which he means, I would guess, the power to invent new systems and hierarchies and "worlds" of value.

The result of all this is that the subject of metaphor is today involved in the utmost confusion, that a mystique of metaphor has developed, in which writers as diverse as I. A. Richards, Monroe Beardsley, and Philip Wainwright, though they disagree on much, all place themselves before the altar of metaphor, within the dread boundaries marked by the sacred veil of poetry. I mention these three writers, for at least each of them has attempted to bring some light and reason into this almost hopelessly confused subject. They, at least, are not content to worship. Richards has offered a terminology, Beardsley has attempted to make a sharp distinction between metaphor and simile, and Wainwright, though not accepting that difference, has endeavored to define two ultimate metaphorical types. Yet I do not believe that any of them has been successful, for the assumption of each is the equation, metaphor=poetry=truth, or at least a special kind of truth. (Beardsley has almost succeeded in ridding himself of this, but not in his discussion of metaphor.)

Though I have never been able to understand twentieth-century critics when they write about metaphor, certainly until a few years ago I accepted the notion that poetry is a special way of using language, with a unique semantic aspect and characteristics, though it is a long time since I have been able to believe that poetry is a means of access to a special kind of "truth" inaccessible to other modes of thought. If we make a distinction between "thinking" and "linguistic behavior"—a distinction very hard to maintain or keep clear yet equally hard to get along without—I could not use "poetic" to modify the first, but I could use it to modify the second. But when I had learned to differentiate sharply among the phonemic, the syntactic, and the semantic aspects of language, I found myself less and less capable of applying "poetic" to the third. Whenever I found myself asserting that a certain kind of behavior is unique to poetry, I asked myself, "But is it so? Is this kind of semantic behavior never found in prose or in ordinary spoken language, at all cultural levels?" Thus I attacked myself and eventually drove myself entirely from the very weakened position which was all I had managed to retain of twentieth-century criticism. I found myself believing that semantically nothing happens in poetry which does not happen as a consequence of perfectly normal and common linguistic behavior. All I can at present assert is that at certain times and places, that is, in particularly poetic styles, certain kinds of linguistic behavior are believed to be appropriate to and therefore characteristic of poetry.

The reasons for this selection have ultimately nothing to do with poetry, but derive from nonpoetic, nonartistic cultural values, subject to change and fashion, mode and style. Whenever a new set of cultural values appears, it affects poetry, and, when it catches up, criticism. One consequence is a radical revaluation of the poetic canon. Modern poetry, some 50 years ago, began to concentrate on the possibilities of metaphor with a purity, intensity, and exclusiveness hitherto unknown. Less than a decade later, criticism was overhauling the canon and rejecting everything which did not show a comparable interest in metaphor. The implicit transcendentalism was revived, and metaphor was made the heart of poetry. That an enormous amount of beautiful English poetry was thrown out on the dump was felt to be a small event in comparison with the mighty modern discovery, at last (and how many times has this not happened?), of the true nature of poetry, of the identity of metaphor, poetry, and truth.

Because metaphor was surrounded with such a bulwark of confusion and transcendentalism, it resisted my attacks for a long time. It is the citadel of modern criticism, and for this reason I was particularly eager to reduce it and, if possible, sow the ground with salt; for it was the very center of the affirmation that poetic thinking makes accessible a unique and uniquely valuable kind of "truth," an affirmation, quite frankly, which I thoroughly detest, for it has been responsible for more nonsense about poetry in the last 40 years than any other notion I am familiar with. I wished to have a clear and sharp notion of metaphor, and to be able to talk about metaphors easily and simply. Only thus, I felt, could the exalted position of metaphor be overthrown, and with it the extravagant and unjustified claims for poetry which have been erected upon it. I feel now that I have something to say upon the subject, and I should like to offer it in the hope that it may be of interest and use to others who, like myself, find the transcendental epistemological claims of the New Critics unacceptable, and even absurd and detestable. Adherents to this kind of criticism I have no hope for; as Richard Foster has shown in his admirable *The New Romantics*, their claims for poetry, and hence for metaphor, are implicitly metaphysical, transcendental, and quasi-religious, and about 20 years ago became overtly so. And to this kind of mind I have nothing acceptable to say.

The first confusion to clear out of the way is that a metaphor is self-contained. This is the basis for Beardsley's distinction between metaphor and simile (in his *Aesthetics*). He is wonderfully inventive in making up metaphors for examples, and I shall use one of his own for my purposes. It is the splendid phrase, "chocolate kilowatt." This is part of a longer phrase which he created to demonstrate that, since it is possible to invent nonsensical metaphors, it follows, if I understand him correctly, that the sense of understandable metaphors arises from within the metaphor and not from their context. In this they differ from similes. To the simile-metaphor problem I shall return, as well as to how we make sense out of metaphors; for the moment I wish only to see if "chocolate kilowatt" can be made to yield any sense. To establish my attitude at once, I shall here make the assertion that it is *impossible* to invent nonsensical metaphors.

The first thing to ask is how we know that we have encountered a metaphor in the sentence, "This is a chocolate kilowatt." What do we mean when we say that the phrase makes no sense? It appears to me that what it violates is the categorial structure of our minds. But the word "mind" always immediately starts one on the way to a dead end of thinking. Rather, it appears to me that no categories are "natural," that all categories are matters of cultural convention. Whatever else they may show, the famous Whorf hypotheses about language certainly seem to demonstrate this. "Chocolate kilowatt," then, violates the categorial structure of our cultural conventions. "Chocolate" and "kilowatt" do not belong to the same category. We perceive a metaphor as a metaphor, therefore, when we encounter words (to keep the problem of metaphor for the time being at a linguistic level) which conventionally do not belong to the same category. A metaphor, then, is an assertion that they do. This is more easily seen if we transform the original phrase into two alternative forms: "This kilowatt is chocolate;" "This chocolate is a kilowatt." In these forms it is easy to see that "is" means, "For the purpose of my present discourse, 'chocolate' and 'kilowatt' belong in the same category." Hence to create a metaphor is to create a novel or emergent category. To the problem of how this can be so, I shall return. Here it is necessary to imagine situations in which the emergent category or metaphor "chocolate kilowatt" would be appropriate.

Let us imagine that I have been driving for three or four hours without stopping. The road has been difficult, narrow, twisting, and mountainous. Weary, and becoming mistrustful of my perceptions and my ability to respond immediately to emergencies, I stop, buy a chocolate bar, and eat it. Whether it is the rest, the food, the gratifying taste of chocolate, the sudden intake of sugar, or the mere act of eating that provides a particular internal experience is not of much importance. Whatever the reason, I feel a relaxation of tension and a corresponding sense of available physical energy which I ascribe to the chocolate. "M-m-m," I say to my companion as we resume our trip, *"that* was a real chocolate kilowatt."

The first thing to be noticed is that "chocolate" is appropriate to the discourse, for it has recently been part of the situation, and indeed, though metamorphosed, still is. But "kilowatt" is not. The referent of "that," as the word "chocolate" reinforces, is the now eaten chocolate bar. "Chocolate" belongs to that category of food called "'candy." But "kilowatt" belongs to the category of things and forces having to do with electricity. A kilowatt is a unit or measure of electrical energy, and in modern civilization a flip of a switch makes immediately available a certain predetermined amount of electric energy. However, chocolate is not electricity. The emergent category includes, therefore, not chocolate and kilowatts but anything which can be interpreted as making available a certain amount of energy. Furthermore, I need not say "chocolate kilowatt." I can just as well remark, as I swallow the last bit of my chocolate bar, "That was a real kilowatt." And I could just as well use this sentence after the performance of a symphony, on reading a poem, on finishing a refreshing swim, after a hot shower or a scalp massage, so long as the referent for "that" is determined by the situation in which the sentence occurs. I can even use the sentence when that referent is obvious only to me, but to no one else, if I wish to be mystifying; or indeed, when the referent is unknown to me, as in, "Whatever that was, it was a real kilowatt." My listener would then know at least that whatever it was, it gave me a sensation which I interpret as the sudden influx of increased energy and physiological resources. So long as the referent, known or unknown, whether said or implied, of "that" is not in fact electricity, as when I am being electrocuted, "kilowatt" is a metaphor.

But we need a terminology for the semantic functions of "chocolate" and "kilowatt." Since "chocolate" is appropriate to the situation and the discourse which emerges from the situation, I shall call it the "local term." And since "kilowatt" is not appropriate, I shall call it the "imported term." (These are equivalent to the "tenor" and "vehicle" of Richards, which I used in *Word, Meaning, Poem*; but I have found these terms unsatisfactory, partly because, since they are themselves metaphors, I find it hard, as do my students, to remember which is which.) It is apparent from the above examples that both local and imported terms may appear, or that the latter may appear. Only the imported term is necessary for a metaphor or emergent category to arise.

So far it would appear likely that Beardsley is in error in asserting that a metaphor is self-contained. Clearly the interpretation of an imported term as a metaphor depends upon the situation in which it appears. This can be made even more evident by another example.

Let us imagine that on a cold, rainy night I have been walking home through streets which are ill-lit, lonely, and dangerous, as they are in any large American city. I come through the door into my warm, cozy house, I switch on the lights, and I say to myself with a smile of amusement and pleasure, "Ah! a chocolate kilowatt." Obviously here "kilowatt" is appropriate to the discourse arising from the situation. It is the local term, and "chocolate" is the imported term. This is even clearer if we imagine my saying, "Ah! kilowatts!" No metaphor would be present; but a metaphor would occur if I said, "Ah! chocolate!" The statement is an assertion that for the purpose of the present discourse, both chocolate and kilowatt belong to the category of sensations and things which provide, on demand, immediate gratification, immediate pleasure and comfort, and that therefore the imported term may be substituted for the local term. What those "purposes of discourse" may be, however, must for the moment be postponed.

These examples seem to me to make it irresistible that a metaphor is not self-contained but depends upon either a verbal or a situational context. Indeed, since no verbal behavior exists without a nonverbal situation, the context for a metaphor is always the circumstances in which it appears. The proper question is not, "What is a metaphor?" but, "Under what circumstances do we interpret an expression as metaphorical?" And the answer is, "When the expression is inappropriate to the categories and terminology conventionally demanded by the situation." To say, in the first example, that the chocolate bar was sweet, or good, or refreshing, or gratifying would be to employ categories and terms conventionally appropriate to the situation, but to call it a kilowatt is to use a conventionally inappropriate term.

That these are matters of convention becomes apparent when we consider the dead metaphor. Why does a metaphor die? Supposing on eating the chocolate bar I had said, "That chocolate gave me a real charge." Here again is a metaphor taken from electricity, and it is probably a humorous reference to electrocution. It is a fairly recent metaphor; I can remember first noticing it sometime within the last decade. It certainly exists at the level of spoken popular language and would be considered a vulgarism in high-level formal written prose. It is slang, as many metaphors are, though I should say less exclusively slang than it was but a few years ago. Certainly it is found in the informal conversation of individuals of the higher cultural levels. It might be found, very self-consciously, in remarks on a paper at a meeting of the Modern Language Association; it would hardly be found in the paper itself. On the other hand, it could easily be found in a fairly earnest address at the meeting of the Rotary Club in a non-metropolitan city. But I think its social status is not entirely independent of the degree to which it is perceived as a metaphor. In popular slang it probably today serves as a mild intensive, and is hardly felt as a metaphor at all. At the highest levels its metaphorical character would still be fairly obvious. Yet it is by no means uncommon to find in serious critical prose an expression such as this: "His poetry is highly charged with striking and original metaphors." Does this mean that there are many metaphors? Or does it mean that the metaphors elicit in the reader a strong and emotional intellectual response? It is hard to say; and I suspect that the reason is that in this instance a metaphor has changed its category. Some decades ago, I suspect, the sentence would have read "heavily charged," and the imported term "charge" would have been taken from shipping and accounting. But this use of "charge" is more or less obsolescent, while the electrical use of "charge" is now the conventional one. Thus the metaphor originally meant that the poetry had a great many metaphors, while now it probably means that the metaphors are powerful and original. In any case the metaphor is nearly dead. That is, when we encounter it we do not think of the category from which it is drawn; in "chocolate kilowatt," of course, we do think of it. A metaphor dies, then, when it has become so well established and conventionalized, along with its accompanying emergent category, that we do not identify it as a term inappropriate to the

situation of the discourse. We think of the attributes of the once
emergent category, not of the attributes of the category to which
the imported term originally belonged.

How this can be is shown by the delightful effects of mixing
metaphors, which is a consequence of ignoring the fact that, faced
with a metaphor, the listener can, if he wishes, make himself
aware of the category from which the imported term is drawn. A
sound old boner is an example. "A virgin forest is one in which
the hand of man has never set foot." There is nothing funny
about, "A virgin forest is one which has been neither economically exploited nor even explored," at least if one reads it without
the boner fresh in one's mind. What makes the boner funny is
that all three imported terms, "virgin," "hand of man," "set foot,"
are taken from the category of the human body. Their juxtaposition makes one aware of that category; by themselves each is
so dead a metaphor that one would not think of the category from
which it is imported. This juxtaposition, then, resuscitates the
dead metaphors, and the perception of the absurdity follows, an
absurdity which becomes more obscene, and funnier, the more
one meditates on it. I do not think it has to be spelled out.

A metaphor, then, is a metaphor if the listener identifies the
imported term as imported. In reading poetry and interpreting it,
one is acutely aware of metaphors if the poetic and critical conventions of the time, as today, are such that one has a high level of
metaphorical expectation. The assumption, then, is that the poet
was equally sensitive to metaphor, an assumption that may or
may not be justified, and often, I should say, at least when it
comes to poetry written more than 50 years ago, is not so justified
as modern critics would insist. The present high metaphorical
expectation combined with the equation metaphor=poetry=truth
and blended with the old notion that truth should be consistent
and unified has lead to the search, especially in Shakespeare
studies, for one big underlying metaphor, the categories of which
shall include all of the metaphors in the poem. I have yet to encounter a thoroughly convincing study of this sort, and on the
face of it, on the basis of ordinary linguistic behavior, which often
is just as metaphorical as the poetry of some periods, and of the
enormous number of dead metaphors, I doubt if such a study can

ever be convincing. This high metaphorical expectation has led also to the value judgment that in a lyric poem all of the metaphors should be derivable from one basic metaphor. Joyce Kilmer's "Trees" has been brutally mangled for this reason, and so has Shelley's poetry; Empson's attempt to justify what he called the nineteenth-century tumbling metaphor seems to have had little influence. I really see no reason why a poet should not use imported terms from as many categories as he likes. He need only be careful not to juxtapose terms imported from the same category (as Kilmer was not) if he wishes to avoid attacks from critics with a high degree of expectation for metaphorical consistency. That a vast number of people have enjoyed and have been moved by "Trees" suggests that such readers are, statistically, fairly rare and that Kilmer, who was by no means from a lower cultural level, did not entertain those expectations himself. Indeed, he wrote and published his poem before that particular critical mode had developed, and he was not himself influenced by the new poetry which that mode was designed to account for.

From this we may conclude that the proper form for the question, "What is a metaphor," is, "Under what circumstances and with what metaphorical expectancies is a term identified as an imported term with the consequent perception of a metaphor?" With this in mind we can return to a postponed question: A meaningful linguistic sequence (by which I mean any sequence to which it is possible to make a response interpreted as appropriate by the originator of the sentence) which includes a metaphor is an assertion that for the purposes of the discourse the imported term may be substituted for the local term. In the chocolate-eating situation they serve to place the local term in a nonconventional category, chocolate in the category of electrical phenomena. But it is clear that this term does not fit entirely into the nonconventional category. The reason is that not only are categories conventional, but the attributes or characteristics of categories are likewise matters of cultural convention. Here the assertion that kilowatt may be substituted for chocolate does not mean that all of the attributes of the category "electrical phenomena" are appropriate and applicable to chocolate. For instance, the capacity of electricity, when directly contacted by the human body, to give it a severe and painful shock and burn, to kill tissue, even to kill the organism, is clearly not appropriate in this situation. The substitution of "kilowatt" for "chocolate" is an assertion that *some* of the characteristics of kilowatts which they have by virtue of being of the category of electrical phenomena are to be considered as applicable to chocolate, but *not all* of them. A metaphor, then, selects *some* of the attributes of the category of the imported term and applies them to the local term. Thus the semantic function of a metaphor emerges, and the purposes become clear. A metaphor functions by attributing certain characteristics to a given phenomenon.

But this assertion immediately gives rise to two more questions. The first is: How do we know which attributes made available by the imported term are to be applied to the local term? How do we know which attributes are to be selected in order to constitute the emergent category? The answer that the appropriate attributes are to be used helps very little. How does my companion *know* that I do *not* mean that my digestion is so bad that eating rich chocolate has made me feel as if I had experienced a disagreeable electrical shock? In truth, he cannot know. He can only reply to my metaphor in a way that will test whether or not he has selected the attributes which I consider appropriate. Or—and this is the technique of much witty, malicious and ironic conversation—he may be able to guess from his knowledge of me which attributes I consider appropriate and to deliberately select others, in such a way as to cast discredit on me, or on Light and Power Companies, as in, "You mean that you paid a lot for a small amount of energy?" Or he might say, more obliquely, "Yes, everything costs more these days." In either case he has selected not the attribute of the immediate availability of a given amount of energy but the attribute of the high cost of electricity. Or he may be neither right nor witty but merely wrong. Indeed, the incorrect interpretation or overinterpretation of metaphors is one of the plagues of reading poetry. In many modern poems which give almost no clues to the situation or the local term, but merely present the imported term, the difficulties are staggering. Clearly the ease and correctness with which the interpreter applies the attributes made available by the imported term are functions of the level of his metaphoric expectation, of his comprehension of the situation, of the amount of information the speaker gives about which attributes are to be applied, of the interpreter's intelligence, and of his experience in interpreting metaphors. And this conclusion sheds considerable light on the distinction between metaphor and simile.

One of the difficulties in explaining the difference between the two has been that investigators attempt to compare different metaphors and similes. (Wainwright is an exception, but he does too little to be of much help. Besides, he is principally interested in the relative merits of simile and metaphor.) Rather, I shall use the method of constructing a series of expressions all of which use the same terms and categories. This will bring out both the differences and the similarities.

(1) In this the listener has no knowledge of the situation. He is to be thought of as overhearing an isolated remark entirely divorced from its situation and verbal context. "That was a real kilowatt." Here the listener obviously cannot even identify the expression as a metaphor.

(2) In this and all subsequent examples, the listener has full knowledge of the situation. "That was a real kilowatt." The listener knows that the referent is chocolate and can identify "kilowatt" as an imported term. However, he has to guess, from his knowledge of the speaker and the situation, which of the various categories "kilowatt" is conventionally put into and which attributes of that category are appropriate.

(3) "I enjoyed that kilowatt." This offers more information about the appropriate category and attributes, but the local term is still only implied by the situation. It contributes very important information about what attributes of the category of the imported term are to be considered appropriate. It rules out, for instance, both cost and pain.

(4) "I enjoyed that chocolate kilowatt." This now includes the local term in the sentence and makes the interpreter less dependent on his knowledge of the situation.

(5) "That chocolate bar was a most enjoyable kilowatt." This transformation returns to the sentence forms of (1) and (2) but with the identification of the local term and an indication of some

limitation of the imported attributes. I have already touched on the special meaning of the various forms of "to be" in this kind of metaphorical sentence. It does not mean, as is so often urged, that two apparently different things are in fact one and the same; it is not an assertion of identity. And to call it an assertion of similarity, though not entirely wrong, is too inadequate to be of much use. Rather, "to be" should be transformed into, "For the purpose of the present discourse the referents of the local term and of the imported term are to be considered as belonging to the same category, a category which does not include all of the attributes of the imported category, insofar as that category may be identified by the interpretation of the situation and the information offered, but only those appropriate, to, that is, an emergent category which, unless other information is given, is to be considered as a category only for this sentence." This may seem a great deal for "is" to mean, but it really is not much when we remember that vast metaphysical systems and religious truths have been built from the various forms of this one verb. Richards has long since demonstrated in *How to Read a Page* that "is" has a number of semantic functions.

(6) "That chocolate bar was like a kilowatt, it was so enjoyable." (Or, "That chocolate bar was as enjoyable as a kilowatt.") This crosses the line between the metaphor as a figure of speech and the simile, but not much has been changed. All that has happened is that some of the burden of meaning has been taken off of "to be." The sentence is an assertion that in certain respects a chocolate bar belongs to the category of kilowatts, but not in all respects. One respect is identified—capacity to give enjoyment; but "enjoyment" has so wide a spread of meaning that it does not put very severe limitations on the attributes to be considered appropriate. It rules out anything which may be regarded as in any way disagreeable, so far as the interpreter understands the character of the speaker, but it does not indicate what conventionally enjoyable attributes of the imported term's category are to be considered appropriate.

(7) "That chocolate bar was like a kilowatt, it was enjoyable. I mean it gave me a sense of renewed energy." Here the attribute of enjoyable is further limited to the sensation of suddenly and eas-

ily renewed energy. From here on the appropriate attributes may be limited and refined indefinitely. For instance, "It changed my mood from depression to elation, just as a release of kilowatts can turn darkness into light." And so on.

Though this series does not by any means exhaust the possibilities, it serves to clarify the difference between a metaphor and a simile. That difference consists simply in providing more detailed information about how some form of "to be" is to be interpreted and which attributes made available by the imported term are appropriate to the interpretation of the sentence. The real difference between (1) and (7) as well as between (5) and (6) lies in the demands the speaker makes upon the interpreter and the latter's power of comprehending the situation and understanding the character of the speaker. Each of the transformations in this series could be given a name, as well as other transformation possibilities I have not used. To a certain extent the Renaissance rhetoricians attempted to do so. But there seems to be little purpose in trying, for not even the older rhetoricians succeeded in identifying all the sentence forms in which a metaphor, to use what appears to be the best generic term, can be presented. Actually, the transformation possibilities are so unlimited as to be, for all practical purposes, infinite. The important matter is to be able to recognize a metaphor as a particular kind of semantic function; in practice, that means to recognize that an imported term has been presented and to raise in one's mind the question as to what category and what attributes are appropriate. Above all I would emphasize that it takes two to make a metaphor, a speaker and an interpreter. It is the traditional neglect of the interpreter's role in this communicative transaction that is more responsible than anything else, I think, for the confusion that has traditionally surrounded the whole problem. (It is worth pointing out that speaker and interpreter are *roles*. Both roles may be played by the same individual. We often create metaphors which we have difficulty in interpreting ourselves.)

We may now turn to the second question raised by the proposition that a metaphor functions by attributing certain characteristics to a given phenomenon. What is the semantic necessity for metaphors? Why are they not only normal but frequent in language behavior? We may begin by observing that no isolated phenomenon is comprehensible in and of itself. It has often been pointed out that a taste cannot be described to a person who has never experienced it. But this is equally true of anything which one has never experienced. When we describe something to a person unfamiliar with it—and this includes describing such phenomena to ourselves—we place it in a category or in categories with which, we presume, they are familiar. If they are not, we try again. Thus, to someone who has never tasted a mango, we might say, "It's a blend of peach and pine." Here the local term—mango flavor— is without meaning to the listener. The speaker therefore uses imported terms, one from the category of fruit flavor and one from that of a tree smell, to give an approximate indication of what the listener may expect when he tastes a mango. Further, "blend" is itself a dead metaphor. Now as soon as we place something in a category we imply that all of the attributes of that category are applicable. This is the difference between identification and metaphor. If a botanist discovers a new kind of object in the vegetable kingdom and calls it a tree, he has identified it. He has asserted that all the attributes of the category "tree," as these attributes are conventionalized within his general culture and botanists' subculture, are applicable. But when, wishing to talk about the relationships among the various members of a family through three or four generations, we refer to a genealogical tree, we do not imply that all the attributes of the category "tree" are applicable, but only some of them. We have used a metaphor.

When Bernini wished to present the ecstasy of St. Teresa as something of moral and religious value not to just the saint but rather to all believing Catholics, he used the metaphor of the theater. He placed the statue of St. Teresa and her dart-throwing angel on a platform at the end of a transept. He framed the scene in a proscenium arch and arranged light from concealed sources to illuminate the figures but to leave the transept itself comparatively dark, for the transept has no windows of its own. Then on either side of the transept he placed theatrical boxes in which are visible, in relief, members of the family who donated the shrine. They are engaged in excited discussion about St. Teresa's appearance. This was not an identification, an assertion that the actors in this spiritual drama were playing a part which should not be regarded as belonging to the same category as real events. Rather, the whole scheme is a metaphor to which the imported term, the theater, brings the attributes of an emotional experience so important that it should be separated from ordinary experiences, isolated in one's consciousness, and discussed and thought about publicly. It was an assertion that St. Teresa's experience belongs to the category of human events of the utmost public importance. On the other hand, an unsympathetic nonbeliever who had decided that Bernini was secretly a Protestant might interpret the complex as an assertion that religious experiences of this sort are as false as acting. This brings out the fact that a metaphor is a transaction, that the interpretation of metaphors can be full of perils, and that the application of the wrong category or the use of the wrong attributes of the correct category can result in a completely inappropriate interpretation.

The basic condition for the creation of a metaphor, then, is the presentation to the speaker's consciousness of a phenomenon for which there is no category and therefore are no attributes, or for which, in his judgment, the conventional category and attributes for that phenomenon are inadequate or, as in the mango situation, unusable. Or, to put it another way, (1) no language exists for talking about the phenomenon, or (2) the speaker is ignorant of that language, or (3) the listener is ignorant, or (4) the speaker judges that current language to be inadequate, a judgment for which there can be innumerable reasons. One of the most important is that the speaker finds the conventional language too vague, too imprecise, inclusive of too many categories or of too many attributes for a single category. For this reason it has often been asserted that the function of metaphor is to make language more precise, or to put phenomena in a fresh and novel light. This is true enough, but by no means the whole story.

A good example of (1) is the language used in talking about the meaning of music, a language so metaphorical that a good many individuals deny that music has any meaning at all. Let us assume, however, that music is a semiotic system, and that its signs refer to psychic processes, "movements of the soul," as they have so often been called. To be sure, major is often identified with happiness and minor with sadness, but apart from the fact that the terms "happy" and "sad" are in themselves utterly inadequate for the purpose of precise psychological discourse, there are good reasons to doubt this identification. Currently, then, there is no conventionalized language which identifies the semiotic processes of music with psychological processes, that is, no language which can put both into the same category with reasonably stable attributes. Consequently, the only way to talk about the meaning of music is to use metaphors. Some of these metaphors are almost dead, as in "the *triumphant* conclusion of the fourth movement," but on the whole there is little stability to this metaphorical language and it enjoys no respectable intellectual status.

Types (2) and (3) are primarily problems of cultural level, explaining why the language of simple people tends to be highly metaphorical when they encounter novel phenomena. It seems to be generally true that the more educated a man is and the more he operates on the highest cultural level, and the more thoroughly he has mastered the existing categories, attributes, and terminologies available in a culture, the less dependent he is on metaphor and the more suspicious he is of it. But he too will have to resort to metaphor when he is confronted with the enormous range of specialized objects in a well-equipped hardware store. For complex cultural reasons the dependence of the naïve mind upon metaphor has often led to the assertion that the folk are more poetical than the urbanized, the sophisticated, and the educated. And this in the teeth of the fact that the richest and most rewarding poets have been highly cultivated and educated. Certainly, from the point of view about metaphor presented here, the dependence of the simple mind upon metaphor is a function not of unsullied natural poetic talent, but of ignorance. Part of the sentimentality over the popular use of metaphor comes from the recognition by sophisticated minds of imported terms. To the speakers themselves they are dead. The sentimentality, then, takes its origin from mere unfamiliarity, and also brief encounters with the lower orders, as our British friends once would have said. And it is also worth adding that (2) is often the result of simple laziness. No honest writer or teacher can deny that he often uses metaphors because he refuses to take the trouble to learn the conventional terminology or to dig it out of his memory. Metaphor can be a trouble-saving device; and their worship of metaphor has led many New Critics to use it instead of less easily available but existing and satisfactory nonmetaphorical language. Metaphor can easily be a vice, a lesson which freshmen are forced to learn but which self-indulgent critics forget. Among modern critics Richard Blackmur is the greatest sinner, though the fuzzy-minded Allen Tate is not far behind him. To conceal a platitude behind a novel metaphor, far-fetched and insufficiently informative to be easily comprehensible, is one of the most successful devices of the pretentious writer.

One of the most frequent uses of (4) is the value metaphor. It often occurs that a category, such as tree, for example, is not conventionally recognized as either good or bad; and likewise it is often the case that a category may be ambivalent, such as alcohol. Again the speaker may wish to reverse a normal valuation, such as that conventionally attributed to drugs. Or he may wish to give an intenser valuation than the conventional one, whether it is good or bad. Some examples are, "A poem lovely as a tree," "That needle gave me a real charge," "She's a dog," "She's an angel," and so on.

The most interesting function of type (4) is a consequence of the speaker's recognition of the descriptive and definitional inadequacy; and language is always ultimately inadequate, since it can talk about phenomena only in terms of categories. As Linnaeus realized, a name is useful only when it presents categorial information. Names of human beings, for example, to be useful must also inform us of what family category the individual belongs to; and one of the commonest categorial efforts has been to attempt to establish stable attributes for particular family categories. As a consequence of the inadequacy of language, linguistic invention and semantic imagination truly emerge. But again, when we consider poetry we must be cautious. As I suggested above, metaphorical density is a function of poetic style, the values of that style not being rooted in poetry but in the cultural situation of the time. Nevertheless, it is true that highly valued poets, whether their style calls for a high or low density of metaphor, are notable for freshness, originality, and precision in creating and using metaphors. But it would be a mistake to assert that their poetic power is a consequence of the high quality of their metaphoric invention. I would be embarrassed at asserting that valued poets are verbally gifted, were it not a simple fact so often neglected. Why an individual is verbally gifted we have no idea, we simply know that some people are. We have all had friends who are not writers, who even have no interest in poetry, but whose conversation is nevertheless a continual delight because of their metaphoric creativity. A verbally gifted individual is extremely sensitive to the inadequacies of language. It is but a tautology to say that he is always trying to improve current linguistic and semantic conventions, to refine them, to free language from inadequate conventions. A poet uses striking metaphors not because he is a poet but because he is verbally gifted. What makes him a poet is not his metaphoric agility but something else. (To my mind it is his power to make emotionally significant correlations between the semantic aspect of language on the one hand and the formal—phonemic and syntactic—aspect on the other.)

Nevertheless, there is one further way for accounting for the frequency of fresh and striking metaphors in highly valued poetry, and even, perhaps, for judging a poet, at least to some extent, on his power to invent such metaphors. In discussing the series of metaphors constructed on "chocolate kilowatt," I pointed out that the degrees in that scale were a matter of the demands made upon the interpreter to provide the appropriate categories and select the appropriate attributes. Any novel metaphor breaks with a semantic convention. This in itself elicits in the interpreter a certain amount of emotional disturbance. But when he encounters a novel metaphor which makes extreme demands upon him, his mental disorientation and accompanying emotional disturbance can be very considerable, intense and even severe. He may, and often does, completely lose control of the thread of meaning in the discourse. The use of novel, remote, and demanding metaphors, then, adds considerably to the emotional power of a poem, as in Hopkins. At periods, therefore, when it is held that poetry ought to be emotionally powerful and disturbing, as among the Metaphysicals, the Romantics, the French Symbolists, and English and American poets of the 30 or 40 years after 1912, poets use a high density of novel, remote, and demanding metaphors. But at other times, such as the period of Enlightenment poetry, from Thomson through Cowper, when poetry is supposed to be sentimental or elevating and sublime, but not profoundly disorienting or disturbing, metaphor tends to be conventional and rather sparse. It is not surprising that the Romantics, who wished to increase the emotional power of poetry, became so deeply involved with metaphor, even to the point of identifying metaphor with poetry and poetry with truth. As I have already indicated, this in turn led to the modern position of identifying metaphor with truth.

That notion I hope to have extirpated, though I know well that my hope is in vain. Nevertheless, I believe I have offered grounds for asserting that metaphor is a perfectly normal and necessary semantic phenomenon and that it is mistakenly identified with the very special kind of linguistic behavior we call poetry. We find our way in the world by applying conventional categories and categorial attributes to familiar and unfamiliar phenomena. When those categories and attributes fail us, because they are not applicable, or because we or others are ignorant or lazy, or because the categories and attributes are insufficiently precise or insufficiently emotional, we resort to metaphor and create new or emergent categories. Sometimes these emergent categories become conventionalized; more often they do not. But whatever happens to them, and no matter how easy or demanding they are, how familiar or how novel, we create them by a kind of thinking and linguistic and semantic behavior which is no different from our normal behavior of this sort, which is indeed—so stupid are we—the only kind we have.

(*Note:* The basic notions of this paper emerged from attempting to meet the stimulating challenges made by Dr. E. Anthony James of Lehigh University to my brief discussion of metaphor—particularly to my adoption of Richard's terminology— in *Word, Meaning, Poem*.)

22

THE

INTENTIONAL? FALLACY?

[1968*]

Nowadays in literary academic circles one hears with increasing frequency such remarks as, "The New Criticism is a dead issue," or "The New Critics have had their day; it's all over with." However, a more accurate statement of the current condition is that the tenets of the New Criticism have so deeply entered current teaching, scholarship, and criticism that, if the issues are dead, it is only because the New Critical solution to those issues has completely triumphed. Certainly, the more sophisticated undergraduate and graduate students I have recently encountered now take as self-evident attitudes which only a generation ago were heatedly argued against by what used to be called the old-fashioned biographical critic. Of the various bits of critical jargon which were once, at any rate, worth fighting about, perhaps the most commonly encountered is the "intentional fallacy."

* Delivered at the University of Kentucky, February, 1968. Reprinted by permission from *The New Orleans Review*, I (Winter, 1969), pp. 116–64. Copyright © 1969 by Loyola University, New Orleans.

The first of two famous articles by Professor Monroe C. Beardsley, then at Yale, now of the Swarthmore Philosophy Department, and Professor W. K. Wimsatt, Jr., of the Yale English Department, "The Intentional Fallacy," was published in the *Sewanee Review*, Vol. LIV (Summer, 1946). At the time that journal was one of the most distinguished and conspicuous places to publish any discussion of literary criticism or any performance of it, and the phrase entered the language of criticism with the utmost rapidity. A good many regarded that essay, and still regard it, as the clincher for the validity of the New Criticism. It has been reprinted several times in anthologies of criticism and aesthetics, and in 1954 it was collected with its companion, "The Affective Fallacy," in Wimsatt's *The Verbal Icon*, published by the University of Kentucky Press. As such things go, it is now a generation old and a critical classic.

Everybody knows, of course, what the phrase means, or at least what he thinks it means; but I daresay a good many people might be a little puzzled if they actually read the essay, for I know from diligent inquiry that a great many who use the term have never read the paper from which it comes. However, Professor E. D. Hirsch is one critic who has read it recently, and it is instructive to observe what he says about it in his recent book *Validity of Interpretation* (New Haven, 1966).

The critic of the arguments in that essay is faced with the problem of distinguishing between the essay itself and the popular use that has been made of it, for what is widely taken for granted as established truth was not argued in that essay and could not have been successfully argued in the essay. Although Wimsatt and Beardsley carefully distinguished between three types of intentional evidence, acknowledging that two of them are proper and admissible, their careful distinctions and qualifications have now vanished in the popular version which consists in the false and facile dogma that what an author intended is irrelevant to the meaning of his text (p. 11).

I admire Hirsch's book, but it has serious weaknesses, and this discussion of the intentional fallacy is among its least convincing sections. He has excellently expressed what he calls "the popular version" in the title of the section in which the discussion occurs,

"It Does Not Matter What an Author Means." The question is, is there any justification in the original essay for this "popular version"?

To begin with, I must say that I do not find "The Intentional Fallacy" either clear, well argued, or coherent. Indeed many of the authors' fundamental propositions are not argued at all. They are merely asserted, by fiat. The essay's success can only be accounted for by the fact that its dogmatisms were uttered in a situation in which a great many people were prepared to accept them without argument. If the "popular version" has indeed been mistaken, it is perhaps because the mere title was enough for a good many critics, teachers, and students; it said all they wanted to have said; it summed up the doctrine of the New Criticism in a brilliant phrase which also gave fairly precise directions for the kind of verbal response one should make to a poem in interpreting it. Actually, the essay is rather careless, and so is Hirsch's account of it. For example, he asserts that the authors "carefully distinguished between three types of intentional evidence." It is not nit-picking to point out that the authors do *not* distinguish between three types of intentional evidence. Rather, they distinguish between three types of "internal and external evidence for the meaning of a poem," and they assert that one of these types, the biographical, which they call external, private, and idiosyncratic, "need not involve intentionalism," but that it usually has, to the distortion of poetic interpretation. That is, when Hirsch writes "three types of intentional evidence," he has ascribed "intentional" to three types of evidence which Beardsley and Wimsatt specifically said were not intentional evidence.

This shows not only that Hirsch was so over-eager to prove that it is correct to talk about intention that he missed the Beardsley-Wimsatt point but also that the essay is easily misunderstood, or at least that it needs to be read with great care. There is, moreover, another reason for bringing up Hirsch. His book is, I believe, going to be widely read and will have a very great influence. It is undeniably an important work. No doubt his version of the Beardsley-Wimsatt essay will be pretty generally accepted as authoritative. Without wishing, therefore, to impugn the value of his work, I think it is of some importance to determine whether or not what Hirsch calls the false and facile popular version of "The Intentional Fallacy" has any justification in the essay itself, and this will serve also to begin an attack on what is a very vexing problem.

Professor Hirsch has subsumed the notion that "what an author intended is irrelevent to the meaning of his text" under the doctrine of "semantic autonomy." It is a good phrase, and I shall adopt it. Beardsley and Wimsatt exemplify it when they write that "the design or intention of the author is neither available nor desirable as a standard for judging the success of a work of literary art." (For "work of literary art" I shall henceforth use the term "poem.") Thus their primary interest is in evaluation, not in interpretation; but their argument amounts to the proposition that intention is irrelevant to evaluation because it is irrelevant to interpretation. At several points in the essay this assumption of the irrelevance of intention comes out very strongly. For example, "In this respect poetry differs from practical messages, which are successful if and only if we correctly infer the intention." Thus it is evident that, according to Beardsley and Wimsatt, the semantic functions of poetry are to be distinguished from those of ordinary language. Again, poetry "is detached from the author at birth and goes about the world beyond his power to intend about it or control it). The poem belongs to the public. It is embodied in language, the peculiar possession of the public." This last would seem to indicate that poetry is not, after all, distinguishable from ordinary language, until we note that the "poem is embodied in language." This certainly seems to indicate that it is other than language. Further, if practical messages require that we infer the intention it would seem that practical messages are not beyond the power of their utterers to intend about them or control them. Moreover, our authors say in a note, "And the history of words *after* a poem is written may contribute meanings which if revelant to the original pattern should not be ruled out by a scruple about intention." From other statements we glean that "pattern" here means "pattern of meanings," for "Poetry is a feat of style by which a complex of meaning is handled all at once." It would certainly be strange for practical messages—in which the authors include such kinds of discourse as science—to be open to new semantic functions. This note, then, seems coherent with the doctrine of semantic autonomy. Finally, at the end of the essay they write that to ask Eliot what "Prufrock" means "would not be a critical inquiry." To ask a poet what he meant would be "consulting the oracle," a superstitious act, presumably. At any rate, it cannot settle a critical inquiry having to do with exegesis.

All this, then, is coherent with the first quotation, which asserts that for practical messages it is legitimate to inquire for the author's intention. It is evident that we do indeed have here an instance of semantic autonomy and that the notion that this famous essay is an exemplification of that doctrine is correct. Hirsch is mistaken in thinking that the doctrine of Beardsley and Wimsatt is different from the popular version. By Hirsch's standards they stand condemned of the "false and facile dogma that what an author intended is irrelevant to the meaning of his text." The popular version is, after all, the correct one.

It is not difficult to refute the doctrine of semantic autonomy. It can be put in the form of asserting that poetry has unique semantic functions, different from those of all other kinds of linguistic utterance. It is evident that, in its radical form, this is not an historical or cultural statement: it does not mean, for example, that in a given cultural epoch poets are, as it were, assigned a class of message that they and they alone are privileged to deliver. No, the poem is embodied in language; presumably, then, either in practical messages something nonpoetic is embodied, and this gives poetry semantic autonomy, or it means that the mode of embodiment is unique, or at least different from the mode of embodiment to be found in practical messages, which is ordinarily taken to mean all nonpoetic messages. In this kind of criticism, as in the essay under consideration, the distinction is ordinarily confused, and perhaps it is unimportant; nevertheless, it is a distinction worth noting for what follows. In either case, however, the consequence is that the critic is privileged, or perhaps required, to employ a special kind of interpretation, called in this essay poetic "exegesis." That is, since poetry has semantic autonomy, there is a corresponding interpretive autonomy. Whether or not this kind of interpretation differs from the interpretational modalities used to interpret all other kinds of discourse depends upon the demonstration that there is a distinction between the two. But that in turn depends upon a basis for the interpretation, namely a general theory of interpretation. But such a general theory of interpretation does not exist. There is, therefore, at the present time no way of demonstrating either interpretive autonomy or semantic autonomy for poetry.

Furthermore, if the language of semantic autonomy differs from ordinary language, it would seem to follow that the language of interpretive autonomy differs from the language of ordinary interpretation. It is the objectors to the New Criticism and to semantic autonomy who claim that the New Critics offer not interpretation but another poem. The latter have always vehemently denied this, thus asserting that the validity of interpretive autonomy is not different from the validity, whatever it may be, of any mode of interpretation. Our authors give an example of this. In objecting to a scholarly interpretation of a metaphor by Donne, they assert that, "To make the geocentric and heliocentric antithesis the core of the metaphor is to disregard the English language, to prefer private evidence to public, external to internal." One of their points is that "moving of the earth" is antithetical to "trepidation of the spheres," not parallel, as their target, Charles Coffin, would have it. Assuming that Coffin is wrong, as I too think he is, it is impossible to use this disagreement for their theoretical purposes. Coffin may have been carried away by his learning and may have violated common sense in making this mistake; but it is only a mistake. "Moving of the earth" can be explained in terms of the Copernican hypothesis, even though it may be wrong to do so here. Galileo is said to have said that, after all, the earth does move, though he was speaking Italian; and it seems quite fantastic to maintain that the geocentric and heliocentric theories are private evidence. The point of all this is that in arguing against Coffin, Beardsley and Wimsatt use the same kind of language that he does, the same kind of evidence, public knowledge, and the same kind of interpretive mode. To assert that a man has failed is not to assert that his method is in error, though Beardsley and Wimsatt seem to think so.

There are other ways of showing the impossibility of the doctrine of semantic autonomy, but it is much more instructive to
examine and if possible to understand what kind of doctrine it is.
It is probable that today Professor Beardsley would consider the
proposition that a poem is embodied in language as exceedingly
incautious, and it is possible that Professor Wimsatt would feel
the same way, but we may be grateful for the statement, for it
tells us a good deal. The notion of something suprasensible being
embodied in something sensible—for both written and spoken
words are phenomenal and sensible—has an irresistibly transcendental ring about it. One could say that all they mean by this is
that something originally in the mind of the poet is now embodied
in language, but their own position, of course, forbids them to
take this way out: it would throw them back on intentionalism.
Now, anyone familiar with Christian doctrine can recognize the
embodiment thesis as structurally identical with the theory of
transubstantiation. Since, however, these days very few are familiar with the thesis of transubstantiation, including a good
many professing and practicing Christians, it may be well to
define it. It is the thesis that in the celebration of the mass the substance of the bread and the wine become changed to the body and
the blood of Christ, though their accidents, such as taste, color,
smell, and so on, remain the same. Thus the consecrated bread
and wine belong, after this metamorphosis, to a unique category
of physical substances.

The structural analogy to the doctrine of the semantic autonomy of poetry is remarkable. A suprasensible quality, poetry, is
embodied in a sensible quality, language, and the result is a
unique category of language, which requires a unique kind of
interpretation. Carlstadt asserted that the bread and wine could
not possibly be put into a unique category of physical substances,
and that the Lord's Supper was a commemorative rite. Zwingli
adopted this thesis, but Luther developed the theory of consub-
stantiation; the substance and accidents are not changed but a
quality is added, as heat is added to an iron bar. In terms of the
structural analogy proposed this changes little or nothing; the
doctrine of semantic autonomy asserts also that a suprasensible

quality is added to a sensible quality. It is noteworthy that the clear-sighted Erasmus felt that the Zwinglian position was irrefutable, but preferred the old doctrine for the sake of peace.

The argument that Carlstadt originated and Zwingli and Oecolampadius and their followers accepted was in fact an instance of semantic analysis, and quite an elegant one. The argument centered on the word "is" in such Gospel passages as that found in Matt. 26:26–28. "And as they were eating, Jesus took bread and blessed it, and brake it, and gave it to the disciples, and said, Take, eat; this is my body. And he took the cup, and gave thanks and gave it to them, saying, Drink ye all of it; for this is my blood of the new testament, which is shed for many for the remission of sins." The new position claimed that in such phrases as "this is my body" and "this is my blood" the word "is" should properly be interpreted as "is a sign of," rather than, as in the orthodox interpretation, "has become in a unique mode." Using the language that is here under question, the reformers were claiming that it was the intention of Jesus that his act should not be so interpreted, while the orthodox claimed that Jesus' intention was as they had defined it. This analysis suggests that to call upon "intention" is a way of explaining and justifying an interpretation rather than a way of using knowledge of intention to control an interpretation. The possibility arises that Beardsley and Wimsatt, in distinguishing language that requires inference of intention from language that does not, have failed to make a sufficiently exacting analysis of the term "intention."

To this possibility I shall return. At the moment I would only remark that for the phrase "the doctrine of semantic autonomy" it would be reasonable to substitute "the doctrine of semantic real presence." This is a metaphor, of course, but that does not necessarily mean that it is a falsification of the semantic state of affairs we find here. Whether theologically correct or not, the reformers were claiming that the orthodox were indulging in bad thinking because the doctrine of transubstantiation was an example of ascribing to the sign of something the attributes of the thing itself. In this case, since the thing itself has ceased to exist— the episode of the last supper having had an historical existence— the body and blood said to be in the bread and wine as a consequence of transubstantiation have no existence. The reformers' denial of transubstantiation amounted to the assertion that the orthodox had made a logical error and had hypostatized or reified the nonexistent referent of a pair of words. Likewise, by the doctrine of semantic real presence, as applied in the assertion that a poem is embodied in language, Beardsley and Wimsatt have hypostatized the term "poem." Having done so, and having decided that poetry has certain attributes and not others, they then ascribe those attributes to a category of utterances. Thus the doctrines of transubstantiation and of semantic autonomy are instances of the same kind of thinking, or, to be a bit more precise, of semantic behavior. Consequently it is a justifiable metaphor to call the doctrine of semantic autonomy the doctrine of semantic real presence.

What kind of thinking is it? In magic we can see the same semantic behavior at work, or at least in certain kinds. Take the old stand-by, the wax image to which you give your enemy's name and which you stick full of pins and knives. Here again we have the sign, the ascription to the sign of the attributes of the thing signified, and behaving accordingly, that is, placing it in a special category of physical substances, or, as in semantic autonomy, verbal signs. On the whole this kind of magic seems intellectually more respectable than does semantic autonomy. After all, the waxen sign is a sign of something, a living enemy, not a sign of a reified verbal sign, poetry. Now it is also worth noting that the practitioner of magic cannot be refuted. Either his enemy dies, in which case he killed him by stabbing his waxen sign, or his enemy lives, in which case he made a mistake in magical technique. If he lives longer than his enemy, and continues his magical technique, he is bound, sooner or later, to have proof that his magic is efficacious. Likewise, any conclusion arrived at by the doctrine of semantic autonomy cannot be refuted. The easiest way to grasp this is to remind oneself of how frequently one sees it asserted that all interpretations of a poem are equally valid, the criterion being "interesting," rather than "true" or more or less "adequate."

Structurally, then, transubstantiation and semantic autonomy are instances of magic. Consequently, the doctrine of semantic autonomy in poetry may be justly called the magical theory of poetry. It is, however, useful to consider all three as examples of the same kind of semiotic behavior and look for a more general statement of that. I think it may be found in the theory of immanent meaning, which is undoubtedly the universal theory, a theory which we are only beginning to see through. It is simply the thesis that words mean, or, alternatively, have meaning. Even so sophisticated a philosophical position as logical positivism accepted this position, as the famous attempt to distinguish between metaphysical or emotional statements and empirical statements witnesses. The former were said to be meaningless, and the latter to have meaning, or to be meaningful. Meaning was said to be immanent in the latter, but not in the former. The inadequacy of this position comes out when we glance at the word "reference." Words are said to have reference. But when I say, "Look at the ceiling," you look at the ceiling, the sentence does not.

It is not difficult to see how the notion of immanent reference should arise. When I generate an overt utterance, and tell you to look at the ceiling, you perform an act of reference, but you do it in response to my instructions. It is a verbal shorthand, therefore, to say that I have referred to the ceiling. But since my utterance is, among its other semantic functions, a sign of me, by another similar slip the act of reference is imputed to the utterance. Or it can go from your reference to the utterance to me, and by "it" I mean the chain of ascribing to the sign of something the attributes of that which it signifies. Thus you have attributed your attribute of reference first to me and then to the utterance, or first to the utterance and then to me.

Human beings, then, refer; words do not. Words are signs to which, on interpretation, we respond by various modes of behavior, verbal and nonverbal. The meaning of a bit of language is the behavior which is consequent upon responding to it. Therefore, *any* response to a discourse is *a* meaning of that discourse. That is why an interpretation arrived at on the basis of semantic autonomy cannot be invalidated. However, language is a matter of conventions. Thus the correct meaning of an utterance is the consequent behavior which, for whatever reasons, is considered appropriate in the situation in which the utterance is generated.

For example, if I say, "There is no God," and my respondent says, "That is a meaningless utterance," the response amounts to a claim that it is impossible that there should exist a situation in which any response at all could be appropriate, except for this response.

Let me sum up this position dogmatically, though not without leaning a bit on authority. Forty years ago Grace Andrus de Laguna, of Bryn Mawr College, published her *Speech: Its Function and Development*, a work which, long neglected, has been reissued and is being given serious attention. Her basic proposition is that both the animal cry and speech "perform the same fundamental function of *coördinating the activities of the members of the group.*" To put it another way, all that the generator of an utterance can do is present a set of instructions for behavior, either his own or another's; and all the responder to an utterance can do is to follow those instructions, or not follow them. That is, if he knows how to interpret those instructions he can, if he so decides, behave in accordance with what in that situation is the conventionalized appropriate responsible behavior. I tell you to look at the ceiling; you look at the floor. You have obeyed only part of my instructions. I tell you to look at the ceiling; you fold your arms and glare at me. Have you disobeyed all of my instructions? Not at all. Any linguistic utterance is first of all an instruction to respond. That response to an instruction is so deeply built into your biological equipment that you cannot possibly avoid it. We may discern, then, three kinds of response to any utterance: inappropriate response, partially appropriate response, appropriate response. These are the meanings of an utterance.

At first glance it may seem that I am about to assert that the doctrine of semantic autonomy opens the way to justifying any inappropriate response. Not at all, and for these reasons. The error of immanent meaning is, for the vast majority of human interactions, not an error at all, or rather is an error of not the slightest importance. When we say, "This is the real meaning of that utterance," we are simply responding to the conventions of appropriateness for the situation in which we respond to the utterance. Obviously, then, uncertainty about meaning arises when the conventions are unknown, are imperfectly known, or are disregarded. But why should they ever be disregarded? Once the magical theory of language has taken root, as it has in all living humans who have progressed through infancy, any utterance becomes a sign the response to which entails conforming one's behavior to a set of conventions appropriate to a situation. Thus, in any sign response there are two ingredients, the sign and the conventionalized behavior patterns. By the magical theory of language, or immanent meaning, we ascribe to the sign the attributes of those behaviors. Thus, in responding to a sign we neglect the complementary circumstance that we are responding to a sign and its situation. To put it another way, the sign on which we focus is but one of many situational signs; it is but one in a constellation of signs. Since all signs are polysemous, that is, since all signs can be, theoretically, responded to by all possible behaviors, the only limit being the conventions we have learned, the sign on which we focus loses its compelling and unitary function to the degree to which we neglect the other signs in the situational constellation of signs. Without trying to trace the history of human semiotic evolution, it is sufficient to point out that the written language preserves an utterance long after the situation in which it was uttered has ceased to exist; this is what Zwingli and his reformers were trying to do, restore the situation in which Jesus' statements about the bread and the wine originally took place and determine their semantic function, that is, the appropriate behavior in response to his words according to the conventions of that situation. Conversely, human beings have the power of imagination, the capacity to create strings of verbal signs to which neither nonverbal response is possible nor nonverbal or verbal response is possible. From that it is but a step to a kind of discourse to which nonverbal overt response is possible but not appropriate. And from there it is but another step to discourse to which overt nonverbal response is currently unknown but for which its situational constellation instructs us to attempt to discover appropriate and overt nonverbal response, as with a scientific theory, with its concomitant situational and conventional instruction to devise an experiment to confirm or disconfirm it.

Thus there are numerous situations in human affairs in which the constellation of supporting situational signs is missing, are conventionally in part disregarded, never existed, or are unconsciously responded to. And here by "unconscious" I mean all signs not focused on, or, more precisely, all signs the attributes of which have been ascribed to another sign or other signs. To respond to a situation thoroughly means to focus in turn on all the signs in that situation, determine whether or not they are appropriate, and to reascribe to each sign its appropriate attributes. Thus, if we go into a chapel to pray and to experience emotional relief as a consequence, a thorough examination of the situation will show that the emotional relief experienced is a consequence of responding not only to the prayer but also to all the religious signs of the setting in which we have played the suppliant's role. Consequently, I do not assert that the use of the doctrine of immanent meaning, or magical meaning, or semantic real presence, or semantic autonomy in interpreting poetry opens the way to any inappropriate response. It is not quite trivial to point out that any interpretive response is, for poetry, frequently, though not always, appropriate. (Some would assert that it is never appropriate.) Nor is it at all trivial to point out that the semantic autonomist focuses on only a very limited number of verbal signs. Even when in theory he claims that a proper interpretation must necessarily provide a unitary explanation for all terms in the poem, in practice he neglects a great many. Furthermore, his interpretation of a good many words such as articles, prepositions, and conjunctions usually conforms to the conventions of interpretation for those terms. In fact, he is usually so taken with the free-wheeling possibilities for novel interpretations of nouns and verbs, with lesser attention to adjectives and adverbs, that he suffers from a singular paucity of seeing alternative possibilities for the lesser words as well as for syntactical relations. This is not surprising. A theory of immanent meaning inevitably leads to the neglect of the situational sign constellation, to, as it were, the neglect of focusing on focusing; the consequence is a compulsive ascription of attributes from what is signified to the sign focused on.

At this point something of a digression may illuminate what I am trying to say and provide a bit of relief from these dreadful abstractions. Professor Hirsch begins his *Validity in Interpretation* with a quotation from Northrop Frye, the source of which, unfortunately, he does not give us. It goes as follows: "It has been said of Boehme that his books are like a picnic to which the author brings the words and the reader the meaning. The remark may have been intended as a sneer at Boehme, but it is an exact description of all works of literary art without exception." It is clear that this statement enrages Professor Hirsch. It enrages me, too; but I do not think that his reply to it is adequate. And his reply, alas, is his book. Certainly, Hirsch was well advised to pick Northrop Frye as his point of departure, for the *Anatomy of Criticism* terminated the theoretical development of the New Criticism, which to be sure was never very powerful. In that book Frye took the doctrine of semantic real presence to its absolute limits: all poems mean the same thing. After that one either decided that the central doctrine of the New Criticism was absurd, as Hirsch probably did; or one concluded that it was now so well protected, so thoroughly proved, that it was not longer arguable and was self-evident. Even if one did not agree with Frye on the thing that all poems mean, he provided a theoretical carte-blanche to make one's own thing that all poems mean.

However, Professor Hirsch has unfortunately attacked Frye and semantic autonomy from an outmoded position, and I fear that his book, for all its many excellencies, will not have the salutary effect I am sure he hoped for, and that I hoped for when I started reading it. For the unfortunate fact is that Frye is right, as far as he goes. He merely does not go far enough. Hirsch's whole effort is to prove that the author brings the meaning as well as the words, and he does as much with this thesis as, I think, is possible, or at least worthwhile. However, Frye's statement is correct if divested of the theory of semantic autonomy and re-written as follows: "It has been said of Boehme that his books are like a picnic to which the author brings the words and the reader the meaning. The remark may have been intended as a sneer at Boehme, but it is an exact description *of all linguistic utterances without exception.*"

Everything said here about the human response to signs points to one fact: the response to a sign requires on the responder's part a decision. To be sure, this statement may seem to need some qualification, and perhaps does. The rapidity of most responses to verbal and nonverbal signs alike certainly seems to indicate that the decision is immediate; that is, if by decision we mean those sign responses in which there is observable hesitation, as well as those in which alternatives are so fully explored that years may elapse before the response actually occurs, then it would indeed seem that the use of "decision" to refer to apparently immediate responses is inaccurate. I think the point is arguable, but until we understand a great deal more than we do about brain physiology, there is little value in arguing it. It is enough to say that a sign which involves the responder in uncertainty requires a decision if it is to be responded to, and that any utterance encountered in a situation other than the one in which it was originally generated offers the possibility of uncertainty and hence decision, unless, as with the bread and the wine, it has been, according to Zwingli, made part of a new situational sign constellation. This explains why Beardsley and Wimsatt can assert that meanings that emerge after a poem is written should not be ruled out by a scruple of intention. Thus, though I do not know if the position has any theological respectability or has ever even appeared in the history of theology, it would be possible to say that what Jesus meant in his remarks to the apostles is irrelevant; and I rather suspect that Newman's idea of the growth of Christian doctrine entails just this, the explanation being that though the Apostles would not have interpreted the remarks as the theory of transubstantiation does, that theory was implicit in Christian doctrine from the moment of its revelation. Thus it is not surprising that Professor Beardsley in his *Aesthetics*, published in 1958, should say that a semantic definition of literature is that "a literary work is a discourse in which an important part of the meaning is implicit" (p. 126). Such is the necessary consequence of any magical use of the theory of immanent meaning. And indeed Hirsch's discussion of "implicit" is not one of his happier passages. In fact, with his fundamental notion that meaning is expression in language of a willed intention on the part of an utterer, it is evident that Hirsch also is working from a doctrine of immanent meaning. Thus, for all his efforts—and many of them are admirable and useful—he cannot dispose of the doctrine of semantic autonomy with complete and unequivocal success. This is what I mean when I assert that his book will not have the salutary effect he hopes for.

Poems that as teachers and students and critics we attempt to interpret do not fall in the same category as transubstantiation; an alternative semantic function has not been conventionalized in an historically emergent situation. We ask what the poem means. That is sufficient evidence for our purpose that uncertainty is present, and that a decision must be made. The poems we deal with were uttered in the past; the situations in which they were uttered are no longer existent. What are we to do? We must make a decision about what is the appropriate verbal response. On what grounds are such decisions properly made? That vast question I do not propose to answer here. My interest here is only to question the function of asking questions about the intention of the poet, and also to question the strategy of denying that such questions are in order when we interpret a poem.

Let us return to the point at which we started, the Beardsley-Wimsatt proposal that for one category of discourse it is improper to ask questions about intention, but for another category we must "correctly infer the intention." It would seem, therefore, that there are such things as correct intentional statements, and that it is possible to locate something properly called "intention." What is the status, then, of statements about intention? As we have seen, all a statement can do is give instructions for responsive behavior. What we call a referential statement—whether it be a book or a word—gives instructions for locating a phenomenal configuration. But it is not so easy as that. All signs are categorial. Thus a referential statement instructs us to locate a category of configurations. To instruct us to infer correctly the intention of the speaker of a particular utterance is to instruct us to locate a specific member of a category. Language, then, apparently can be specific in this qualified sense. But it must be observed that specificity is achieved, and a categorial member located, only because that particular member shares attributes with other members of the same category. Further, it is possible to tell one member from another only if the instructional statement includes other categorial instructions. Here the good old game of fish, flesh, or fowl is helpful, as is the recently deceased "What's My Line?" The person or persons having to guess the correct word proceed, within certain rules, by piling up categories the partially shared attributes of which gradually eliminate all but one specific term. In locating nonverbal specificities we proceed in the same way. On the other hand, interlocking categories need not be included in the instruction if the respondent is previously trained to do the locating without such instructions. If I say to someone in a room, "Bring me the chair," he would be at a loss to know which one I meant. However, if my instructions were to bring me the chair which is the darkest in color, the interlocking categories of chair, color, and shade would make it possible to respond appropriately to my instructions, even though I myself did not yet know which chair corresponded to these specifications. Likewise, one member of a group can respond correctly to a simple, "Bring me the chair," if at some previous time I have instructed him sufficiently in the interlocking categories necessary for his appropriate response.

Beardsley and Wimsatt, then, have instructed us to infer the intention of a speaker. Thus in the situation just outlined an already instructed member of the audience infers that when I say, "Bring me the chair," his appropriate response is to take to me the previously designated chair. Now a problem arises, first, if it is the case that in my judgment his response is in fact inappropriate, and that my response to his action is to assert, "I didn't mean you, blockhead"; and second, if the speaker of the instructions is no longer present in the situation in which the utterance is responded to. The normal test for appropriate behavior—the response of the speaker of the uttered instructions—is under these conditions impossible. Inference, therefore, is a term used to categorize this last kind of situation, one in which the instructions for response are incomplete and the authoritative judge of appropriateness of response is no longer present. What is the appropriate response in a situation of this sort, one which is characterized by uncertainty about what response is appropriate?

The Beardsley-Wimsatt proposal to infer the intention of a speaker seems at first glance to be a referential statement. It seems to instruct us to locate something, namely an intention. The word "intention" is like such words as "will," "desire," "meaning," and "purpose." They are said to be mental activities; they are supposed to occur in the mind. However, if, as we have seen, all terms are categorial and cannot bear a specific reference to a unique phenomenal configuration, then the status of the mind as such a phenomenal configuration is called in doubt. Indeed, when we ask what the mind is we are often given a list of its attributes, such as will, desire, meaning, purpose, and so on; and these are said to be the mind's contents. But this is nothing but a spatial metaphor, and these terms are but the attributes of the verbal category "mind." We may see this from another point of view. Every semiotic response involves interpretation, since we do not respond to a meaning immanent in the sign; and one of the most obvious things in the world is interpretational variability, the easily and constantly observed phenomenon that two people in the identical situation, judging by their overt responses, have interpreted that situation's signs differently. That is, all the word "interpretation" does is to draw attention to the actuality and possibility of difference of response to a given sign, or, more generally, to difference in sign response. "Mind," then, categorizes all responsive activity which exhibits differences in sign response, that is, for reasons suggested earlier, all responsive activity, which is all activity. The word "mind" then is a category which ascribes to human beings, at least, behavioral differences in the same situation. And words like "will," "desire," "meaning," "purpose," and "intention" are terms which discriminate various subcategories of behavioral difference. It follows, then, that the Beardsley-Wimsatt proposal to infer the intention of a speaker is not a referential statement; it does not and cannot give us instructions to locate a phenomenal configuration. If they believe it can, they are guilty of that common consequence of the theory of immanent meaning, hypostatization.

What kind of instruction, then, is their proposal? What would be an appropriate response? Some utterances instruct us to locate phenomenal configurations, to be sure; but others instruct us to generate verbal behavior. Such responses are the most mysterious and fascinating that human beings perform. Since language is tied to the world only by behavior, when the response to a generated utterance is only to generate another verbal response, it is not tied to the world at all, or at best only at various points, most frequently at the beginning of a chain of utterances, and, hopefully, at the end. One semantic function of the term "mind" is precisely to draw attention to this transcendence of the world by language. It is not mind that is metaphysical but language, and it can be said with justice that all language, by itself, is metaphysical. It is not, then, that language is the product of the mind; "linguistic behavior" is one semantic function of the word "mind."

To see what kind of instructions Beardsley and Wimsatt have given us in their proposal that for practical messages we infer the intention it is only necessary to examine the ordinary use of the word "intention" from this orientation. When in ordinary circumstances, that is, situations in which the speaker of the utterance we are responding to is actually present, we ask the speaker what he meant when we do not understand the utterance, that is, when we are uncertain as to what verbal or nonverbal response we should offer in response to his utterance, ordinarily he will give us additional instructions; this is one mode of explanation. "Bring me the chair!" "What do you mean?" "Pick up that chair, which is the darkest in color in the room, and bring it to me!" But instead of answering, "What do you mean?" we could elicit the same response, or get the same set of additional instructions, by asking, "What do you intend me to do?" or "What is your intention?" We will have, then, a general understanding of the term "intention" if we recognize that it instructs us how to categorize a certain kind of explanation, one given in response to a demand for additional instructions. But what does intention instruct us to do if the original speaker is not present? This is a more subtle problem.

Let us imagine that when I ask you to bring me a chair, instead of asking me what my intention is, you turn to a neighbor and ask him, "What does he mean? What does he intend me to do? What is his intention?" Let us assume that the neighbor has privileged information and gives the answer I gave when I was asked. Supposing that you carry out the instructions, make the appropriate response. When it comes to judging that appropriateness, which, as we have seen, is the only way possible to judge whether or not the response is correct, does the neighbor's statement of intention have as much authority as mine? Perhaps so, since we defined him as having privileged information, that is, information I gave him. However, if he does not have the information, but generates his intentional statement from his interpretation of the situation, including his prior knowledge of the sort of thing I am likely to say in such situations, does his statement of intention now have as much authority as mine? Again, in terms of your response, yes; but possibly no, since at first glance it would seem that I must know my intention better than he could. Supposing now that you ask me, as you probably feel like doing, what my intention is in going through all this analytical rigamarole merely to demolish a position which by my account I have long since demolished? Presumably my answer—and at the end of this paper I shall offer an answer—is a report on what I intended to do when I set out to write this paper. This means, first, that I must have stated my intention to myself, because "intention" categorizes a class of statement, and second, that I consider that I have carried it out, that I have obeyed those self-directing instructions. Now as it happens in this particular instance the statement of intention I shall give as my conclusion was not generated as covert verbal behavior before I began to write but occurred to me only after the above question about my intention had occurred to me as a very sensible question to ask.

We may speak of two kinds of intention. One is accessible, a class of instructions or a class of explanations, that is, further instructions. But psychic intention is inaccessible. It happens, whatever it is, between the stimulus and response; it is responsible for those variations in interpretation and behavior which "mind" in one of its semantic functions categorizes. But in the sense that "mind" refers to what happens between stimulus and response, it is a word that we use as a bridge to cross an abyss of absolute ignorance. But furthermore, in actual behavior, psychic intention is doubly inaccessible. When we seem to be reporting on psychic intention we are in fact reporting on an historical event; the psychic intention happened before our statement about it, which we take to be a report on it. But, as we all know, historical events are phenomenally no longer existent. Whatever we say about them is not a report but a linguistic construct of a report of an event, and, for psychic intention, an inaccessible event.

Suppose you say to me, "It is obvious from the tone of your paper that your deliberate intention was to bore me to distraction while confusing me." Whether I agree with you or disagree, my answer will be, like yours, an explanation of a verbally constructed historical event, not of a phenomenally existent event. That is, both of us have responded to the ongoing situation; we have interpreted that situation; and we have offered an explanation of what is happening in that situation. That is, when you surmise a psychic intention that occurred in the past and I say that I am reporting such a psychic intention, neither of us is doing either of these. We are both making an historical construct in order to provide an explanation for the discourse we are currently encountering. Hence it follows that "to infer an intention" means to make a linguistic construct of an historical situation so that by responding to the semiotic constellation of that constructed situation we may gain additional instructions for deciding the appropriate verbal response to an utterance to which our initial response was decisional uncertainty. And this is true whether the utterance under consideration was originally uttered two minutes ago or two thousand years ago. The difference is one of relative difficulty, not of kind of behavior. Briefly, an inference of intention is a way of accounting for or explaining the generation of an utterance; it can never be a report. The speaker of an utterance has greater authority than anybody else in his so-called intentional inference only because he is likely to have more information for framing his historical construct, *not* because he generated the utterance.

From this point of view it is not difficult to understand what has happened when you assert that my intention was so-and-so, and I respond, "I wasn't aware of it, but I guess you're right; indeed, as I think the matter over, I'm sure you are right. What you are saying *was* my unconscious intention." In such cases I am simply admitting that your responsiveness to the reconstructed situation is superior to mine. The very fact that such chains of linguistic utterance can occur indicates that it is only probable that an utterer has superior authority in generating an intentional explanation; it is never certain; it is, then, always a matter for investigation, never for a priori fiat.

It is now possible to see with some clarity, I hope, the kind of error that Beardsley and Wimsatt have made. It is not merely that the doctrine of semantic autonomy is an error; just as important is their error in thinking that it is *ever* possible to locate an historical psychic intention. The inference of intention is an attempt to provide additional instructions for determining our response to the stimulus of a verbal utterance when we are uncertain. Even so fantastic an instance of providing additional instructions for interpreting poetic utterances as the *Anatomy of Criticism* is only that: an attempt to provide additional instructions. The doctrine of semantic autonomy, untenable on other grounds, is also untenable because it attempts to assert by a priori fiat that a certain class of additional instructions is, for the interpretation of poetry, inadmissible. But such a distinction is untenable because both semantic autonomous interpretation and so-called intentional interpretation do nothing more than construct a situation in order to derive additional instructions. And the failure of the Beardsley-Wimsatt distinction comes out in several places. It shows up in their attack on Charles Coffin, the interpreter of Donne, in which they confuse a theoretical error with a simple mistake; and again in their denial that the author is an oracle who can settle problems of interpretation. As we have seen, the generator of an utterance only has a pragmatic and probable superior access to information; he is not, by the mere fact of being the author, in a position of superior authority. It emerges in their assertion that "even a short lyric poem is dramatic, the response of a speaker to a situation. We ought to impute the thoughts and attitudes of the poem immediately to the dramatic *speaker*, and if to the author at all, only by an act of biographical inference"; as we have seen in our analysis of the neighbor's instructions, the author of any statement is always, from the point of view of the responder, a construct. That is, for every statement we always do what Beardsley and Wimsatt say we ought to do only in interpreting poetry. Finally it emerges in their avowed failure to make any sharp distinctions among their three kinds of evidence, and in their nearby statement that "the use of biographical evidence need not involve intentionalism, because while it may be evidence of what the author intended, it may also be evidence of the meaning of his words and the dramatic character of his utterance." The fact is that "evidence of what the author intended" and "evidence of the meaning of his words and the dramatic character of his utterance" are merely two different sets of verbal instructions for the same kind of verbal behavior.

Thus we may conclude, to put it broadly, that the trouble with "The Intentional Fallacy" is that its authors are not talking about intention and it is not a fallacy. The doctrine of semantic autonomy, or semantic real presence, or semantic magic, or immanent meaning is untenable; and equally untenable is their attempt to distinguish between two kinds of interpretation. When we interpret poetry, we go through the same behavioral process that we go through when we interpret any utterance. Whether or not we use the word "intention" in going through that process is not of the slighest importance.

Finally, let me offer an *ex post facto* statement of *my* intention in going through all this analytical rigamarole. This kind of analysis is, for me at least, very amusing and profitable to write. That it is tedious to read I would not attempt to deny—even for those who have a passionate interest in this kind of verbal analysis, even if that passionate interest has been a result, as mine has been, of a profound dissatisfaction with the confusion into which their training in the study of literature has plunged them. The unhappy fact is that the language of literary criticism is filled with unanalyzed terms, and for the most part it consists merely of pushing around worn-out verbal counters to create pretty new patterns; and this kind of intellectually unsatisfactory and even pointless activity will go on forever unless we put a stop to it. And the only way to stop it that I can see is to engage in the kind of excruciatingly painful, exacting, and wearisome verbal analysis which I have offered here as an example, if not a model, of what we must do. We have indulged ourselves for so long that penance for our sins cannot be anything but humiliating and dreary.

23

ON THE HISTORICAL

INTERPRETATION OF LITERATURE

[1969*]

A theory of historical interpretation depends upon a theory of interpretation. And a theory of interpretation depends upon a theory of meaning. A theory of meaning depends upon a theory of language, and a theory of language depends in turn upon a theory of mind. If we had these theories in reasonably satisfactory shape we could begin to grapple with the effect the attribute "historical" has upon the term "interpretation." An initial confusion can be cleared up by distinguishing between "historical" and "historiographical." "History" is "past events," and "historiography" is "discourse that purports to discuss history." A literary work is an event if some human being is connected with it by behavior; either it is the deposit or consequence of writing behavior, or it is the stimulus of reading behavior. Of reading events two kinds may be distinguished: immediate, and

* Written for *Romantic and Victorian: Studies in Memory of William A. Marshall*. Copyright © 1970 by the University of South Carolina Press.

mediated. To make this distinction it is necessary to return to the ground of theory construction: mind.

The word "mind" is the source of a common, virtually universal confusion. (1) One semantic function is "what happens between stimulus and reponse." (2) The other is "covert verbal or other semiotic behavior, such as subjective images, verbal, aural, tactile, dreams, and so on." (Henceforth the discussion will be confined to verbal behavior.) When an individual says, "I thought so," it is never clear to others whether he engaged in covert verbal behavior before making the utterance, or whether the stimulus responsible for the utterance fulfilled certain expectancies, that is, simply seemed "right" to him. It is not clear if he is reporting that the prediction of covert verbal behavior has been confirmed, or if he is merely reporting a sense of gratification elicited by the stimulus responsible for his saying, "I thought so." Thus the same duality of semantic function is to be found in the various forms of "thought" as well as in the various forms of "mind." In the sense of "response" as "observable response," if only to the person generating it, that is, "private" or "privileged verbal response," what happens between stimulus and response is unobservable and inaccessible. "Observable response" is equivalent to "phenomenal response," while "what happens between stimulus and phenomenal response" is "physiologic response." Between physiological response and phenomenal response it is currently impossible to make a connection, and it is likely to remain impossible. The most recent research has shown the "stochastic or indeterminate behavior of nerve cells, requiring statistical analysis in terms of probabilities of firing, and thus making any meaningful statement of the relation between an individual [phenomenal] response and a particular single stimulus impossible . . ." ". . . the neurones at all levels of the nervous system are continually and spontaneously active." (M. A. Boden, review of *The Uncertain Nervous System*, by B. Delisle Burns, *Mind*, LXXVIII, p. 313, April, 1969.) (It is to be noted that the term "stimulus" now becomes in itself extremely vague; it depends upon the assumption that direct connection between stimulus and response is ascertainable. Since it is not, it is therefore impossible to identify a stimulus; one must speak of a "stimulus field.")

Immediate verbal response is the direct consequence—how we do not and probably cannot know—of physiological response, or brain activity. Mediated verbal response is response preceded by verbal behavior, covert or overt, from the individual generating the immediate verbal response. This is feedback. Any given utterance may be a mixture of the two; i.e., while the speaker is performing the utterance, the utterance itself may enter his stimulus field and by feedback affect the rest of the utterance. Thus whether reading behavior is immediate or mediated depends on whether the reader generates verbal behavior which affects his reading behavior.

From this several conclusions may be drawn. First, it is consistent with Grace Andrus de Laguna's proposal that language functions by coordinating behavior. Since response is always after stimulus, language functions in time. Thus a higher explanatory level of language function is that it gives directions for controlling behavior; but since the relation between stimulus field and response is stochastic, language gives directions only to one who has been conditioned to obey those directions, or to disobey them. Second, for this same reason of the indeterminate connection between stimulus and response it cannot be said that "meaning" is something immanent in language which the "mind" "extracts" from language. "Meaning" is an attribute of response, not of stimulus field. That is, meaning is a matter of cultural convention, or protocol. The question is not, "What is the meaning of the term or utterance?" but, "What is the appropriate response to the term or utterance?" In its most radical form, "the meaning of an utterance is all possible responses." By this is meant not "all possible responses to that utterance" but quite nakedly, "all possible responses." This is the full consequence of the proposition that meaning is a matter of cultural convention, or protocol.

A response to a verbal utterance, then, is either appropriate or inappropriate. It can be inappropriate in various ways, according to the judgment of the observer of the response, including the generator of the response. If we judge that the responder is ignorant of the appropriate response, then "inappropriate" means "incorrect," "wrong," "in error." If we judge that the responder is capable of the appropriate response but makes an inappropriate response, we call his response "ironic." Irony is possible because inappropriate responses are possible, and inappropriate responses are possible because responses are cultural conventions. Irony is of several sorts. (1) If we judge that the ironist is capable of the appropriate response, then our judgment includes a judgment that he has judged the utterance to which he is responding to be a response inappropriate for the situation in which it was generated. We may call this "judgmental irony." (Thus we can call an incorrect response "ironic" if we judge that the response reveals the stimulus utterance as inappropriate for its situation, even though the responder, we assume, did not so judge it.) (2) If our judgment is that the ironist is unconcerned with the appropriateness of the stimulus utterance for the situation in which it was generated, but only with the appropriateness of his response for the situation in which he generates that response, then we may call such irony "indifferent irony." In either kind of irony, given a situation in which the factors of the generative situation are identical with the factors of the response situation, except for the entrance of the utterance into the situation, we judge that the utterer and the ironist have judged the situation differently. The term we use to categorize the factors we judge to be responsible for the difference in these two judgments is "interests." (This again recognizes the conventionality of response, that is, meanings.) "Interpretation" categorizes the factors of situation, interests, and utterance. Any utterance necessarily involves interests, including the interests of the responder. In appropriate response the interests of utterer and responder are identical; in error, judgmental irony, and indifferent irony, they are divergent.

A response in which the only factor in the response situation different from the factors in the generative situation is judged to be the original utterance, and in which the original utterance has not been mediated by verbal or other semiotic behavior, covert or overt, on the part of the responder, is a "current situation."

Any response situation in which the response is immediate but which factors beyond the utterance are judged to have entered is an "ironic situation." Any response situation in which the response is mediated by covert or overt verbal or other semiotic behavior on the part of the responder is an "historical situation." In historical situations the responder generates a further set of directions to control his behavior in responding to the original utterance. Such directions may be constructs of factors of the generative situation, of the response situation, of the interests of the utterer, or of the interests of the responder, or of all four. (Analysis of syntax and grammar of the utterance is a construct of factors of the generative situation.)

Loosely, "historical interpretation" may mean any one of these, or any combination of them. Hence the extreme confusion over the term. "Objective historical interpretation" is response mediated by a construct of the interest factors of the utterer, of the factors of the generative situation, and of the relation between the two. "Augustinian historical interpretation," which I have named for the practitioner most responsible for its currency in European culture, is response mediated by a construct of the factors in the responder's situation, in his interests, and of the relation between the two. " 'Contextualist' or 'New Critical' historical interpretation" depends on the judgment that an ironic situation is a current situation. These last two are modes of indifferent irony. Any interpretational construct which omits any one of the four interpretational factors is influenced by those factors, since they are operant in all responses, even though they are not factors in the construct.

"Complete historical interpretation" attempts to include all four factors of interest and situation of utterer and responder. Complete historical interpretation can never be final. Since the response in an historical response situation which the generative situation preceded by a brief interval—say thirty seconds, or even less, so long as a mediated response took place—can be appropriate, there is no theoretical objection to the possibility of appropriateness for a response in an historical response situation which the generative situation preceded by hundreds or even thousands of years. The difficulty of appropriateness, however, is undeniably increased by the degree to which the situation has become ironic. The more ironic the situation, the greater the number and complexity of factors to be included in the interpretative construct and the greater the cultural distance to be overcome in establishing an identity of interests for speaker and responder, or complete historical interpreter. To establish such an identity requires a mediating construct.

"Historiography" is written discourse which is the deposit or consequence of historical interpretation. Confusion would be alleviated if "historiography" were confined to the deposit or consequence of complete historical interpretation.

The ambition of the complete historical interpretation of literature is to make a construct of an ironic and historical situation such that the attributes of the construct are those of a current situation. So long as it is remembered that the construct as an event is not identical with the original utterance as an event, confusion can be avoided, though certainty can never be achieved. The function of "historical research" is the improvement of the construct by identifying the factors of ironic situations. The function of "historical theory" is the improvement of the construct by identifying the interest factors of the complete historical interpreter.

Index

Psychic insulation as condition for artistic behavior, 262

Rational, definition of, 247
Reading events, immediate and mediated, 445–46
Realism, architectural, 137
Reassurance as goal of interpretation, 378
Re-orientation, requirements for, 192
Response: appropriate, 438–39; appropriate and inappropriate verbal, 447–48; immediate and mediated verbal, 447; kinds of ironic verbal, 448; in verbal, current, and ironic situations, 449
Richards, Ivor A., on metaphor, 402
Richter, Jean-Paul Friedrich, 301
Robertson, D.W., 309, 366
Robinson, Henry Crabb, and Constable, 109–10
Role and self, 31, 38, 40
Romanticism: anti-metaphysical character of, 33, 37, 78; author's definition of (1950), 14; author's definition of (1960), 33; compatability of, with science, 249–50; correct mode of defining, 83; cultural logic of, 246; as equivalent of Enlightenment, 31; heroicism of, 212; historical, 3; impact of Origin of Species on, 196; importance of definition of, 59; and involvement with metaphor, 420; and modern culture, 35; necessary character of definition of, 65; need for definition of, 64; new roles of, 37; as opposite of Pop-Op-Mini, 242; organistic episode of, 34; originality in, 234; of Pop-Op-Mini, 250; procedure for defining, 65; proper construction of definition of, 76–78; psychological basis of, 162; and reality, 35; realization of program of, 203; as redemp-

tion, 33; Romantic transcendence of, 244, 246; and self, 33; strategies for pressure of, 215; tight artistic control in, 170; tough-mindedness of, 215; transcendental stage of, 49–51; value task of, 237
anti-roles of, 142; Bohemian, 42–43; Byronic Hero, 41; Dandy, 43–44; Historian, 44–46; Poet Visionary, 41–42; Virtuoso, 43–44
Negative: defense of concept of, 73–75; definition of, 16, 21–23, 31; disorientation of, 193; lack of imperative for action in, 48; and metaphysical evolutionism, 185; psychological basis of, 162
stages of, 49; American, 163–64; Analogism, 47–50; Nietzscheanism, 55–57; Objectism, 51–52; Stylism, 52–55; Transcendentalism, 49–50
Rossetti, Dante Gabriel, and Stylism of House of Life, 220–22
Ruskin, John, architectural functionalism in, 139
Russell, Bertrand, and idea of permanence, 182
Rymer, Thomas, on Othello, 392

St. Augustine: interpretational interests of, 353; as interpreter of classical myths, 353; plot explanation in, 309. See also Interpretation
Saporta, Marc, 314
Schleiermacher, Friedrich, Romantic heroicism of, 212
Schmutzler, Robert, 218
Schönberg, Arnold: external discontinuity in Pierrot Lunaire, 276; Gurrelieder, 211; and Mahler, 203
Schopenhauer, Arthur, Romanticism of, 69
Science as strategies of decision-making, 375
Scientific law, Darwin's notion of, 190

THE TRIUMPH OF ROMANTICISM

Composed in Linotype Palatino by Heritage Printers and printed by offset lithography by the Halliday Lithograph Corporation on Warren's University Text specially watermarked with the University of South Carolina Press colophon. The two-piece binding is in Columbia Bayside vellum and linen. The book was designed by Robert L. Nance.